The George W. Bush Presidency
Appraisals and Prospects

edited by

Colin Campbell
University of British Columbia

and

Bert A. Rockman
The Ohio State University

CQ PRESS

A Division of Congressional Quarterly Inc.

Washington, D.C.

CQ Press
1255 22nd Street, N.W., Suite 400
Washington, D.C. 20037

Phone, 202-729-1900
Toll-free, 1-866-4CQ-PRESS (1-866-427-7737)

www.cqpress.com

♾ The paper used in this publication exceeds the requirements of the American National Standard for Information Sciences—Permanence of Paper for Printed Library Materials, ANSI Z39.48-1992.

Printed and bound in the United States of America

07 06 05 04 03   5 4 3 2 1

LIBRARY OF CONGRESS CATALOGING-IN-PUBLICATION DATA

The George W. Bush presidency : appraisals and prospects / edited by
Colin Campbell and Bert A. Rockman.
p. cm.
Includes bibliographical references.
ISBN 1-56802-909-8 (alk. paper)
1. United States—Politics and government—2001–   2. Bush, George W.
(George Walker), 1946–   I. Campbell, Colin.   II. Rockman, Bert A.
III. Title
  E902.G47 2004
  973.931'092—dc22

                                                              2003025522

We dedicate this book to Richard E. Neustadt (1919–2003), who founded the modern study of the presidency and who once said of holders of that office:

The most informed and most alert President needs something more: he needs the means to make himself take time. He needs the means of putting pressure on himself, of imposing new deadlines on himself. To come to grips with those things he would want to make his own if he were free to interfere and pick and choose at will. Deadlines self-imposed are no less helpful to a President than tangible details. The one informs his mind, the other arms his hand. Together they contribute what he needs when he seeks power.

—*Presidential Power: The Politics of Leadership with Reflections on Johnson and Nixon,* 1976

Contents

George W. Bush could not have experienced a shakier rise to power. Losing the popular vote, he ascended to the presidency amid controversy and questions about his presidency's legitimacy and mandate. But the nation's forty-third and the Bush family's second presidency came out of the chute about as single-minded in pursuit of its agenda as any on record, pursuing ideological principle intensely on many fronts. And that was before September 11th transformed both the nation and the administration.

The George W. Bush administration has been a surprise to many observers who underestimated both the president's character and his political skills. The tragic events of September 11, 2001, propelled Bush to levels of public approval unmatched in the lifetimes of most Americans. Moreover, both before that date and since, Bush has been extraordinarily focused and active in seeking to mobilize his party's base of supporters. What has been the effect of Bush's high standing in the polls on his drive for public and congressional support for his policies?

*The U.S. Constitution was designed to promote power
sharing. "Separated institutions, sharing powers," in
Richard Neustadt's classic phrase, demand that others be
accommodated. Presidents who ignore this risk undermining
not only the delicate fabric of freedom and mutual
accommodation that is the basis of the American political
system but also, in extreme situations, their own
administrations, as Nixon did in Watergate and as Reagan
nearly did in Iran-contra. Students of the presidency should
therefore find the remainder of the Bush administration of
great interest, both because of what it reveals about our
understanding of the contemporary presidency and because
of the stakes involved.*

*Unrestrained ideological entrepreneurship flourishes in the
Bush administration's advisory system, both because the
president seems detached from open discourse about the
crucial issues he faces and because the administration, more
generally, seems to include a surfeit of doctrinaire players but
invests very little structure or effort in ensuring that policy
initiatives receive intense collegial scrutiny.*

*In times of crisis, members of Congress are loath to seem to
second-guess and hinder a popular president who claims he is
simply doing what is necessary to safeguard the American
people. Nevertheless, the Bush administration's reassertion of
executive authority vis-à-vis Congress has led to a tug-of-war
that is likely to persist and, barring more terrorist attacks,
become more prominent.*

Delays and the hotly contested confirmation hearings and votes in the Senate inexorably reflect how the confirmation process for judicial nominees has been transformed over the past few decades, as presidents have made federal judgeships both symbols and instruments of their own power. They are also the results of an increasingly polarized Congress and the vigorous interventions of conservative and liberal interest groups in both advocating for and opposing candidates for judgeships.

Bush's domestic record is disappointing from the standpoint of substantive accomplishment and the implementation of a compassionate-conservative agenda. For the most part, that reflects constraints beyond the president's control. Judging from their decisions on education, the faith-based initiatives program, homeland security, and tax cuts, however, Bush and his advisers did not deliberate carefully about the actual consequences of their policies.

George W. Bush entered the White House emphasizing the importance of U.S. interests close to home and the primacy of a domestic agenda. Reflecting popular conservative sentiments, he initially expressed reservations about becoming deeply involved in nation-building, especially in the Middle East. September 11th changed that, making foreign policy and homeland security the defining issues for the Bush presidency. In the highly charged atmosphere following 9/11, popular mobilization for war and imperial moral missions to change the nature of politics in far-off lands were conceivable in ways they had not been before the attacks on New York and Washington.

Bush has led, and is often influenced by, a readily identifiable set of corporate, small business, and social conservative interests. As the president made it clear that he would pursue his policy agenda aggressively in both the legislative and administrative realms, Republicans on Capitol Hill quickly showed their determination to enact laws much desired by the conservative and business interests that work in close collaboration with the White House. After Republican gains in the 2002 midterm elections, Bush's partisan, ideological coalition of interests entered 2003 chomping at the bit.

Calls for demographic diversity among presidential appointees and administration policy leaders implicitly assume that a diversity of ideas will follow. Critics of the George W. Bush administration argue that the promise of diversity was hollow because the demographic diversity of the Bush White House did not result in a diversity of ideological perspectives. The solution to the need to appeal to women and racial and ethnic minorities, as well as to Bush's conservative base, was to create a diverse administration descriptively but not substantively.

Bush II was vividly aware of the possibility that a president could succeed overseas and be rejected at home; his own father was a case in point. It is striking that in spite of the need to create and maintain an international coalition to combat al Qaeda, the Bush administration did not fully retreat from its original foreign policy views—the concerns of even the closest allies would continue to be subordinated to domestic politics and the quest for reelection, and U.S. interests would continue to be asserted vigorously even if doing so conflicted with its own principles or with the urgings of international organizations that the United States had supported in the past.

*Bush must be reckoned a successful party leader but a
failed national leader. In view of the unusual opportunities
he was given to do what he said he would do—reduce
partisan distemper in Washington, create conditions of
political civility, and promote national cohesion—his failure
on these matters has been profound, but also apparently
intended. The conditions of his accession and those of
national crisis created openings that were ignored.*

Tables and Figures

Preface

This book will issue from the printer on or about Christmas Eve 2003—more than six months later in its subject's term of office than its predecessor volumes. Students of the U.S. presidency will know that those works included *The Bush Presidency: First Appraisals*; *The Clinton Presidency: First Appraisals*; and *The Clinton Legacy*. All of those books came out during the summer after the midterm elections. Given the event-filled third year of the George W. Bush administration, we find it fortuitous that *The George W. Bush Presidency: Appraisals and Prospects* was delayed, allowing the authors of these essays to update their work and to continue to take stock of the U.S. campaign to bring about regime change in Iraq. In few cases is later better, but this may be one of them, since it permits more current and complete coverage than other, comparable books on the George W. Bush presidency.

All of the previous assessments edited by us appeared under the Chatham House imprint. One of the most highly esteemed, perhaps legendary, individuals known to the political science profession, Edward Artinian, created that publishing firm. Chatham House hosted an outstanding collection of works, written by prominent scholars but directed to students in the classroom as well as those who taught them from the lectern. The list, in other words, boasted some of the best political science scholarship in forms readily understandable to college students.

Ed Artinian knew as intimately as any publisher in the United States the demands faced by faculty seeking excellent teaching materials. He worked vigorously to encourage academics to write accessible books and equally vigorously to make sure that their colleagues around the nation became aware of the books' availability. He would buttonhole academics—whether book-prize recipients or fresh Ph.D.'s who had written brilliant dissertations—at conventions and urge them to write for a wide audience. If the scholar rose to the challenge, Ed would then call virtually everybody teaching a large course in the field to ensure that the author's work would win adoption in courses across the country.

Ed Artinian passed away in 1997. His list continued to operate independently under the Chatham House imprint until October 2003. We take special delight in the fact that it has now found its way to CQ Press. Indeed, had Ed lived to retirement age and decided to sell his list, we have no doubt that all of those scholars would have received jubilant calls—probably late in the evening—announcing the sale and proclaiming that he could not have found a better home for his treasures (authors and books alike!).

CQ Press has produced our book in record time, so that it can reach the hands of students by January 2004. But we know that those at the Press would want us to thank two people at Chatham House, as well, for their roles in making this book possible: First, Ted Bolen, Ed Artinian's successor as publisher, kept alive Ed's pride in this series of presidential administration appraisals. He continued to move the book along even though he ultimately would pass the list on to CQ Press. Second, Katharine Miller gave new meaning to the expression "above and beyond the call of duty" by putting the chapter manuscripts through her typically rigorous and judicious copy editing before handing them over to CQ Press.

In the past month, we have gotten to know three people at CQ Press who have shown us through their professionalism that Ed's list will thrive under its new owner. Brenda Carter and Charisse Kiino have handled exquisitely and with lightning-fast dispatch the transfer of our book and its authors to CQ Press. Nancy Geltman took direct control of production and guided superbly the intricate task of obtaining last-minute updates and revisions from our widely dispersed authors.

Just as we were putting this book to bed, the most recognized presidency scholar of the last half of the twentieth century, Richard E. Neustadt, passed away. Professor emeritus of government at Harvard University, he was a scholar whose work and example touched profoundly all of the authors in this book. Neustadt's scholarship animates this book and the series of which it is a part. We dedicate this volume to his memory.

CHAPTER 1

Managing the Presidency or the President?

Raising Some Issues Concerning the Bush II Administration's Approach to Executive Leadership

Colin Campbell

> . . . for practical purposes after 1717 the Cabinet ceased to be a body meeting with the King. . . . The chief reason was that George's personality altered the situation. He was . . . ignorant of English affairs . . . and could never be at ease presiding over a wide-ranging discussion among ten or twelve Cabinet ministers . . . he was suspicious and preferred to lean on his . . . [trusted confidants]. The politicians, for their part, sensing this situation, preferred to consult with the King in private and not at the Cabinet where misunderstandings and animosities could so rapidly arise and flourish.
>
> —*John P. Mackintosh*

THE QUOTED PASSAGE has been considerably redacted from the original text of Mackintosh's *The British Cabinet.*[1] Unabridged, that work contains language that would offend in our current era and, more important, would not pertain to George W. Bush, who both reveals considerable intelligence through his political maneuvering and maintains a personal lifestyle that is seemingly beyond reproach. However, Mackintosh, the twentieth century's most influential authority on British cabinet government, succinctly captured just why King George I of England (1714–27) had presided over the diminution of the British monarchy's salience to executive leadership in his country. And some of Mackintosh's assertions about George I touch upon defects that commentators have noted in the presidential character of George W. Bush.

Even before he became president, many observers registered concern that George W. Bush would fail to bring to the most powerful position in the world sufficient knowledge of policy issues, intellectual curiosity, and comfort with open discourse. They doubted, in other words, that he possessed the qualities that could enable him to effectively lead an administration.

Partially in response to such concerns, George H.W. Bush, the current president's father, actively involved himself in the selection of his son's running-mate, Richard Cheney. He had received a tip from his own former national security adviser, Brent Scowcroft, that Cheney wanted to become vice president.[2] The senior Bush even consulted with a cardiac surgeon to assess whether Cheney's heart condition would curtail his ability to immerse himself in a presidential campaign. The soundness of this choice, given concerns about George W. Bush's preparedness for the presidency,[3] even prompted former president Gerald R. Ford and 1996 Republican presidential candidate Bob Dole to contribute a *New York Times* op-ed piece extolling its wisdom. They clearly wanted to enshrine in the attentive public's mind that Cheney would serve both as a steadying influence on George W. Bush should he become president and a guarantor of the restoration of dignity to the White House:

> He is an unconventional choice if only because of the transparent merit which motivated his selection. This makes him a refreshing alternative. He was selected less because he could help Bush get elected than because he could help a president govern—in a way that will help restore popular respect for tarnished institutions.[4]

In the event, George W. Bush could not have experienced a shakier rise to power. He lost the popular vote for the presidency in November 2000 but nevertheless ascended to the office on the back of a highly partisan Supreme Court decision, which only seemed to add credence to those who questioned the legitimacy of his election. But, the nation's forty-third and the Bush family's second presidency came out of the chute about as single-minded in pursuit of its agenda as any on record. Even before the Supreme Court's ruling, the administration-in-litigation engaged exquisitely in the ancient art of mandate confection. One could see strong parallels to Newt Gingrich's claims, after the 1994 midterm elections, to a clear electoral mandate in support of the Contract with America.[5] Namely, the Bush team began to justify each step toward preparing the nation for its game plan, by consistently harking back to the specifics of its campaign platform as if they formed part of an itemized commission that had been sanctioned by an overwhelming majority of voters. The Bush team had concluded that acting as if it had a strong electoral mandate would rapidly establish its legitimacy. As one Bush adviser noted, "The feeling is that the country deserves governance and if you don't assert the sovereignty and legitimacy of your administration from the outset, you undermine your ability to achieve your goals later."[6]

Harvard's Richard E. Neustadt—the nation's preeminent presidency scholar—saw a wisdom in this tack so long as Bush proceeded in a dignified manner: "If he can manage graciousness in this transition period, and if he can get two or three events that permit him to look very presidential, then by summer he'll be the president, and it won't matter how he got there."[7] In the end, it took one event—the September 11th terrorist attacks—to turn Neustadt's prophecy into reality.

In pressing its agenda, the Bush team cashed in the obvious resonance of the impending president's view that a very substantial proportion of the projected budget surpluses—which, of course, have since evaporated into thin air—should go back to the people on the grounds that "it is their money." Once in the White House, the new administration acted audaciously in pursuit of this agenda item, making it clear that it would press for as large a ten-year aggregate figure as possible—originally requesting $1.6 trillion, it ultimately attained $1.35 trillion in tax cuts. Further, it justified this determination by brilliantly buttressing its demands for tax cuts with a heavy dose of crisis inflation.[8] That is, it talked down the economy by speaking in bleak terms about the apparent lag in growth before it had actually fulfilled the technical definition of a recession (two successive quarters of shrinking rather than expanding production). To be sure, the actual ballot counts left uncertain the voters' preferences regarding the disposition of the surplus—whether it should stay in Washington or go back in their pockets—but the Bush team sought to assuage these doubts by drawing the nation's attention to a looming economic downturn.[9] In flashback to the Keynesian economics of the middle part of the past century, it assigned great urgency to tax cuts on the premise that putting more cash in the hands of consumers and investors would stimulate the economy.

It did not seem to matter to those in Congress stampeded by this gambit that the gradual staging of these cuts over a period of ten years preordained that they would have very little immediate stimulative effect. During the electoral quandary and the transition, the Bush team very astutely backed doubters into a corner, in the process establishing a fiscal framework with a built-in shortfall between spending and revenues that would seriously constrain expansionary possibilities in domestic spending for the foreseeable future. Thus, despite a dubious electoral mandate, they had accomplished precisely the feat that Ronald Reagan had achieved after his decisive defeat of President Jimmy Carter in 1980. That is, they successfully pressed for a fiscal framework that would seriously constrict the funds available for domestic programs.

To be sure, much of the Bush administration's success in the early months was similarly based on nerve and bluff. By the summer of 2001, the president's approval ratings had begun to soften, while the defection of Vermont's Jim Jeffords from the Republican Party had tipped control of the Senate over to the Democrats, making pursuit of further items on the administration's domestic agenda exponentially more difficult. The administration realized that it had to get back on message—a Bush II version of the first Clinton campaign's "It's the economy, stupid."[10] But we will never know how this mildly ponderous phrase might have worked itself out, for the horrific terrorist attacks of September 11th brought an abrupt close to the summer doldrums—and transformed both the nation and the administration.

Not every observer has ascribed to George W. Bush particular genius at leading the United States in these perilous times. The image that most often comes to mind in recalling the disaster's immediate aftermath is that of the president being bundled about the country by the Secret Service, leaving the American public to their own devices in making sense of the events both for their private lives and for the nation. So far as whose hands grasped the rudder, the spin from no less a personage than Vice President Cheney showcased his personal role during the crisis.[11] That assurance would comport eerily with the pre-inaugural musings that Cheney was to operate as "prime minister" while Bush would function as a "ceremonial head of state"[12]—except for the fact that the president did not seem to be performing especially robustly in the latter role either.

The context in which President Bush first joined the nation in grieving itself struck some as somewhat distant. It was a memorial service in Washington's National Cathedral, to which only the great and the good were invited—very much along the lines of the British monarchs historically leading their nation in mourning. Indeed, the prominent presence of the president's father in the proceedings gave the occasion the aura of a crown prince's long-delayed coronation. In any case, New York's Mayor Rudy Giuliani completely overshadowed Bush in the immediate aftermath of 9/11, hugging and pressing the flesh reassuringly as the nation struggled with its shock and grief.[13] And Britain's Tony Blair turned phrases that evoked memories of Winston Churchill capturing the peril faced by civilization.[14] Indeed, Blair's words proved so effective—even with the domestic U.S. audience—that the American and British administrations began to orchestrate closely their statements on the war against terror.[15]

Top officials in the White House seemed to relish the spectacle of "Bush being Bush" in his unvarnished utterances at the early stages of the crisis.[16] Still, the use of terms such as *folks* for the terrorists, *crusade* for the U.S. countereffort, *the evil one* for Osama bin Laden, and *Pakis* for the citizens of Pakistan—whose cooperation would become indispensable in eradicating al Qaeda—seemed an impoverished response at best, especially if the United States was to garner enthusiastic support in the war against terrorism beyond its shores—in which attempt it still has not succeeded conspicuously. Nonetheless, the nation itself rallied almost unanimously behind its president. Criticism from the chattering classes has about as much effect on presidential approval ratings as hometown favoritism has on the outcome of an athletic competition, and, at the end of the day, foreign nationals do not get to vote in U.S. elections. Bush, therefore, reaped the mother of all rallies. His approval ratings shot to the highest levels recorded since the beginning of polling and sustained themselves for an unprecedented duration.

Just Quibbling with Success?

In November 2002 the president bucked historical patterns by gaining seats in both the House of Representatives and the Senate in a midterm election. We can say that Bush defied history because he personally staked his reputation in this eventuality by articulating the importance of adding to the numbers of Republicans in both houses—in the case of the Senate, in order to regain control of that chamber. He then invested a huge proportion of any president's scarcest resource, time, in ensuring that he obtained the desired result.

Following this accomplishment, the press began to lionize Bush's position. Indeed, Adam Clymer, writing in the *New York Times*, pondered out loud the specter of a continued Bush dynasty: ". . . Jeb Bush's easy victory [in Florida] made him an obvious presidential candidate for 2008, and President Bush's announcement that he would keep on Dick Cheney as vice president avoided anointing a rival to his brother."[17] Simultaneously, dismissive treatments of the Democrats' relevancy began to surface. For instance, in the same issue of the *New York Times* the highly-regarded foreign affairs columnist Thomas L. Friedman cut to the chase: "Let's be blunt: the Democratic Party as a force in shaping U.S. foreign policy is out of business, until that party undergoes regime change."[18]

We have seen such adulation and scorn before in recent political history. After her landslide victory in May 1987—her third in eight years—the press invested Britain's Prime Minister Margaret Thatcher with iconic status, speculating that she would lead her party to its fourth electoral mandate in succession, thereby enhancing the prospect that the Conservatives would lead the United Kingdom into the twenty-first century. As it happened, the Conservatives ousted Thatcher unceremoniously in 1990 and lost control of the House of Commons in 1997; they have drawn ever since precisely the type of derision that is now directed toward Democrats in the United States. Fortunes can change rapidly in politics. Witness the case of George W. Bush's father, who drew stratospheric approval ratings in the aftermath of the resounding 1991 victory in the Persian Gulf but then lost the 1992 presidential election to Bill Clinton.

One can scarcely open the *New York Times* or *Washington Post* without finding fresh evidence that the Bush I presidency serves as a constant model of what not to do for Bush II. Bush I did not coddle sufficiently his conservative base, and he seemed detached from the concerns of average Americans—especially the stress they faced from the economic downturn of the early 1990s. Therefore, Bush II rarely pivots without one foot firmly planted in his base, and he gushes endlessly about the central place that the average American holds in his heart. But Bush II could benefit greatly by bearing in mind as well that his father's failures owed in considerable degree to the lax management of his administration. Indeed, they stemmed substantially from a lack of clarity about whether Bush I's White House apparatus was functioning as an instrument for implementing the president's agenda or had instead become a captive machinery manipulated by subordinates who were pursuing their own agendas.

Even with respect to the 1990 war against Iraq, George H.W. Bush had proven decidedly flat-footed in responding to the increasingly bellicose language of Saddam Hussein.[19] Indeed, only Thatcher's prodding immediately after the Iraqi invasion of Kuwait prompted the president to consider rolling back rather than simply containing the occupying force.[20] On the domestic side, Bush I delegated great responsibility to his chief of staff, John Sununu, who regularly antagonized rival administration officials as well as key senators and congressmen with his brash and presumptuous pronouncements, in at least one notorious instance actually scheming behind the president's back.[21] By the time he summoned the courage to replace Sununu, in December 1991, Bush I had already squandered valuable months that should have been devoted to translating the enormous Desert Storm bounce in his approval ratings into a concerted program to address the domestic ills that increasingly absorbed the electorate. Giving further weight to the argument that chief executives neglect the internal organization of their administrations at their own peril, it was precisely such issues—in her case an increasingly autocratic approach toward the cabinet—that led to Thatcher's own early demise.[22]

The dynamics of the tenure of Thatcher's successor, John Major, who led the conservatives to their nadir, offers further evidence that an administration basically manages itself to its ultimate fate and place in the history books.[23] Independently, Bert A. Rockman and Peter Jenkins resorted to the term *pastel* to characterize the political personas of, respectively, George H.W. Bush and John Major.[24] According to Rockman and Jenkins, both leaders appeared to lack what Bush I dismissively termed "the vision thing." Ironically, this very trait had contributed to each man's rise to power when the U.S. and British electorates seemed to want time out from the decidedly ideological stances of their predecessors. However, the seeming lack of vision eventually presented difficulties for each man as issues began to emerge in both countries that could not be deferred, no matter how much their tentative instincts counseled caution.

Significantly, Major differed sharply from Bush I in the strongly ideological composition of his cabinet. Notwithstanding Sununu and some other committed neoconservatives, Bush had incorporated in his cabinet and White House several notable moderates, and this inclusiveness cut back substantially on the partisan stridency of his administration. Major, on the other hand, resigned himself to a cabinet filled with Thatcher protégés who delighted in straying as far from the reservation as possible on key issues. What emerged was a tendency within the government toward unrestrained ideological entrepreneurship.[25] This trait took root in the depth of ideological commitment of the Thatcher protégés, in their view that they owed their careers to Thatcher—not Major—and therefore had a high sense of free-agency in a Major cabinet, and in the immense leverage they exerted over Major because of the difficulty of his brokering deals that would sustain his electoral support. In a U.S. administration, we might expect such unrestrained ideological entrepreneurship to assert itself especially when two conditions prevail: (1) when the appointment process for key members of the administration has displayed a strong bias toward the ideological extremes of the president's party; and (2) when the president's advisory system does not place a high value on submitting policy proposals to countervailing review.

With respect to the ideological composition of a chief executive's team, one finds a much stronger parallel between Bush II and Major than between Bush I and Major. Two factors seem operative here. First, the current president, as we have noted, displays unfailing cognizance of a lesson garnered from his father's failure to win reelection—namely, that he must always pivot from his conservative base. Second, even before the Florida standoff, Bush II realized that the political elite and the public alike harbored doubts about whether he would bring sufficient intellectual acuity to function effectively as president and that he had to counter this uncertainty by surrounding himself with a team of advisers with indisputable credentials. Most critically here, he selected Richard Cheney to be his running mate. While this decision clearly helped silence concerns about the top candidate's competency, it also would work monumental effects on the ideological composition of his eventual administration. It also provided an element of free-agency similar to that found in the Major government. Especially in light of Bush II's struggle for legitimacy after the disputed election, we can see how some members of the political executive—hawks in the Pentagon, for instance—might see themselves as beholden as much to the skillful machinations of Dick Cheney as to Bush II's prerogatives as president.

In some quarters, much has been made of the similarities between the ideological thrusts of the Bush II and Reagan administrations. Indeed, some have argued that Bush II is Reagan's and not his father's political son.[26] That might well be the case with regard to personal ideological proclivities. Yet Reagan's first-term administration, like Thatcher's in the U.K., significantly moderated its pursuit of ideological entrepreneurship. During their first terms, both administrations operated with relatively heterogeneous cabinets that were required because their neoconservative positions had not reached mainstream status within their respective parties. Thus, ideological entrepreneurship required measured approaches to achieving reform. Indeed, during his first term, Reagan tempered ideological entrepreneurship somewhat by imposing a "roundtabling" norm whereby significant policy commitments usually required vetting by cabinet councils. The Bush II administration has resembled more the Major government in the license it offers to unrestrained ideological entrepreneurship. One key difference presents itself here, however. Major was essentially a moderate whose weakness as a leader engendered a cacophony of position-taking. Bush II, on the other hand, is a committed neoconservative who has exploited the ascendancy of his world view in the United States to cater to his base in a manner that would have been unthinkable in the 1980s.

Disconcerting Signs

Has its strong rightward skew set up the Bush II administration for unrestrained ideological entrepreneurship? A substantial amount of the analysis provided in the chapters that follow points in that direction. It seems that often the judgment of the president—and of those in his administration—becomes clouded by position-taking that adheres almost idiosyncratically to stimuli from the far right and receives little or no critical scrutiny from within the political executive. However, not all of the authors commenting here emphasize this order of difficulty with how the administration has managed itself.

In raising the specter of unrestrained ideological entrepreneurship, this chapter clearly goes beyond mere quibbles about issue management in the Bush II administration to some relatively serious concerns. But, even if these concerns prompt significant "arguments" with success, what would such problems add up to in the larger scheme of an administration that appears, at this writing, destined for reelection? We seem, thus, not to be dealing with concerns that, barring significantly worsening fortunes either in the economy or in foreign affairs, will likely impinge on George W. Bush's currently bright prospects for a second term, but instead to be raising questions about the long-range viability and effects of his policies, many of which will not come fully into view until after the 2004 election.

In his chapter, "Riding High in the Polls: George W. Bush and Public Opinion," George C. Edwards III provides an overview of the continued support for George W. Bush notwithstanding his shaky mandate. Edwards notes from the outset a "positivity bias," which seemed to rest both on a willingness on the part of voters to forget about the electoral debacle and on an attraction to Bush as a person. The public's favorable attitude toward the president laid the groundwork for his stunning victory in pressing for tax cuts. However, Bush did not do well during the late spring and summer of 2001 in keeping his agenda at a boil; observers had started speaking of the "disappearing president." The 9/11 attacks, however, turned this trend around so dramatically that Bush soon broke all records for both strength and duration of poll-measured approval ratings. Still, Edwards registers concern that the president seems unable to convert his political capital very effectively into fulfilling his agenda, except, of course, in matters associated with national security and tax cuts. Notwithstanding this strategic weakness, Edwards gives Bush's White House public relations strategies very high marks for keeping his approval ratings at such high levels.

Joel D. Aberbach's chapter, "The State of the Contemporary American Presidency: Or, Is Bush II Actually Ronald Reagan's Heir?" examines George W. Bush as a practitioner of adversarial politics even within the executive branch. In this regard, the current president differs clearly from his father, who brought an exceptionally strong resumé to the Oval Office and essentially followed traditional codes prizing cooperativeness for relations with advisers, cabinet officers, and the standing public service. In contrast, Bush II has pursued a hard-right orientation both in terms of aggressive intervention in executive branch affairs and in a degree of responsiveness to core conservative constituencies that surpasses in some respects even that of Ronald Reagan. Aberbach notes that Vice President Cheney's critical role in the administration has more than compensated for George W. Bush's relatively meager exposure to Washington, but he also registers concern that the Bush II administration has departed from efforts of the Bush I and Clinton administrations to accept some degree of power-sharing with Congress. The tendency for Bush II to "govern alone" seems, to Aberbach, to run against the checks and balances prescribed by the U.S. Constitution.

In "Unrestrained Ideological Entrepreneurship in the Bush II Advisory System: An Examination of the Response to 9/11 and the Decision to Seek Regime Change in Iraq," I provide an assessment of the Bush II advisory system—especially the roles of the White House staff and the cabinet. My chapter employs a case study of the administration's response to 9/11 and the subsequent invasion of Iraq to probe the degree to which unrestrained ideological entrepreneurship asserted itself in this especially crucial policy area. My analysis finds that a lack of coherence in the administration's issue management system led, in the first place, to a pre–9/11 response to the al Qaeda threat that was in many respects less vigorous than that of the Clinton administration. After 9/11, the Bush administration clearly departed from its stated commitment to a systematic effort to root out terrorism by deeply personalizing the struggle as one of "getting" Osama bin Laden.

When the failure of this approach became obvious early in 2002, the administration's attention shifted to regime change in Iraq. However, unrestrained ideological entrepreneurship visited a series of mishaps upon the process that culminated in the invasion, including an abortive attempt to win the support of other Islamic states in the Middle East; critical interventions during summer 2002 by moderates, which led to a largely symbolic and ultimately unsuccessful effort to assemble a multilateral alliance; the distortion and hyping of evidence against Iraq; a significant alienation of the military leadership over both the size of the force required to do the job and its timely deployment; and a clear underestimation of the difficulty of occupying Iraq. While focusing on this one case, the chapter points up the degree to which unrestrained ideological entrepreneurship and weak countervailance to strongly articulated views can lead to poor issue management. The president's aloofness from open discourse within the administration seems to compound these difficulties. It also leads him often to stick with a vengeance to strongly-held positions adopted ostensibly at the service of his base.

In her chapter, entitled "Context, Strategy, and Chance: George W. Bush and the 107th Congress," Barbara Sinclair assesses Bush's relations with Congress and argues for attention to the context that prevails as a presidency begins, rather than too strong a focus on the incumbent's leadership skills. At the outset of the Bush II administration, a Republican president faced two Republican-controlled houses for the first time since Eisenhower's first two years in office (1953–55). In addition, Republicans, who had controlled both houses of Congress since 1995, had pent-up frustrations over their failure to enact their agenda in the face of Bill Clinton's "triangulation" strategy. George W. Bush, however, had strongly advocated bipartisanship during his campaign, and he came to office under the shadow of a disputed victory. Sinclair finds that, notwithstanding his campaign rhetoric, Bush has, with few exceptions—such as the 2001 education bill—pursued a strongly partisan approach in his relations with Congress. This confrontational strategy persisted despite the loss of control of the Senate for over a year and a half due to the defection of Jim Jeffords in May 2001 and regardless of the national trauma resulting from the terrorist attacks of 11 September 2001. In fact, during the 2002 midterm elections Bush bet the farm on a personal drive to win back the Senate with highly partisan interventions in campaigns throughout the nation.

One finds clear evidence of the single-minded, hard-right thrust of the Bush II administration in David M. O'Brien's chapter, "Ironies and Disappointments: Bush and Federal Judgeships." O'Brien outlines the existing divide in the Supreme Court that underlies the close *Bush v. Gore* decision and then demonstrates how the administration has moved assertively to consolidate the position of conservatives throughout the judiciary—primarily by advancing members of the Federalist Society, an interest group founded by Antonin Scalia and Robert Bork when the two were conservative legal scholars pressing for action against a perceived liberal bias in law schools and on the federal bench. Members of that group now control all senior Department of Justice and White House positions responsible for vetting and selecting candidates for the federal judiciary. The administration also has terminated formally the role of the American Bar Association in evaluation of the qualifications of nominees. The Jeffords defection stymied the administration strategy just as it was gaining altitude, however, giving the Democrats time to dig themselves in in preparation for trench warfare once the Republicans regained control of the Senate.

In "Deliberations of a 'Compassionate Conservative': George W. Bush's Domestic Presidency," Gary Mucciaroni and Paul Quirk review the track record of the Bush II administration in domestic policy—focusing on its political strategies and the quality of its deliberations on tax and economic policy, faith-based initiatives, education, and homeland security. The chapter begins by situating the administration within the wider framework of a polarized national politics in which the number of moderates in Congress has declined to the point that no president can easily govern from the center. This leaves presidents with two options, each of which can undermine moderate, deliberative policymaking. Bill Clinton pursued opportunistic policies that appealed to swing voters or powerful interest groups but largely abandoned his promise to find workable, effective measures that would transcend ideological cleavages. Alternatively, a president can pander to his ideological base, overlooking substantive problems with its pet policies and leveraging its enthusiasm to pressure the few congressional centrists to cut deals. In most respects, George W. Bush has stressed this latter approach. According to insider reports, his White House has been exceptionally casual in substantive deliberation about domestic policy, and his legislative strategy has encountered the predictable risk of the center digging in its heels (a special problem in the Senate, with its requirement of sixty votes to overcome a filibuster). The administration's domestic policy initiatives have introduced a serious threat to the nation's fiscal rectitude, creating projected deficits so large that they may hamper long-term economic growth; overlooked obvious difficulties in reconciling faith-based programs with religious freedoms; settled for empty declarations of lofty goals and unenforceable requirements for education; and lurched from one dubious solution to another in developing a program for homeland security. "Bush and his administration," Mucciaroni and Quirk conclude, "appear to have given less than adequate attention to issues and information about the real-world consequences of their policies."

Richard K. Herrmann, in collaboration with Michael J. Reese, offers an assessment of "George W. Bush's Foreign Policy," and their treatment will remind readers how important it is to know the backgrounds and the responsibilities of key political appointees in any administration. While my chapter 4 asks whether the Bush II foreign policy team was so deeply wired in the neoconservatives' favor that the invasion of Iraq became inevitable, Herrmann and Reese argue that traditional conservatives held important posts as well and that the administration was not following the neoconservative agenda before 9/11. They contend that the shock of the terrorist attacks shifted the foreign policy agenda and the distribution of influence within the administration in a hard-line direction. In this situation, Colin Powell struggled to balance a desire to advance the war on terrorism with concern for Arab nationalism and traditional U.S. allied relationships. Although Condoleezza Rice, who had links to both the more moderate conservatives and the hawkish neoconservatives, served as a broker, it became increasingly clear that on the issue of war, Bush II's heart was with the neocons. Herrmann and Reese acknowledge that without oil, the Persian Gulf would not have enjoyed the strategic importance it was granted, but they maintain that concerns about Israel's security and plans for inducing far-reaching political change in the region moved the neoconservatives more than oil. Belief in the threat of so-called weapons of mass destruction, even if misplaced, they contend, is what finally won the day both in the White House and with the general public.

The next two chapters, by Mark A. Peterson and by David Canon and Katherine Walsh, offer considerations of the Bush II administration's relations with interest groups and of its dealings in issues of gender and race. In "Bush and Interest Groups: A Government of Chums," Peterson outlines the options available to a president in crafting a strategy toward interest groups and then ponders why Bush II, burdened as he was by the appearance of a tainted mandate, eschewed an inclusive liaison with groups that would have bolstered the legitimacy of his administration. Such an approach, Peterson notes, would have comported well with rhetorical flourishes Bush employed during the 2000 campaign about his "compassionate conservatism" and his desire to be "a uniter, not a divider." As Peterson acknowledges, however, other forces within the Republican Party—including the determination of congressional Republicans to run with their agenda now that their party controlled the White House and the emergence during the 1990s of the far right as a mainstream movement within the party—preordained that the administration would employ liaison selectively, that is, in the service of its operating like a governing executive. Peterson then provides a detailed inventory of position-taking in the administration that has produced substantive policies targeted to core supporters rather than the inclusiveness hinted at in Bush's campaign rhetoric.

Canon and Walsh provide additional evidence of selectivity in their examination of "George W. Bush and the Politics of Gender and Race." Indeed, they find that the administration has abandoned all but symbolic gestures toward the "big tent" approach to women and minorities that it outlined during the 2000 campaign. The decidedly noninclusive Florida election strategy that deployed regulations and techniques to limit minority participation certainly cast a dark cloud over the administration-in-litigation. Once in power, the Bush White House proved almost as punctilious in achieving visual representativeness as had the Clinton administration. Yet, starting with the appointment of John Ashcroft as attorney general, it lodged in critical places enough resisters of gender and racial progress to more than cancel out any potential thrust toward what Canon and Walsh term "substantive" representation.

In "Bush II and the World," Graham Wilson analyzes how the Bush administration has used the U.S. position as the world's dominant superpower. Wilson notes the irony that Bush, who early on was determinedly uninterested in other countries, has, because of September 11th, benefited enormously from the prominence of foreign policy in terms of his political and popular standing. Still, even when seeking allies for his military campaigns, Bush retained a strong tendency toward unilateralism, asserting American interests and goals without much regard for the sensitivities or interests of other nations. The fact that the "coalition of the willing" that supported the United States in the Second Gulf War was much smaller than that assembled for the first—or for ousting the Taliban from Afghanistan—was due in part to the insensitivity with which the administration had treated its allies on topics such as the Kyoto climate change agreement and the creation of the International Criminal Court. Unlike most of his predecessors, Bush used U.S. dominance to act unilaterally and not to build a network of international organizations and agreements through which U.S. strength could be expressed. However, the realities of world politics and global economics acted as a powerful counterweight to these unilateralist instincts.

Finally, in "Leadership in an Era of Party Polarization," Bert A. Rockman places George W. Bush's presidential candidacy and leadership in a context of strident partisanship and polarization, perceiving therein a striking similarity to the disputed incumbency of another former president's son—John Quincy Adams. In the run-up to the 2000 election, Bush had to appear moderate and broadly appealing in order to make himself electable, but when it came time to govern, he had to provide red meat for his right-wing constituencies. Thus, he campaigned to the center but governed to the right—in part, to solidify his standing with his party's activists and, in part, because his own thinking appears to reflect many of their fundamental beliefs. Bush II's lesson from his father's administration—whether correct or not—was not to ignore the party base. However, as re-election time drew closer, Bush began increasingly to reposition himself back toward the center, moving away from his party's stridently right-wing leadership in the House of Representatives on hearth-and-home issues such as prescription drugs and tax credits for low-income working families.

The events of 9/11 would have left a powerful marker in any president's administration. In George W. Bush's case, the terrorist attacks came as the economic bubble of the late 1990s was bursting, and they served to accelerate the economy's decline. All things being equal, without the terrorist trauma and Bush's repeated vows to wage war on it (and much else), his approval ratings would likely be mediocre at best. Ironically, therefore, the ongoing security threat and the war-making response have saved the Bush II presidency, and it may be that such a presidency must sustain an aura of bellicosity to remain politically viable. In contrast to the Clinton administration, which liked to argue about options long into the night, often without choosing any, the Bush II presidency reflects the style of the business school–graduate at its head—it makes decisions quickly, decisively, and without benefit of significant analysis.

Although the individual commentators employ differing terminologies, much of what this book reveals about Bush II fits broadly within my own preferred emphasis on the importance of unrestrained ideological entrepreneurship. One finds in the chapters to come myriad policy areas wherein that concept might prove useful in an attempt to assess where the administration is headed at this stage. The answer to any question about what will ultimately come of the George W. Bush presidency perhaps rests in its tendency to pursue ideological principle with such intense entrepreneurship and on so many fronts. It seems inevitable that an administration acting with such heavily value-laden zeal in so many realms, domestic and international, most certainly runs the risk of overextension and ignominious collapse. One can only hope that, if this danger should be realized, the resulting train wreck(s) will cause minimal collateral damage to the political system, the well-being of Americans, and the long-term standing of the United States with the rest of the world.

Notes

I am immensely grateful to Jamie Gillies, a graduate student in the Department of Political Science at the University of British Columbia, for his assistance on the research for this chapter and chapter 4 of this book. I am also indebted to Joel D. Aberbach, Bert A. Rockman, and Graham K. Wilson for their comments on each chapter.

1. John P. Mackintosh, *The British Cabinet* (London: Stevens & Sons, 1977), 51.
2. Frank Bruni and Eric Schmitt, "Looking for Just the Right Fit," *New York Times*, 25 July 2000.
3. Richard Berke, "A Safe Pick Is Revealing," *New York Times*, 26 June 2000.
4. Gerald R. Ford and Bob Dole, "The Wisdom of Choosing Dick Cheney," *New York Times*, 31 July 2000.
5. Colin Campbell, "Demotion? Has Clinton Turned the Bully Pulpit into a Lectern?" in *The Clinton Legacy*, ed. Colin Campbell and Bert A. Rockman (New York: Chatham House, 2000), 53.
6. Mike Allen, "Bush's Choices Defy Talk of Conciliation," *Washington Post*, 31 December 2000.
7. David S. Broder, "For Bush, Desire to Unite Will Be Tested," *Washington Post*, 14 December 2000.
8. Colin Campbell, *Managing the Presidency: Carter, Reagan and the Search for Executive Harmony* (Pittsburgh: University of Pittsburgh Press, 1986), 10–13.

9. Richard W. Stevenson, "On Cloudy Economic Horizon, Bush's Silver Lining," *New York Times*, 7 December 2000.

10. David E. Rosenbaum, "Like Father, Bush Is Caught in a Politically Perilous Budget Squeeze," *New York Times*, 9 September 2001; and Richard L. Berke and David E. Sanger, "Bush's Aides Seek to Focus Efforts on the Economy," *New York Times*, 9 September 2001.

11. Eric Schmitt, "Cheney Describes His Nerve-Center Role in the First Hours of Crisis," *New York Times*, 17 September 2001; and Mike Allen, "Quietly, Cheney Again Takes Prominent Role," *Washington Post*, 17 September 2001.

12. Dana Milbank, "The Chairman and the CEO," *Washington Post*, 24 December 2000.

13. Mary McGrory, "Rudy Unlimited," *Washington Post*, 30 September 2001.

14. Jim Hoagland, "Two Who Seized the Moment," *Washington Post*, 7 October 2001; and "Mr. Blair's Vision," editorial, *Washington Post*, 8 October 2001.

15. Dana Milbank and T.R. Reid, "New Global Threat Revives Old Alliance," *Washington Post*, 16 October 2001.

16. Mike Allen, "An Unvarnished President on Display," *Washington Post*, 19 September 2001.

17. Adam Clymer, "Defying Expectations, a Bush Dynasty Begins to Look Real," *New York Times*, 10 November 2002.

18. Thomas L. Friedman, "Colin Powell's Eyebrows," *New York Times*, 10 November 2002.

19. Larry Berman and Bruce W. Jentleson, "Bush and the Post–Cold War World: New Challenges for American Leadership," in *The Bush Presidency: First Appraisals*, ed. Colin Campbell and Bert A. Rockman (Chatham, N.J.: Chatham House, 1991), 119–21.

20. Michael R. Gordon and General Bernard E. Trainor, *The General's War: The Inside Story of the Conflict in the Gulf* (Boston: Little, Brown, 1995), 36.

21. Colin Campbell, "The White House and Presidency under the 'Let's Deal' President," in Campbell and Rockman, *Bush Presidency*, 213–16.

22. Colin Campbell and Graham K. Wilson, *The End of Whitehall: Death of a Paradigm?* (Oxford: Blackwell, 1995), 124–25, 132.

23. Colin Campbell, *The U.S. Presidency in Crisis: A Comparative Perspective* (Oxford: Oxford University Press, 1998), 122–28.

24. Rockman penned the words deploying this imagery in the preface to Campbell and Rockman, *Bush Presidency*, viii. See also Peter Jenkins, "The Shift of Key to Major May Not Be Enough," *The Independent*, 14 November 1991.

25. Campbell, *U.S. Presidency in Crisis*, 131–32.

26. Bill Keller, "Reagan's Son," *New York Times*, 26 January 2003.

CHAPTER 2

Riding High in the Polls
George W. Bush and Public Opinion

George C. Edwards III

THE PRESIDENT'S RELATIONS with the public lie at the core of the modern presidency. Both politics and policy revolve around presidents' attempts to garner public support, both for themselves and for their policies. Three fundamental and widely shared premises about the relationship between public opinion and presidential leadership underlie this mode of governance. The first is that public support is a crucial political resource for the president, that it is difficult for others who hold power to deny the legitimate demands of a president with popular support. A president who lacks the public's support is likely to face frustration and perhaps humiliation at the hands of his opponents. As Bill Clinton exclaimed after he was acquitted in his impeachment trial, "Thank god for public opinion."[1]

The second premise supporting the White House's intense focus on public opinion is the view that the president not only must earn public support with his performance in office but also must actively take his case to the people. Moreover, he must do it not only at reelection time but all the time. As Clinton adviser Dick Morris put it:

> Once upon a time, elections settled things for the term of office. Now, they are mere punctuation marks in an ongoing search for public support and a functioning majority. Each day is election day in modern America. . . . A politician needs a permanent campaign to keep a permanent majority.[2]

The third (and least analyzed) premise sustaining the public presidency is that through the permanent campaign the White House *can* successfully persuade or even mobilize the public. Commentators on the presidency in both the press and the academy often assume that the White House can move public opinion if the president has the skill and will to effectively exploit the "bully pulpit." As a result, modern presidents choose to engage in a permanent campaign for the public's support as their core strategy for governing.

For most of the period since 11 September 2001, George W. Bush has enjoyed extraordinarily high levels of public approval. He has also enthusiastically adopted the permanent campaign of his predecessors. In this chapter I explore the public's evaluations of George W. Bush, his efforts to lead the public, and the impact his public support has had on congressional response to his policy proposals.

Public Evaluations

Certainly one of the highest priorities of presidents is to obtain the public's support for themselves. Presidents believe that public approval increases the probabilities of obtaining the passage of legislation in Congress, positive coverage in the press, and even responsiveness in the bureaucracy. As a result of their belief in the importance of public approval, they devote an impressive amount of time, energy, and money to obtaining it. How has the public evaluated George W. Bush?

The "Honeymoon" Period

The unusual nature of George W. Bush's election had a substantial potential to weaken the start of his presidency—and eliminate any potential for a honeymoon. Receiving neither a majority nor even a plurality of the vote, Bush became the first candidate since 1888 to be elected with fewer popular votes than his principal opponent. In light of the election results, the new president could not credibly claim a mandate from the people. Moreover, the Republicans lost seats in both houses of Congress, undermining any claim to presidential coattails.

Many (mostly Democrats) saw his victory as illegitimate, because he received more than a half-million fewer votes than Al Gore and because of the peculiar circumstances surrounding the determination of the winner of Florida's electoral votes. A Gallup poll taken just before the inauguration found that 31 percent of Americans thought Bush "won on a technicality" and 24 percent thought he "stole the election," while 45 percent said he "won fair and square." Thirty-eight percent of Americans still considered Gore to be the "real winner of the election."[3]

Nevertheless, Americans were optimistic that the new president would succeed in the core activities of the presidency (see table 2.1). In addition, the public had confidence that the president would make progress on important issues such as improving the country's security and education and keeping America prosperous. The public was less sanguine regarding other specific policy accomplishments, however. Most people did not feel that the president would succeed

TABLE 2.1. Early Expectations of President George W. Bush (in percentages)

Confident that the president can:

Set a good moral example	81
Use military force wisely	78
Prevent major scandals in his administration	77
Manage the executive branch wisely	77
Work effectively with Congress to get things done	74
Fulfill the proper role of the U.S. in world affairs	72
Handle an international crisis	71

Source: CNN/*USA Today*/Gallup poll, 15–16 January 2001.

TABLE 2.2. Expectations of the George W. Bush Administration (in percentages)

Q: Do you think the Bush administration will or will not be able to do the following?

	Will	*Will Not*
Improve military security for the country	81	16
Improve education	66	32
Keep America prosperous	63	33
Increase respect for the presidency	61	36
Improve respect for the United States abroad	58	38
Improve moral values in the United States	55	41
Keep the federal budget balanced	50	46
Ensure the long-term strength of the Social Security system	50	44
Cut your taxes	49	46
Ensure the long-term strength of the Medicare system	49	44
Improve the healthcare system	46	49
Improve race relations	44	51
Reduce the crime rate	44	50
Improve conditions for the disadvantaged and the poor	44	51
Improve the quality of the environment	42	52
Heal political divisions in this country	41	53

Source: Gallup poll, 15–16 January 2001.

at improving race relations, the environment, or conditions for the poor; reducing crime; or healing the country's political divisions. A plurality did not anticipate that the president would succeed in improving the health care system, and majorities did not believe the president could deliver on a tax cut, ensuring the long-term health of the Medicare and Social Security systems, or keeping the federal budget balanced (see table 2.2). Indeed, only 46 percent of the public felt the country would be better off in four years.[4]

There were forces working in the new president's favor, however. The "positivity bias"—the tendency to evaluate positively public figures and institutions—has the greatest potential for influence in ambiguous situations, such as the beginning of a president's term, when the new occupant of the Oval Office is unknown to the public as chief executive. There tends to be a national consensus following a presidential campaign: people want their new president to succeed and usually give him the benefit of the doubt.

In addition, as people have little basis on which to evaluate the president, they may turn elsewhere for cues. The press generally treats a new chief executive favorably. Moreover, there is excitement and symbolism inherent in the peaceful transfer of power, the inaugural festivities, and the prevalent sense of "new beginnings." All this creates a positive environment in which initial evaluations of elected presidents take place, buttressing any effect of the positivity bias.

Bush may have lost the popular vote for president, but he received positive reviews immediately after taking office. Although he had won only 48 percent of the vote the previous November, 57 percent of the public approved his performance in the first two polls taken after his inauguration. Bill Clinton began his tenure with a similar 58 percent approval rating. As is typically the case in presidential approval polls, party identification was the best predictor of approval. For example, in the 9–11 February Gallup poll, Bush received approval from 88 percent of Republicans and 54 percent of Independents, but only 31 percent of Democrats. His approval level held reasonably steady, increasing slightly to 62 percent near the symbolic 100-day mark.

Another advantage for Bush was that at the beginning of his term 65 percent of the public approved of him as a person. Ninety-one percent of Republicans, 63 percent of Independents and 40 percent of Democrats said they approved of Bush as a person. Perhaps reflecting the acrimony of the election controversy, however, 49 percent of Democrats disapproved of Bush as a person.[5]

Bush also enjoyed positive evaluations on a number of personal character dimensions, particularly as someone with a vision for the country's future and who was strong and skilled enough to achieve this vision (see table 2.3). The public's opinion of Bush seemed consistent with the image of a straight-talking chief executive officer that he had tried to project during the campaign. Contrary to the views of his most vocal detractors, majorities of the public felt that Bush understood complex issues, and only 26 percent of the public felt he was not working hard enough to be an effective president.[6] In light of the public's negative evaluations of his predecessor's character, it is worth noting that large majorities saw the new president as honest and trustworthy.

Positive evaluations of Bush's personal characteristics proved to be important, because in its 20–22 April 2001 poll, Gallup found that 52 percent of Americans considered leadership skills and vision to be the most important criterion for evaluating the president's job performance—compared to 36 percent who felt that the

TABLE 2.3. Evaluations of Bush Characteristics and Qualities

Q: *Thinking about the following characteristics and qualities, please say whether you think each one applies or doesn't apply to George W. Bush.*

Characteristic	Percentage saying it applies					
	9–11 February 2001	20–22 April 2001	5–6 October 2001	29 April–1 May 2002	26–28 July 2002	10–12 January 2003
Has vision for country's future		74				68
Can get things done		69				
Is tough enough for the job	68	68				
Is honest and trustworthy	64	67		77		
Is a strong and decisive leader	61	60	75	77	69	70
Can manage the government effectively	61		79	75	70	76
Shares your values	57	58	75	67	66	67
Inspires confidence	57	55	69	66	60	54
Cares about the needs of people like you	56	59	69	68	66	65
Understands complex issues	55	56	60	64	60	56
Generally agrees with you on issues you care about	53			64	60	
Is a person you admire	49					
Keeps his promises		57				
Is sincere in what he says				76		
Provides good moral leadership			84	84		
Puts the country's interests ahead of his own political interests			72			
Is not a typical politician				54		

Source: Gallup polls, various dates.

TABLE 2.4 Issue Approval for George W. Bush (in percentages)

Issue	20–22 April 2001	10–11 July 2001	22–24 March 2002	26–28 July 2002	10–12 January 2003
Overall	62	57	79	69	58
Economy	55	54	65	52	53
Foreign affairs	56	54	71	63	48
Defense	66		80		63
Education	62	63	63	62	57
Taxes	54	60	64		49
Budget	52		51		43
Unemployment	47		57		
Environment	46	46	53		
Abortion	43		49		39
Energy	43	45	57		
Social Security		49	47		
Health care			52	47	41

Source: Gallup poll, various dates.

president's stance on issues was the most important criterion. Gallup found that a plurality of all key subgroups, including Bush's natural opponents—Democrats and liberals—assigned more importance to leadership skills and vision than to agreement on issues. The importance the public accorded Bush's personal characteristics may partly explain why his overall job approval rating was higher than support for his job performance in the more specific policy-related areas.

Indeed, Bush's overall approval rating exceeded his approval rating on many specific issues. Table 2.4 presents results of five Gallup polls taken during his presidency. Focusing on the two polls in the pre–September 11, 2001, period, we see that the president was rated most highly on the issues that were his highest priorities: taxes, education, and defense. It is reasonable to conclude that these issues were the most salient to the public in the early months of the Bush administration. Conversely, less than 50 percent of the public approved of his performance on Social Security, unemployment, abortion, the environment, and energy. These issues evidently were less salient in evaluations of the president.

Thus, President Bush appeared to be well positioned in his relations with the public early in his term. The public accorded him reasonably high levels of approval for his job performance, liked him as a person, and perceived him as having a wide range of positive personal characteristics that it valued in a chief executive. Ratings of his performance on issues were more mixed, but were positive on his priority issues.

As presidents perform their duties, citizens obtain more information and thus a more comprehensive basis for judging them. Moreover, as time passes, people may begin to perceive greater implications of presidential policies for their own lives. Overall, the president's approval held reasonably steady in the mid–50s, but it dipped to 51 percent in the Gallup poll that concluded on 10 September 2001. (Bill Clinton was at 47 percent approval at this point in his tenure.) Things were not going well for the president.

As Congress returned to session following its summer recess, Democrats were beginning to blame Bush's tax cut for "defunding" the federal government and forcing Congress to spend the surplus provided by Social Security contributions. These funds were to have been placed in a "lock box," off limits for paying current expenses. At the same time, unemployment was climbing and news about the country's economic recession was becoming more prominent in the media. The president's initiatives on education and funding for faith-based charities were stalled, and stories were circulating that Secretary of Defense Donald Rumsfeld was being thwarted in his efforts to reform the U.S. defense posture.

The public was also giving the president low marks on the environment and energy (see the 10–11 July 2001, Gallup poll results in table 2.4). In March Bush made a series of environmental decisions that were widely viewed as pro-industry, including reversing a campaign pledge to seek a reduction in carbon dioxide emissions from power plants, rescinding Bill Clinton's regulations lowering the level of arsenic acceptable in drinking water, rejecting the Kyoto accords on global warming, withdrawing the ban on building roads in 60 million acres of federal forests and limits on logging in those areas, and canceling higher efficiency standards for air conditioners. The White House also sought to permit drilling for oil in the Arctic National Wildlife Refuge. Then the administration launched a national energy policy that was seen as emphasizing exploration and production rather than conservation and the development of alternative energy sources. Bush's actions thus played into the stereotype of a conservative Republican former energy company executive who was too cozy with special interests. In April Gallup found that 63 percent of the public felt that big business had too much influence over the administration's decisions. 7

The Rally

As figure 2.1 shows, President Bush stood at an unimpressive 51 percent approval rating in the Gallup poll that concluded on 10 September 2001. The terrorist attacks the following day, however, provided him an opportunity to remake his image and build a new relationship with the American people.

Within days (perhaps hours) of the attack, questions about the president's legitimacy or competence disappeared in the outburst of patriotism for which the commander in chief served as the focal point. In a poll taken on the day of the

FIGURE 2.1   George W. Bush Job Approval Rating (in percentages)

Q: Do you approve or disapprove of the way George W. Bush is handling his job as president?

Source: Gallup polls, various dates.

attacks, *prior* to Bush's short nationwide address, a Gallup poll found 78 percent of Americans expressing confidence in Bush's ability to handle the situation. The 14–15 September Gallup poll showed 91 percent of Americans approving of the way the president was handling the response to the terrorist attacks—nearly a week *before* his address to a joint session of Congress. The ABC News/*Washington Post* poll on 13 September found the same level of approval.

Equally important, Americans overwhelmingly saw the president as rising to the occasion. After a shaky start, he performed well, appearing confident, reassuring, and resolute. As R.W. Apple Jr. wrote in the *New York Times*, Bush "sought to console the bereaved, comfort the wounded, encourage the heroic, calm the fearful, and . . . rally the country for the struggle and sacrifices ahead."[8] There was no more talk of a stature gap in the presidency.

Following the terrorist attacks, approval of Bush's job performance soared to 86 percent—an increase of 35 percentage points that represents the largest rally effect ever recorded by the Gallup Poll. The second highest jump recorded by Gallup in the past half century was during the Gulf War, when approval of the president's father, George H.W. Bush, jumped by 20 percentage points after the launching of Operation Desert Storm in January 1991.

The surge in support was not limited to the president's overall approval rating. In addition to the 91-percent approval of the way Bush was handling the events subsequent to the terrorist attacks, almost nine in ten Americans expressed confidence in the U.S. government's ability to protect its citizens from future attacks. The administration also benefited in another way from the rally around the president. Although Americans overwhelmingly blamed Osama bin Laden and other countries for the terrorist attacks, a majority also blamed airport security, the CIA, and the FBI. Forty-five percent blamed the Clinton administration, but only 34 percent blamed the Bush administration.[9]

Shortly after September 11th, the public saw Bush in a new light. Large majorities regarded him as sincere, strong, and decisive, an effective manager, inspiring confidence, caring about average people, and understanding complex issues (see table 2.3). The following spring, the public still saw his personal characteristics and qualities in a very positive light.

The president's overall job approval level rose another 4 percentage points, reaching 90 percent in the 21–22 September 2001 Gallup poll. This approval rating was one point higher than the previous high point, registered by his father at the end of hostilities in the Persian Gulf War.[10]

The rally for Bush was based on changes in the evaluations of Democrats and Independents. Republicans had accorded the president strong support from his first days in office, typically providing more than 90 percent approval. Thus, there was little potential for Republicans to rally.[11] The potential was much greater for Democrats and Independents, only a minority of whom (44 percent of Independents and 27 percent of Democrats) had approved of his performance before the terrorist attacks. Immediately afterwards, their approval levels rose to more than 80 percent.

Between September 11th and the end of March 2002, the president retained the approval of more than 79 percent of the public, a level unprecedented in the past half century. This high overall approval rating was undoubtedly driven by the strongly positive evaluations of his performance on the issues of defense and foreign policy, but these impressive approval levels seem also to have had a halo effect, increasing his support on unrelated issues as well. The results of the 22–24 March 2002 Gallup poll (see table 2.4) show that the public's evaluation of Bush's handling of issues rose substantially not only on defense and foreign affairs, but also on the economy, unemployment, energy, and the environment. He maintained the strong support he had previously achieved on education and taxes. In that same poll, the president received 86 percent approval for his performance on preventing terrorism in the United States and also for fighting terrorism abroad. Seventy-two percent of the public approved of his handling of the Middle East.

The terrorist attacks and the resulting war on terrorism's dominance of the public agenda, then, had the perverse consequence of solving several intractable problems facing the president. After September 11th, the recession gave way as a news story to terrorism and preparations to wage war in Afghanistan. Later, Bush could lay blame for economic problems at the feet of Osama bin Laden and his supporters. Everyone seemed to forget about the Social Security lock box as Congress raced to provide whatever was needed to aid the victims of terrorism and to fight terrorists abroad. When consensual policy dominates the political landscape, presidents do well in the polls.

Bush's approval ratings may have also inoculated him from being blamed for bad news. For example, in January 2002 only 20 percent of the public blamed the Bush administration "a lot" or "fairly much" for the current recession.[12] In May 2002 most people agreed with the administration's contention that the information available to it prior to September 11th had not been sufficient to prevent the terrorist attacks on the World Trade Center and the Pentagon.[13] Bush's defense of his failure to file notification of his sale of Harken stock on time and of the accounting practices at Harken seemed to put that potentially damaging story to rest.

After the Rally

Although the rally that began on 11 September 2001 was the most sustained in modern times, an eventual decline was inevitable. Americans seemed to grow uneasy amid terrorism warnings, a stagnant economy, and the failures of such prominent institutions as the FBI, the CIA, major corporations, and the Catholic church. The Gallup poll of 3–6 June 2002 found that the president's approval rating had dropped 7 points in a week, and that of 21–23 June showed that only one-third of the public believed the United States was winning the war on terrorism. These concerns were reflected in the drop in public approval of the president's performance on foreign affairs, the economy, and health care (see the 26–28 July 2002 results in table 2.4). As in the previous summer, the administration seemed to be adrift.

The decline in Bush's overall job approval rating during this period was the result in large part of losses among those who had rallied earlier: Democrats and, to a lesser degree, Independents. By the end of the summer, the president had fallen to 50 percent approval among Democrats and 56 percent among Independents. On the other hand, his ratings among Republicans remained in the 90s.[14]

Having drifted down in the Gallup poll as far as 65 percent in August 2002 (and even lower in the polls of a number of other organizations), Bush's overall approval ratings increased slightly in September. As the spotlight turned from the economy, corporate malfeasance, and failures in the intelligence community to responses to the Iraqi threat against the United States, the president's approval ratings stabilized and even rose slightly. This approval level diminished slightly in the first quarter of 2003, but the president benefited from a 13 percentage point rally once the war with Iraq began.

After the war, the public focused on both the economy and the pacification and reconstruction of Iraq. Although the economy was growing, unemployment levels remained stable, depressing the evaluations of the president's handling of the economy. Similarly, the continued violence in Iraq and the high cost of reconstruction weakened the president's standing in the foreign policy realm. Together, these trends left him just above the 50 percent mark in overall approval.

Going Public

Every president must choose a strategy for governing within the context in which he finds himself. One approach is to seek to pass legislation through relatively quiet negotiations with congressional leaders. The president's father, George H.W. Bush, provided an example with his administration's efforts regarding environmental, education, and budget policy. An alternative strategy is to take the case to the people, counting on public opinion to move Congress to support the president. The second President Bush, surprisingly to some, chose the latter course.

Soon after taking office, the president launched a massive public relations campaign on behalf of his priority initiatives. At the core of this effort was the most extensive domestic travel schedule of any new president in American history. By the end of May, Bush had spoken in 29 states, often more than once.

Despite a severely truncated transition, Bush lost no time in sending priority bills to Congress. Proposals for a large cut in income taxes, education reform, and increased support for faith-based charities went to Congress in short order. The White House also launched an extensive review of the nation's defense posture.

The president not only spoke extensively about each initiative, but he also went to considerable lengths to focus attention on each proposal in the early weeks of the administration. The faith-based initiative received attention in the week after the inauguration, followed in successive weeks by education, tax cuts, and defense.

The White House employs a "rolling" announcement format in which it alerts the press that it will be making an announcement about a legislative initiative in coming days, sparking stories on the upcoming news. Then it makes the announcement, generating additional stories. Finally, the president travels around the country repeating the announcement he just made, obtaining both local and network coverage of his media events.

Public Relations Efforts

There are less-direct ways of going public than the president's giving a speech. The White House employs some public relations techniques in ways that it hopes will affect broad perceptions of the Bush presidency or structure thinking about issues. There are some characteristic patterns in the Bush White House's public relations efforts.

Control the Venue.   Although the president has gone public actively, he has done so in controlled venues. As the *Washington Post* reported in September 2002, Bush had devoted far more time to golf (fifteen rounds) than to solo news conferences (six). [15] After holding three news conferences in his first four months, he held only three more in his next twenty–four months—not counting the question-and-answer sessions he had with foreign leaders during this period. [16]

Emphasize the Bright Side.   One pattern of White House public relations efforts is what one journalist described as "compromise quietly, claim victory loudly." Bush is a pragmatist who makes the best deal he can with Congress and then declares victory. The White House knows that few Americans will notice or care that he did not get all, or even most, of what he wanted. Regarding education policy, for example, the Heritage Foundation complained on 5 July 2001 that "key elements of the president's plan—accountability, choice, flexibility and structural change—have been eliminated or weakened to the point that his design for educational reform is barely recognizable." Two weeks earlier, however, Bush had projected a more optimistic view. "I'm pleased to say that we're nearing historic reforms in public education," he said. "This is a victory for every child and for every family in America." The administration would rather public commentary focus on the size of the president's victory rather than on whether there *was* a victory. [17] Naturally, the White House hopes that its claims of victory will be self-fulfilling, improving its reputation and thus the chances for future successes.

The White House serves up its upbeat diagnosis each day and again at week's end. Bush's aides send the talking points throughout the White House, to allies on Capitol Hill, and to Republican opinion leaders around town. Interest groups receive customized talking points, such as a list of Bush victories for Hispanics. In an era of 24-hour cable and Internet news, the administration hopes that its talking points, repeated by administration officials or allies, will be reported by outlets too pressed for time to put the claims in context.

Manage the Image.   The Bush White House is also skilled at using the powers of television and technology to promote the president. "We pay particular attention to not only what the president says but what the American people see," said Office of Communications director Dan Bartlett. Thus the White House has hired experts in lighting, camera angles, and backdrops from network television to showcase the president in dramatic and perfectly lighted settings. In May 2003, at a speech in Indianapolis promoting his economic plan, White House aides went so far as to ask people in the crowd behind Mr. Bush to take off their ties so they would look more like the ordinary people the president said would benefit from his tax cut. For a speech that the president delivered in the summer of 2002 at Mount Rushmore, the White House positioned the platform for television crews off to one side so that the cameras caught Mr. Bush in profile, his face perfectly aligned with the four presidents chiseled in stone.[18]

Perhaps the most elaborate White House event was Mr. Bush's speech aboard the *Abraham Lincoln* announcing the end of major combat in Iraq. The Office of Communications choreographed every aspect of the event, even down to arraying members of the crew in coordinated shirt colors over Bush's right shoulder and placing a banner reading "Mission Accomplished" to perfectly capture the president and the celebratory two words in a single shot. The speech was specifically timed for the sun to cast a golden glow on Mr. Bush. One of the president's aides proclaimed, "If you looked at the TV picture, you saw there was flattering light on his left cheek and slight shadowing on his right. It looked great."[19]

Change Justifications.   The Bush administration has been skillful in adapting rationales for its policy proposals to changing circumstances. The president advocated tax cuts as a way to return money to taxpayers when the government ran a budget surplus, as a way to constrain future government growth, as an insurance policy against an economic downturn, and as a means of stimulating a stagnant economy. The facts that the surplus soon disappeared, that government had to grow substantially as a result of the war on terrorism, that an economic downturn occurred, and that most of the tax reductions would not occur for years (and thus could not provide a stimulus) were ignored.

On the issue of regime change in Iraq, the administration sought first to link

Iraqi President Saddam Hussein to al Qaeda and the September 11th attacks. When those links proved tenuous, the administration proclaimed a shift in U.S. strategic defense doctrine from deterrence and containment to preemption of those who would use weapons of mass destruction. When critics at home and abroad complained that the United States was ignoring its allies in pursuit of unilateral action, the president went to New York and declared that Iraq's refusal to comply with United Nations resolutions *required* multilateral action to preserve the viability of the world organization. Similarly, Bush responded to criticism that he had usurped the legislature's war powers by going to Congress and asking for a strong resolution of support for the use of force against Iraq. After the war, when weapons of mass destruction had not been found, the president focused on destroying the *capability* to produce such weapons rather than the weapons themselves.

Stay Resilient. The Bush administration has continually demonstrated resilience in its relations with the public. The summer of 2002 provides an excellent example of this pattern. By June, only 54 percent of the respondents felt Bush had strong qualities of leadership. Even worse, only 42 percent expressed confidence in his ability to deal wisely with an international crisis and only 45 percent thought he had the skills necessary to negotiate effectively with world leaders. Fifty-seven percent felt the administration favored the rich.[20] The next month, the same poll found the public evenly split on whether Bush or his aides were running the government. A plurality of 48 percent felt the United States was on the wrong track, 58 percent viewed business as having too much influence on Bush, and 66 percent felt the same way about business influence on the administration. Sixty-one percent of the public felt the administration's proposal for reforming corporate accounting practices showed it was more interested in protecting the interests of large corporations than those of ordinary Americans.[21]

The White House did not allow events to overtake it, however. In the week following its biggest drop in the Gallup poll since the September 11 rally began, it announced—"hurriedly" in the minds of critics—its proposals for a new Department of Homeland Security. This returned it to a proactive stance and also provided a distraction from congressional hearings that were critical of the federal bureaucracy's performance.

In August, the administration again seemed to be adrift. As it stepped up its rhetoric against Saddam Hussein and advocated a unilateral strategy for regime change, the United States found its allies reluctant partners. Indeed, many were openly critical of the president's policy. Even more damaging were highly visible cautionary warnings from Republican establishment figures such as James Baker, Brent Scowcroft, and Lawrence Eagleburger. Moreover, more than two-thirds of the public signaled that it was necessary to obtain resolutions authorizing going to war with Iraq from both Congress and the United Nations—authorizations the administration argued it did not require. Fifty-eight percent of the public felt the White House had not done a sufficient job of explaining to the American public why the United States might take military action to remove Saddam Hussein from power.[22] In addition, the public remained quite pessimistic about the economy.

Once again, the administration turned the tide. Putting on a full-court press, Bush turned the tables on his critics by asking the UN for multilateral action and Congress for a resolution authorizing force. In short order, a majority of the American public concluded that the administration had made its case for going to war clearly.[23] As the public became convinced that there would likely be a war with Iraq and that the White House was meeting its critics at least halfway, it began moving behind the president and his approval ratings reversed some of the losses sustained over the summer.

As the UN weapons inspectors searched for illegal weapons of mass destruction in Iraq early in 2003, the administration yet again found itself in danger of losing control of events. As international pressure built to give the inspectors more time, it appeared that opponents of the war in the UN were setting the terms of debate. In response, the administration launched a carefully coordinated series of speeches by leading figures in January and February, culminating in the presentation to the Security Council by Secretary of State Colin Powell.[24] As a result, support for invading Iraq with ground troops rose to its highest point since 2001 (see table 2.7).

Focus on Values.   The Bush White House copied a page from Bill Clinton's (and Dick Morris's) playbook by frequently focusing on values rather than issues. For example, it has staged events around the country that focused on family-friendly concerns such as fitness, homeownership, reading, and adoption—typically providing largely symbolic support. Such efforts were designed to appeal to suburban women, one of the most sought-after groups of votes, and to reach people who do not focus on politics by relating to the issues in their personal lives. Local media typically gave substantial coverage to these events.

Such events were natural outgrowths of the 2000 presidential campaign, in which Bush emphasized returning dignity and integrity to the presidency, "an era of responsibility," "leave no child behind," and, of course, "compassion." The war on terrorism provided new symbols for the president to exploit, focused around the most basic of public concerns, that of safeguarding people from attack in their homes and workplaces.

Influencing the Agenda

A major goal of every administration is dominating the political agenda. Usually this means focusing public attention on its top-priority issues and, if possible, keeping lower priority and potentially politically damaging issues off the agenda. Karl Rove, the president's wide-ranging senior adviser, maintained that Bush campaigned on six key issues: tax cuts, education standards, military upgrades and a missile defense shield, federal support for faith-based charities, partial privatization of Social Security, and Medicare reforms and prescription drug coverage for seniors.[25] If these were Bush's priorities, he did a good job of focusing on them, helping to secure them a place on the national agenda.

Tax cuts were the administration's highest priority, but education reform, an overhaul of defense policy, and greater federal support for faith-based social welfare programs were also high on the list. As we have seen, the president not only spoke extensively about each initiative, but he also went to considerable lengths to focus attention on each proposal in the early weeks of the administration. Not surprisingly, a study of the first sixty days of news coverage of the Bush and Clinton administrations found that Bush was more successful than Clinton in controlling his message. Each of the five most reported stories about Bush was on his priority initiatives, amounting to more than a third of all stories.[26]

During the first months in office the president has the greatest latitude in focusing on priority legislation. After the transition period, other interests have more influence on the White House agenda. Congress is quite capable of setting its own agenda and is unlikely to defer to the president for long. In addition, ongoing policies continually force decisions to the president's desk.

The George W. Bush presidency is no exception to the challenge of controlling the national agenda. At the same time that the president was seeking support for his priority items, he had to engage in legislative battles on important issues such as campaign finance reform and a patients' bill of rights and make a highly visible decision on stem cell research. In fact, he had to devote one of only two nationally televised addresses (scarce presidential resources) of his first seven months in office to the latter. Bush also inevitably became embroiled in the issue of navy practice bombings in Vieques, Puerto Rico.

More damaging were his responses to the unexpected energy shortage in California and his decisions on environmental regulations, many of which were proposed by his predecessor. His and Vice President Cheney's energy plan was widely viewed as a sop to the oil-and-gas industry the two had served, and many people saw the administration as having a weak commitment to environmental protection.

Despite the administration's organization and discipline regarding its legislative agenda, the need to respond to the terrorist attacks of September 11th immediately dominated the president's agenda. The emphasis on national unity in the weeks that followed the tragedy and the inevitable focus of the president's energies on national security limited opportunities for him to push hard for his most contentious proposals. We have already noted how the change in agenda solved potentially significant problems for Bush. As the recession and the Social Security lock box gave way as news stories to terrorism and preparation to wage war in Afghanistan, the public focused on consensual issues on which it rated the president highly.

When the president proposed a Department of Homeland Security on 6 June 2002 and when he made his case for regime change in Iraq later in the summer, he had no difficulty dominating the nation's agenda. Issues dealing with the security of Americans, recently shocked by terrorist attacks, easily captured the media's and the public's attention. Even a looming war with Iraq, however, could not stop people from placing the sagging economy at the forefront of their concerns.[27]

Success in Moving the Public

It is one thing to go public. It is something quite different to succeed in moving public opinion. How successful has George W. Bush been in his efforts to govern through a permanent campaign?

Taxes

The president made tax cuts the centerpiece of his campaign in 2000, and he wasted no time in proposing substantial tax cuts once he was inaugurated. He advocated them both frequently and forcefully. Table 2.5 shows responses to Gallup Poll questions on the president's tax-cut proposal. The results show that public opinion did not change in response to Bush's efforts.

In 2003, the president proposed a fundamental change in the tax structure, one that would eliminate taxes on most stock dividends and allow people to establish tax–free savings accounts. The policy did not gain traction with the public, however. The Pew Research Center for the People and the Press found that only 42 percent of the public approved of Bush's handling of taxes despite a high-profile White House campaign on behalf of its policy.[28] At the beginning of May, Pew found that only 40 percent of the public favored the president's tax cut.[29] Most respondents to a CBS/*New York Times* poll in early May said they did not think it was important to cut taxes or that doing so would stimulate the economy.[30] Similarly, the *Washington Post*-ABC News Poll found that tax cuts were of low importance to the public and that when given the choice between tax cuts and increased domestic spending, the public favored the latter by 67 percent to 29 percent.[31] Shortly before the president signed the truncated bill that eventually passed, Gallup found that more people felt the tax cuts were a bad idea than thought they were a good idea.[32]

The president originally requested a ten-year total of $726 billion in tax cuts. He repeatedly railed against the strategy of making tax cuts temporary and phasing them in over time. At the center of his proposal was the elimination of taxes

TABLE 2.5. Support for George W. Bush Tax Cut (in percentages)

Q: Based on what you have read or heard, do you favor or oppose the federal income tax cuts George W. Bush has proposed?

Poll date	Favor	Oppose	No opinion
9–11 February 2001	56	34	10
19–21 February 2001	53	30	17
5–7 March 2001	56	34	10
20–22 April 2001	56	35	9

Source: Gallup polls, various dates.

on stock dividends. In the end the president signed a tax bill that cut taxes $320 billion, that was temporary and phased in, and that did not eliminate the dividend tax.[33]

Four republican senators refused to support the full package: John McCain (Arizona), Lincoln Chafee (Rhode Island), Olympia Snowe (Maine), and George Voinovich (Ohio). The administration did not even try to pressure McCain and Chafee, knowing that it would be useless, but it did target Voinovich and Snowe. In addition, the White House did not object when the Club for Growth ran advertisements aimed at them in their home states. The administration also targeted Democrats John Breaux (Louisiana), Blanche Lincoln (Arkansas), and Ben Nelson (Nebraska).

The White House staged dozens of events around the country with administration officials and mobilized friendly interest groups to pressure senators. Sometimes these efforts seemed to equate tax cuts with patriotism. More importantly, the president took to the road, attempting to exploit his 70 percent approval ratings following the cessation of fighting in Iraq. In Ohio, the home of Republican holdout Voinovich, the president derided the Senate bill that provided $350 billion in tax cuts as a "a little bitty tax relief package" and insisted that senators who did not support him "might have some explaining to do."

In the end, the efforts had little impact and may even have backfired. Ben Nelson was the only Democrat (aside from long-time tax cut supporter Zell Miller) who supported even the $350 billion tax-cut bill the Senate passed. Of the four Republican opponents, only Voinovich voted for the final bill—after holding out for $32 billion of relief for the states and insisting that it be subtracted from even the scaled-down Senate bill. The White House declared victory, of course, but in reality Bush concluded that it was more important to have a tax cut than to stand on principle over its size and content.[34] The lack of success of his strategy of going public had left him no choice.

Televised Addresses

President Bush faced similar frustrations in attempting to increase his public support with his nationally televised addresses. Presidents do not speak directly to the American public over national television often, and when they do, they frequently are seeking support for themselves and their policies. Table 2.6 shows the difference in presidential approval in the Gallup polls taken most closely before and after each of George W. Bush's live televised addresses to the nation in his first thirty-two months in office. (In a comparison of survey results of two samples such as these, the results must reflect a gap of about 6 percentage points before we can be reasonably sure that they indicate any real difference.)

The figures in the third column of the table show that a statistically significant change in Bush's approval rating following a televised presidential address occurred only twice. The first was an increase of 35 percentage points following the terrorist attack on 11 September 11, 2001. Few would attribute the public's rallying around the commander in chief to the president's brief comments that evening. There was another rally, this time of 13 percentage points, following the president's address on March 17, 2003, announcing the invasion of Iraq. Again, it would be stretching to attribute the rally to the president's short statement.

Bush's approval rating went up only one percentage point in the Gallup poll following his address to a joint session of Congress on 27 February 2001, and only two percentage points following his 9 August 2001 address on his decision regarding federal funding of stem-cell research. After September 11th, when his approval was very high, there was less potential to increase his support.

There are many possible explanations for this repeated failure to move the public, but part of the reason for the modest response to Bush's early addresses may be that he drew equally modest audiences. A total of 39.8 million viewers saw at least part of his nationally televised address in February 2001. This audience compares unfavorably with the 67 million viewers for Bill Clinton's first nationally televised address in 1993. Moreover, there was a substantial fall-off in viewership during the president's speech.[35] The September 11th terrorist attacks increased interest in the president's messages, however. More than 80 million watched his address to a joint session of Congress on 20 September 2001, and his 2002 State of the Union message drew about 54 million viewers.[36] A live televised press conference on 11 October 2001 (his only one that year) drew 64.8 million viewers.

Bush compensated for the increased difficulty of obtaining time on television for presidential speeches and of gaining an audience when television provides coverage by traveling extensively around the country. If the increase in local appearances was intended to increase news coverage for the president and his policies, early indications are that it did not succeed. A comparative study of the news coverage of the first sixty days of the Clinton and George W. Bush presidencies

TABLE 2.6. Changes in George W. Bush Approval Ratings after National Addresses

Date of speech	Subject of speech	Change in approval (in percentages)
20 January 2001	Inaugural	NA
27 February 2001	Administration goals	+1
9 August 2001	Stem-cell research	+2
11 September 2001	Terrorist attacks	+35
20 September 2001	Terrorist attacks	+4
7 October 2001 (afternoon)	War in Afghanistan	+2
8 November 2001	War on terrorism[a]	0
29 January 2002	State of the Union	-2
6 June 2002	Department of Homeland Security	+4
11 September 2002	Anniversary of terrorist attacks	+4
7 October 2002	War with Iraq[b]	−5
28 January 2003	State of the Union	1
1 February 2003	Columbia space shuttle disaster	−2
26 February 2003	War with Iraq	1
17 March 2003	War with Iraq	13
1 May 2003	War with Iraq	−1
11 September 2003	Reconstruction of Iraq	−7

Source: Gallup polls, various dates.
[a]Broadcast by only one network.
[b]Broadcast only by Fox—not ABC, NBC, CBS, or PBS.

found that there was a dramatic across-the-board drop-off in coverage on television, newspapers, and news weeklies (see figure 2.2). Network television coverage was down 42 percent and newspaper coverage (*New York Times* and *Washington Post*) was off 38 percent. *Newsweek* magazine had 59 percent fewer stories about Bush in its pages than it carried about Clinton eight years earlier. Although the president was still a dominant figure on op-ed and editorial pages, he was less visible in the front pages, newscasts, and financial pages.[37] This lower profile was not an asset in advancing the president's agenda, and talk of a "disappearing presidency" began to be heard inside the Beltway.

The presidency reappeared in force following the September 11th terrorist attacks, however. The prominence of the commander in chief in wartime and the nation's need for reassurance and action against terrorists compelled the media to cover his words and actions and allowed him to dominate the news.

War with Iraq

The president's most important initiative in 2002 was preparation for war with Iraq. In the late summer, the White House decided it should move on regime

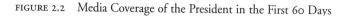

FIGURE 2.2 Media Coverage of the President in the First 60 Days

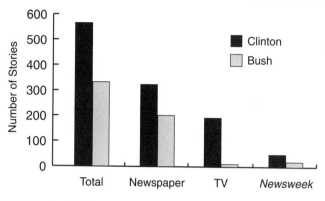

Source: The Project For Excellence in Journalism, *The First 100 Days: How Bush Versus Clinton Fared in the Press,* 2001.

change in Iraq and sought the public's backing. The context in which Bush sought this support was certainly favorable. In surveys conducted over the previous ten years, stretching back to the end of the Gulf War, majorities had generally supported U.S. military action to remove Saddam Hussein from power in Iraq. The American public had long held strongly negative perceptions of Iraq and its leader. In a December 1998 poll, Saddam Hussein received the worst rating of any public figure tested in Gallup poll history—1 percent positive and 96 percent negative.[38] In early 2002, the country of Iraq received a 6 percent favorable and 88 percent unfavorable rating, the worst of any of the twenty-five countries tested in that poll.[39] Since 1991, Iraq had never received even a 10 percent favorable rating.[40] Asked in February 2001 what country was America's worst enemy, Americans named Iraq significantly more often than any other country.[41]

In September 2002, Gallup reported that most Americans believed that Iraq had developed or was developing weapons of mass destruction. Many Americans felt that if left alone, Iraq would use those weapons against the United States within five years. Most Americans felt that Saddam Hussein sponsored terrorism that affected the United States. A little more than half of Americans took the additional inferential leap and concluded that Saddam Hussein was personally and directly involved in the September 11th terrorist attacks.[42]

On 26 August 2002, Vice President Cheney delivered a hard-hitting speech laying out the administration's case for invading Iraq, and then, on the anniversary of the terrorist attacks, the president delivered a nationally televised address. The next day he addressed the United Nations, demanding that it take action to disarm Iraq. Later, he asked Congress to pass a resolution authorizing him to use force against Iraq. On 7 October, Bush addressed the nation again, delivering his most comprehensive case for the need to use force against Saddam Hussein's regime in Iraq. On 26 February and 17 March 2003, the president again made national addresses on Iraq.

It is interesting to note that although Bush's 7 October speech was strictly nonpartisan, delivered in a venue chosen for the absence of a statewide election in the midterm elections, and focused on what is perhaps the most important decision a nation can take, ABC, CBS, NBC, and PBS nevertheless chose not to carry the president's remarks. The White House was reluctant to make a special request for airtime out of concern for fanning fears of an imminent invasion, but it would have welcomed coverage. The networks argued that the president's speech contained little that was new. In the absence of breaking news, the commander in chief was unable to obtain airtime to discuss his thinking about going to war. As a result, only about 17 million people viewed the speech.[43]

Table 2.7 shows public support for the invasion of Iraq, indicating that public opinion did not change in response to the administration's blitzkrieg. Gallup used the phrase "sending American ground troops" in the question about invading Iraq. Some other polling organizations simply asked about "military action"—an easier threshold—and found higher levels of support. The president, of course, sought support for the use of ground troops as well as other means of projecting force. Nevertheless, surveys by the Pew Research Center and the CBS/*New York Times* poll found little or no change in public support for invading Iraq since before the White House's public relations effort. Indeed, Pew found that between mid-August and the end of October support for taking military action in Iraq to end Saddam Hussein's rule decreased by 9 percentage points.[44]

Furthermore, Americans expressed reservations and listed conditions for their support. They had strong preferences for both a congressional authorization of the use of force and securing the participation of allies.[45] They also preferred to wait for weapons inspectors to attempt to disarm Iraq before the United States took military action. At the same time, respondents said they were more concerned with the economy than with Iraq, and 69 percent (including 51 percent of Republicans) complained that Bush should be paying more attention to the economy.[46]

Public support for invading Iraq with ground troops stayed within a narrow range throughout the fall and winter until early February. At that point it increased five percentage points. This increase was not in response to the president, however, but to Secretary of State Colin Powell's presentation of evidence against Iraq to the United Nations. In the month following Powell's speech, support for an invasion drifted downward until the middle of March, when the president issued the final ultimatum to Saddam Hussein that marked the beginning of a rally in support of war.

Midterm Elections

In the month following the president's speech, Bush engaged in the most active midterm campaigning of any president in history. In the end, the Republicans

TABLE 2.7. Public Support for Invasion of Iraq (in percentages)

Q: Would you favor or oppose sending American ground troops to the Persian Gulf in an attempt to remove Saddam Hussein from power in Iraq?

Poll date	Favor	Oppose	No opinion
19–21 February 2001	52	42	6
26–27 November 2001	74	20	6
17–19 June 2002	61	31	8
19–21 August 2002	53	41	6
2–4 September 2002	58	36	6
5–8 September 2002	58	36	6
13–16 September 2002	57	39	4
20–22 September 2002	57	38	5
3–6 October 2002	53	40	7
14–17 October 2002	56	37	7
21–22 October 2002	54	40	6
8–10 November 2002	59	35	6
22–24 November 2002	58	37	5
9–10 December 2002	55	39	6
16–17 December 2002	58	35	7
19–22 December 2002	53	38	9
3–5 January 2003	56	39	6
10–12 January 2003	56	38	6
23–25 January 2003	52	43	5
31 January–2 February 2003	58	38	4
7–9 February 2003	63	34	3
17–19 February 2003	59	38	3
24–26 February 2003	59	37	4
3–5 March 2003	59	37	4
14–16 March 2003	64	33	3

Source: Gallup polls, various dates.

gained seats in both houses of Congress, maintaining the majority in the House and regaining it in the Senate. The historic nature of these gains (exceeded only once—in 1934—during the previous century) generated considerable commentary about the president's public leadership.

Bush campaigned relentlessly, covering fifteen carefully chosen states in the last five days alone, and he rallied his party. The most significant factor in the Republican success was the heavy turnout in the Republican base, not Democratic abstentions. A Gallup poll taken the weekend before the election found that 64 percent of Republicans were "more enthusiastic" about voting than in the past, while only 51 percent of Democrats responded that way.[47] On the other hand, the

Democrats failed to rally—they had little to rally around, lacking both a message and a messenger. Voters did not necessarily support the Republicans on the issues, but the White House succeeded in turning the election into a referendum on a popular president.[48]

Most people who entered the booths did not have terrorism on their minds. More were concerned about the economy and the prospect of war with Iraq. But the minority who did have terrorism on their minds were overwhelmingly Republican, and the Democrats were not able to establish positioning on enough of the other issues to counter this strong GOP advantage. The war on terrorism had shifted the public debate to national security issues that favored the Republicans and shielded the president from criticism on domestic issues that favored the Democrats.

It is important to view the Republican success with some perspective. The election was actually very close—the *Washington Post* reported that a change of 41,000 votes in only two states, out of 77 million votes cast nationwide, would have kept the Senate in Democratic hands. As political analyst Charlie Cook put it, "This was a year of very close races that, for the most part, broke toward Republicans but in no way reflected a significant shift in the national direction."[49]

In addition, the Republicans enjoyed several advantages. Because the president had lacked coattails in 2000, there was less chance for setbacks in the midterm elections. Few Republicans held seats that lacked a substantial Republican base. In fact, since Al Gore received the most votes in 2000, we would have expected the Democrats to lose seats.

Republicans also had gained as a result of redistricting following the 2000 census. Both the *National Journal* and *Congressional Quarterly Weekly Report* concluded that the Republican gains in the House almost exactly matched these territorial gains.[50] (The Republicans were successful, however, in boosting the security of representatives who had won narrowly in 2000.)

Democrats were also forced to play on Republican turf, trying to pick up seats in traditionally Republican areas. For example, twenty-six of the country's forty-five competitive House seats were in districts where Al Gore had gotten less than 50 percent of the vote in 2000.[51] The Democrats' seven strongest bids to take over Republican-held seats were in states Bush had won in 2000, and four of the six vulnerable Democratic seats were in states won by Bush, while Gore had only narrowly carried the other two, Minnesota and Iowa.

The Republicans raised more money than the Democrats (although not in Georgia), and in a handful of hotly contested races, the money helped. Having more money also allowed the Republicans to concentrate their funding in battleground states and districts.[52] The Republicans also enjoyed an advantage with candidates. The White House actively recruited quality candidates, including Senate winners Norm Coleman (Minnesota), Jim Talent (Missouri), and Saxby

Chambliss (Georgia). The Democrats, on the other hand, had a weak cohort of challengers to Republican incumbents.[53] The memorial service for Minnesota Senator Paul Wellstone, who died in a plane crash a few days before the election, turned into a political rally that alienated some voters in a closely contested election and gave Coleman an excuse to resume his campaign.

Charlie Cook found no Republican wave except perhaps in Georgia. Instead, he concluded that the midterm elections in 2002 were mainly decided by the basics of getting out the vote.[54] Indeed, the Republicans operated a finely engineered voter-mobilization effort. In Georgia, the state with the biggest Republican successes, the party implemented a meticulous organizational plan that included computer analysis, training programs for volunteers, and a voter registration drive followed by massive mailing, telephone, and neighborhood canvasses in the closing days of the campaign. The president visited as late as 2 November to energize the Republican ranks. Aiding this grassroots mobilization were the National Rifle Association and United Seniors (an organization heavily underwritten by the drug industry).[55]

The Impact of High Approval on Congress

One of the perennial questions about presidential-congressional relations is the impact of the president's public approval on the support he receives in Congress. Did George W. Bush's extraordinarily high approval ratings following the terrorist attacks provide him significant political resources in his attempts to obtain congressional support for his policies? Did the patriotic response to the attacks help him to mobilize the public on behalf of his programs? Bush certainly seemed aware of the potential advantages of public support—as well as its ephemeral nature. As the president put it, "It is important to move as quickly as you can in order to spend whatever capital you have as quickly as possible."[56]

Where the public supported his policies—on fighting the war on terrorism abroad, on investigating and prosecuting terrorism at home, and in reorganizing the government to enhance domestic security—the president ultimately won most of what he sought. Even on security issues, however, the going was not always easy. He lost on the issue of privatizing airport security workers, although Congress considered the bill in the immediate aftermath of the September 11th attacks. Bush also faced a protracted battle over the new Department of Homeland Security, when his proposal for additional flexibility in personnel policy in the department infuriated labor unions, a core Democratic constituency.

Passing legislation was even more difficult on the divisive domestic issues that remained on Congress's agenda, including health care, environmental protection, energy, the economy, government support for faith–based social programs, corporate malfeasance, judicial nominees, and taxes. The politics of the war on terrorism did not fundamentally alter the consideration of these issues, which continued to divide the public and their representatives in Congress as they had before. The inevitable differences between the parties emerged predictably, exacerbated by the narrow majorities in each chamber and the jockeying for advantage in the midterm elections.

Bipartisanship in one arena (the war on terrorism) does not necessarily carry over into another. As the parties in Congress have become more homogeneous over time and as the number of competitive seats has shrunk, especially in the House, the differences between the parties have increased. The opposition party does not offer very fertile ground for presidents on most issues—even during wartime. Thus, President Bush failed to obtain many of his top-priority items in 2002, including making the 2001 tax cuts permanent and passing his fiscal stimulus program, providing government funding for a robust faith-based programs initiative, and obtaining drilling rights in the Arctic National Wildlife Reserve. No progress was made on partially privatizing Social Security, banning human cloning and certain kinds of abortion, or passing private-school tax credits, and the president experienced plenty of frustration on obtaining confirmation of his judicial appointees. He also had to sign a farm bill that was much more costly than he wanted.

In December 2001 the president concluded quiet negotiations with the Democrats led by Senator Edward Kennedy and signed a bill on education reform. He was thus able to claim victory on one of his top-priority issues, even though he had given up many of the most controversial elements of his original proposal. It is significant that to accomplish even this much, the president chose to negotiate in private rather than to go public.

In 2003, following the historic results of the 2002 midterm elections, many observers predicted that the president would be more successful in Congress. Such predictions were illusory, however. With Bush focused mostly on the war in Iraq, a small but crucial number of Republican moderates in the Senate broke ranks and dealt significant blows to several of his highest-profile policies, reducing by more than half the president's $726 billion tax cut proposal and defeating his plan for oil drilling in the Arctic National Wildlife Refuge in Alaska. Democrats were no easier to deal with, forcing the president to accept a faith-based plan stripped of its essential features and to put on hold his proposals for providing a prescription drug program for seniors and for capping medical malpractice lawsuit damages. The opposition also continued to oppose effectively his nominations to appellate courts.

The modest impact of Bush's high approval ratings is not surprising. The president's public support must compete for influence with other, more stable factors that affect voting in Congress, including members' ideology, party, personal views and commitments on specific policies, and constituency interests. Although constituency interests may seem to overlap with presidential approval, they should be viewed as distinct forces. It is quite possible for constituents to approve of the president but oppose him on particular policies, and it is opinions on these policies that will ring most loudly in congressional ears. Members of Congress are unlikely to vote against the clear interests of their constituents or the firm tenets of their ideology solely in deference to a widely supported chief executive.[57]

It is interesting that at the beginning of his term, Bush's travels seemed motivated more by demonstrating his support in states where he ran well in the election than in convincing more skeptical voters of the soundness of his proposals. He did not travel to California until May 29 and visited New York even later. Instead, the White House gave priority to states that Bush had won and that were represented by Democratic senators, including Georgia, Louisiana, Arkansas, Missouri, North and South Dakota, Montana, and North Carolina.

The goal of these trips seemed to be to demonstrate preexisting public support in the constituencies of members of Congress who were potential swing votes. Whatever the president's motivations, he obtained the support of only one Senate Democrat—Zell Miller of Georgia, who had announced his support for the tax cut before Bush was inaugurated—in the 4 April bellwether vote on his full tax cut.

In 2003, the president seemed to be following the same strategy as he campaigned for his tax cut proposal. His travel seemed designed to work at the margins to convince moderate senators of both parties that his tax cut proposal enjoyed public support in their states.

Conclusion

The tragic events of 11 September 2001 propelled George W. Bush to levels of public approval unmatched in the lifetimes of most Americans. Even before that date, Bush had been extraordinarily focused and active in seeking public support for his policies, moving the permanent campaign to new heights. Despite the advantages of the greatest rally event in polling history, the public has typically been unresponsive to the president's pleas for support. In addition, his high standing in the polls has not led to equally impressive successes in obtaining support in Congress. It is one thing to go public. It is something quite different to succeed.

Nevertheless, as Bush reached the fourth year of his term, he had the benefit of working with Republican majorities in each house of Congress. The president's high approval ratings and his persistent efforts at mobilizing his party's base of supporters provided the critical difference in the historic midterm elections of 2002. Divided government matters.[58] In a closely divided legislature, marginal change in the party balance can significantly increase the probability of the White House winning on its priority issues, ranging from nominations to tax cuts.

The George W. Bush administration has been a surprise to many observers, who underestimated both the president's character and his political skills. Overnight can be a lifetime in politics, but as the president completed his third year in office, he seemed to be well positioned to run for reelection in 2004.

Notes

1. Quoted in Bob Woodward, *Shadow* (New York: Simon and Schuster, 1999), 513.
2. Dick Morris, *The New Prince* (Los Angeles: Renaissance Books, 1999), 75, 72.
3. Gallup poll, 15–16 January 2001.
4. Gallup poll, 15–16 January 2001.
5. Gallup poll, 9–11 February 2001.
6. Gallup poll, 20–22 April 2001.
7. Gallup poll, 20–22 April 2001.
8. R.W. Apple Jr., "After the Attacks: Assessment; President Seems to Gain Legitimacy," *New York Times*, 16 September 2001, A1.
9. Gallup poll, 14–15 September 2001.
10. Gallup poll, 28 February–3 March 1991.
11. On this point, see George C. Edwards III and Tami Swenson, "Who Rallies? The Anatomy of a Rally Event," *Journal of Politics* 59 (February 1997): 200–12.
12. Gallup poll, 11–14 January 2002.
13. Gallup poll, 20–22 May 2002.
14. Gallup poll, 19–21 August 2002.
15. Dana Milbank, "Bush by the Numbers, as Told by a Diligent Scorekeeper," *Washington Post*, 3 September 2002, A15.
16. Martha Joynt Kumar, "'Does This Constitute a Press Conference?' Defining and Tabulating Modern Presidential Press Conferences," *Presidential Studies Quarterly* 33 (March 2003): 221–237.
17. Dana Milbank, "No Lemons; It's All Lemonade in Bush's White House," *Washington Post*, 22 July 2001, B1.
18. Elisabeth Bumiller, "Keepers of Bush Image Lift Stagecraft to New Heights," *New York Times*, 16 May 2003, pp. A1, A8.
19. Bumiller, "Keepers of Bush Image Lift Stagecraft to New Heights."
20. CBS News/*New York Times* poll, 14–18 June 2002,
21. CBS News/*New York Times* poll, 13–16 July 2002,
22. CNN/*USA Today*/Gallup poll, 2–4 September 2002.
23. The switch was from 37 percent agreeing the administration had made a clear case in late August to 52 percent in mid-September. Pew Research Center poll, 12–16 September 2002.
24. Elisabeth Bumiller, "War P.R. Machine Is on Full Throttle," *New York Times*, 9 February 2003, p. 13.
25. Alexis Simendinger, "The Report Card They Asked For," *National Journal*, 21 July 2001, 2335.

26. The Project for Excellence in Journalism, *The First 100 Days: How Bush Versus Clinton Fared in the Press*, 2001.

27. See, for example, the Gallup polls for 13–16 January 2003; 3–6 February 2003; and 3–5 March 2003.

28. Pew Research Center for the People and the Press poll, 12–18 February 2003.

29. Pew Research Center for the People and the Press poll, 30 April–4 May 2003

30. CBS News/*New York Times* poll, 9–12 May 2003.

31. Dana Milbank and Dan Balz, *Washington Post*, 11 May 2003 (Web site).

32. Gallup poll of 19–21 May 2003. These results are based on a question asked of half the sample ($N = 509$). Forty-six percent responded that the tax cuts were a bad idea, one percent more than thought they were a good idea.

33. It is possible, of course, that the tax cuts would be made permanent in the future. The point here is the contrast between what the president wanted and what he got.

34. Dana Milbank and Jim VandeHei, "Bush Retreat Eased Bill's Advance," *Washington Post*, 23 May 2003, p. A5.

35. *Washington Post*, 1 March 2001, C1.

36. Lisa de Moraes, "President Bush Has America Tuning In," *Washington Post*, 21 January 2002, C7.

37. The Project for Excellence in Journalism, *The First 100 Days*.

38. Gallup poll, 28–29 December 1998.

39. Gallup poll, 4–6 February 2002.

40. Chris Chambers, "Americans Most Favorable Toward Canada, Australia and Great Britain; Iran, Libya and Iraq Receive the Lowest Ratings," Gallup Poll News Release, 16 February 2001.

41. Gallup poll, 1–4 February 2001.

42. Frank Newport, "Public Wants Congressional and U.N. Approval Before Iraq Action," Gallup Poll News Release, 6 September 2002.

43. Jim Rutenberg, "Speech Had Big Audience Despite Networks' Action," *New York Times*, 9 October 2002, A13.

44. See Pew Research Center survey report of 30 October 2002.

45. Editors of the Gallup Poll, "Nine Key Questions about Public Opinion on Iraq," Gallup Poll News Release, 1 October 2002; Lydia Saad, "Top Ten Findings about Public Opinion and Iraq," Gallup Poll News Release, 8 October 2002.

46. CBS/*New York Times* poll, 3–5 October 2002.

47. William Schneider, "The Bush Mandate," *National Journal*, 9 November 2002, 3358.

48. William Schneider, "A Popularity Contest," *National Journal*, 16 November 2002, 3346; Adam Nagourney and Janet Elder, "Positive Ratings for the G.O.P., If Not Its Policy," *New York Times*, 26 November 2002, A1 and A22.

49. Charlie Cook, *Off to the Races*, "So Much for the GOP Sweep," 10 December 2002, Washington, D.C. [email newsletter]

50. Richard E. Cohen, "New Lines, Republican Gains," *National Journal*, 9 November 2002, 3285; Gregory L. Giroux, "Redistricting Helped GOP," *Congressional Quarterly Weekly Report*, 9 November 2002, 2934–35. See also Gary C. Jacobson, "Terror, Terrain, and Turnout; Explaining the 2002 Midterm Elections," *Political Science Quarterly* 118 (no. 1, 2003): 8–11.

51. Charlie Cook, "A Landslide? That Talk Is Mostly Just Hot Air," *National Journal*, 9 November 2002, 3346–47.

52. Bob Benenson, "GOP Won Midterm by Winning Series of Small Battles," *Congressional Quarterly Weekly Report*, 9 November 2002, 2890. See also Jim VandeHei and Dan Balz, "In GOP Win, a Lesson in Money, Muscle, Planning," *Washington Post*, 10 November 2002, A1, A6, A7.

53. Jacobson, "Terror, Terrain, and Turnout: Explaining the 2002 Midterm Election."

54. Cook, "A Landslide?"

55. Peter H. Stone and Shawn Zeller, "Business and Conservative Groups Won Big," *National Journal*, 9 November 2002, 3355.

56. Quoted in Dana Milbank, "Bush Popularity Isn't Aiding GOP Domestic Agenda," *Washington Post*, 16 June 2002, A4.

57. On the question of the impact of presidential approval on presidential support in Congress, see George C. Edwards III, *At the Margins: Presidential Leadership of Congress* (New Haven: Yale University Press, 1989); and idem, "Aligning Tests with Theory: Presidential Approval as a Source of Influence in Congress," *Congress and the Presidency* 24 (Fall 1997): 113–30.

58. George C. Edwards III, Andrew Barrett, and Jeffrey S. Peake, "The Legislative Impact of Divided Government," *American Journal of Political Science* 41 (April 1997): 545–63.

CHAPTER 3

The State of the Contemporary American Presidency: Or, Is Bush II Actually Ronald Reagan's Heir?

Joel D. Aberbach

TWO SPECTERS DOMINATE the political science literature on the presidency. In one, the president is weak. This president's office is faced with numerous competing offices, each with its own constituency and interests. The president must govern by persuasion. His job—hopefully, some day, her job—is to convince others, including the bureaucracy, to do what he wants by showing them how cooperation is in their own interest. Commands tend to backfire. Others may not obey, or other institutions, such as courts, may step in and hand the president a costly setback. Because of the constitutional system, in fact, this president has little claim to lead by command. He must win over the other power brokers in Washington and teach the general public realism, or he will be overwhelmed. It's a hard job. Only the president can fully grasp how hard. And only the president can truly protect his own interests.

The second specter has much in common with the first. But the differences are crucial. The second president, like the first, faces a difficult situation because of the system of separate institutions sharing powers. Like the first, this president has potential opponents all about him, including many in the bureaucracy. Like the first, this president must figure out a way to get others to do what he would like them to do. Like the first, this president must deal with great expectations. Like the first, this president has a hard job, one that would overwhelm most of us.

But this president differs from the first in some crucial respects. With growing public expectations over the years, the president is increasingly held responsible for government policy and performance. Yet this president does not try to teach the public realism; rather, he feeds on (and stimulates) the public's need for successful leadership. Driven by public expectations and his own ambition, he is an election and legacy maximizer. The maximizing perspective leads him to a different strategy than the first. Rather than bargain, this president seeks to command. Since command is difficult, this president must build a loyal cadre of officials about himself and find ways to overcome potential adversaries. This president dominates the system; the system does not dominate him. While the first president adjusts to weakness, the second president seeks to dominate despite the obstacles the system places in his path.

The first president has strong leadership capabilities (or should have them) and is a hard bargainer, but he is also basically a rule-abiding leader. He does his best to overcome obstacles, but he knows that there are bounds to what he can do. The second president is also a strong leader and a hard bargainer, but the demons of maximization and the strong expectations he feels he must satisfy force him to do whatever is necessary to overcome his adversaries. The first president moves the bureaucracy at times by inspiration but mainly by bargaining, wheedling, and targeting those he wants especially to affect. The second president also seeks to inspire and target, but his aim is to remove obstacles and make his subordinates do what he wants. Responsive competence is the goal, but responsiveness above all is the key.

The two presidencies described in the literature have quite different implications for the way the institution is organized and for the nature of the relationship between the president and the bureaucracy. While the first president holds his own interests tightly—he is the best judge of his own power prospects and, in the end, is well-advised to be his own chief of staff—the second is surrounded by a set of like-minded advisers who pursue his interests. The first president expects to bargain with his cabinet and subcabinet appointees (who represent a variety of interests). The second expects a tightly knit team. The first president casts a wary eye on the bureaucracy but is, despite sometimes difficult struggles, resigned to its pursuit of interests that are often different from his own. The second president takes on the bureaucracy and insists that it serve his interests and do what he wants it to do. Where the first president aims to live with what Richard Hofstadter has called "a harmonious system of mutual frustration,"[1] the second president will not accept frustration. He expects to get his way with Congress and the bureaucracy. If he cannot get Congress to go along, he expects the bureaucracy to do his bidding and structures his administration with this in mind.

These two views of the presidency will be quite familiar to those who follow the literature on the subject, particularly that on the president's relationship with the bureaucracy and other branches of government. The first is identified with Richard Neustadt's classic study, *Presidential Power*, and it dominated in the period when pluralist political science stood astride the field.[2] The second, found in the literature on the "administrative presidency" that followed in the wake of Richard Nixon's administration, is most closely identified with Richard Nathan's book on the subject and with a broader theoretical treatment by Terry Moe.[3] In a nutshell, Moe's argument is that changing expectations of the president as the one nationally elected leader, reinforced by changes in popular, political and media expectations, have led to an incongruence between structures, incentives, and resources. This, in turn, has inevitably led presidents to seek greater control over the structures and processes of government in an effort to create a systemic balance more satisfactory to them. It is not primarily a question of failed moral-ity—that is, simply violating the norms of the system—but an imperative of the situation, and will continue until a new balance is established and accepted.

I return to this issue in my conclusion. Before that, though, I want to exam-ine the Bush II administration in light of the two perspectives on the presidency outlined above. My focus is on administrative issues germane to the debate. First, I look at the appointments process, paying particular attention to the pace and methods of appointments, the nature of the cabinet and subcabinet officials cho-sen, and the argument that the appointments system is broken, an assertion that links directly to questions about presidential rights and prerogatives. Second, I examine George W. Bush's management agenda, comparing it to Bill Clinton's ef-forts to "reinvent" the way U.S. government works and evaluating its place in the Bush II presidency. I then turn to what I think is the core of the issue—what I call "governing alone." Here I consider issues central to the questions of how much the president can act independently of the other branches in a system that is, constitutionally, one of separation of powers and how much control the pres-ident has been able to exert over the executive branch, an issue that is intimately related to his relationship with other government institutions. Before the main part of the analysis, however, it is important to look at Bush's political views and place them in the context of other recent presidents.

Bush II in the Context of Recent Presidents

An uneasy relationship between the president and Congress is a staple of Ameri-can politics, even when the same political party controls both branches. And at least some tension is common in the relationship between the president and the executive branch, a product of differences in needs and time horizons and of the fact that Congress has a say in what the bureaucracy does and how it works. Richard Nixon and Ronald Reagan had notably assertive approaches to the bu-reaucracy. Nixon established the "responsiveness program" and developed what Richard Nathan has labeled the "administrative presidency," a strategy entailing use of creative regulation-writing, budget impoundments, personnel policy, and administrative reorganization to "take over the bureaucracy" and achieve "policy objectives through administrative action."[4] Reagan refined this strategy and made particularly good use of the provisions of the 1978 Civil Service Reform Act.[5] Unlike Nixon's first cabinet, Reagan's first cabinet was not designed to represent a broad range of political views, and his White House staff maintained tight control over subcabinet-level appointments. Administration was increasingly politicized, with policymaking increasingly centralized in the White House. For Terry Moe, Reagan's administration is a model of the way a contemporary president must operate. Moe, in fact, lionizes Reagan as "the most administratively influential president of the modern period."[6] In addition, unlike Nixon, Reagan had a well-structured, ideologically driven, and clear agenda—something of immense importance in signaling the bureaucracy about the president's preferences.

Moe is surely correct that presidents in the modern period have adopted elements of the administrative presidency strategy. But some have done so more than others. Gerald Ford and Jimmy Carter were, for the most part, more traditional than others, and Bush I (George H.W. Bush) and Clinton, while certainly assertive in many areas, followed what we might call the Reagan strategy with less vigor and consistency. For example, Bush I used "signing statements" as a way to assert a right to veto parts of bills, and Clinton used executive privilege (rather ineffectively), regulation-writing, and acting appointments in his efforts to influence policy or escape the clutches of his institutional opponents. But both were mainstream politicians, with a deep commitment to fiscal responsibility and essentially moderate administrations.

To focus on Bush I for purposes of comparison, he had a much easier relationship with the career civil service than did Ronald Reagan, his predecessor. One cannot imagine him uttering the famous Reagan remark, "When you're up to your eyeballs in alligators, it's sometimes hard to remember that you're here to drain the swamp."[7] Bush I did not routinely appoint cabinet officials hostile to the roles and missions of their agencies, and he gave his cabinet much greater leeway than Reagan had done in selecting their subordinates.[8] Most important in explaining Bush I's general tendencies is that he was, to quote Nelson Polsby's felicitous phrase, an "American Tory." That is, he was a traditional conservative who valued and respected the role of civil servants. As Polsby notes, such people value conventional wisdom and have a deep commitment to "keep[ing] the boat afloat." [9] And as Burt Solomon commented at the time, Bush filled his administration with people who were "civil, cautious and conciliatory," problem solvers who did not have a fixed agenda such as that found in the Reagan administration, but who did want to "do something" prudent when the situation suggested action was needed.[10] Bush I raised taxes because that was the conventional and "responsible" thing to do. A leading scholar of the presidency tellingly labeled him "an effective President of Consolidation."[11]

How should one characterize George W. Bush? Certainly, it would be wrong to label him a traditional conservative (an American Tory, as Polsby defines the term). An excellent article in *National Journal* on "W's" reported interest in Theodore Roosevelt made the following argument:

> In many ways, TR and Bush [II] are considerably less simpatico than, say, TR and Bush's father. The former president is a Connecticut Yankee more than a transplanted Texan, while the younger Bush, who was raised in West Texas, is more genuinely conservative, closer to business, less of a latter-day Progressive. . . . TR was hands-on; Bush likes to delegate. TR was a Renaissance man; Bush isn't known for intellectual curiosity. . . . TR distrusted Big Business; until Enron Corp. collapsed, Bush thrived on it.[12]

And in another interesting article in *National Journal*, John Maggs struggled with finding an adequate way to compare the two Bushes:

> It would be easy to sum up the differences between the two Bushes by saying that the son is more conservative than his father. The elder Bush was certainly more willing to compromise with his opponents, and one effect was his ability to find a degree of consensus that has been greatly lacking in government lately. Forty-one's willingness to break his no-new-taxes pledge was distasteful to most conservatives, but it may have been more important than anything Bill Clinton did to secure the prosperity of the 1990s.
>
> Even in his much-criticized handling of the economy, Bush was conservative in the old-fashioned sense. Some advisers wanted to push a showy and expensive economic plan . . . but Bush believed that the deficit deal had laid the groundwork for a strong, inflation-free recovery, which indeed began in the fall of 1992. Contrast that with the current president's support for a long-delayed economic stimulus plan, which most economists now say was a waste of $50 billion.[13]

What is clear is that Bush II is not, to use Maggs's phrase, an "old fashioned conservative" like his father. He appears to be more hostile to many established policies (environmental policies, for example), more of a jingoist, go-it-alone type on foreign policy, and his tax cuts helped turn the country's budget from surplus to deficit in short order. In sum, the populist conservative style and policies that were prominent in his first two years—and, as we shall soon see, his administrative conduct—suggest that politically he has more in common with Ronald Reagan than he does with his father.

Appointments

Pace and Method

It was widely assumed that George W. Bush would tread very lightly in making appointments to his administration. He had, after all, lost the popular vote nationally, and it is likely that he was not the choice of the voters of Florida, though this is one of those debates that will never be settled. In the end, it took a highly controversial Supreme Court decision to put him in office. With this as background, the *New York Times*'s Frank Bruni reported on 28 November 2000 Republican officials as saying that Bush was likely to appoint "several Democrats to his cabinet." Indeed, Dick Cheney was quoted in the story as saying that Bush's actions "are likely to be influenced by the fact that it's been a very close election, that the nation is, if anything, evenly divided, if you will."[14]

Close election or not, only a token Democrat (Secretary of Transportation Norman Mineta) was appointed to the cabinet. The general decision process was well underway before the election, and few other bones were thrown to those who opposed Mr. Bush. Indeed, as John Burke notes, "Florida notwithstanding, by January 2, Bush had finished up with the selection of his cabinet. That date placed him only about a week behind Clinton's schedule in 1992. More notable in fact, the Bush team was actually ahead of Clinton in naming the White House staff."[15] Burke also points out that the Bush team drew on the work of the Reagan transition, drawing up an action plan for the first 180 days of the administration, and that it put great emphasis on loyalty and discipline, using the transition to instill this as a major feature of the "organizational culture" Bush favored.[16]

Clay Johnson, who managed the transition, makes clear why the senior White House staff was named quickly: "Cabinet officers can only receive clear direction from the White House staff if there are senior staff members in place to do so."[17] Cabinet members were given a say in choosing the subcabinet, but, as has now become standard, they did not have control in this regard. Far from it. Johnson says that a presidential personnel person was assigned to each secretarial nominee and worked in "collaboration" with him or her to select subcabinet members. As he put it, "We were going to do it *with* them, not *to* them.[18] The process appears to have been somewhere between the highly centralized decision process for choosing the subcabinet employed by the Reagan administration and the Bush I process, in which the administration "decided to give significant leeway to cabinet secretaries to choose, in consultation with the Office of Presidential Personnel, their own management teams at the subcabinet level.'[19]

Nature of the Cabinet and Subcabinet

Following recent trends, the Bush appointees are quite diverse, especially for a Republican administration. This can be seen in table 3.1, comparing appointments of women and racial minorities made by June in the first years of the Bush I, Clinton, and Bush II administrations. Bush had not chosen as high a percentage of women or minorities as had Clinton, who made it a centerpiece of his administration that it "look like America," but he was ahead of his father in this regard.

TABLE 3.1   Appointee Diversity in the Bush I, Clinton, and Bush II Administrations (in percentages of total appointees to senior positions in the executive branch through June of first year of administration)

	Bush I[a]	Clinton[b]	Bush II
Women	19	34	26
Racial minorities	17	25	20

Source: James E. Barnes, "White House: Bush's Insiders," *National Journal,* 23 June 2001.
[a] Tallied in June 1989.
[b] Tallied as of 5 June 1993.

And a paper on his appointments of women indicated that he appointed them to higher ranking positions than had Clinton.[20]

Bush ran as an "outside the Beltway" candidate, but the profile of his appointees is one indicating substantial Washington experience. According to the *National Journal,* more than 50 percent of his appointees (as of 14 June 2001) had addresses inside the Beltway, 86 percent had previously worked for the government, 20 percent had worked for Washington lobbying firms, and 43 percent had worked in the Bush I administration. The White House staff, however, had a lower percentage of people who served in the Bush I administration (38 percent) than did other executive branch appointees (44 percent). While the "Texas crowd" is more prevalent on the White House staff, the cabinet, the *Journal* article concludes, is marked by strong ties to Vice President Cheney, a man with long experience in Washington. And, the article argues, "While the new President's government isn't one of Washington outsiders as Reagan's was, it lacks the clubby feel that characterized his father's administration," since only Commerce Secretary Donald Evans is a longtime friend of the President.[21]

Bob Herbert, a liberal columnist for the *New York Times,* argues that Bush's cabinet is "Far, Far From the Center," saying, "George W. Bush's cabinet may look like America, but on a host of important domestic issues it sure doesn't think like America."[22] While Herbert might arguably not be the best person to make such judgments, since his ideas about what is far from the center might include people others would label as moderates, the head of Americans for Tax Reform and a leading conservative strategist, Grover Norquist, concurs: "There isn't an us and them with this administration. They is us. We is them."[23] And the president of the conservative Heritage Foundation, Edwin J. Feulner, readily agreed, holding that the Bush II administration is "more Reaganite than the Reagan administration."[24]

One widely accepted argument about why the administration might seem more Reaganite than Bush I-like is that Bush II took as a lesson from the fate of his father's administration that he had to protect his right flank.[25] Another is that he grew up in a more conservative period than his father did and that his views are deep-seated and, as he sees things, have a wide appeal. Whatever the case, the noted rightist Paul Weyrich summed things up as follows: "I've been through five

Republican administrations, and the effort to communicate with conservatives and to understand our concerns and address our concerns and involve us in the process is the best of any of the Republican administrations, including Ronald Reagan. In fact, far superior to Ronald Reagan."[26]

A mark of the Reagan administration was its tendency to appoint people who were hostile to the programs they were there to advise on or administer. Reliable evidence about the prevalence of this practice in the Bush II administration is as yet unavailable, but there are some publicized cases. For example, on 5 September 2002 the *Washington Post's* Dana Milbank wrote, "The Bush administration plans to appoint to its domestic-violence advisory committee two representatives of a group vigorously opposed to the law the committee oversees."[27] And another press account, this time of Bush's nominees for key environmental policy jobs, emphasized how much his nominees resembled those of Ronald Reagan as opposed to his father's:

> In 1989, the elder Bush chose an environmentalist, William K. Reilly, to head the Environmental Protection Agency and filled other regulatory jobs with experts from academia, environmental groups and state pollution agencies, as well as from industry.
>
> The younger Bush appears to be embracing, instead, the practice of his father's conservative predecessor, Ronald Reagan, who tended to fill regulatory jobs with representatives of the businesses being regulated. Some examples of Bush's appointees:
>
> The deputy administrator for the Environmental Protection Agency, Linda Fisher, was a chief lobbyist and political fund-raising coordinator for Monsanto Co., a biochemical and pesticide producer. . . .
>
> The Interior secretary's two newly named envoys to Alaska are the top lobbyist for drilling in the Arctic National Wildlife Refuge and a former state lawmaker who has championed the same cause.[28]

Overall, then, the personnel of the Bush II administration are definitely more diverse than those in his father's (and in Ronald Reagan's) administrations, but they are also apparently more conservative. Feulner's enthusiastic claim that they really are "more Reaganite than the Reagan administration" may be overstating the case, but the current administration is clearly very open to the sorts of people who supported Ronald Reagan, and its personnel policies have at least as much in common with those of Reagan as they do with those of the Bush I administration, and probably more.

Is the Process Broken?

There seems to be general agreement among scholars and others that the appointments process is broken.[29] Available data certainly seem to support that conclusion, particularly with respect to delays in putting a team of political appointees in place.[30] One widely used statistic, for example, the number of months from inauguration to confirmation for first-year appointments, shows a dramatic increase over time. As table 3.2 shows, in the Kennedy administration the average number of months from inauguration to appointment was 2.4. That interval increased steadily in subsequent administrations for which data are readily available, reaching 5.3 in the Reagan administration and then jumping to 8.1 in the Bush I administration. It has remained essentially unchanged since then.

Those are stunning statistics, and they are supported by other available indicators. Data on the average and median number of days between Senate receipt of a nomination and confirmation show that the Clinton numbers were higher than the Bush I numbers. Averaging the number of days to confirmation in the two Bush I Congresses yields figures of 52 mean days and 46 median days. For Clinton's four Congresses, the figures are 76 and 67 respectively.[31] Comparable data for the Bush II administration are not yet available, but I suspect that they will look more like those for the Clinton administration than those for the Bush I administration.

One clear indicator of difficulty is the average number of days it takes an administration to get nominations to the Senate. As table 3.3 shows, this figure has increased over time. It took the Reagan administration an average of 50 days to submit a nomination, while the Clinton administration took 69 and the Bush II administration took 75.

The fact that the Bush II administration was only slightly behind the Clinton administration is in many ways remarkable, given the 2000 election. That, however, is not what I want to focus on here. Rather, the increase in time to submit nominations is part of a general problem discussed in the literature.

The litany of problems is quite large. The number of positions requiring Senate confirmation has increased over time. Extensive background checks are conducted, including complex disclosure forms. And then, of course, there are often huge problems with the Senate confirmation process, particularly holds and disputes about nominee qualifications. The literature offers suggestions for dealing with these problems: The number of appointed positions could be decreased. Background checks could be simplified and so could disclosure forms. The Senate could forbid holds and be required to schedule hearings within some reasonable time frame after the submission of a nomination.[32]

All of these suggestions would surely help, but it is important to keep in mind that the underlying difficulty is political and not procedural. A leading scholar on the appointments process, commenting on the long wait for confirmation of Bush II appointees, noted: "It's become more and more difficult for well-qualified candidates to get through just on the basis of merit."[33] That is undoubtedly true, but merit is usually not the issue. As administration has become more and more self-consciously a tool in the raw politics of government, the ap-

TABLE 3.2   Average Time to Fill a Senate-Confirmed Nomination from Inauguration Day to Confirmation

President	Average number of months
Kennedy	2.4
Nixon	3.4
Carter	4.6
Reagan	5.3
Bush I	8.1
Clinton	8.0
Bush II	8.3

Sources: Kennedy–Carter, 25 July 2002 press release from the Brookings Institution, "Presidential Appointee Initiative Urges Senate to End Confirmation Drought," www.appointee.brookings.org/news/July2402-newsrelease.htm; Reagan–Bush II, G. Calvin Mackenzie, "The Real Invisible Hand: Presidential Appointees in the Administration of George W. Bush," *PS: Political Science and Politics* 35, no. 1 (March 2002):28.

TABLE 3.3   Nominations and Confirmations to Policy Positions in the First 100 Days of the Reagan, Clinton, and Bush II Administrations

President	Average days to submit a nomination	Nominations submitted	Positions to be filled	Nominations as a percentage of positions
Reagan	50	137	384	35.7
Clinton	69	155	476	32.6
Bush II	75	140	476	29.4

Source: Rogelio Garcia, "Nominations and Confirmations to Policy Positions in the First 100 Days of the George W. Bush, William J. Clinton, and Ronald W. Reagan Administrations," Congressional Research Service, 17 July 2001.
Note: Policy positions are "all positions [requiring Senate confirmation] in executive departments, independent agencies, and agencies in the Executive Office of the President" (Garcia 2001, 2). Data exclude U.S. attorney and U.S marshal positions and ambassadorships.

pointments process cannot be divorced from the rest of the administrative process (which itself has become an overt part of the political process).

Obviously, we are dealing here with a matter of degree; politics and administration have never existed in isolated spheres. But intense conflicts over appointments are inevitably an integral part of what Terry Moe calls "the politicized presidency" and Richard Nathan labels "the administrative presidency." As the trend has developed for administrators appointed by the president to help him "govern alone" according to his preferences, it is hardly surprising that confirmations are bogged down in controversy. Nor is it surprising that senators and others demand huge amounts of data about each nominee. The nominations are an opening round in a battle that often lasts until the nominated individual either fails to be confirmed (actually a relatively rare occurrence), leaves the government early, or the term of the administration has come to an end. The litany of problems with the process, in other words, is often as much a function of the underlying political controversy as a cause of it. Ban one type of procedural problem and another will likely soon be devised to replace it, because the struggle is really about issues and actions taken through the administrative process that people feel strongly about and interest groups have invested in heavily. The Bush II administration has certainly done little or nothing to calm the heated administrative atmosphere and associated patterns of behavior that have built up over time. A difficult appointments process, with delays in getting personnel confirmed, is one cost of the efforts of assertive presidents to get their way by using administration in a forceful and uncompromising way.[34]

The Management Agenda

One of the defining marks of the Clinton administration was its program for "reinventing" the government. Reinvention had three phases. Its elements were sometimes inconsistent, but the basic thrust was to secure a government that "works better and costs less."[35] The National Performance Review (NPR), as the program was originally called, was the American version of New Public Management (NPM), a worldwide movement to make governments more "efficient" by using market-like mechanisms where possible and cutting extraneous governmental activities. Reinvention aimed to cut red tape, put government's "customers" first, empower employees to get results, and cut government back to basics. After the Republicans won the 1994 congressional elections, the Clinton administration put a particularly heavy stress on what government ought to do— the cutting back government part of reinvention—and reiterated its commitment to performance management through implementation of the 1993 Government Performance and Results Act (GPRA).

"The goal [of NPM reforms] is a lean state performing only needed functions effectively and efficiently."[36] Republicans would be hard-pressed to disagree with such a goal, and in his presidential campaign Bush II embraced it in concept without at the same time crediting the Clinton administration or, in particular, Al Gore, who was the major Clinton administration figure in the reinvention effort. Instead, Bush criticized the Clinton administration's reinvention efforts for ineffectiveness. He said that the Clinton administration had "simply reshuffled" the government bureaucracy, not reinvented it.[37] He promised, according to an article in *GovExec.com*, to save $88 billion over five years by opening "to competition from the private sector at least half of the 900,000 federal government jobs not classified as inherently governmental under the Federal Activities Inventory Reform (FAIR) Act," eliminating about 40,000 middle-management jobs, linking program funding levels to performance as called for by GPRA, and using effective performance incentives to make the federal civil service system work better and attract people from the private sector.[38]

When it came to putting forth his management message, Bush announced, "Government should be citizen-centered, results-oriented and, whenever possible, market-based."[39] As Stephen Barr, the federal page columnist of the *Washington Post*, correctly noted, however: "Many federal employees will not find much new in Bush's approach. For several years, they have heard directly from Gore on much of this, as well as variations on these themes from dozens of government reformers."[40]

In short, Bush's management program was hardly a major break from that of the Clinton administration (except for his abolition of Clinton's Labor-Management Partnership Councils and his job outsourcing targets). Indeed, he has a fairly standard NPM-type management agenda, featuring budget and performance integration, competitive sourcing, expanded e-government, leaner government, and the like.[41] The reason he resembles his Democratic predecessor in this respect is not that he is an imitation Democrat on management issues. Rather, Clinton and Gore adopted a management agenda that most Republicans, including quite conservative Republicans, would find congenial. When Clinton famously announced to Congress that "the era of big government is over," the Gingrich Republicans roundly applauded him because he was using their rhetoric and endorsing their basic view. That announcement fit quite comfortably into the National Performance Review and could have been the slogan for Phase II, with its emphasis on program changes (especially cutbacks in personnel and the like), terminations, and privatizations.

Where Bush has run into difficulty (apart from the fun poked at the administration's color scheme for grading management performance) is in attempts to set numerical targets for outsourcing federal jobs and in issues related to civil service protection and union rights in the Homeland Security area. The FAIR Act required the government to inventory federal jobs where the same functions were available from the private sector, but it did not require that any percentage of these jobs—jobs held by about half of the federal civilian workforce are not identified as "inherently governmental"—actually go to the private sector. Bush, however, announced plans to outsource or hold public-private competitions on 5 percent of the federal jobs considered "commercial in nature" in fiscal 2002. The target was 15 percent by the end of fiscal 2003, with a goal "that agencies must eventually compete 50 percent of their commercial jobs," a target Office of Federal Procurement Policy Administrator Angela Styles said in a Senate hearing was set by Bush himself.[42]

These plans have generated repeated controversy in Congress, where they have been countered with proposals to ban targeted contracting-out of federal jobs and to determine which of the currently contracted federal activities could be more effectively performed in-house.[43] There have also been proposals to "subject equal numbers of contractor and government jobs to public-private competitions each year."[44] And even certain Republican members, including Representative Tom Davis, who is from a Virginia district with a large population of federal employees, and Senator George Voinovich of Ohio, have expressed alarm at the administration's contracting targets.[45] The bill to establish a Department of Homeland Security also became enmeshed in disputes about federal jobs, in this case over Bush's desire to curtail union rights.

My point here is not to focus on these controversies per se, but to indicate that Bush has a federal management program that fits the conservative Republican agenda quite well. It resembles the Clinton administration program because that program had its origins in New Public Management doctrines that, as Donald Kettl summarizes them,

> stemmed from the basic economic argument that government suffered from the defects of monopoly, high transaction costs, and information problems that bred inefficiencies. By substituting market competition—and market-like incentives—the reformers believed that they could shrink government's size, reduce its costs, and improve performance.[46]

Adding a dash of antilabor sentiment and an emphasis on targets for contracting out, Bush has put his administration's stamp on the program. These are controversial additions that probably reinforce his appeal among the right wing of his party, but the foundation was already in place.

Governing Alone

The clearly articulated goal of the Bush administration is to enhance presidential powers. Vice President Cheney did not mince words when he said, in explaining his refusal to turn over to congressional investigators his records on the development of the administration's energy policy, "I have repeatedly seen an erosion of the powers and ability of the president of the United States to do his job." Indeed, Cheney claimed, "We are weaker today as an institution because of unwise compromises that have been made over the last 30 to 35 years."[47] Similar sentiments were openly voiced by a "senior administration official" who said, in reference to a variety of disputes with Congress over the scope of congressional oversight rights, "There's no question that there's a recognition within the administration that the presidential authority has eroded over the years beyond the proper constitutional separation of powers. And this is a matter of principle for the presidency."[48] The White House counsel made the following broad claim: "The framers of the Constitution, I think, intended there to be a strong presidency in order to carry out certain functions, and he [President Bush] feels an obligation to leave the office in better shape than when he came in."[49]

In short, a major thrust of Bush II has been to act assertively, to be, in terms of the two views of the presidency outlined in the introduction to this chapter, a president in the manner described by Moe, one who is seeking significantly greater control over the structures and processes of government—indeed, to have an administration that is dominant in the manner of the "administrative presidency" described by Nathan. While it is true that most recent administrations have employed a variety of assertive tactics to overcome congressional, court, and bureaucratic impediments,[50] my argument here is that the Bush II presidency has been extraordinarily active in this regard. Bush II officials, in other words, have, at least so far, produced what is arguably the most assertive presidency since Ronald Reagan's.

One would need to present more evidence than I can possibly assemble in this chapter to make a definitive case for this contention. And the Bush II administration may ease its approach over time. That said, what I can do is buttress the remarks of administration officials quoted in the first paragraph of this section with examples of the administration's behavior.

Dick Cheney and the General Accounting Office

In 2001 Vice President Cheney chaired an administration task force whose mission was to help formulate a national energy policy. The General Accounting Office (GAO), "a legislative agency created to assist Congress in the performance of its constitutional responsibilities, including the enactment of legislation and oversight of the executive branch," sought to investigate and evaluate the activities of the task force, seeking information from the administration about the composition of the task force, the people with whom it met, notes and minutes of its meeting, and cost data about the task force's operations. GAO argued that it sought such information "to determine how the NEPDG's [National Energy Policy Development Group] energy policy recommendations were developed, in order to aid Congress in considering proposed legislation, assessing the needs and merits of future legislative changes, and conducting oversight of the executive branch's administration of existing law."[51]

After some negotiation with the vice president's office in the spring and summer of 2001, the GAO narrowed its request to a list of those present at the various meetings, an explanation of how it was determined who would be invited, and an accounting of the task force's costs, in order to accommodate what it labeled "the Vice President's asserted need to protect executive deliberations." GAO argued that it was entitled to all of the information originally requested, but that it

> voluntarily eliminated its request for minutes or notes of meetings that NEPDG support staff and the Vice President held, and for information that was presented at these meetings. [Further, GAO noted,] Despite its efforts to reach a reasonable accommodation, GAO has been denied access to information it has a statutory right to obtain.[52]

As a result, GAO brought a lawsuit against the vice president, a lawsuit that was dismissed on 10 December 2002 by Judge John D. Bates, who had been appointed to the bench in 2001 by the sitting President, George W. Bush.[53] Bates held that since neither house of Congress (nor any of its committees) had issued a subpoena for the information or formally authorized a suit, there was no standing to sue.[54]

Aside from the complex legal issues that any such suit inevitably entails, there were some unusual aspects of this case. First, the lawsuit marked the first time in GAO's "80 [now 81] year history that it sued the executive branch for failing to cooperate with an inquiry."[55] Second, GAO's head, Comptroller General David M. Walker, is a Republican. (In fact, he was a delegate to a Republican National Convention.) Third, the GAO is widely respected as a nonpartisan group. Fourth, and most important, "the politically charged lawsuit . . . raise[d] important constitutional questions, including whether the vice president can ignore a request for information from the G.A.O. without the President's decision to exercise executive privilege."[56] The fact that executive privilege was not invoked is especially important in that it makes the decision to ignore the GAO request a particularly strong assertion of administration prerogatives. Cheney argued vigorously that "what's really at stake here is the ability of the president and vice president to solicit advice from anybody they want in confidence—get good, solid unvarnished advice without having to make it available to a member of Congress."[57] In short, the administration in this case was seeking to expand greatly its right to keep information secret, and in doing so it was clashing with one of the most respected and least partisan institutions in Washington.

Executive Privilege

Bush II did, however, invoke executive privilege in a rather unusual case. A congressional committee sought "prosecutors' records related to a 30 year-old Boston mob case and the Clinton administration campaign finance probe."[58] This type of information (for closed cases) had evidently been disclosed routinely in the past if requested by Congress, and the administration's refusal to do so in this case set off a set of vitriolic exchanges between the branches. In a memo signed by the president to Attorney General John D. Ashcroft, Bush wrote that release of the documents would "inhibit the candor necessary" to executive branch deliberations and therefore "be contrary to the national interest."[59] The fiery conservative Republican Rep. Dan Burton of Indiana, chair of the House Government Reform Committee, retorted: "This is not a monarchy. The legislative branch has oversight to make sure there is no corruption in the executive branch."[60]

Protecting Clinton campaign finance probe records may seem an odd cause for a Republican administration, but White House press secretary Ari Fleischer made clear that the case had deeper meaning to the administration: "The pendulum probably shifted too far toward the Congress, in terms of probing the Administration, during the Clinton years. . . . I think there's been a healthy rebalancing so the executive branch can have the authority to get the job done."[61] Mark Rozell, a scholar of executive privilege, argued that the Bush administration "may be trying to establish the principle of executive privilege and may believe they are upholding this executive power, but they are using some very nontraditional cases to do that. Right now the Administration is almost using executive privilege as an opening bid to engage in a battle with Congress."[62]

Invoking executive privilege is almost always provocative, so congressional opposition is not too surprising. However, the instances cited above are unusually provocative because they seem to stretch the power so far and also because of the stance taken by the administration's spokesman (reflecting, of course, the stance of the administration) that the Bush administration must somehow rebalance power in light of challenges to executive privilege that occurred during probes of a predecessor Democratic administration, probes strongly backed by congressional Republicans. Court decisions during the Clinton presidency weakened executive privilege, so Bush's actions are a particularly pointed way to declare that the presidency is regaining strength. Right or wrong in legal terms, it represents a potent political statement of the Bush II administration's views about the power of the presidency. And, as Mark Rozell points out, it is clearly "clever politics"—"What better way to do it than to win a dispute with Burton's committee over a Clinton administration scandal?"[63]

Congressional Testimony by Tom Ridge

Following September 11th, President Bush established the Office of Homeland Security and the Homeland Security Council. On 8 October 2001, Tom Ridge was sworn in as the country's first Assistant to the President for Homeland Security. Ridge's job was, in the words of his bio, to "coordinate a comprehensive national strategy to strengthen protections against terrorist threats or attacks in the United States."[64]

This sounds like something relatively uncontroversial in the context of the times, but Ridge soon ran into a major flap over whether or not he should testify before Congress. The administration held strongly that, as an adviser to President Bush, he did not have to testify. Congress had other ideas. Democratic Senator Robert C. Byrd of West Virginia and Republican Senator Ted Stevens of Alaska wrote a letter to Ridge requesting that he testify before the Senate Appropriations Committee, of which they are chair and ranking minority member, respectively: "You are the single executive branch official with the responsibility to integrate the many complex functions of the various federal agencies in one formulation and the execution of homeland defense programs. Your views and insights on the policies necessary to meet these objectives are critical to the committee and to the nation."[65] The White House refused to let Ridge give formal testimony.

This sparring over the power balance between the branches reached an almost absurd climax when Bush sent his plan to establish a cabinet-level homeland security department to Congress. Congress wanted Ridge to testify, but if the White House assented, in what capacity would he testify? Ridge did testify, but he drew an almost Talmudic distinction between his roles:

> The president has directed me to testify not as an adviser . . . but to go to the Hill to testify—to formally testify—about the reorganization of the executive branch, the creation of the Department of Homeland Security. The testimony on the Hill will not be as an adviser—there will not be any discussion relative to the advice and counsel that may have been shared with the president.

The notion was that this would "'preserve the prerogative' of a president to make his advisers 'accessible' to Congress but not make them 'subject to the call of the chair.'"[66]

One can evaluate this dispute in a variety of ways, but it is clear that it represents another strong—if, to an outside observer, somewhat bizarre—example of the Bush II administration taking an assertive stand on presidential power and prerogatives.

Recess Appointments

Recess appointments—appointments made when the Senate is in recess—are a way for a president to get into a position a controversial nominee who has failed to win Senate confirmation. Some examples should suffice. The Bush II administration used this procedure to appoint Otto J. Reich as assistant secretary of state for Western Hemisphere Affairs and Eugene Scalia as solicitor of the Labor Department. The controversy over the Reich nomination had its roots in the Reagan administration, where "Mr. Reich led a covert program to generate public support in the United States for the anti-Sandinista rebels, or *contras*, in Nicaragua."[67] Scalia, son of the Supreme Court justice, was controversial because of his views on worker-protection issues. "He once denounced as 'quackery' and 'junk science' a Clinton administration regulation on ergonomics designed to reduce injuries due to repetitive motion; the Bush administration repealed it in March."[68] In another appointment of this type, Bush chose "a vocal critic of affirmative action [Gerald Reynolds] as civil rights chief at the Education Department."[69]

The Bush II administration, it is fair to say, is not unique in using recess appointments—indeed, they are authorized by the constitution. Bill Clinton, for example, made use of this device to appoint such people as Bill Lann Lee, his controversial acting assistant attorney general for civil rights, and the tool was a favorite of Presidents Reagan and Bush I.[70] I include them here because they are part of a dense web of devices that the Bush II administration has employed.

Executive Orders

Executive orders are an important tool for presidents in their efforts to make policy choices and impact government structures.[71] Bush II is hardly alone in using them. Again, however, he has used them in quite an assertive manner. A future study on this subject should be well worth the effort, but two examples will suffice here.

Most important has been the issuance of executive orders to allow the government to use military tribunals to try noncitizens charged with terrorism, monitor communications between some detainees and their lawyers, and take related steps in the wake of September 11th.[72] Speed, the administration has argued, is essential to counter terrorist threats.[73] Attorney General John Ashcroft said bluntly,

> Foreign terrorists who commit war crimes against the United States, in my judgment, are not entitled to and do not deserve the protections of the American Constitution, particularly when there could be very serious and important reasons related to not bringing them back to the United States for justice. I think it's important to understand that we are at war now.[74]

The same *New York Times* story that contained this quote went on to say that some lawmakers were "increasingly concerned" about the administration's approach to such constitutionally charged issues.[75] And there was even opposition reported from some senior law enforcement officials.[76]

In testimony to the Senate Judiciary Committee, Ashcroft was scathing in his reactions to those who questioned the wisdom, let alone the constitutionality, of administration antiterrorism proposals and actions: "To those who scare peace-loving people with phantoms of lost liberty, my message is this: your tactics only aid the terrorists."[77] Comments like this would probably have brought a smile of recognition to the face of Senator Joe McCarthy when he served in that body, but several of the senators were not amused.

One of the country's leading constitutional scholars, Louis Fisher, has argued that the widely cited precedent of Franklin Roosevelt's order of a secret trial for eight captured Nazi saboteurs is not appropriate for this case. Roosevelt's proclamation "was limited to persons from 'any nation at war with the United States.'"[78] Bush's order, in contrast, is much wider and covers any noncitizen in an open-ended war without a named national opponent. As Fisher correctly warns, "The risk of miscalculation and error under the Bush order is high. A system of justice that depends on secret trials without a reviewing court cannot assure fairness or inspire confidence in verdicts."[79]

An executive order of particular interest to academics is Bush's order severely undermining the 1978 Presidential Records Act, which provided for most presidential papers to be released twelve years after the end of an administration. On 1 November 2001, "President Bush signed an executive order . . . to allow a sitting president to keep secret the papers of a previous president, even if a previous president wants his papers made public."[80] A suit challenging the order was filed by Public Citizen, but regardless of its outcome, the White House explanation that the order was issued to provide an "orderly process" for handling requests lacks credibility. More likely the case—in the view of critics cited in the *New York Times* story on the order—is that it was issued to protect the president's father (who was vice president under Ronald Reagan, whose presidential papers were to be released) and current administration officials who also served under Reagan from embarrassing revelations.[81] Whatever the correct explanation, the order appears to be an arbitrary and inappropriate use of presidential power.

Is Bush II Actually Reagan's Heir?

In a provocative article published before September 11th, Thomas Friedman wrote that George W. Bush ran as "Clinton-minus," by which he meant a "compassionate conservative" who would provide "Clinton-like policies on key issues" minus Mr. Clinton's personal baggage. Instead, Friedman argued, "once in power, Mr. Bush has ruled not as 'Clinton-minus' but as 'Reagan-squared,' not as a compassionate conservative but as a radical conservative."[82]

It is still perhaps too early to make a definitive judgment about the administrative side of the Bush II presidency, but the evidence from its early years suggests that Bush's administration shares more with Reagan's in this regard than with his father's. His administration has been—like that of the second president outlined in the introduction to this chapter—one with distinct, clear, and dominant features of the "administrative presidency" described by Nathan and analyzed by Moe.

Observers were struck almost immediately by the assertiveness of the Bush II administration. After a few gracious comments about the need to recognize the implications of the closeness of the election, the Bush administration put forth an "agenda that would significantly alter domestic and foreign policies dating back decades and whose ambitiousness belies the narrowness of the victory that brought [Bush] to the White House."[83] Tax cuts, Social Security reform, energy policy, and defense were all areas in which the administration set out to make major changes, or, as the director of OMB, Mitchell Daniels put it: "It's not going to be a presidency of miniature gestures."[84] This was, in short, not going to be the administration of an "old fashioned conservative" (an American Tory) like Bush I, but a more radical administration that rattled some settled cages and made some major changes.

A key concept behind the administrative presidency is that the president has received a mandate to govern through his election. This mandate is unique because the president is the one official in U.S. government who is elected nationally.[85] That, in this view, gives the president a legitimacy that no other institutional actor has and the right to use the levers of power aggressively, riding roughshod over others who stand in his way.[86] One remarkable thing about the Bush II administration is that it acted almost from the start as if it had a popular mandate rather than a delicate problem because of the circumstances accompanying Bush's selection. As Thomas Mann of the Brookings Institution said of the administration's early behavior, "It reminds you that this is the farthest thing from a caretaker administration you could get. It's the farthest thing from a president saying I lost the popular vote, I'm here because of a 5 to 4 vote on the Supreme Court, I'd better stake out some centrist positions."[87]

The lack of a majority from the voters did not keep Bush II from an appointments process and policy that from the start gave his administration a decidedly conservative cast, one that noted Reagan supporters have found most congenial—"more Reaganite than the Reagan administration," as the Heritage Foundation's president, Edwin J. Feulner, said with great enthusiasm. The final proof of the Feulner proposition will only come in time, but the available evidence points in that direction. And the Bush administration has accomplished this even while achieving a significant level of diversity, especially for a Republican administration. Just as the Clinton administration demonstrated that diversity and political moderation were not incompatible,[88] so the Bush administration shows that appointee diversity need not conflict with the building of a quite right-wing administration.

In his management agenda, Bush has continued most of the NPR initiatives of the Clinton administration because these initiatives already appealed to those suspicious of many government programs, especially on the domestic side. The rhetoric of cutbacks in personnel, program downsizing, "getting back to basics," marketlike systems, and privatization that marked much of the New Public Management–inspired National Performance Review was not foreign to those who wanted to see major changes of the type that a Reaganite would find congenial. In his campaign, Bush criticized the NPR effort for ineffectiveness in implementation, not for its stated goal of reinventing the government. In office, the Bush administration then added highly publicized efforts to use performance management techniques, and it tried to mandate a set of escalating targets in contracting out government jobs, a goal that Republican Senator George Voinovich criticized for unsettling the federal workforce and sending a "negative message" that would dissuade "college graduates and mid-career professionals from pursuing jobs in the federal government."[89] That was mixed with some steadfastly anti–labor union initiatives in the Homeland Security area. All of this helped communicate to the right wing of his party that Bush II was firmly in their camp.

Most important, the Bush II administration has assertively sought to "govern alone," to use the tools of the "administrative presidency" to get its way. This chapter has examined many of these tools and the enthusiastic and, frankly, aggressive style with which the Bush II administration has often employed them in an attempt to impose its will. This effort began before 11 September 2001, although the events of that day have obviously accelerated the trend and made it easier for the administration to get its way. Indeed, Vice President Cheney, who is apparently the architect of the administration and much of its strategy, and others in the administration have been open almost from the beginning about their desire to assert what they believe are appropriate and important presidential prerogatives.

The administration resisted inquiries from the General Accounting Office, resulting in an unprecedented lawsuit filed by that agency. The underlying constitutional claim here is quite strong; after all, the administration is asserting that it can refuse a request for information from the GAO without even bothering to claim executive privilege. It invoked executive privilege against requests from a Republican-led House committee and has been quite public about its desire to promote a "healthy rebalancing" in its relationship to Congress so the "the executive branch can have the authority to get the job done."[90] It engaged in a questionable and rather convoluted effort to keep Tom Ridge, when head of the Office of Homeland Security, from testifying before Congress due to his capacity as adviser to the president. It has used recess appointments to put controversial appointees into office. It seems fair to characterize its use of executive orders as quite audacious, particularly in regard to actions taken after September 11th. When lawmakers expressed some concern, the administration's attorney general, John Ashcroft, accused opponents of aiding terrorists.

It is at least possible that the general thrust of the first half or so of the Bush II administration will prove somewhat misleading once the full record is before us. But then again, Bush may even prove to be "Reagan squared," as Thomas Friedman suggested. Analysis of the period covered by this chapter indicates that this has been an administration much in line with the "administrative presidency" model outlined by Richard Nathan and the "politicized presidency" that Terry Moe asserts is inevitable in the modern period. The overall pattern—the web of evidence—is more than suggestive, and some of the individual actions are quite striking. Certainly, Bush and his associates fashioned an administration that, in the words of an incisive *National Journal* article, "has flexed all the muscles the Constitution gave him and, some would say, a few it didn't."[91] Whatever else the Bush II administration may be, it is not one that a traditional conservative, an American Tory, could be expected to readily embrace; rather, it is one that would appeal to a more radical conservative willing to take great liberties with traditional ways of doing things and to challenge established institutions.

The question remains whether the assertiveness of the Bush II administration is a sign that the second model of the presidency is not so much a question of choice as of necessity. One can at least make an argument, in line with the Moe analysis, that the George W. Bush administration behaved the way it did during its first two years because it had little or no choice, that "systemic" forces pushed it in that direction.[92] The course of the next few years, with Republican majorities in both houses of Congress and an increasingly conservative judiciary, should provide much suggestive evidence about the choice versus necessity issue, though debate will surely continue long after the Bush II administration is over. Clearly, in the highly partisan and contentious political climate that has prevailed in Washington in recent times—and was made even more contentious by split-party control of the Senate and the presidency such as that obtaining during much of Bush's term in office prior to the 2002 election—and in a period of great uncertainty brought on by new challenges such as terrorism, presidents are sorely tempted to "govern alone."[93] The U.S. constitution, however, was designed to promote power sharing. "Separated institutions, *sharing* powers," in Richard Neustadt's classic phrase,[94] demand that others be accommodated. Presidents who ignore this risk undermining not only the delicate fabric of freedom and mutual accommodation that is the basis of the American political system, but also, in extreme situations, their own administrations, as Nixon did in Watergate and as Reagan nearly did in Iran-*contra*. Students of the presidency should therefore find the remainder of the Bush II administration of great interest, both because of what it reveals about our understanding of the contemporary presidency and because of the stakes involved.

Notes

The author is grateful to Colin Campbell, Helene McCarren and the members of the American Politics luncheon group at UCLA for their very helpful comments on earlier drafts of this chapter.

1. Quoted in James MacGregor Burns, *The Deadlock of Democracy: Four-Party Politics in America* (Englewood Cliffs, N.J.: Prentice Hall, 1963), 22.
2. Richard E. Neustadt, *Presidential Power and the Modern Presidents: The Politics of Leadership from Roosevelt to Reagan* (New York: Free Press, 1990). The book was originally published in 1960 under the title *Presidential Power*.
3. Richard Nathan, *The Plot That Failed: Nixon and the Administrative Presidency* (New York: Wiley, 1975); Richard Nathan, *The Administrative Presidency* (New York: Wiley, 1983); and Terry M. Moe, "The Politicized Presidency," in *The New Direction in American Politics*, ed. John E. Chubb and Paul E. Peterson (Washington, D.C.: Brookings Institution, 1985), 235–71.
4. Nathan, *Plot That Failed*, 80.
5. See Nathan, *Administrative Presidency*; and Joel D. Aberbach and Bert A. Rockman, *In the Web of Politics: Three Decades of the U.S. Federal Executive* (Washington, D.C.: Brookings Institution, 2000).
6. Moe, "Politicized Presidency," 271.

7. Quoted in the National Commission on the Public Service (Volcker Commission), *Leadership for America: Rebuilding the Public Service,* 63.

8. James P. Pfiffner, "Establishing the Bush Presidency," *Public Administration Review,* January/February 1990: 68–69; and Joel D. Aberbach, "The President and the Executive Branch," in *The Bush Presidency: First Appraisals,* ed. Colin Campbell and Bert A. Rockman (Chatham, N.J.: Chatham House, 1991), 238–40.

9. Nelson Polsby, comments in "IGS Panel Assesses Bush Administration," *Public Affairs Report,* September 1990, 5.

10. Burt Solomon, "A Gathering of Friends," *National Journal,* 10 June 1989, 1402.

11. Erwin C. Hargrove, "The President Who Can't Lead Unless He Hears the Roar of the Crowd," *Los Angeles Times,* 21 October 1990, M1.

12. Burt Solomon, "The Cult of TR," *National Journal,* 16 February 2002, http://nationaljournal.com, 7.

13. John Maggs, "41, Reconsidered," *National Journal,* 20 July 2002, http://nationaljournal.com, 9.

14. Frank Bruni, "Quietly, but Confidently, Bush Pushes Ahead," *New York Times,* 28 November 2000, www.nytimes.com, 3.

15. John P. Burke, "The Bush Transition in Historical Context," *PS: Political Science & Politics* 35, no. 1 (March 2002): 24.

16. Ibid., 25.

17. Clay Johnson, "The 2000–2001 Presidential Transition: Planning, Goals, and Reality," *PS: Political Science & Politics* 35, no. 1 (March 2002): 51.

18. Ibid., 53 (emphasis in text).

19. Pfiffner, "Establishing the Bush Presidency," 68–69.

20. Janet M. Martin and Mary Anne Borrelli, "Campaign Promises and Presidential Appointments: Women in the George W. Bush Administration," paper presented at the annual meeting of the American Political Science Association, San Francisco, 30 August–2 September 2001. See Table 7, p. 22.

21. James A. Barnes, "Bush's Insiders," *National Journal,* 23 June 2001, http://nationaljournal.com, 2.

22. Bob Herbert, "Far, Far From the Center," *New York Times,* 8 January 2001, www.nytimes.com, 1.

23. Quoted in Robin Toner, "Conservatives Savor Their Role as Insiders in the White House," *New York Times,* 19 March 2001, www.nytimes.com, 1.

24. Ibid., 1.

25. See Richard L. Berke, "Political Memo: Bush Shapes His Presidency With Sharp Eye on Father's," *New York Times,* 28 March 2001, www.nytimes.com.

26. Toner, "Conservatives Savor Their Role," 2.

27. Dana Milbank, "Ashcroft Appointment Assailed," *Washington Post,* 5 September 2002, A29.

28. Elizabeth Shogren, "Bush Environment Jobs Are Skewed to Business," *Washington Post,* 24 June 2001, www.latimes.com.

29. See, for example, the articles in the *Brookings Review* issue on "The State of the Presidential Appointment Process," Spring 2001, and related pieces in G. Calvin Mackenzie,

ed., *Innocent Until Nominated: The Breakdown of the Presidential Appointments Process* (Washington, D.C.: Brookings Institution, 2001).

30. Critics are concerned about the time it takes to fill positions (something that is relatively easy to measure), but they also worry about the currently drawn-out process "frightening away talent" and making it more difficult to hold presidents accountable for governmental performance. (For a good, brief presentation of this point of view, see G. Calvin Mackenzie, "Nasty & Brutish Without Being Short: The State of the Presidential Appointment Process," in *Brookings Review*, Spring 2001, 4–7.)

31. These data come from Burdett Loomis and are based on CRS Reports. See table 5–1 of Burdett Loomis, "The Senate: An 'Obstacle Course' for Executive Appointments," in Mackenzie, *Innocent Until Nominated*, 160–72.

32. See, for example, G. Calvin Mackenzie, "The State of the Presidential Appointments Process," in Mackenzie, *Innocent Until Nominated*, esp. 44–47.

33. Paul Light, quoted in Brian Faler, "For Bush Choices, Wait Grows," *Washington Post*, 25 July 2002, www.washingtonpost.com, 2.

34. Whether the delays in getting appointees confirmed has a large impact on the quality of those who are willing to accept appointments is still an open question. As for accountability, another concern of critics of the current process (see note 30), that is also a complex issue since the struggle over confirming appointees is itself tied to issues of presidential accountability through the link between appointees and the administrative presidential strategy of "governing alone."

35. See National Performance Review, *From Red Tape to Results: Creating a Government That Works Better and Costs Less* (Washington, D.C.: Government Printing Office, 1993).

36. Aberbach and Rockman, *In the Web of Politics*, 136.

37. Alison Mitchell, "Bush Criticizes Gore Record on Trimming Bureaucracy," *New York Times*, 10 June 2000, www.nytimes.com, 1.

38. Tom Shoop, "Bush Proposes to Cut Middle Management Jobs," *GovExec.com*, 12 June 2000, www.govexec.com, 1–2.

39. Quoted in Stephen Barr, "Don't Worry About the Job Cuts in Bush's Plan, Adviser Says: Think Hefty Bonuses," *Washington Post*, 12 June 2000, www.washingtonpost.com, B2.

40. Ibid.

41. The administration describes its management program as "an aggressive strategy for improving the management of the Federal government" (www.whitehouse.gov/omb/budgetintegration). Its formal management agenda focuses on five initiatives: 1. strategic management of human capital; 2. competitive sourcing; 3. improved financial performance; 4. expanded electronic government; and 5. budget and performance integration. See Office of Management and Budget, *The President's Management Agenda: Fiscal Year 2002*, 11–30.

42. See Jason Peckenpaugh, "Senators Blast Bush Competitive Sourcing Plan," *GovExec.com*, 6 March 2002, http://govexec.com.

43. Jason Peckenpaugh, "Bush Administration Blasts Proposed Freeze on Contracts," *GovExec.com*, 29 June 2001, http://govexec.com.

44. Jason Peckenpaugh, "House Democrats Plan 'In-sourcing' Amendment for Defense Bill," *GovExec.com*, 30 April 2002, http://govexec.com.

45. Peckenpaugh, "Bush Administration Blasts Proposed Freeze on Contracts." Note that

Rep. Davis is chair of a House subcommittee central to securing legislation in this area. See also Peckenpaugh, "Senators Blast Bush Competitive Sourcing Plan," 1, on Sen. Voinovich's (R-Ohio) concern that "the benchmarks the administration has adopted for its competitive sourcing plan are arbitrary and potentially damaging."

46. Donald Kettl, *The Global Public Management Revolution: A Report on the Transformation of Governance* (Washington, D.C.: Brookings Institution, 2000), 13–14.

47. Dana Milbank, "Cheney Refuses Records' Release," *Washington Post*, 28 January 2002, A1.

48. Alison Mitchell, "Cheney Rejects Broader Access to Terror Brief," *New York Times*, 20 May 2002, www.nytimes.com, 2.

49. Ibid.

50. See, for example, Joel D. Aberbach, "President and the Executive Branch"; and idem, "A Reinvented Government, or the Same Old Government?," in *The Clinton Legacy*, ed. Colin Campbell and Bert A. Rockman (New York: Chatham House, 2000).

51. Both quotes are from p. 2 of the GAO filing in U.S. District Court for the District of Columbia in *Walker v. Cheney*, Civil Action No. 1:02cv00340, dated 22 February 2002.

52. Ibid.

53. Judge Bates was appointed to the D.C. Circuit in December 2001. In a delicious irony, he was Deputy Independent Counsel for the Whitewater investigation from 1995 to mid–1997. For a biographical sketch of Judge Bates, see www.dcd.uscourts.gov/bates-bio.html.

54. Adam Clymer, "Judge Says Cheney Needn't Give Data on Energy Policy to G.A.O.," *New York Times*, 10 December 2002, www.nytimes.com. Comptroller General David M. Walker subsequently decided not to appeal this ruling. He wrote, "Despite GAO's conviction that the district court's decision was incorrect, further pursuit of the NEPDG information would require investment of significant time and resources over several years." And he held that the "court's decision is confined to the unique circumstances posed by this particular case and does not preclude GAO from filing suit on a different matter involving different facts and circumstances in the future." Quoted in Dana Milbank, "GAO Backs Off Cheney Lawsuit: Accounting Office Will Not Appeal Federal Court Ruling," *Washington Post*, 7 February 2003, www/washingtonpost.com.

55. Don Van Natta Jr. and Terence Neilan, "Agency Will Sue White House to Obtain Cheney Records," *New York Times*, 30 January 2002, www.nytimes.com, 1.

56. Don Van Natta Jr., "Cheney Argues Against Giving Congress Records," *New York Times*, 28 September 2002, www.nytimes.com, 1.

57. Quoted in Dana Milbank, "Cheney Refuses Records' Release," A1.

58. Ellen Nakashima, "Bush Invokes Executive Privilege on Hill: Records on Clinton, Mob Case Barred," *Washington Post*, 14 December 2001, www.washingtonpost.com.

59. Ibid., A43.

60. Ibid.

61. Quoted in Alexis Simendinger, "Power of One," *National Journal*, 26 January 2002, http://nationaljournal.com, 4.

62. Ibid., 5. See also Mark J. Rozell, *Executive Privilege: Presidential Power, Secrecy, and Accountability*, 2d ed., rev. (Lawrence: University of Kansas Press, 2002), 147–55.

63. Quoted in Ellen Nakashima and Dan Eggen, "White House Seeks to Restore Its Privileges," *Washington Post*, 10 September 2001, www.washingtonpost.com, A2.

64. See the Ridge biography on the White House web site at www.whitehouse.gov/home-land/ridgebio.html. See also Section 3 of the Executive Order [13228] Establishing the Office of Homeland Security which stated, "The functions of the Office [to be headed by the Assistant to the President for Homeland Security] shall be to coordinate the executive branch's efforts to detect, prepare for, prevent, protect against, respond to, and recover from terrorist attacks within the United States" (October 8, 2001, www.whitehouse.gov/news/releases/2001).

65. Alison Mitchell, "Letter to Ridge Is Latest Jab in Fight over Balance of Power," *New York Times*, 5 March 2002, www.nytimes.com, 1.

66. Keith Koffler, "Ridge to Testify, Within Limits, on Cabinet Creation Plan," *GovExec.com*, 7 June 2002, www.govexec.com, 1.

67. Christopher Marquis, "Bush Bypasses Senate on 2 More Nominees," *New York Times*, 12 January 2002, www.nytimes.com, 2.

68. Ibid.

69. Associated Press, "Bush Makes Recess Appointment of Campaign Law Critic," *New York Times*, 29 March 2002, www.nytimes.com, 1. The story covered several recess appointments, including the appointment of Michael E. Toner, described as the "top lawyer" of the Republican National Committee (RNC) to the Federal Election Commission. The RNC had opposed "the ban on unlimited contributions in the bill that Bush reluctantly signed Wednesday."

70. See Aberbach, "A Reinvented Government, or the Same Old Government?" 124–26.

71. For a recent study, see Kenneth R. Mayer, *With the Stroke of a Pen* (Princeton: Princeton University Press, 2001).

72. See especially the military order of 13 November 2001 on "the detention, treatment, and trial of certain non-citizens in the war on terrorism" listed on the White House web site under Executive Orders Issued by President Bush, http://whitehouse.gov/news/orders/.

73. As of January 2003, no trials had yet been held under this procedure, a fact that administration spokesman Ari Fleischer actually cited as evidence that the president is an advocate of openness. He was reported as saying that this openness "was exemplified by the fact that while 'the president reserved the authority to try people under military tribunals, nobody has been tried under military tribunals.'" Adam Clymer, "Government Openness at Issue as Bush Holds onto Records," *New York Times*, 3 January 2002, www.nytimes.com, 3.

74. Robin Toner and Neil A. Lewis, "White House Push on Security Steps Bypasses Congress," *New York Times*, 15 November 2001, www.nytimes.com, 1.

75. Ibid.

76. Matthew Purdy, "Bush's New Rules to Fight Terror Transform the Legal Landscape," *New York Times*, 25 November 2001, www.nytimes.com, 1.

77. Neil A. Lewis, "Ashcroft Defends Antiterror Plan and Says Criticism May Aid Foes," *New York Times*, 7 December 2001, www.nytimes.com, 1.

78. Louis Fisher, "Bush Can't Rely on the FDR Precedent," *New York Times*, 2 December 2001, www.nytimes.com, 1. Also see Louis Fisher, "Military Tribunals: The Quirin Precedent," Congressional Research Service, 26 March 2002.

79. Fisher, "Bush Can't Rely on the FDR Precedent," 3.

80. Elisabeth Bumiller, "Bush Keeps a Grip on Presidential Papers," *New York Times*, 2 November 2001, www.nytimes.com, 1.

81. Ibid.

82. Thomas L. Friedman, "Reforming Success," *New York Times*, 7 September 2001, www.nytimes.com, 1.

83. Dan Balz, "Next on Bush Agenda: Bigger Policy Changes," *Washington Post*, 6 May 2001, www.washingtonpost.com, 1.

84. Ibid.

85. Moe stresses the idea that the president is the single official elected nationally ("Politicized Presidency," 238).

86. See, for example, Joel D. Aberbach and Bert A. Rockman, "Clashing Beliefs Within the Executive Branch: The Nixon Administration Bureaucracy," *American Political Science Review* 64 (June 1976): 456–68, esp. p. 468, where we argue that Nixon saw himself "not as the preeminent contender for power, but as the holder of an exclusive mandate to command" and discuss some implications of that view.

87. Ibid.

88. See, for example, Joel D. Aberbach, "The Federal Executive under Clinton," in *The Clinton Presidency: First Appraisals*, ed. Colin Campbell and Bert A. Rockman (Chatham, N.J.: Chatham House, 1996).

89. Quoted in Stephen Barr, "Opening Jobs to Private Competition: Why 1 in 4?" *Washington Post*, 7 March 2002, B2.

90. Administration Press Secretary Ari Fleisher, quoted in Simendinger, "Power of One," 4.

91. Ibid., 1.

92. Moe asserts that because the "expectations surrounding presidential performance far outstrip the institutional capacity of presidents to perform," the resulting imbalance pushes them away from the bargaining behavior featured in Neustadt's treatment of the presidency and toward what Moe labels "politicization and centralization." Presidents may vary in the degree to which they follow this strategy, but "there will likely be no turning back from the general path of historical development" because "the basic causes are systemic," i.e., presidential behavior in this regard is basically a matter of necessity, not choice. See Moe, "Politicized Presidency," 269–70.

93. Ironically, the reluctance of a Republican Congress to investigate its own president could embolden the administration to "govern alone" even more than in its first two years. Add to this the fact that the Senate requires extraordinary majorities to get things done and one has a ready opportunity for dissenters to obstruct administration initiatives, meaning that the 2002 election results are unlikely to produce a smooth-running institution consistently bowing to White House requests. Contention and presidential frustration, therefore, are likely to continue, though the levels ought to be at least somewhat reduced. Assuming the above, such a complex situation is not likely to provide a clear-cut answer to the choice versus necessity question.

94. Richard E. Neustadt, *Presidential Power and the Modern Presidents*, 29 (italics in original).

CHAPTER 4

Unrestrained Ideological Entrepreneurship in the Bush II Advisory System

An Examination of the Response to 9/11 and the Decision to Seek Regime Change in Iraq

Colin Campbell

UNDERSCORING THE IMPORTANCE and legitimacy of policy entrepreneurship among government officials, John W. Kingdon outlines two crucial steps toward pressing a policy agenda. Officials get policy innovation rolling initially through a pre-decisional process of specifying available alternatives.[1] They then position themselves for the opportunity to drive home their case, much like a surfer waiting for the perfect wave—"ready to paddle, and their readiness combined with their sense for riding the wave and using the forces beyond their control contribute to success."[2] A difficulty presents itself here: the policy entrepreneur may often find it hard to maintain a balance between the advocacy inevitably associated with entrepreneurship and a thoroughgoing canvassing of the possible implications of the options that he or she has chosen to promote. Terry Moe, noting this tension, has greatly influenced presidential studies by highlighting the legitimacy of presidential appointees' opting for "responsive competence"—that is, stances that will advance an administration's political support—even if this comes at the expense of "neutral competence"—namely, doing what a relatively detached assessment would suggest as the correct course of action.[3]

To be sure, one invariably finds it difficult to differentiate ideological from policy entrepreneurship. The former, however, usually entails a very strong depth of adherence that makes compromise very difficult. It also often relates to a narrowly defined yet politically leveraged segment of the president's perceived base. Finally, its advocates frequently display exceptional persistence—in other words, they surf until dark no matter how bad the conditions may appear to the onlooker.

Ideological entrepreneurship becomes "unrestrained" within an administration when two conditions prevail. First, the selection of political appointees has been influenced to a substantial degree by the ideological commitments of nominees. Second, the administration's decision-making process lacks conscious efforts to ensure that policy proposals receive testing under fire through intense countervailing review. Unrestrained ideological entrepreneurship stands in sharp contrast to "multiple advocacy," which gained great currency through two important works on the presidency published in 1980. First, Alexander L. George pointed up the benefits of providing a level playing field for the advocacy of ideas within an administration.[4] Second, Roger B. Porter provided an analysis of multiple advocacy at work during the Ford administration.[5]

George W. Bush's chairman of the Council of Economic Advisers, N. Gregory Mankiw, provided in the first edition of his economics text an apt description of ideological entrepreneurship under the Reagan administration.[6] In a section of the book headed "Charlatans and Cranks," Mankiw dwelt on the dangers of "fad economics," whereby "a small group of economists advised presidential candidate Ronald Reagan that an across-the-board cut in income tax rates would raise revenue." He noted that "when politicians rely on the advice of charlatans and cranks, they rarely get the desirable results they anticipate." These circumstances prove most lethal, with respect to the potential for deleterious effects, when the administration lacks the inclination and/or the capacity to place strongly advocated policy propositions under rigorous collegial review.

To What Degree Is Unrestrained Ideological Entrepreneurship a Worry in the Bush Administration?

Early in December 2002, the *New York Times* revealed that the January 2003 issue of *Esquire* would quote very negative reflections by John DiIulio—a former Harvard professor who had served briefly as an assistant to the president for faith-based and community initiatives—on the operation of the Bush II White House.[7] The *Times* reported that the yet-to-be published *Esquire* article focused on the dominant role of Karl Rove—the senior adviser to the president for strategic initiatives—in White House policymaking.[8] It noted that DiIulio had asserted that Rove had introduced a reign of "Mayberry Machiavellis" that was nearly devoid of systematic consideration of policy issues. As if to verify this somewhat jaundiced view of Rove's not-so-hidden hand, DiIulio recanted his remarks on the day the *Times* story appeared. Indeed, he used terms ("groundless and baseless due to poorly chosen words and examples") that, despite slightly different ordering, corresponded exactly with those employed by press secretary Ari Fleischer ("baseless and groundless due to poorly chosen words and examples") in denouncing DiIulio's characterization of the Bush White House.[9]

Esquire then released the e-mail message in which DiIulio had outlined his view of the Bush White House.[10] DiIulio's assault had targeted the administration's lack of direction on domestic strategy: "Besides the tax cut, which was cut-and-dried during the campaign, and the education bill, which was really a Ted Kennedy bill, the administration has not done much . . . on domestic policy." He added, "There is a virtual absence as yet of any policy accomplishment that might, to a fair-minded non-partisan, count as the flesh on the bones of so-called compassionate conservatism." DiIulio expressly pinned the problem on a lack of White House organization as a policymaking apparatus, which led, he believed, to "on-the-fly policy-making by speech-making"—"nice" and "extremely gifted" people "organized in ways that make it hard for policy-minded staff, including colleagues (even secretaries) of cabinet agencies, to get much West Wing traction, or even get a non-trivial hearing." DiIulio asserted, thus, that those wanting to base their arguments on analysis found it hard to make themselves heard in the Bush II White House, while those crafting words that captured the president's imagination would find relatively smooth sailing.

DiIulio specifically underscored the tendency within this framework—or lack thereof—for what I have termed unrestrained ideological entrepreneurship to prevail in deliberations. Citing his own experience as the official responsible for preparing administration proposals seeking legislation in support of faith-based initiatives, he describes an unruly policymaking process:

> . . . over-generalizing the lesson from the politics of the tax cut bill, they winked at the most far-right House Republicans who, in turn, drafted a so-called faith bill (H.R.7, the Community Solutions Act) that (or so they thought) satisfied certain fundamentalist leaders and beltway libertarians but bore few marks of "compassionate conservatism" and was, as anybody could tell, an absolute political non-starter.

DiIulio's e-mail painted a portrait of Karl Rove that was strongly evocative of Bush I's John Sununu—the clear distinction being that the former displays exquisite political judgment, whereas the latter let his hubris get him into an endless succession of pratfalls.[11] Rove, according to DiIulio, instills fear without having to be nasty about it:

> Some in the press view Karl as some sort of prince of darkness; actually, he is basically a nice and good-humored man. And some staff members, senior and junior, are awed and cowed by Karl's real or perceived powers. They self-censor lots for fear of upsetting him, and, in turn, few of the president's top

people routinely tell the president what they really think if they think that Karl will be brought up short in the bargain.

The administration on occasion has tried to draw attention away from Rove's pervasive influence. For instance, a *New York Times* column, published early in 2003 right after the administration unveiled its proposed $670 billion tax-cut package and reflecting substantial spin by normally taciturn White House officials, floated the name of another aide said to be performing the role of White House policy ringmaster.[12] Josh Bolten, who served as White House deputy chief of staff for policy until appointed director of the Office of Management and Budget later in 2003, at least notionally reported to White House chief of staff Andrew H. Card Jr. The notoriously tight-lipped administration was attempting in the interviews granted for the *Times* piece to draw attention away from Rove's pivotal role by hinting at a purportedly wide-ranging consultative process. The *Times* proclaimed, thus, that Bolten "coordinated the ideas coming out of two competing White House entities, the Domestic Policy Council and the National Economic Council." However, a difficulty immediately arises here, for unlike cabinet-level councils in the Reagan administration,[13] these bodies rarely meet. Indeed, accounts of trouble in the Bush economic team had since the summer of 2002 claimed, inter alia, that Bolten had eclipsed Lawrence Lindsey—who was, until December 2002, the director of the National Economic Council—as Bush's favorite economic adviser, that Bush had to become his own chief economic spokesman, that Rove wanted to get rid of both Lindsey and Paul H. O'Neill— the treasury secretary until December 2002—and that the National Economic Council had faded into irrelevance.[14] Strangely, the administration's tax-cut package went through gestation just as these players in normally key roles for development of economic policy became aware that they soon would be twisting in the wind. Under the circumstances, one would have to ask, "Was Bolten ringmaster of consultations between phantom cabinet-level stakeholders?"

The *Times* piece asserted that Bolten controlled the agendas and attendance at a forty-five-minute "policy time" in which the president meets with leading advisers—Card, Rove, the assistant to the president for legislative affairs, affected cabinet officers, and, often, the vice president—on most days when he is in Washington. Mention of this process puts the spotlight on the role of the president in leading such discussions. Franklin Delano Roosevelt and John F. Kennedy serve as one possible model for this kind of advisory procedure. They brought to such sessions clear intellectual acuity and an ability to narrow participation in and bring closure to deliberations without embracing positions before canvassing thoroughly the options at hand.[15]

Dwight Eisenhower and Ronald Reagan present another model. Of course, the former clearly was a quicker study on the examination of issues—although he proved maddeningly evasive to anybody trying to pin him down on them. Both presidents, however, brought to policy deliberations a strong requirement of inclusion. Eisenhower's experience in the Pentagon and his exposure to a collective approach to decision making in the United Kingdom during World War II had made him a strong believer in structured cabinet deliberations.[16]

While his intellect was no match for Eisenhower's, much less Kennedy's, Reagan, too, differed substantially from Bush II in the practice of decision making. The principles behind Reagan's policy views became widely known even before he attained the presidency. Indeed, his former domestic policy adviser, Martin Anderson, has edited—along with his wife and a colleague—a collection of papers that reveals the great deal of thought and effort, if not a high degree of intellectual sophistication, that went into Reagan's speeches before he became president.[17] (One must suspect that the George W. Bush Presidential Library will be bereft of any comparable documents.) Furthermore, while governor of California, Reagan had become enamored of structures for collective consultation between cabinet secretaries.[18] Interestingly, these two important distinctions between the decision-making styles of Bush II and Reagan seem to have escaped a recent *New York Times Magazine* article that posits a nearly one-to-one fit between the two presidents.[19]

In his first term as president, Reagan imposed a strict "roundtable" norm, whereby cabinet secretaries usually could not bring matters directly to the president without their going first to the relevant cabinet council.[20] In addition, the president frequently would chair these bodies when they had reached the critical decision point on administration policies. Significantly, however, Reagan and his closest aides let the roundtable norm lapse substantially during the second term, primarily because the president was then becoming somewhat detached from reviewing the details of policy. An additional factor, though, was that James A. Baker III—the first-term White House chief of staff, who was a firm believer in the norm—switched positions at that time with Donald Regan—the first-term treasury secretary, who instead viewed the top White House job as a command position.[21]

The notorious Iran/*contra* affair stands almost as a monument to the consequences of the decline of roundtabling during Reagan's second term. This episode involved a scheme, concocted and driven from within the National Security Council staff, that had the U.S. government arranging through third parties to send weapons to Iran in exchange for funds that were then funneled covertly to the U.S.-supported *contra* forces seeking to overthrow a leftist regime in Nicaragua. While aware of this effort and even party to some discussions associated with it, Secretary of State George Shultz and Secretary of Defense Caspar Weinberger essentially nodded and winked at what ultimately became a debacle from the standpoint of the administration's credibility.[22] The Tower Commission's report on the affair placed the blame squarely at the feet of a president who had become overly indulgent of the machinations of his immediate White House advisers:

> The President's management style is to put the principal responsibility of policy review and implementation on the shoulders of his advisors. Nevertheless, with such a complex, high-risk operation and so much at stake, the President should have ensured that the NSC system did not fail him. He did not force his policy to undergo the most critical review of which the NSC participants and the process were capable. . . the most powerful features of the NSC system—providing comprehensive analysis, alternatives and follow-up—were not utilized.[23]

In the Bush II administration, we are seeing once again a high degree of presidential detachment from the heavy lifting required in policymaking. We find as well little evidence of decisional conventions—such as a roundtabling norm and its associated structures—that could effectively compensate for any shortfall in presidential engagement.

In their media appearances, two chroniclers of the Bush II administration—the *Washington Post's* Bob Woodward and Bush's own former speechwriter, David Frum—have time and again found themselves defending the president's intelligence.[24] However, most such attacks miss the point. George W. Bush clearly operates at the outer limits of brilliant political maneuver, but this obvious tactical intelligence does not seem to translate into the consistent concentration and rigor required for grasping the key elements of policy issues and the processes whereby they might be resolved. This lack of deliberative effort should cause concern, especially at moments when the president is receiving strong external reinforcement for his performance, such as high approval ratings or gaining seats in midterm elections. Such reinforcement may easily lull an inattentive executive into excessive docility toward the advice bubbling up from his most trusted aides.

President Bush's inability to express the reasons for his positions unless heavily scripted exacerbates concerns that he has acquired little authentic mastery of the issues. This perception has even prompted seriously alarmed treatises that raise questions about the nature of presidential campaigns that can produce such a poorly informed incumbent.[25] More troubling than such worries about the president's grasp of issue details, however, is the sense that his words often betray shaky foundations even for his most firmly held beliefs. Why, for instance, did he limit himself to dismissive epithets in response to our traditional allies' skepticism about the justification for invading Iraq? Do not remarks such as, "This looks like a rerun of a bad movie and I'm not interested in watching it . . . "[26] take the level of discourse—here involving international relations at the very highest levels—down to that of television interviews of participants in a professional wrestling match?

A further example of this problematic ineloquence occurs in the context of the religious commitment that Bush II often posits as operating at the core of his philosophy of life.[27] Indeed, in the weeks immediately following 9/11, those close to Bush underscored how his Christianity had steeled his resolve.[28] The *Times* quoted a friend as saying, "I think, in this frame, this is what God has asked him to do. It offers him enormous clarity." By late December 2001, Ralph Reed, the former head of the Christian Coalition, claimed that providence had intervened in the 2000 election to ensure that a godly man would lead the nation in its time of crisis: "I've heard a lot of: 'God knew something we didn't.' . . . He had a knowledge nobody else had: He knew George Bush had the ability to lead in this compelling way." The White House jumped at the chance of confirm Reed's view, as Tim Goeglein, a special assistant to the president for public liaison, incanted: "I think President Bush is God's man at this hour." Michael Gerson, Bush's speechwriter and a religious conservative, gushed—perhaps without realizing that effectively he was admiring his own craftsmanship—that the president "speaks the language of religion better than any president since Jimmy Carter. . . . "

It would appear, thus, that spirituality might stand as the president's strongest suit, on which even his nonscripted remarks should reveal a true depth of intellectual engagement. No such evidence was on display, however, at a presidential appearance on 5 January 2002 in Ontario, California, where Bush led a town-hall style forum with a highly sympathetic audience. The session attracted special press attention because it came the day after Senate Majority Leader Tom Daschle had attacked the Bush-approved $1.35 trillion tax cut program for "causing the most dramatic fiscal deterioration in our nation's history."[29] In the event, the president characteristically retorted with a malapropism, "Not over my dead body will they raise your taxes."

Most subsequent press accounts translated Bush's misstatement to say what he actually meant.[30] However, the official White House transcript of the session—during which the president spoke almost entirely ad lib—reported two exchanges that revealed a rather underdeveloped spirituality. In response to the question, "How can we . . . pray for you and your family [in this time of national crisis after 9/11]?" the president answered, ". . . to pray . . . that there is a shield of protection, so that if the evil ones try to hit us again, that we've done everything we can, physically, and that there is a spiritual shield that protects the country." Then, perhaps prompted by this answer, another member of the audience asked, "What was the first thing that went through your head [after the terrorist attacks]?" The president began his response by saying, ". . . I was sitting in a schoolhouse in Florida. I had gone down to tell my little brother what to do—just kidding." He then plugged his reading program and shared a paragraph of thoughts about "getting" the "evil ones," before ending his answer with the comment, "Anyway, it was an interesting day."

Coming from the nation's leader less than four months after an attack on the United States unrivaled since Pearl Harbor, these words might strike many readers as astoundingly pedestrian. And, although they received, apparently, no comment in the national press, even under the most generous interpretation such detached and evasive remarks must raise questions about the president's ability to provide a reasoned account of the principles behind his actions. While any private citizen might by reflex deflect efforts by others to peer into his soul, such a reflexive tendency on the part of the president might deter as well White House advisers, cabinet secretaries, and other senior administration officers from attempting to engage him in deep discourse about the principles behind his policy stances. The Bush administration frequently shows the president wearing his spirituality on his sleeve in his prepared texts. A personal unwillingness to enter into open discourse at any depth that might reveal his inner thoughts would therefore constitute a true paradox.[31]

We have already seen that significant tensions emerged in the president's economics team and that structures for collective deliberation over issues had become more honored in the breach than the observance. We know as well that the president's relations with Secretary of State Colin Powell had become somewhat strained by the summer of 2002.[32] Indeed, Powell did not attend the critical meeting in Crawford, Texas—ostensibly held to review the Pentagon budget proposals for fiscal year 2004 —where the administration made a commitment to continue its efforts to seek regime change in Iraq notwithstanding caveats from two Republican former national security advisers, Henry Kissinger and Brent Scowcroft.[33]

By that summer, Attorney General John Ashcroft had also blotted his copybook with the White House. In the immediate aftermath wave of 9/11, the White House had pulled Ashcroft up short when he started to negotiate with senators and congressmen over the details of the proposed USA Patriot Act.[34] Eventually, the administration made it clear that Timothy Flanigan, the deputy White House counsel, would take the lead in such negotiations—although Flanigan, in a *Times* interview, characterized Ashcroft's role as that of "full partner." Nevertheless, Ashcroft stayed in the media spotlight by making frequent announcements. Ultimately, one of these—the declaration that a "dirty bomber" had been apprehended, when in fact the individual involved had merely been caught in the planning stages of a plot—prompted a spate of negative leaks from the White House.[35] The complaint: Ashcroft was stealing attention from the president.

Serious Problems with Issue Management: An Examination of Regime Change in Iraq

So far, two questions crucial to any evaluation of the Bush II presidency have presented themselves in this chapter. First, has the president established and led a rigorous dynamic for the review of policy issues? Second, has he revealed in his non-scripted remarks a deep engagement in discourse over policy? Insofar as the answers to these two questions appear to be negative, we might expect fertile soil for unrestrained ideological entrepreneurship within the administration. Other chapters in this book probe in greater detail the Bush II administration's handling of domestic and foreign policy issues, but even a quick survey of the matters on the administration's plate in early 2003 discovered relatively strong indications that some policies seemed to emanate from especially assertive position-taking by key players. These entrepreneurial policies often seemed to fly in the face of thoroughgoing assessment of the dangers they posed, and sometimes to tarnish the attractiveness of ideologically motivated stances as well.

As the Bush II presidency moved past its midpoint, at least three issues loomed as matters in which the administration had taken strongly ideological stances that were fraught with incalculable danger. These matters included the administration's pursuit of regime changes in the Arab world, the consequences of its early refusal to negotiate with the North Korean leader, and its determination to seek further cuts in taxes despite the inevitable result of ever-deeper deficit spending. Because space allows an in-depth look at only one of these issues, we now examine the decision to invade Iraq from the standpoint of issue management, especially with regard to unrestrained ideological entrepreneurship.

If Bush II Wants to Avoid the Failures of His Father, Two Issues Might Still Haunt Him

As I noted in chapter 1, most assessors of an administration's performance hesitate to argue with success. With respect to Iraq, the reader knows that in early 2003 the United States led a relatively efficient invasion that it had mounted with support from a handful of allies self-consciously termed the "coalition of the willing." Despite one tense week during which the force's advance overstretched its supply lines, the operation proceeded with surprisingly surgical precision, resulting in far fewer civilian casualties than had been feared. Soon after toppling Saddam Hussein's government, however, the administration began to appear very much like the dog that caught the bus. That is, it seemed not to know how to advance its putative goal, establishing a stable democracy, without running the risk of ensnarling itself in chaos. At a minimum, the circumstances on the ground in Iraq pointed to a long and tortuous road toward the envisioned transformation of Baghdad into a beacon for democracy in the Arab world.

Still, much of the nation seemed anxious to chalk up the invasion itself as a policymaking triumph closely paralleling that of George H.W. Bush in 1990–91. Others cautioned against judging the episode too hastily, for two reasons. First, the Bush I victory in the Persian Gulf did not itself rate as an unqualified policy success; the American-led allied forces had pushed Iraq out of Kuwait but stopped short of expelling Saddam Hussein from Baghdad, because the allies had become fearful of negative fallout from media coverage of the infamous "Highway of Death," along which the bodies of the fleeing Iraqi army were strewn in one of the most horrific scenes of carnage known to history. And, in any case, the UN Security Council's Resolution No. 678 had only sanctioned expulsion of Iraqi forces from Kuwait. To many, thus, the Gulf War had left unfinished business.

Second, the war effort had proved a huge distraction to George H. W. Bush. To be sure, Bush I went on record several times declaring that he relished trying to solve the crisis.[36] Unfortunately, he also left the enduring impression that domestic issues seemed trivial in comparison. More fatally, some highly regarded observers—spanning the political spectrum from the left-leaning David S. Broder to the right-wing George F. Will—saw a connection between the reactive role Bush I had taken in response to the Iraqi threat and his approach to intractable domestic issues that ultimately boiled over.[37] Indeed, Will quoted approvingly two Bush I administration officials whose deep concerns could as readily apply to George W. Bush—especially with regard to a leader's tendency to allow personalization of conflict to cloud his judgment:

> A "top official" tells *The New York Times*, "It's the budget mess all over again—flip-flops, a message out of control and nobody in charge." Another official says, "We seem to be zigzagging because sometimes it's less a matter of a game plan and more a matter of the president's moods."

What Do Elephants and Paul Wolfowitz Have in Common? Answer: Long Memories

The elements of unrestrained ideological entrepreneurship run deep in the emergence of the administration's commitment and resolve to invade Iraq. Immediately after 9/11, Paul Wolfowitz, the deputy defense secretary, pressed for making regime change in Iraq a centerpiece of the war against terrorism.[38] Indeed, Wolfowitz advocated his position so strenuously at a Camp David meeting on 15 September 2001 that the White House chief of staff, Andrew Card, had to admonish him not to interrupt Defense Secretary Donald Rumsfeld. Wolfowitz—who served as undersecretary for defense policy during the Bush I administration—had, as a young Pentagon analyst, led the development of a secret 1979 document warning of the emerging Iraqi threat to Middle East security.[39] When, during the 1991 Gulf War, the televised "Highway of Death" images had begun to trouble the Bush I administration, Wolfowitz had adamantly opposed the chairman of the Joint Chiefs of Staff, Colin Powell, and the top general in the Persian Gulf campaign, H. Norman Schwarzkopf, in their determination to abruptly end the allied attack. The visual horrors being transmitted around the globe had even in-duced qualms back home in the United States. Still, Wolfowitz argued, contin-ued pressure could prompt a coup in Iraq that would lead to Saddam Hussein's ouster even without the ground war having to continue on to Baghdad.[40] Ironi-cally, the tension between Wolfowitz and Powell would play a significant role dur-ing the buildup for the 2003 invasion of Iraq as well.

Although at the Camp David meeting following 9/11 the president cut short consideration of an invasion-of-Iraq option,[41] the idea apparently intrigued him. Indeed, *New York Times* journalist Bill Keller asserts that when Wolfowitz had registered his concerns privately to the president during a break in the discus-sions, Bush had admonished him to speak up.[42] As Keller notes, Wolfowitz en-joyed excellent wiring for spreading his perspective widely within the adminis-tration,[43] for he shared a mentor with Richard Perle—who resigned in 2003 as the chairman of Rumsfeld's Defense Advisory Board due to conflict of interest—in that both men had received their socialization as neoconservatives under the tute-lage of the late Senator Henry M. "Scoop" Jackson (D-Wash.).

Wolfowitz, in turn, had nurtured the generation of neoconservatives by men-toring two critically placed administration hawks. While at Yale he taught I. Lewis "Scooter" Libby, who currently serves as Dick Cheney's chief of staff and who aligned himself soon after 9/11 with those seeking regime change in Iraq.[44] Then, in the Pentagon during the Bush I administration, Wolfowitz had supervised Stephen J. Hadley, Condoleezza Rice's deputy, who chairs the crucial National Security Council's deputies' committee, which meets several times a week to prepare issues for cabinet-level consideration. Drilling one level down in the NSC staff, we found at the time another Wolfowitz protégé in Zalmay Khalilzad, Rice's senior director for Southwest Asia, Near East, and North African Affairs. Close to both Rumsfeld and Cheney—he headed up the former's transition team—Khalilzad doubled as the administration's most senior Muslim and strongest proponent of the view that a de-mocratized Baghdad would serve as a beacon for the transformation of the Arab world.[45] At this writing Khalilzad serves as the administration's special envoy to Afghanistan and ambassador designate to that nation.[46]

Earlier in this chapter we argued that ideological entrepreneurship becomes "unrestrained" when two conditions prevail: when the selection of appointees al-lows for pockets of officials who share strongly held programmatic commitments, and when the administration does not sufficiently test these advocates' views under the fire of countervailance. Especially given the neoconservative reflexes of Rumsfeld and Cheney, only Colin Powell stood in the way of Wolfowitz and his cohorts in their determination to use the war on terrorism as a pretext for going after Saddam Hussein. What resulted was a skewed process that pretty much pre-ordained flawed implementation. However, before examining how the adminis-tration eventually committed to the invasion of Iraq and the consequences this process would have upon the outcome, let us back up to assess the administration's pre–9/11 handling of the terrorist threat from the Arab world.

Easier than Swatting Flies

Before the 9/11 attacks, as the administration considered what to do about al Qaeda, President Bush, according to Condoleezza Rice, once characterized the effort as "swatting flies."[47] The administration, apparently, straddled two strategies. While, on the one hand, the Bush II White House did not entirely abandon the Clinton administration's emphasis on decapitating al Qaeda by getting rid of Osama bin Laden, on the other hand, it had become mired in a ponderous examination of how to target the network and not just the man.[48] By June 2001 the air force and the CIA had perfected the technology that would allow an armed drone to kill bin Laden—assuming, of course, that he would continue to move around Afghanistan with relative ease, as was the case before 9/11. This development amounted to a quantum leap over the previous administation's several failed efforts to target bin Laden with Cruise missiles.[49] However, the more encompassing strategic approach benchmarked by the administration in January still had not worked its way through the National Security Council's interdepartmental process. And even when the review culminated, on 4 September, with NSC principals' approval, its recommendations simply distilled for the president a series of incremental steps that would seek elimination of the al Qaeda network through "phased escalation."[50] The president was supposed to review the NSC recommendations on 10 September, but he did not do so because he was "on travel."

In articles cited earlier, *Washington Post* reporter Barton Gellman and *New York Times* journalists Judith Miller, Jeff Gerth, and Don Van Natta Jr. attempted to discover how the Bush II administration's pre–9/11 response to the al Qaeda threat differed from that of its predecessor. Gellman's account alleges that Condoleezza Rice had labeled the Clinton administration's approach as "feckless." However, both articles report that Samuel R. ("Sandy") Berger, who had held Rice's post under Clinton, had warned his successor that she would "spend more time during your four years on terrorism generally and al Qaeda specifically than any other issue."[51] Despite both this alert and her own apparent conviction that Bush II must pursue the challenge more strategically than had Clinton, the actual follow-through proved lethargic, if not downright feckless.

From the first week of February until 7 June, the new administration's strategic review of the al Qaeda threat languished in the Counterterrorism Strategy Group (CSG)—a body composed mainly of assistant-secretary-level officials representing NSC principals. Much of the delay owed to the issue's back burner status at the cabinet level. Army Lt. Gen. Donald Kerrick, whose service on the NSC staff bridged both the Clinton and Bush II administrations, conveyed to

Gellman a stark contrast between the high priority granted to al Qaeda under the former and the low level of attention under the latter:

> He noticed a difference on terrorism. Clinton's Cabinet advisers, burning with the urgency of their losses to bin Laden in the African embassy bombings in 1998 and the [USS] Cole attack in 2000, had met "nearly weekly" to direct the fight, Kerrick said. Among Bush's first-line advisers, "candidly speaking, I didn't detect" that kind of focus, he said. "That's not being derogatory. It's just a fact. I didn't detect any activity but what Dick Clarke [Richard A. Clarke, the NSC counterterrorism chief who also bridged both administrations] and the CSG were doing."[52]

It then took nearly two months—from 7 June to 4 September—for the NSC principals to review and forward to the president the CSG recommendations. Meanwhile, al Qaeda "chatter"—communications traffic—had reached such intensity and prompted so many warnings of impending attacks by CIA director George J. Tenet (another Clinton administration holdover) that key administration players had begun to discount his concerns. Post–9/11, hindsight-is-20/20 controversy bubbled up during the spring of 2002 over the administration's apparent failure to collate evidence that al Qaeda operatives were planning to use airliners as weapons in terrorist attacks. In addition, by that time, further revelations provided clear indications that the FBI and CIA had fumbled coordination of their intelligence gathering and also raised concerns that the president himself had failed to give sufficient guidance in response to briefings on the matter—especially during one session held on 6 August 2001 while he was on vacation in Crawford, Texas.

The issue of the president's prior knowledge of terrorist threats prompted Rice's exquisite effort to dispel suspicion, in a 16 May 2002 news conference, by alleging that the intelligence had been too vague, lacking information assembled by the FBI and other agencies.[53] Rice seemed essentially to be saying that the NSC did not usually dig for answers to questions that were not going to be on the exam, but a docile press bought the line. In any case, the stir over the administration's all too apparent lapses ultimately caused Bush in June to reverse his opposition to creation of the Department of Homeland Security.[54] This move, along with the windup to the invasion of Iraq, thereafter drowned out most discussion of the (mis)handling of intelligence that might have tipped the administration to the 9/11 attacks.

It thus appears that before 9/11 the administration proceeded lethargically both in devising an encompassing strategy for dealing with al Qaeda and in its response to signals, however ambiguous, that the terrorist organization had targeted the United States for horrific attacks using commercial airliners as weapons. Elements of the new administration's fecklessness are discernible even earlier, in a brief survey of the specific actions it undertook in response to the al Qaeda threat following the inauguration of the president in January 2001.

Barton Gellman provides an inventory of known lapses in this period.[55] First, the Bush II administration suspended the covert deployment of Cruise missiles, submarines, and gunships that its predecessor had placed on six-hour alert to strike should the exact location of any of al Qaeda's top leadership be ascertained. Second, it took no concrete action once it was determined in February that al Qaeda had been responsible for the October 2000 attack of the USS *Cole*. Third, it provided no new funds for the Northern Alliance even though the CIA had ascertained in the spring of 2001 that the Afghan opposition group—the Taliban's main opponent—had fallen seriously short of resources. Fourth, it assigned only a smidgen of additional resources to counterterrorism. Indeed, it diverted $600 million of the Pentagon's homeland security funds to its pet project, the missile defense system. At Justice, Attorney General John Ashcroft seriously downgraded the institutional commitment to counterterrorism while still assuring Congress that his department had "no higher priority."[56] Fifth, although the president announced on 8 May that the vice president would head a government-wide review on managing the consequences of a domestic attack, neither that review nor promised meetings of the NSC on the subject actually took place.

Finally, a center of unrestrained ideological entrepreneurship outside the national security community asserted itself to confound another critical element of the counterterrorism effort—cutting off the cash flowing to al Qaeda and other terrorist organizations. In response to concerns expressed by conservative groups about market economics and privacy issues, then–Treasury secretary Paul H. O'Neill fought the assault against money laundering in support of terrorists on three fronts. He put existing enforcement tools under a cost-benefit review, opposed attempts to tighten U.S. legislation, and stymied global efforts to strengthen antilaundering laws and regulations.[57]

In light of all this, there is a huge irony in the administration's immediate response to the 9/11 attacks. To be sure, it made a great show of slamming the barn door shut so that future terrorists intent on attacking U.S. targets would find it much more difficult to get in and out of the country or to operate within it. In reality, of course, the administration has displayed both parsimony in actually meting out resources for homeland security and hesitancy in imposing rationality in their use.[58] But the truly jarring irony rests in the fact that an administration that, before 9/11, was intent upon not personalizing the antiterrorism effort suddenly focused its sights on getting Osama bin Laden "dead or alive."[59] Edward Cody, an editor at the *Washington Post* and a highly regarded observer of the Arab world—writing with colleagues—filed two prescient reports in the fall of 2001.[60] Each outlined exactly how circumstances in Afghanistan and, relatedly, in Pakistan made the Bush II administration's designs upon bin Laden difficult, if not impossible, to achieve.

The reports' skepticism rested upon two facts: Pakistan's Inter-Service Intelligence Agency controlled access to the lawless tribal regions of Afghanistan and Eastern Pakistan, and that agency would have to reverse a culture deeply supportive of the Taliban and al Qaeda before it could help the U.S. forces in tracking down bin Laden. In the meantime, the porousness of the border areas would allow bin Laden to maneuver with sufficient freedom to avoid capture.

In the event, U.S. Special Forces outsourced the effort to flush out bin Laden from Tora Bora—where he was thought to have fled in an effort to reach Pakistan—to Afghan guerillas who proved more intent on humoring their American patrons than on thwarting bin Laden's escape. The al Qaeda leader vanished into Eastern Pakistan sometime in December 2001.[61] He soon all but disappeared from the administration's rhetoric as well. Having tried swatting flies and failed, the Bush II White House turned its focus toward rogue regimes it thought capable of unleashing weapons of mass destruction (WMDs)—specifically, the trinity of Iraq, Iran, and North Korea, which it styled the "axis of evil." Subsequently, two key National Security Council aides responsible for counterterrorism resigned their positions, registering, in one case publicly, their dismay over the administration's shift of focus from al Qaeda to Iraq.[62]

Anatomy of a Regime Change

A rhetorical flourish issuing from the keystrokes of a journeyman speechwriter captured the impulse that would lead eventually to the U.S. invasion of Iraq in March 2003. As the Canadian journalist David Frum recounted, he had mulled over the "fascism" of some Mideast regimes and movements and had come up with the concept that they comprised an "axis of hatred."[63] According to Frum, this turn of phrase caught fire not just with Condoleezza Rice and her deputy Stephen Hadley but with the president as well. To be sure, the president's State of the Union address eventually spoke of the "axis of evil" and granted membership to a trio of states—two Muslim (Iran and Iraq) and one Asian (North Korea).

The adoption of the axis image (evocative of the World War II alliance of Germany, Italy, and Japan) and its galvanizing impact serve as an excellent example of what John DiIulio, as noted earlier, characterized as "on-the-fly policy-making by speech-making." The rhetoric also provided a timely streetcar for the neoconservatives who were bent upon invasion of Iraq, giving an immense boost to those in the administration wanting to cast the conflict with rogue states in black-and-white rather than in shades of gray.[64] Chris Patten, the European Union's external affairs chief, put his finger on the dangers of such a posture in facilitating the impetuous assertion of power, remarking, "The Afghan war [has] perhaps reinforced some dangerous instincts: that the projection of military power is the only basis of true security; that the U.S. can rely on no one but itself; and that allies may be useful as optional extras."[65] The events that unfolded between the State of the Union address and the U.S. invasion of Iraq seem to justify Patten's concerns.

The administration's initial attempt to follow through on its rhetoric on Iraq proved abortive. In March 2002, Vice President Cheney embarked upon an eleven-nation tour of the Middle East in an effort to garner support for a confrontation with Iraq. However, Arab frustrations over the lack of progress toward resolving the Israeli-Palestinian conflict—exacerbated by Prime Minister Ariel Sharon's contemporaneous heightening of pressures upon the Palestinians—made it impossible for Cheney to stay on message in discussions with Arab leaders.[66]

This roadblock turned some minds in the administration, during the spring of 2002, toward rejoining the languishing peace process. But because Bush had, since his inauguration, studiously avoided entanglement in the Israeli-Palestinian struggle—on the grounds that Bill Clinton had become excessively mired in the issue[67]—not only did he encounter an exceedingly sharp learning curve when prompted to engage the issue, but his advisers divided deeply on the matter.[68] The results were less than optimal coherence just when clarity was most needed and a futile Mideast mission by Colin Powell that was stillborn before the secretary of state even reached the region.[69] While no less formidable a figure than Bush I's national security adviser Brent Scowcroft opined that the administration was "in real danger of being overextended," James B. Steinberg, a senior fellow at the Brookings Institution and a former deputy national security adviser under Clinton, saw peril in the prospect of an administration that was deeply divided on ideological grounds trying to address quotidian issues in black-and-white terms:

> Below [Cabinet] level, it's not working at all. You have people with intense ideological convictions and such trench warfare . . . that it's hard for them to get anything done. . . . they have this . . . grand Bush doctrine to fight evil, but they haven't developed an elaborate set of policies on the second order problems. If it can't be fit into the template of counterterrorism and the fight against evil, they haven't any strategies.[70]

One might have expected the continued intractability of the Mideast peace process to bring an end to pressures for a confrontation with Iraq. Instead, it cleared the field for still more aggressive advocacy on the part of administration proponents of regime change in Iraq. A quasi-theological thrust behind the hawks' arguments—with their emphasis of the putative ripeness of Iraq for conversion to democracy[71]—stuck readily on the flypaper of providential destiny that had lodged itself in the president's mind after 9/11.[72] Even staunch supporters of the invasion thus voiced concerns about the way in which Bush tended to eschew explaining his position on Iraq and to present his views almost as articles of faith.[73] The president's uncommunicativeness suggested, again, that he had not gone through an elaborate thought process before embracing the views put forward by the neoconservatives. To borrow from a career Office of Management and Budget official's account of why his agency rarely won conflicts with the Pentagon during the Reagan administration, "Now the biggest hawk in the administration happens to be the president himself. So, when the issue goes that far, the outcome is predictable."[74]

As Bush flirted with embracing the invasion option, his obvious lack of interest in a thoroughgoing canvassing of alternatives gave opponents a sense that the neoconservatives would prevail no matter what. Glenn Kessler of the *Washington Post* quoted an official close to the deliberations who described the resignation that seized skeptics of regime change: "The issue got away from the president. He wasn't controlling the tone or the direction. . . . [He was being influenced by people who] painted him into a corner because Iraq was an albatross around their necks."[75] In the same story, Kessler reports an awkward July 2002 meeting between Condoleezza Rice and Richard N. Haass, the State Department's director of policy planning, who left the administration in June 2003 to head the prestigious Council on Foreign Relations. When Haass inquired of Rice whether they should discuss the pros and cons of confronting Iraq, Rice apparently replied, "Don't bother. The president has made a decision."

By the summer of 2002, the administration notably intensified its focus on planning an invasion of Iraq.[76] However, in mid-August, formidable Republicans in the foreign policy community began to air both privately and publicly their reservations about the haste with which the president appeared to have opted for an invasion over further diplomatic efforts. Key among these was Brent Scowcroft, who registered his concerns in a *Wall Street Journal* op-ed piece on 16 August. Because Scowcroft had served as Bush I's national security adviser, observers believed that he would not have gone public with his concerns without conferring first with the former president.[77] (Indeed, shortly before the actual invasion, Bush I himself publicly lodged his preference for multilateral approaches to threats such as those posed by Iraq.)[78]

Although the vice president countered almost immediately with strenuous defenses of preemptive action,[79] the concerns expressed by Republican foreign policy experts clearly caused a diversion of the administration's strategy. James A. Baker III—former White House chief of staff and treasury secretary under Reagan and secretary of state and chief of staff under Bush I—had directly challenged such reasoning in a 25 August op-ed piece that some also believed to have been prompted by Bush I.[80] Baker urged the president to "do his best to stop his advisors and their surrogates from playing out their differences publicly." He then outlined the costs associated with military confrontation of Iraq, an inevitability in his mind, and stressed that these would increase exponentially if the United

States were to act alone. In an eerily insightful premonition of the difficulty of seeking regime change militarily, Baker noted that the invasion would have to include sufficient ground troops to get the job done and not simply try to get by "on the cheap," that the occupation could prove challenging, and that Saddam Hussein might elude capture.

The concerted effort of the Olympians succeeded in resurrecting Colin Powell's preference for a multilateral approach. By late September, Powell had worked a deal with the hawks whereby they would support seeking an additional UN resolution and a rigorous regime of inspections, while he would promise to support an invasion should Iraq remain defiant.[81] By November, observers were hailing Powell's diplomatic coup in negotiating through the UN Security Council a resolution calling for Iraq to eliminate its weapons of mass destruction and submit to comprehensive inspections.[82] No sooner had the ink dried on that resolution, however, than neoconservatives and, eventually, the president began questioning the likelihood that Iraq would comply.[83] This set the stage for a single-minded campaign by the administration to find Iraq in "material breach" of the resolution. The remaining debate would center on the veracity of the administration's evidence.

This stage of the regime change saga could easily take up a chapter on its own. Indeed, by the summer of 2003, the Monday-morning quarterbacking centered on evaluating the grounds for the invasion of Iraq seemed about to eclipse the swiftness of the military conquest itself in the minds of many commentators.[84] This controversy prompted not only congressional inquiries into the intelligence that had fed the administration's arguments but also an internal CIA review of the accuracy and integrity of the agency's data analysis.[85] The British Parliament launched parallel inquiries into whether Tony Blair's staff had spun U.K. intelligence in favor of the case for material breach.[86] This issue takes on special importance in terms of this chapter's analysis, for a common manifestation of the effects of unrestrained ideological entrepreneurship involves the constricting of the values at play in critical decision-making processes. In this case, some observers felt that they had found evidence that both the U.S. and the U.K. administrations had compromised the integrity of career intelligence gathering services in their eagerness to build arguments in support of the invasion of Iraq.[87]

Indeed, it became clear during summer and fall 2003 that both the Bush and Blair administrations even resorted to jeopardizing the anonymity of officials in their zeal to discredit those who disagreed with their characterization of evidence concerning weapons of mass destruction. Aides in the former appear to have revealed the identity of a CIA operative in order to undermine the credibility of her husband.[88] The Blair administration—in a maneuver now traced to the prime minister himself—disclosed the name of a senior arms control scientist who objected to the inflation of evidence that Iraq could readily deploy weapons of mass destruction.[89] In the case of the British official, David Kelly, his suicide triggered an investigative process much more vigorous than comparable efforts in the United States.

The administration's determination to marshal support for its argument that Iraq remained in breach of successive UN resolutions ultimately left the impression that it viewed inspections as temporary diversions. Both the president and Colin Powell expended notably less effort—either through travel or phone contacts—to make their case for the invasion of Iraq directly with foreign leaders than George H.W. Bush and James Baker had done during the Persian Gulf crisis.[90] Powell's commitment to the process, indeed, often appeared halfhearted, fueling the belief that he had concluded that the hawks would ultimately prevail no matter how Herculean his efforts to pursue a diplomatic resolution to the crisis.[91] With respect to the allies, however, he clearly had become irritated by indications that France and Germany would remain intractable toward action against Iraq whatever the evidence.[92]

As the U.S. administration's lead spokesman at the UN, Powell found himself, by late January 2003, increasingly cornered in the position of arguing that inspections would ultimately fail, and he began to proffer evidence that did not stand up well to independent scrutiny. For instance, Bush, Cheney, and Rice had all declared that aluminum tubes ordered by Iraq but not actually delivered had been intended for its nuclear weapons program. This assertion, first offered in an 8 September 2002 appearance by the vice president on *Meet the Press*, proved on closer analysis to be a self-licking ice cream cone.[93] Cheney cited a *New York Times* article published the same day, but the article itself—which began by implying that U.S. intelligence officials had reached a determination regarding the purpose of the tubes—eventually lapsed into discussion of concerns among administration "hardliners" that "Washington dare not wait until analysts have found hard evidence that Mr. Hussein has acquired a nuclear weapon."[94] Despite the thundering *Times* headline, "U.S. Says Hussein Intensifies Quest for A-Bomb Parts," the hard-liners' worries actually had no official standing as intelligence findings.

In January, UN inspectors determined that the tubes would be suitable only for artillery rockets—a judgment that both the Departments of Energy and State had made in opposition to the CIA before the administration began pressing its nuclear weapons assertion.[95] Nevertheless, Powell joined the debate in February by introducing the technical term *adonization*, in reference to the fact that the tubes were to be coated with a thin outer film, which, he alleged, made them suitable for use in centrifuges employed in uranium enrichment. In fact, the adonization argued strongly on behalf of the tubes being intended for rockets; indeed, a group of independent experts had briefed Powell's staff on this pivotal technical conclusion.[96]

By July 2003, the administration was admitting that the president himself had inflated the veracity of intelligence reports alleging that Iraq had tried to obtain uranium in Africa as part of an effort to reconstitute its nuclear weapons program.[97] In his January 2003 State of the Union address, Bush had declared, "the British government has learned that Saddam Hussein recently sought significant quantities of uranium from Africa." In fact, the CIA had determined in February 2002 that the documents upon which the claim was based might have been forged.[98] A finding of the U.K. House of Commons Foreign Affairs Committee that chastised the Blair government for making the uranium claim despite shaky grounds provoked the Bush administration's belated acknowledgment of its error.[99] However, the International Atomic Energy Agency (IAEA) had brought the suspicions of forgery to light even before the invasion of Iraq.[100] Indeed, when it handed the documents over to the IAEA on 4 February 2003, the U.S. State Department noted, "We cannot confirm these reports and have questions regarding some specific claims."[101]

Following the White House admission, a debate developed over why the CIA did not prevail upon the White House speechwriters to excise the questionable uranium claim from drafts of the State of Union address.[102] Some well-placed intelligence officials blamed sloppy handling of the evidence for the lapse, while others registered the view that the failure fit with the ethos of an administration that does not want to entertain conclusions that will not support its defined positions on issues. In the words of one senior CIA analyst, "Information not consistent with the administration agenda was discarded and information that was [consistent] was not seriously scrutinized."[103] On 11 July the director of the CIA, George J. Tenet, placed his sword under his chest and admitted that he should have objected to the State of the Union claim.

The National Security Council (NCS) staff itself had proposed including the questionable material in drafts of the speech.[104] On 11 July Condoleezza Rice implied that the White House had stood at the mercy of the CIA verdict on the contentious passage, although both the CIA and the State Department had previously registered their reservations. Indeed, Tenet noted in his admission of CIA responsibility that the agency had not used the doubtful claim in any of its classified or unclassified reports, even after the submission of the British allegations in September 2002.[105] The NSC operates upon a statutory mandate, inter alia, to integrate intelligence advice submitted to the president. Rice, not Tenet, held the ultimate responsibility for the veracity of the claims made by the president. Given her critical role as the eyes and ears of the president on national security matters, one might have expected her to urge upon him the same caution that she herself exercised in a *New York Times* opinion piece appearing on 23 January—five days before the State of the Union address.[106] In that article, she simply stated that Iraq had engaged in "efforts to get uranium from abroad" without providing specifics.

The British became embroiled in such disputes over the credibility of information because they often made the case for material breach on behalf of the "coalition of the willing." They did so because it was believed that evidence provided by U.K. sources would appear less tainted than that put forward by U.S. sources.[107] In February 2003, the British government released a report—now widely known as the "dodgy dossier"—alleging evidence of a link between the Iraqi regime and the promotion of terrorism. That report eventually turned out to be a sham. It plagiarized—including spelling and punctuation errors—an article published by a research associate at the Monterey Institute of International Studies in California.[108] The student's analysis, in turn, relied mostly on material dating back to 1990 and 1991. The U.K. report's version, however, departed at critical points from pure plagiarism. For instance, it embellished the student's characterization of the role of the Iraqi directorate of intelligence, by changing the operative phrase from "aiding opposition groups in hostile regimes" to "supporting terrorist organizations in hostile regimes."

In July 2003 the committee of the British House of Commons examining the basis for the invasion of Iraq styled the document "counterproductive."[109] It especially chided the government about the unacceptability of plagiarizing and amending material derived from previously published documents. The discovery of such unethical activity would ruin any scholar's career or place a student in dire academic difficulty. We can imagine, thus, the embarrassment felt by the British intelligence community in what many public administration experts consider the most professional civil service in the world. Indeed, Prime Minister Blair had specifically invoked the credibility of the British intelligence service when he announced the release of the dossier to Parliament on 3 February 2003:

> We issued further intelligence over the weekend about the infrastructure of concealment. It is obviously difficult when we publish intelligence reports, but I hope that people have some sense of the integrity of our security services. They are not publishing this, or giving us this information, and making it up. It is the intelligence that they are receiving, and we are passing it on to the people.[110]

Of course, the dubious provenance of the dossier—which, in fact, included no new intelligence—became known within days. The document's contents thereby subverted entirely the Blair government's objective of painting a veneer of British credibility on the American-led coalition's allegations about Iraqi obstruction of efforts to discover its weapons of mass destruction.

The dodgy dossier episode takes us to the heart of this chapter's inquiry into the integrity of the contribution of career public servants to policy discussions. It fits within a framework whereby the Bush and Blair administrations coordinated efforts to release selectively information that supported their case against Saddam Hussein even though in doing so they were ignoring or overriding the judgment of their respective governments' intelligence services. One would have expected that the British intelligence agency would have become outraged over the appearance that it had had a hand in producing such subterfuge. Indeed, the head of the U.K.'s Secret Intelligence Service (MI6), Sir Richard Dearlove, must have lodged a protest. He received a fulsome written apology from Tony Blair's director of communications, Alastair Campbell, who later resigned in the aftermath of the Kelly affair mentioned above.[111]

Thus, the cases so far brought into the public eye serve as testimony to the politicization of the advisory systems of both George W. Bush and Tony Blair. Normally in the British cabinet system, a document purporting to distill available intelligence would have issued from an integrative process in the nonpartisan Cabinet Office. Instead the dodgy dossier had issued from a cut-and-paste exercise conducted by a task force in the Foreign and Commonwealth Office (FCO, or Britain's equivalent to the State Department) that reported directly to Campbell, who worked out of No. 10 Downing Street (the equivalent to the White House). The U.K. Foreign Affairs Committee was able, in light of the fact that neither an FCO minister nor the Cabinet Office Joint Intelligence Committee chairman had signed off on the dodgy dossier, to get the government to agree that the latter at least would in the future have to approve government intelligence before its release. While Congress proved slower to respond to parallel problems with politicization of intelligence by the Bush administration, the issue reached a boil in the summer of 2003 and seemed likely to lead in the United States to a reenshrinement of the principle that the professional intelligence community must operate with freedom from political interference.

Space limitations do not permit a detailed discussion here of all such episodes connected with the invasion of Iraq, but three other examples in which the administration's judgment appears to have been clouded by unrestrained ideological entrepreneurship suggested themselves during the buildup to the invasion of Iraq. The first of these concerned arranging for Turkey to grant access to the army's 4th Infantry Division so that the U.S. forces could invade Iraq from the north as well as from the south. The negotiations collapsed, with recriminations all around, when a Turkish parliamentary resolution failed on a technicality and it became clear that the United States would have to pay much more than had been offered for the access. The Turks maintained that the outcome would have been different had U.S. representatives not behaved in such a heavy-handed manner.[112] One sticking point even revealed unrestrained ideological entrepreneurship bearing the fingerprints of the Department of the Treasury—the administration had insisted that Turkey's acceptance of the access funds would trigger a renegotiation of its current loans with the International Monetary Fund, of which the United States is the dominant member. Also, when the Bush I team had successfully gained similar access for U.S. forces through Turkey in 1990 during the Persian Gulf crisis, its effort included three visits to Turkey by James Baker and upwards of fifty-five telephone calls by President George H.W. Bush.[113] By contrast, Colin Powell failed to visit Turkey even once during the buildup to the invasion of Iraq, and President George W. Bush logged a total of three calls or meetings with Turkish leaders.

The second area in which ideology clouded judgment arose in the determination of the force structure and size that would be required to carry off the invasion. Observers have styled Defense Secretary Rumsfeld a staunch advocate of the *transformation* of the military, but questions had arisen even before discussion of the invasion of Iraq as to whether he entirely grasped the meaning of this term. Strictly speaking, it refers to the adjustments that the Pentagon must make in its medium and long-term resource commitments in order to position itself for the emergence of a peer competitor to the United States—most likely China—that would be able to operate with a large exclusionary zone. That is, the peer competitor would control air space and the seas so far beyond its shores (say 1,000 miles) that it would make warfare from U.S. bases in its region, aircraft carriers, fighters, and ground attacks much more difficult than now.[114] Rumsfeld's version of transformation, in contrast, fits more into the "reinvention" movement of the 1990s, whereby political leaders expected to do the same things as before but for less.[115]

This reinvention thrust came through loud and clear even at the beginning of discussions with the military about what would be required to invade Iraq. When, in the summer of 2002, the military pegged the requirement as some 250,000 troops, the administration countered with a "Baghdad first" strategy, whereby it would land 80,000 to 100,000 troops in Baghdad and have them fan out from there to pacify Iraq.[116] In the end, the administration settled for roughly the force that the military had originally recommended, but because of the failure to gain access through Turkey, it had to press the invasion from only one direction and with the 4th Infantry Division out of position.[117] Even before the loss of the northern salient, military analysts had expressed concern that the war plan placed too much stress on a speedy advance to Baghdad that might overreach supply lines.[118] Once the invasion began—certainly during the second week when major supply problems emerged—these concerns became known through remarks made by retired generals who were doubtless acting as surrogates for serving military leaders who could not go public. The view came through clearly that Rumsfeld's force was inadequate for the task and that the administration had seriously hobbled the armed forces by its failures in diplomacy, especially regarding access to Turkey and the use of bases in Saudi Arabia.[119] Observers noted that Rumsfeld's determination to conduct the war "on the cheap" extended even to an unprecedented interference in appointments to top positions on the Joint Staff—the operating arm of the Joint Chiefs of Staff—as well as parsimonious micromanagement of the Pentagon's deployment plan.[120] By May 2003, tensions between Rumsfeld and the army leadership had reached the point where a bipartisan group of senators wrote the secretary to express concerns that he was encountering too much difficulty in finding successors for the army chief and vice chief of staff.[121] Within ten days, Rumsfeld brought closure to the speculation about the reasons behind the delayed transition by appointing a three-year retiree after at least two serving army generals had declined to serve under him as chief.[122]

Once the U.S. force captured Baghdad, much of the criticism of the actual war plan subsided. Soon, however, our third issue—the influence of ideology in planning for the occupation of Iraq—asserted itself. The invading force began to encounter difficulties not only in the pacification of Iraq but also in securing important sites such hospitals, archeological treasures, oil industry infrastructure, munitions sites, and, most crucially, nuclear facilities.[123] To add to the disarray, the occupation force seemed suddenly unable to locate convincing evidence of the weapons of mass destruction whose alleged proliferation and readiness for deployment had served as the administration's primary justification for the invasion of Iraq.[124] Indeed, by late October 2003, the administration finally began to ponder whether it should shift assets focused on the search for weapons of mass destruction to counterinsurgency intelligence where, obviously, the need for greater resources had become acute.[125]

Even neoconservative members of the Defense Policy Board, including then-chair Richard Perle and former Speaker of the House Newt Gingrich, had raised alarm in October 2002 over the lack of preparation for the occupation of Iraq.[126] Much of the difficulty appeared to stem from conflicts between State and Defense over how to foster a successor to Saddam Hussein's regime. The vice president seemed to have taken control of the planning by January—personally attending to many detailed matters.[127] Then, once the administration decided its game plan for the occupation, it was up to Paul Wolfowitz to defend it against critics. Wolfowitz took especially strong exception to the congressional testimony of General Eric Shinseki, the outgoing army chief of staff, to the effect that a force of "several hundred thousand" troops would be needed to return stability to Iraq.[128] Just as events subsequently flew in the face of the vice president's 16 March prediction that "from the standpoint of the Iraqi people, my belief is we will . . . be greeted as liberators,"[129] they also seemed effectively to demolish Wolfowitz's claim that Shinseki's testimony was "far off the mark" because Iraq had no history of ethnic strife comparable to that found in Bosnia or Kosovo.[130] Once again, unrestrained ideological entrepreneurship had clouded key aides' judgment about a crucial dimension to regime change in Iraq.

Some top analysts have lauded the performance of the military in the invasion of Iraq notwithstanding the constraints imposed by the political leadership in the Pentagon.[131] The odds against such an outcome in the occupation of Iraq have appeared substantially less fortuitous. Informed observers, thus, have begun increasingly to fault the failures of the Pentagon in incorporating informed cautions into their scenarios about how auspiciously the occupation of Iraq might unfold.[132]

Conclusion

This chapter has probed the Bush II administration's handling of its most momentous policy initiative in order to assess what this tells us about this president's capacity for issue management. The analysis has focused on the extent to which the administration's advisory system has proven to be a breeding ground for unrestrained ideological entrepreneurship, both because the president seems detached from open discourse about the crucial issues he faces and because the administration, more generally, seems to include a surfeit of doctrinaire players but invests very little structure or effort in ensuring that policy initiatives receive intense collegial scrutiny.

The administration seemed to acknowledge its problems with its countervailing of advice from the Pentagon in October 2003 when it assigned Condoleezza Rice the task of directing an Iraq Stabilization Group to coordinate the occupation of Iraq.[133] However, defense secretary Donald Rumsfeld's immediately registering umbrage at not being informed of the change and dismissing the new wrinkle as window dressing for the National Security Council's traditional role did not bode well for the group's likely effect.[134]

The case study suggests that the administration, notwithstanding its loud disdain for the Clinton administration, performed, if anything, worse than its predecessor had done in pre-9/11 efforts to counter the al Qaeda threat. In the immediate aftermath of 9/11, however, it leapt to embrace exactly the position that it had viewed as the weakest element of the Clinton approach, namely, personalizing the struggle against al Qaeda as a matter of "getting" Osama bin Laden. When bin Laden's escape, probably to Pakistan, proved that approach a failure, the political impasse thus created left the road open for administration hawks who had long been interested in overthrowing Saddam Hussein to change the subject and press for regime change in Iraq. This gambit played so well to the president's natural reflexes that it gained primacy within the political executive without a rigorous examination of the complexities of its implementation or the potential damage that it could do to U.S. standing in the global community.

Unlike the Bush II administration's domestic initiatives—apart from the successive tax cuts—which proffered facile ideological fixes but ultimately faced the vagaries of congressional review, the policy of regime change in Iraq drew concerted challenges only from foreigners. Only after the fact did observers at home begin to examine with some critical edge both the way in which the war-making commitment was engaged and its implications for democratic governance, both at home and abroad. However, between regime change in Iraq and serial tax cutting, the administration's penchant for unrestrained ideological entrepreneurship had put two huge runs on the board that would surely spin off unintended and very possibly insuperable consequences for years to come.

Notes

1. John W. Kingdon, *Agendas, Alternatives, and Public Policies*, 2d ed. (New York: Harper-Collins, 1995), 94.
2. Ibid., 181.
3. Terry M. Moe, "The Politicized Presidency," in *The New Direction in American Politics*, ed. John E. Chubb and Paul E. Peterson (Washington, D.C.: Brookings Institution, 1985).
4. Alexander L. George, *Presidential Decisionmaking in Foreign Policy: The Effective Use of Information and Advice* (Boulder, Colo.: Westview, 1980), 193–94.
5. Roger B. Porter, *Presidential Policy-Making: The Economic Policy Board* (Cambridge: Cambridge University Press, 1980).
6. Edmund L. Andrews, "A Salesman for Bush's Tax Plan Who Has Belittled Similar Ideas," *New York Times*, 28 February 2003.
7. National Desk, "Ex-Aide Insists White House Puts Politics Ahead of Policy," *New York Times*, 2 December 2002. DiIulio currently teaches political science at the University of Pennsylvania.
8. Ron Suskind, "Why Are These Men Laughing?" *Esquire*, January 2003.
9. Scott Lindlaw, "Former Aide Tones Down Criticism," *Washington Post*, 2 December 2002.
10. See "The DiIulio Letter," at http://www.esquire.com/features/articles/2002/021202_mfe_diiulio_1.html.
11. Colin Campbell, "The White House and Presidency under the 'Let's Deal' President," in *The Bush Presidency*, ed. Colin Campbell and Bert A. Rockman (Chatham, N.J.: Chatham House, 1991), 199, 214.
12. Elisabeth Bumiller, "White House Letter: An Invisible Aide Leaves Fingerprints," *New York Times*, 6 January 2003.
13. Colin Campbell, *Managing the Presidency: Carter, Reagan, and the Search for Executive Harmony* (Pittsburgh: University of Pittsburgh Press, 1986), 140–48.
14. See, for instance, David E. Rosenbaum, "Wary Eye on Wall St. and Washington," *New York Times*, 21 July 2002; Elisabeth Bumiller, "A Role Unfulfilled," *New York Times*, 12 August 2002; and Elizabeth Bumiller and David Sanger, "Bush in Shake-Up of Cabinet, Ousts O'Neill as Secretary of Treasury," *New York Times*, 7 December 2002.
15. Richard F. Fenno Jr., *The President's Cabinet: Analysis in the Period from Wilson to Eisenhower* (Cambridge, Mass.: Harvard University Press, 1959), 39–40; Richard E. Neustadt, *Presidential Power: the Politics of Leadership with Reflections on Johnson and Nixon* (New York: Wiley, 1976), 224–26, 270–71; and Stephen Hess, *Organizing the Presidency* (Washington, D.C.: Brookings Institution, 2002), 29–30, 76–77.
16. Fred I. Greenstein, *The Hidden-Hand Presidency: Eisenhower as Leader* (New York: Basic Books, 1982), 113–16.

17. Kiron K. Skinner, Annelise Anderson, and Martin Anderson, eds., *Reagan in His Own Hand: The Writings of Ronald Reagan that Reveal his Revolutionary Vision for America* (New York: Free Press, 2001).

18. Campbell, *Managing the Presidency*, 72.

19. Bill Keller, "Reagan's Son," *New York Times Magazine*, 26 January 2003.

20. Campbell, *Managing the Presidency*, 73.

21. Ibid., 108–11.

22. John P. Burke, *The Institutional Presidency: Organizing and Managing the White House from FDR to Clinton*, 2d ed. (Baltimore: Johns Hopkins University Press, 2000), 153–54.

23. President's Special Review Board (Tower Commission), *Report* (New York: Bantam Books, 1987), 79–80.

24. Bob Woodward, *Bush at War* (New York: Simon & Schuster, 2002); and David Frum, *The Right Man: The Surprising Presidency of George W. Bush (An Inside Account)* (New York: Random House, 2003).

25. Mark Crispin Miller, *The Bush Dyslexicon: Observations on a National Disorder* (New York: Norton, 2001).

26. President Bush used this analogy on 21 January 2003 in rebuking members of the U.N. Security Council for seeking further arms inspections in Iraq. A month later, a top aide to Tony Blair specifically cited this characterization of the inspections as illustrative of the type of rhetoric that might strike much of the president's base as "folksy and direct" while appearing to Europeans to be "flippant and disdainful." See Warren Hoge, "Blair's Stand on Iraq Hurts Him Politically but Seems Unlikely to Topple Him," *New York Times*, 21 February 2003. Bush's words also provoked a cautionary op-ed piece by E.J. Dionne Jr., who argued that, with polls at that stage showing for the first time a clear majority of Democrats against military action to remove Saddam Hussein, such language in presidential discourse about the crisis could undermine the potential for bipartisan support for the invasion of Iraq. See "A Wartime Leader Can't Be Partisan as Usual," *Washington Post*, 26 January 2003.

27. Miller, *Bush Dyslexicon*, 111.

28. Frank Bruni, "For President, a Mission and a Role in History," *New York Times*, 22 September 2001.

29. Alison Mitchell, "Democrat Assails Bush on Economy," *New York Times*, 5 January 2002.

30. David Sanger, "Bush, On Offensive, Says He Will Fight to Keep Tax Cuts," 6 January 2002.

31. See, for instance, Dana Milbank, "Bush Links Faith and Agenda in Speech to Broadcast Group," *Washington Post*, 10 February 2003; and Richard Cohen, "The Crude Crusader," *Washington Post*, 10 February 2003.

32. Todd S. Purdum, "Embattled, Scrutinized, Powell Soldiers On," *New York Times*, 25 July 2002.

33. Adam Nagourney, "White House Denies Texas Session Is about Iraq," *New York Times*, 21 August 2002; Mike Allen, "Exerciser Bush Finds Himself on War Footing," *Washington Post*, 22 August 2002; and Adam Nagourney with Thom Shanker, "A 'Patient' Bush Says He'll Weigh All Iraq Options," *New York Times*, 22 August 2002. See as well Todd Purdum and Patrick Tyer, "Top Republicans Break with Bush on Iraq Strategy,"

New York Times, 16 August 2002; and Elisabeth Bumiller, "President Notes Dissent on Iraq, Vows to Listen," *New York Times*, 17 August 2002.

34. Neil A. Lewis, "Traces of Terror: The Attorney General," *New York Times*, 24 July 2002.

35. Dan Eggen, "Ashcroft's High Profile, Motives Raise White House Concerns," *Washington Post*, 17 June 2002.

36. Campbell, " 'Let's Deal' President," 204–6.

37. David S. Broder, "Reactive President," *Washington Post*, 19 August 1990; and George F. Will, "Still a Line in the Sand: Did You Ever See a Policy Go This Way and That?" *Washington Post*, 7 November 1990.

38. Woodward, *Bush at War*, 49, 83–85.

39. Michael R. Gordon and General Bernard E. Trainor, *The General's War: The Inside Story of the Conflict in the Gulf* (Boston: Little, Brown, 1995), 6.

40. Ibid., 418, 424, 448.

41. Woodward, *Bush at War*, 83–85.

42. Bill Keller, "The Sunshine Warrior," *New York Times Magazine*, 22 September 2002, 52.

43. Ibid., 54, 84.

44. Judith Miller and Lowell Bergman, "Calls for New Push into Iraq Gain Power in Washington," *New York Times*, 13 December 2001.

45. Barrie McKenna, "The Pashtun Prophet Who Shapes U.S. Policy," *Toronto Globe and Mail*, 1 March 2003.

46. Pamela Constable, "Envoy to Afghanistan Is a Force of Nurture," *Washington Post*, 11 October 2003.

47. Judith Miller, Jeff Gerth, and Don Van Natta Jr., "Planning for Terror but Failing to Act," *New York Times*, 30 December 2001.

48. Barton Gellman, "A Strategy's Cautious Evolution Before Sept. 11," *Washington Post*, 20 January 2002.

49. Miller, Gerth, and Van Natta, "Planning for Terror."

50. Gellman, "A Strategy's Cautious Evolution."

51. Ibid.

52. Ibid.

53. David E. Sanger and Elisabeth Bumiller, "Traces of Terrorism: The Overview," *New York Times*, 17 May 2002.

54. Patrick E. Tyler, "Reaction, Then Action," *New York Times*, 7 June 2002; and Elisabeth Bumiller and David E. Sanger, "Traces of Terror," *New York Times*, 7 June 2002.

55. Gellman, "A Strategy's Cautious Evolution."

56. Adam Clymer, "How Sept. 11 Changed Goals of Justice Department," *New York Times*, 28 February 2002.

57. In addition to Gellman, "A Strategy's Cautious Evolution ," see Richard W. Stevenson, "Three Countries Are Warned to Limit Money Laundering," *New York Times*, 23 June 2001; and Joseph Kahn and Kurt Eichenwald, "A Nation Challenged: The Antiterror Bill," *New York Times*, 17 October 2001.

58. Phil Shenon, "Threats and Responses, Domestic Security," 3 March 2003; Bill Keller, "Defense! Defense! Defense!," *New York Times*, 19 April 2003; and Ceci Connolly, "Readiness for Chemical Attack Criticized," *Washington Post*, 4 June 2003.

59. Woodward, *Bush at War*, 100–102; and Jane Perlez, David E. Sanger, and Thom

Shanker, "A Nation Challenged: The Advisers," *New York Times*, 23 September 2001.

60. Edward Cody and Kamran Khan, "U.S. Struggles to Revive Crucial Cold War Alliance," *Washington Post*, 17 October 2001; and Molly Moore and Edward Cody, "Hunting bin Laden: U.S. Stymied by Slippery Target," *Washington Post*, 4 November 2001.

61. Edward Cody, "Manhunt Uncovers No Traces of Bin Laden," *Washington Post*, 26 December 2001. See also Eric Schmitt and Michael R. Gordon, "New Priorities: Hunt for bin Laden Loses Steam As Winter Grips Afghan Caves," *New York Times*, 30 December 2001; Barry Bearak, "Sanctuary: Tribal Area of Pakistan Gives Refuge to Qaeda Fighters Fleeing Caves," *New York Times*, 31 December 2001; and Eric Schmitt, "The Dragnet: Tribes Balking at Cave Hunt, Pentagon Says," *New York Times*, 17 January 2002.

62. Barton Gellman, "Anti-Terror Pioneer Turns in Badge," *Washington Post*, 13 March 2003; Karen DeYoung and Peter Slevin, "Counterterror Team's Turnover Continues," *Washington Post*, 20 March 2003; and Laura Blumenfeld, "Former Aide Takes Aim at War on Terror," *Washington Post*, 16 June 2003.

63. Frum, *Right Man*, 235.

64. David E. Sanger, "Bush Aides Say Tough Tone Put Foes on Notice," *New York Times*, 31 January 2002; and Michael R. Gordon, "Cheney Rejects Criticism by Allies over Stand on Iraq," *New York Times*, 16 February 2002.

65. Gordon, "Cheney Rejects Criticism."

66. Karen DeYoung and Alan Sipress, "A Rush to Act on the Mideast," *Washington Post*, 14 March 2002; and Alan Sipress, "Cheney Plays Down Arab Criticism over Iraq," *Washington Post*, 18 March 2002.

67. Richard Cohen, "The Undoing of Mideast Diplomacy," *Washington Post*, 19 April 2001.

68. Dan Balz and Dana Milbank, "Bush Doctrine Begins to Blur," *Washington Post*, 3 April 2002; and Dana Milbank and Karen DeYoung, "The Birth of a Balancing Act," *Washington Post*, 6 April 2002.

69. Steven R. Weisman, "President Bush and the Middle East Axis of Ambiguity," *New York Times*, 13 April 2002; Elisabeth Bumiller, "Seeking to Stem Growing Political Fury, Bush Sends Conservative to Pro-Israel Rally," *New York Times*, 16 April 2002; and Patrick E. Tyler, "A Rising Toll for Bush: No Peace, More Blame," *New York Times*, 18 April 2002.

70. Karen DeYoung and Walter Pincus, "Crises Strain Bush Policies," *Washington Post*, 21 April 2002.

71. George Parker, "Dreaming of Democracy," *New York Times Magazine*, 2 March 2003.

72. Dana Milbank, "Bush Links Faith and Agenda in Speech to Broadcast Group," *Washington Post*, 10 February 2003; and Jackson Lears, "How a War Became a Crusade," *New York Times*, 11 March 2003.

73. See Richard Cohen, "The Crude Crusader," *Washington Post*, 10 February 2003; and "Kirkpatrick Was Right," *Washington Post*, 8 May 2003.

74. Campbell, *Managing the Presidency*, 70.

75. Glenn Kessler, "U.S. Decision on Iraq Has Puzzling Past," *Washington Post*, 12 January 2003.

76. Thom Shanker, "Bush Hears Options Including Baghdad Strike," *New York Times*, 7 August 2002.

77. Bumiller, "President Notes Dissent."

78. James Dao, "Senior Bush Defends '91 Decision on Iraq," *New York Times*, 1 March 2003.

79. Dana Milbank, "Cheney Argues for Preemptive Strike on Iraq," *Washington Post*, 26 August 2002; and Howard Kurtz, "Cheney Rattles His Saber," *Washington Post*, 27 August 2002.

80. James A. Baker III, "The Right Way to Change a Regime," *New York Times*, 25 August 2002. See also Neil Lewis and David Sanger, "Bush May Request Congress's Backing on Iraq," *New York Times*, 29 August 2002.

81. Patrick Tyler, "U.S. and Britain Drafting Resolution to Impose Deadline on Iraq," *New York Times*, 26 September 2002.

82. Michael O'Hanlon, "How the Hard-Liners Lost," *Washington Post*, 8 November 2002; and Steven R. Weisman, "How Powell Lined Up the Votes, Starting with the President's," *New York Times*, 9 November 2002.

83. Dana Milbank, "Conservatives Wary of Arms Inspections," *Washington Post*, 14 November 2002; and "U.S. Voices Doubts on Iraq Search," *Washington Post*, 2 December 2002.

84. For instance, Paul Krugman, "Waggy Dog Stories," and Nicholas D. Kristof, "Save Our Spooks," *New York Times*, 30 May 2003. See also Dana Priest and Walter Pincus, "Bush Certainty on Iraq Arms Went Beyond Analysts' Views," *Washington Post*, 7 June 2003; and Judith Miller and William J. Broad, "Some Analysts of Iraq Trailers Reject Germ Use," *New York Times*, 7 June 2003.

85. James Risen, "Iraq Arms Report Now the Subject of a C.I.A. Review," *New York Times*, 4 June 2003.

86. Warren Hoges, "Blair Accused of Distorting Intelligence on Iraqi Arms," *New York Times*, 5 June 2003.

87. Bill Keller, a supporter of the invasion, registers precisely this concern in "The Boys Who Cried Wolfowitz," *New York Times*, 14 June 2003.

88. Mike Allen and Dana Milbank, "Bush Vows Action if Aides Had Role in Leak," *Washington Post*, 30 September 2003.

89. Ewen MacAskill, "PM Deeply Involved in Outing of Kelly," *The Guardian*, 25 August 2003; and Richard Norton-Taylor, "Blair Chaired Meeting that Led to Unmasking of Kelly, Inquiry Told," *The Guardian*, 13 October 2003.

90. Glenn Kessler, "Secretary's Style Raises Questions," *Washington Post*, 20 February 2003; and Glenn Kessler and Mike Allen, "U.S. Missteps Led to Failed Diplomacy," 15 March 2003.

91. Steven R. Weisman, "Powell at New Turning Point in His Evolution on Iraq War," *New York Times*, 14 March 2003.

92. Glenn Kessler, "Moderate Powell Turns Hawkish on War with Iraq," *Washington Post*, 24 January 2003.

93. John MacArthur, "All the News That's Fudged to Print," *Toronto Globe and Mail*, 6 June 2003.

94. Michael R. Gordon and Judith Miller, "U.S. Says Hussein Intensifies Quest for A-Bomb Parts," *New York Times*, 8 September 2002.

95. Joby Warrick, "U.S. Claim on Iraqi Nuclear Program Is Called into Question," *Washington Post*, 24 January 2003.

96. Joby Warrick, "Some Evidence on Iraq Called Fake," *Washington Post*, 7 March 2003.

97. Walter Pincus, "Claims of Purchase by Iraq an Error White House Says," *Washington Post*, 8 July 2003.

98. Walter Pincus, "C.I.A. Did Not Share Doubt," *Washington Post*, 12 June 2003.

99. Foreign Affairs Committee, House of Commons, *The Decision to Go to War in Iraq*, Ninth Report of Session 2002–3, Volume 1 (London: The Stationery Office Limited, 7 June 2003), 24.

100. Warrick, "Some Evidence on Iraq"; and Felicity Barringer, "U.N. Splits as Allies Dismiss Deadline on Iraq," *New York Times*, 8 March 2002.

101. David E. Sanger and Carl Hulse, "Bush Charge on Iraq Arms Had Doubters, House Told," *New York Times*, 9 July 2003.

102. Dana Milbank and Mike Allen, "Bush Skirts Queries on Iraq Nuclear Allegation," *Washington Post*, 10 July 2003.

103. Pincus, "C.I.A. Did Not Share Doubt."

104. Walter Pincus and Dana Milbank, "Bush, Rice Blame CIA for Iraq Error," *Washington Post*, 12 July 2003. See also David E. Sanger and James Risen, "C.I.A. Chief Takes Blame in Assertion on Iraqi Uranium," *New York Times*, 12 July 2003.

105. "In Tenet's Words: 'I Am Responsible' for Review," *New York Times*, 12 July 2003.

106. Condoleezza Rice, "Why We Know Iraq Is Lying," *New York Times*, 23 January 2003.

107. Warren Hoge, "Iraq Arms Report Mishandled, Blair Aide Concedes in Letter," *New York Times*, 9 June 2003. See also Dominic Evans, "Blair Criticized for 'Dodgy Dossier' on Iraqi Arms," *Washington Post*, 11 June 2003.

108. Sarah Lyall, "Britain Admits That Much of Its Report on Iraq Came from Magazines," *New York Times*, 8 February 2003.

109. Foreign Affairs Committee, *Decision to Go to War in Iraq*, 35–42.

110. Ibid., 41.

111. Hoge, "Iraq Arms Report."

112. Dexter Filkins, "Turkish Deputies Refuse to Accept American Troops," *New York Times*, 2 March 2003; and "Turkey Will Seek a Second Decision on a G.I. Presence," *New York Times*, 3 March 2003.

113. Kessler and Allen, "U.S. Missteps Led to Failed Diplomacy."

114. Michael Barzelay and Colin Campbell, *Preparing for the Future: Strategic Planning in the U.S. Air Force* (Washington, D.C.: Brookings Institution, 2003).

115. See, for instance, David Osborne and Ted Gaebler, *Reinventing Government: How the Entrepreneurial Spirit Is Transforming the Public Sector* (Reading, Mass.: Addison-Wesley, 1992). A critique of reinvention that highlights the need for political leaders to frame transformation more generally within the context of policy guidance is found in Joel D. Aberbach and Bert A. Rockman, *In the Web of Politics: Three Decades of the U.S. Federal Executive* (Washington, D.C.: Brookings Institution, 2000), esp. 187.

116. Shanker, "Bush Hears Options."

117. Thom Shanker and Eric Schmitt, "Rumsfeld Seeks Consensus through Jousting," *New York Times*, 19 March 2003.

118. Eric Schmitt and Thom Shanker, "War Plan Calls for Precision Bombing Wave to Break Iraqi Army Early in Attack," *New York Times*, 2 February 2003.

119. Thomas E. Ricks, "War Could Last Months," *Washington Post*, 26 March 2003; and Merrill A. McPeak, "Shock and Pause," *Washington Post*, 2 April 2003.

120. Vernon Loeb, "Rumsfeld Faulted for Troop Dilution," *Washington Post*, 29 March 2003; and Seymour M. Hersh, "Annals of National Security: Offense and Defense," *The New Yorker*, 7 April 2003.

121. Vernon Loeb, "Rumsfeld Queried on Nominees," *Washington Post*, 31 May 2003.

122. Bradley Graham, "Retired General Picked to Head Army," *Washington Post*, 11 June 2003.

123. R.W. Apple Jr., "A New Way of Warfare Leaves Behind an Abundance of Loose Ends," *New York Times*, 20 April 2003; Elizabeth Becker, "Baghdad Hospitals Face a Crisis, Groups Warn U.S.," *New York Times*, 3 May 2003; Douglas Jehl and Elizabeth Becker, "The Looting: Experts' Pleas to Pentagon Didn't Save Museum," *New York Times*, 16 April 2003; John Malcolm Russell, "We're Still Missing the Looting Picture," *Washington Post*, 15 June 2003; Neela Banerjee, "Widespread Looting Leaves Iraq's Oil Industry in Ruins," *New York Times*, 10 June 2003; Patrick Tyler, "Barrels Looted at Nuclear Site Raise Fears for Iraqi Villagers," *New York Times*, 8 June 2003; Raymond Bonner, "Iraq Arms Caches Cited in Attacks," *New York Times,* 14 October 2003; and Raymond Bonner and Ian Fisher, "At Iraqi Depot, Missiles Galore and No Guards," *New York Times*, 17 October 2003.

124. Eric Schmitt, "Rumsfeld Echoes Notion That Iraq Destroyed Arms," *New York Times*, 28 May 2003; and Paul Krugman, "Who's Accountable?" *New York Times*, 10 June 2003. See also Jane Harman, "WMD: What Went Wrong?" *Washington Post*, 11 June 2003.

125. Eric Schmitt and Douglas Jehl, "Weapons Searchers May Switch to Security," *New York Times*, 29 October 2003.

126. Michael Gordon, "U.S. Aides Split on Assessment of Iraq's Plans," *New York Times*, 10 October 2002.

127. Elisabeth Bumiller and Eric Schmitt, "Cheney, Little Seen by Public, Wielding Influence on Security," *New York Times*, 31 January 2003.

128. Rick Atkinson and Thomas E. Ricks, "War's Military, Political Goals Begin to Diverge," *Washington Post*, 29 April 2003.

129. Dana Milbank, "Upbeat Tone Ended with War," *Washington Post*, 28 March 2003.

130. Eric Schmitt, "Pentagon Contradicts General on Iraq Occupation Force's Size," *New York Times*, 28 February 2003.

131. Williamson Murray and Robert H. Scales, Jr., *The Iraq War: A Military History* (Cambridge: Harvard University Press, 2003).

132. Walter Pincus, "Spy Agencies Warned of Iraq Resistance," *Washington Post*, 9 September 2003; Eric Schmitt and Joel Brinkley, "State Dept. Study Foresaw Trouble Now Plaguing Iraq," *New York Times*, 19 October 2003; and David Rieff, "Blueprint for a Mess: How the Bush Administration's Prewar Planners Bungled Postwar Iraq," *New York Times Magazine*, 2 November 2003.

133. Glenn Kessler and Peter Slevin, "Rice Fails to Repair Rifts, Officials Say," *Washington Post,* 12 October 2003.

134. David E. Sanger and Thom Shanker, "Rumsfeld Quick to Dismiss Talk of Reduced Role in Iraq Policy," *New York Times*, 9 October 2003.

CHAPTER 5

Context, Strategy, and Chance
George W. Bush and the 107th Congress

Barbara Sinclair

MOST AMERICANS EXPECT their president to be the nation's premier legislative leader, to present Congress with a program and to engineer its passage. How well has George W. Bush fulfilled this expectation? This chapter attempts both to answer that question and to explain Bush's degree of success.

In assessing a president's record, journalists often imply that intrinsic leadership skill makes the difference between success and failure; that some presidents have "it" and others don't. In contrast, I argue that the context in which the president acts and the resources the president commands as a result of that context are much more important as determinants of presidential success. To be sure, skill can make a difference. But while a president may play his hand well or badly, the hand he is dealt is crucial and over that he has little control.

Some facets of the context—such as our constitutional system with its division of powers—are more or less constant and confront all presidents. Others, however, vary. Elections are a critical shaper of context, providing some presidents with ample resources in the form, for example, of big partisan margins in Congress, and others with only meager resources. The first two years of the George W. Bush presidency demonstrate more starkly than any in recent history that, in addition, unanticipated events can drastically change the context within which the president acts.

The Contextual Determinants of Presidential-Congressional Relations

Understanding the relationship between a particular president and Congress and the policy outputs that ensue requires understanding how incentives and behavior are shaped by the constitutional, institutional, and political context. We have come to expect the president to act as policy leader: to set the agenda and to engineer passage of legislation to deal with the country's major problems. The Constitution, however, establishes a relationship of mutual dependence between the president and Congress and, in terms of policymaking, puts the president in the weaker position.[1] The president is dependent upon Congress not just for new programs but also for money to carry out already existing programs, for approval of top-level personnel to staff the administration, and for acquiescence in many of the decisions he makes that Congress, through legislation or less formal means, could hinder.

The Constitution and the undisciplined and decentralized party system that it fostered provide the president with no basis for commanding Congress, but they do give him leverage. By virtue of his veto power, his control of the executive branch, and his access to the media, the president can advance or hinder the goals of members of Congress. Given his dependence upon Congress, his inability to command yet his potential capacity to influence, every president needs a strategy for dealing with Congress—a plan or approach for getting Congress to do what he wants and needs it to do in order to accomplish his goals.

A president's strategies vis-à-vis Congress are shaped and constrained by his legislative goals and by the resources he commands. The extent to which a president's policy preferences and those of a congressional majority coincide or conflict influences how a president sets out to get what he wants from Congress as well as his probability of success. So too do the resources the president commands for eliciting support beyond that based purely upon policy agreement.

Even within the United States's weak party system, members of a party tend to share policy preferences; consequently, when members of the president's party make up the congressional majority, they and the president will often agree at least on the general thrust of policy, providing a basis for presidential-congressional cooperation.[2] Furthermore, the members of his party have an interest in the president's success that transcends any specific legislative battle. Because many such members believe a strong president will be able to help them attain various of their goals in the future, they may be willing to support him even when their policy preferences do not coincide with his. To the extent that presidential success in the legislative arena breeds a perception of strength that translates into future success, a member of the president's party may believe supporting the president today will pay off in terms of the passage of preferred legislation in the future. To the extent that presidential success has an electoral payoff—increasing the chances of holding the White House or increasing congressional representation—a fellow party member has an incentive to provide support for the president beyond that based purely upon policy agreement.

Congressional leaders of the president's party are especially likely to see presidential success as in their best interest; they must concern themselves with the party's image and are likely to be judged by their success in enacting its leader's program.[3] Thus, when the president's party is in the majority, the very considerable institutional and procedural advantages of control of the chamber are usually available to the president.

Members of the other party, in contrast, are likely to see a strong, successful president as a threat to their future goal advancement. They are less likely to share his policy preferences, so an increase in his legislative effectiveness may threaten their policy goals. Their electoral goals are diametrically opposed to his; the president wants his party to hold the White House and increase its congressional representation. To the extent that the president's legislative success advances his party's electoral success, contributing to that success is costly for members of the other party.

When the policy differences between the parties are not very great or the opposition party is ideologically diverse, the president may gain significant support from opposition party members solely on the basis of their agreement with his policy stances. However, for the president to elicit support from members of the opposition party beyond that based purely upon policy agreement, such members must be persuaded that the costs of opposing the president are higher than the costs of supporting him. The most likely basis for doing so is by posing a threat to the member's personal reelection chances. Circumstances that make that threat credible provide a president with significant resources for influencing Congress; their lack leaves a president with little leverage for persuading opposition party members to support him.

Under conditions of unified partisan control, cooperation is the dominant strategy for the president and the congressional majority. The president's success furthers the policy goals of members of his party directly (when they agree with him on the policy at issue) and indirectly (because they expect in the future to agree with him more frequently than they expect to disagree). Presidential success may indirectly further members' electoral goals by convincing the public that the party can govern effectively.

However, while the incentives to support the president are ordinarily considerable for members of his party, incentives to oppose him may also be present and may, for a portion of the membership, outweigh those dictating support. Neither of the major parties is monolithic; on any given issue, some members will disagree with the president. Policy priorities will certainly differ, and electoral priorities will differ as well. Members want to see their party do well in congressional and presidential elections, but their own reelection is their first priority. If the vote required to bring about the president's success would hurt a member's reelection chances, this direct cost may well outweigh the benefits to the member of presidential success. A member's best reelection strategy may dictate voting against a president of his own party on some major issues. The political context determines whether incentives to defect dominate and for how many members.

Consequently, although cooperation with and reliance on the members of his party is the best strategy for a president whose party controls Congress, the strategy does not assure success. In the American political system, numerical majorities in Congress do not automatically translate into policy majorities. Winning coalitions must be constructed. Depending on the issue, his party's cohesion, and the size of the partisan majorities, the president may need to reach across the aisle.

When one or both chambers of Congress are controlled by the opposition party, the president's strategic situation becomes even more complex, especially when the parties are ideologically polarized. Unless he has the resources to threaten the goals of a significant number of the members of the other party and thus induce them to support him, he will need to bargain and compromise with the opposition party. Yet doing so may alienate members of his own party.

The Political and Institutional Context at the Beginning of the George W. Bush Presidency

Elections strongly influence the context within which a president attempts to govern.

George W. Bush received fewer popular votes than his chief opponent, Democratic nominee Al Gore; his narrow electoral college majority depended on questionable counts in the state governed by his brother and on a 5–4 decision by an ideologically split Supreme Court. His party lost seats in both chambers of Congress. Republicans held on to control of the House of Representatives by a razor-thin majority of 221–211;[4] the Senate, which before the elections was 54–46 Republican, emerged from the 2002 elections with an even split. Clearly Democrats and impartial commentators would not find credible any claim that the voters had given Bush a mandate for his program.

Yet Bush did enjoy unified partisan control of both chambers of Congress, something no Republican president since Eisenhower in 1953–54 had had. In that sense, Bush began his term much better situated than did his father, who faced substantial opposition party majorities in both chambers, and better than Ronald Reagan, who had a Republican Senate but confronted a Democratic House.

The Republican congressional party Bush would be working with was more ideologically homogeneous and more cohesive than the party of either Reagan's or his father's time. Between 1991 and 2000, the average Republican voted with his party colleagues on 88 percent of party votes in the House and on 87 percent in the Senate. Furthermore, party votes—those on which a majority of Republicans voted against a majority of Democrats—were much more frequent in the 1990s than before. In the 1990s, 58 percent of the roll-call votes in the House and 57 percent in the Senate were party votes. In contrast, between 1961 and 1980, Republican and Democratic majorities opposed each other on 40 percent of the recorded votes in the House and 42 percent in the Senate. In the 1980s, from 1981 to 1990, the frequency of party votes was 51 percent in the House and 45 percent in the Senate.[5]

Congressional Republicans were eager to work with Bush. When Republicans won control of Congress in the 1994 elections, many of them believed they could govern from Congress. The new Republican House majority, the first in forty years, believed itself to be mandated by the electorate to make "revolutionary" policy change. Led by firebrand Newt Gingrich, this ideologically fervent, strongly conservative majority passed its ambitious program, the "Contract with America," in record time, only to see the Senate and, especially, President Clinton prevent their bills from becoming law. When both House and Senate passed legislation balancing the budget in seven years and making dramatic changes in public policy, including revisions in major entitlement programs such as Medicare, President Clinton vetoed the legislation and succeed in convincing the public that Republicans were to blame for the shutdown of the national government that ensued. This largely set the tone for the remaining years of the decade. Republicans held their majorities in both chambers, though by decreasing margins. Yet they were able to accomplish few of their policy goals because Clinton frustrated them at every turn. Republicans came to understand that in the U.S. system, making nonincremental policy change requires the presidency as well as Congress. Electing a Republican president was the answer to congressional Republicans' dreams. As Senator Phil Gramm (R-Tex.) expressed it, "I've been waiting all my life to have a Republican president and a Republican Congress."[6] Congressional Republicans wanted to cooperate and work with Bush, to help him pass his agenda, with which they largely agreed, and to see him succeed.

Despite their narrow margin, House Republican leaders were in a good position to aid Bush. The House is a majority-rule institution—a reasonably cohesive majority can work its will; minorities lack effective ways of blocking action. The Speaker of the House, who is the chamber's presiding officer and the leader of the majority party, exercises considerable power if backed by a cohesive majority. As the parties became more ideologically homogeneous and more polarized in the 1980s and then even more so in the 1990s, the House majority party leadership became stronger and more actively engaged in all aspects of the legislative process; the leadership commands procedural, organizational, and informational resources invaluable for passing legislation.[7]

Because the vice president of the United States is the president of the Senate and as such casts the tie-breaking vote, the Republicans would be able to organize and thus "control" the Senate. Yet, the Senate would certainly present greater challenges for Bush than the House, and not just because of its 50–50 seat split. The Senate has always operated under highly permissive rules—amendments to most legislation need not be germane, and cutting off debate over any senator's objection requires a supermajority. In the 1950s and early 1960s, senators were quite restrained in using their prerogatives, but by the 1970s that restraint had given way to an activist style that saw senators as individuals much more willing to offer multitudes of amendments on the floor and to use extended debate.[8] The 1990s saw these prerogatives increasingly being employed by the parties, especially, of course, by the minority party.[9] In 1993–94, when Democrats controlled both Congress and the presidency, Republicans used Senate rules to kill many majority-supported bills and to extract substantive concessions on others.

When Republicans gained the Senate majority, Democrats returned the favor, killing or forcing concessions on legislation they opposed. In addition, they became increasingly adept at combining their prerogative to offer nongermane amendments with extended debate to seize agenda control from the majority party. In the late 1990s Senate Democrats used this strategy to enact a minimum-wage increase and to force highly visible floor debate on tobacco regulation, campaign-finance reform, gun control and managed-care reform, all issues the majority party would have preferred to avoid.

The leader of the majority party in the Senate becomes the Senate majority leader and, by precedent, gains the right of first recognition, through which he manages the floor schedule. However, because motions to proceed to consider legislation (as well as legislation itself) can be filibustered, true control of the Senate agenda, much less of outcomes, requires sixty votes. The Senate only runs smoothly when the majority leader and the minority leader cooperate—and not always then.

Bush's Agenda and Initial Strategy Choices

George W. Bush had run for election as a "compassionate conservative," a somewhat fuzzy label that allowed voters considerable latitude for projecting their own wishes on him. Nevertheless, Bush's two top priorities were clear—a huge tax cut and major education reform. Congressional Republicans strongly supported tax cuts; they had, in fact, passed big tax-cut packages several times only to see them vetoed by Clinton. Most also backed education reform, though with some differences over the form such reform should take. Whatever voters may have believed, most congressional Republicans agreed with Representative Jim DeMint (R-S.C.) when he said, "Bush has set a conservative agenda, moderated not so much in philosophy as in tone."[10] Thus the largely conservative Republican congressional party supported Bush's agenda and saw much of it as their own.

A majority of Democrats, on the other hand, had opposed much of the tax-cutting agenda in the past. Getting their support would probably require considerable compromise. The prospects for support from Democrats for Bush's education reform program were certainly better, though there were elements of the Bush proposal that most Democrats adamantly opposed.

A component of Bush's agenda that got considerably less attention early on—though Bush and his vice-presidential running-mate, Dick Cheney, had spoken of it during the campaign—was a reassertion of executive authority vis-à-vis Congress. Cheney especially had argued forcefully that presidential prerogatives had been allowed to atrophy or slip away dangerously and that, for the good of the country, they needed to be reclaimed by the president. The Bush administration's attempts to do so would lead to conflicts with Congress, but this was in the future. In January of 2001, congressional Republicans were giddy with anticipation. "There's a real optimism," a senior leadership aide said about congressional Republicans. "They are jazzed about having the Pres; in DC he's the rock star."

In determining his strategy vis-à-vis Congress, Bush also had to weigh his promises to change the often nasty and bitterly partisan tone of 1990s Washington. Calling himself "a uniter not a divider" during the campaign, Bush had vowed to restore civility and bipartisanship to policymaking and political debate, pointing repeatedly to his cooperative relations with Democratic legislators during his tenure as Texas governor and promising to operate similarly in Washington.

Bush did reach out to Congress; even before he was declared the winner in Florida, he met with congressional Republican leaders at his Texas ranch. Once he was assured of becoming president, he began to court congressional Democrats strenuously. He met with large numbers of Democrats, inviting them to the White House, often in small groups. He attempted to establish personal relationships with as many as possible, even giving nicknames to many of them.

A true strategy of bipartisanship required more than cordiality, however. From the perspective of Democrats, bipartisanship meant Republicans and Democrats working together in the drafting of legislation and, consequently, demanded a willingness on the part of Bush and congressional Republicans to compromise on the substance of policy. Bush's vaunted bipartisanship in Texas had consisted mostly of working with conservative Democrats whose positions were not very far from his own. In Congress, by contrast, the number of conservative Democrats had shrunk to a tiny fraction of their former numbers. Thus the compromises required for true bipartisanship would be substantial. Bush had to decide whether he either needed or was willing to pay the price.

Further complicating Bush's strategic calculations was the character of the Republican Party, the activist core of which consisted of far-right groups and individuals who tend to regard compromise as selling out. From his father's experience, Bush understood the importance of keeping the base satisfied. Congressional Republicans, with few exceptions, ranged from conservative to far-right and had a large unrealized agenda of conservative policy changes in which they believed fervently. Their view of a bipartisan strategy was articulated by House Whip Tom DeLay (R-Tex.) when he said, "We'll write conservative bills and ask Democrats to participate."[11]

Different Issues, Different Strategies: Tax Cuts and Education Reform Pre–9/11

On its two top priorities, the Bush administration employed diametrically opposite strategies. A highly partisan strategy was used on the tax cut; in contrast, the administration's strategy on education reform was characterized by compromise and bipartisanship. These strategy choices were shaped by the characteristics of the issues, by the varying constraints of the legislative process, and by the president's political objectives.

For a great many Republicans, big tax cuts were the number one priority. Since the Reagan tax cut of 1981, the issue had increasingly become one that sharply divided the parties. After barely squeaking into office, Bush was advised by many—including some Republicans as well as most Democrats and many unaffiliated commentators—to cut back the size of his proposal so as to make it more broadly acceptable. Bush and his political advisers, however, decided that doing so would be seen as an admission of weakness and would alienate his core supporters. Bush therefore determined to stick with his figure of $1.6 trillion over ten years. That decision largely dictated a partisan strategy. Democratic congressional leaders had signaled that they were willing to accept some tax cut but not such a huge one and not one so heavily targeted to the well-off. Furthermore, the "Blue Dog" Democrats, a group of relatively conservative House Democrats and as such the Democrats most likely to work with Republicans, were most concerned with reducing the size of the federal debt; consequently the size of Bush's tax-cut proposal alarmed them as well and made cooperation less likely.

The rules governing the budget process in Congress also figured into the decision on strategy. Unlike most legislation, reconciliation bills are protected from nongermane amendments and from a filibuster in the Senate. The tax cut could be passed as part of a reconciliation bill and thus would require only a simple majority, not sixty votes, to pass the Senate. Consequently, if Republicans could maintain perfect cohesion, they could pass Bush's huge tax cut without help from Democrats.

The normal budget process requires that both chambers first pass a budget resolution to set guidelines for future legislative action, including possibly a tax cut. Then the chambers are expected to pass a reconciliation bill that actually enacts into law the instructions included in the budget resolution. Bush and House Republican leaders decided, however, to pass the first and biggest part of the Bush tax cut—the across-the-board cut in income tax rates—in the House even before the budget resolution was passed. Fearing that the budget resolution might highlight less popular elements of Bush's budget plan, such as spending cuts, they wanted to establish momentum.

On 1 March, the House Ways and Means Committee approved HR 3 on a 23–15 party-line vote. President Bush undertook a campaign-style tour around the country to promote his agenda but seemed to have little impact on Democrats. "When members were home last week, they were feeling no pressure on tax cuts," an aide to a Blue Dog reported. A Gallup poll showed that Democrats in the electorate opposed the Bush plan by more than 2 to 1.[12]

On 8 March the House passed the bill without amendments on a vote of 230–198. The leadership had brought up the bill under a rule that allowed only one Democratic substitute and no other amendments, thus protecting the legislation from possible killer amendments. Although many conservative Republicans would have preferred an even bigger tax cut, all voted for the bill. The administration had convinced the many Republican interest groups to support the Bush bill even if it did not include their favorite provisions; big business, for example, agreed to lobby for the legislation and not to try to alter it. Their turn would come in later legislation, they were promised. Only ten Democrats voted for the bill. Democrats cried foul about the lack of real bipartisanship. "At no time were the Blue Dogs consulted about these things," said Charlie Stenholm (D-Tex.), a senior leader of the group. "We weren't even consulted. What's bipartisan about that?"[13]

Bush's campaigning for his tax plan in the states of electorally marginal Democratic senators had produced no results. Democrat Zell Miller of Georgia had come out in support of the tax cut early in the year, but no other Democrats followed. Republican Lincoln Chafee of Rhode Island was on record as opposed, and a number of other moderate Republicans were expressing anxiety about the size of the cut and proposing tying reductions to continuing budget surpluses, a notion that Bush rejected. As the economy weakened, Democrats began advocating an immediate tax rebate as a substitute for the Bush plan, which economists argued would have little stimulative effect. It became clear that passing the Bush plan in the Senate would be difficult and would certainly require the protections afforded a reconciliation bill. And that required passing a budget resolution. The House Republicans quickly moved their budget resolution through the budget committee on a party-line vote and passed it on the floor, with only three Democrats and two Republicans defecting from their party's positions.

A much rockier road lay ahead in the Senate. The 50–50 Senate split had forced Republicans to enter into a power-sharing agreement with Democrats specifying equal numbers of members on every committee; Republicans would, however, chair committees. The evenly split Senate Budget Committee was unable to agree on a resolution, so Majority Leader Trent Lott bypassed the committee and brought a Republican resolution directly to the floor. The Senate majority leader is not, however, able to protect even budget bills from floor amendments, as House leaders are. On the second full day of debate, liberal Democrat Tom Harkin of Iowa offered an amendment reducing the tax cut by $488 billion and shifting the money to education and debt relief. When three Republican moderates—Chafee, Jim Jeffords of Vermont, and Arlen Specter of Pennsylvania—deserted their party, the amendment passed. Vice President Dick Cheney, OMB head Mitch Daniels, and other White House officials scurried around trying to figure out how to reverse the setback. Nevertheless, the vote simply broke the dam, and before the resolution could be passed, a number of other amendments altering the president's program had been added.

Republicans hoped to recoup some of their losses in conference with the House. When Democrats complained about being excluded from the negotiations, Senate Budget Committee Chairman Pete Domenici (R-N.M.) baldly replied, "We don't expect you to sign [the conference report], so we don't expect you to be needed."[14] The administration focused on getting the support of just enough moderate Senate Democrats to pass the conference report in the Senate. That strategy dictated not substantially increasing the Senate's tax-cut figure, but it did allow other changes, including cutting the Senate's figure for discretionary spending. Bush had proposed an increase of 4 percent, and the House had essentially approved that figure. The Senate, however, had gone up to 8.4 percent, an amount totally unacceptable to conservative House Republicans. The partisan strategy resulted in largely party-line votes on the budget resolution conference report in both chambers. It passed the House on a 221–207 vote, with six Democrats and three Republicans crossing party lines. The Senate vote was 53–47; while fifteen Democrats had supported the budget resolution as amended on the Senate floor, only five supported the conference report. This was enough, however, to offset the two Republican defections.

With a budget resolution calling for tax cuts in place, the Senate could now proceed to write a tax bill, assured that it would be protected by budget rules from a filibuster. The Senate Finance Committee has jurisdiction over tax legislation, and Chairman Charles Grassley (R-Iowa) and ranking Democrat Max Baucus (D-Mont.) very much wanted the committee to take the lead role in drafting the tax legislation. As the tax issue had become a party-difference-defining issue during the 1990s, party leaders had increasingly usurped the committee's role. In addition to his desire to reestablish the committee's prestige, Baucus was concerned about his own upcoming reelection battle in a state that Bush had won handily. Grassley and Baucus could maintain control over the legislation only if they worked together and crafted a plan with bipartisan support in the committee.

Grassley and Baucus managed to put together a compromise measure and steered it through Finance, getting approval on a 14–6 vote, with all Republicans and four of the ten Democrats voting for it. A majority of both Republicans and Democrats, including the leaders on both sides, were dissatisfied with the bill; their committee leaders had given away too much in the negotiations, they believed. Yet, despite a barrage of amendments on the floor, the bill passed largely intact. Grassley and Baucus had put together a package that could pass—neither liberal Democrats not conservative Republicans had the votes to move the bill significantly in their preferred direction. On 23 May, twelve Senate Democrats joined all fifty Republicans to pass the legislation.

Under pressure from Bush, the conference committee moved with unusual speed to approve a compromise bill. The result was legislation that largely tracked the Senate bill: it called for a somewhat smaller tax cut than Bush's initial request; it distributed that tax cut somewhat differently, giving more to those in the lower income brackets; it provided immediate tax rebates to act as a stimulus; and it "sunsetted," that is automatically repealed, the entire bill in 2010.[15] Nevertheless, enactment represented a huge victory for Bush. No only had the largest tax cut since Ronald Reagan's first year in office become law, but it included many of the provisions—across-the-board rate cuts, alleviation of the "marriage penalty," and eventual ending of the estate tax—that Bush had advocated and that the Republican core had long desired.

From the beginning, the administration pursued a completely different strategy on education reform. That education legislation, unlike budget reconciliation bills, can be filibustered in the Senate was one factor in favor of a bipartisan approach. There was considerable agreement that more accountability for results should be required in return for federal education funds, that this required some sort of testing, and that at least some more money would be needed. Yet a number of ideologically-charged issues divided the parties and, in some cases, split moderate from conservative Republicans as well. Conservative Republicans strongly advocated issuing vouchers for children in failing schools to use at a school, even a private school, of their choice; Democrats strongly opposed vouchers as taking money away from already underfunded public schools, and many moderate Republicans agreed. Republicans wanted to give states much more freedom to apply federal education funds as they saw fit so long as they showed results; Democrats opposed such block grants, concerned that less money would go to the children and schools that needed it most. Republicans who were social conservatives opposed nationally mandated testing as a mechanism of accountability, fearing too much federal intrusion into education. Bush's education reform program included vouchers, flexibility, some increase in funding, and a heavy emphasis on periodic testing. Thus, while education may have been an easier issue than tax cuts on which to maintain a bipartisan strategy, the education debate certainly had the potential to relapse into partisan warfare. The determining factor in the administration's decision to insist on the bipartisan route seems to have been that Bush and his political advisers decided to use education, as they had during the campaign, as their primary issue for reaching out to moderates and swing voters. As long as the bill included the testing and accountability provisions about which Bush seemed to care most, the president would be willing to trade away anything else to get a bill.

On education, the Senate acted first. In early March, the Health, Education, Labor and Pensions Committee (HELP) reported out a bill by a 20–0 vote. The bill included neither vouchers nor block grants. Chairman Jim Jeffords (R-Vt.), not a voucher supporter and with an evenly split committee, decided to put off those fights until floor consideration. The bill that House Education and the Workforce chairman John Boehner (R-Ohio) introduced did include both Bush objectives, but even though Boehner is a strong conservative, his comments were conciliatory toward Democrats. In April, Bush began to publicly push for action but also signaled that he would not press for private-school vouchers.

Boehner and George Miller (D-Calif.), the ranking minority member of the committee, reached a bipartisan compromise on legislation to present to the committee. It increased funding and severely weakened the block-grant provisions. Vouchers stayed in the draft, but Miller knew he could win on that issue during committee mark-up, where vouchers were deleted on a 27–20 vote. The committee approved the bill on a 41–7 vote.

Why would Boehner, a strong conservative, make a deal with Miller, one of the most liberal members of the House—especially when doing so required jettisoning much that conservatives most intensely wanted? Boehner had just become chair of the committee and he knew from past experience that the highly contentious committee could easily stalemate. Passing legislation is generally the test of success for a committee chair, and Boehner understood that passing the education bill would be a great deal more likely if the committee came to a bipartisan agreement. As Bush himself seemed flexible on many of the provisions in his initial proposal, Boehner could make such a deal.

Such flexibility was, however, not without cost. Conservative Republicans were extremely unhappy; six of the seven "no" votes in committee were cast by conservative Republicans. From their perspective, the attractive parts of Bush's program—vouchers and strong flexibility provisions—had been traded away, while the testing provisions remained and Democrats had gotten more spending. And Bush had not lifted a finger to stop that from happening.

On 23 May the House passed the bill 384–45, with 34 of the "no" votes cast by Republicans. Because of the conservatives' discontent, the party leadership had had to allow them to offer a number of amendments restoring their favorite provisions. Even though Bush nominally supported the voucher amendment, it was easily defeated. Conservatives charged that Bush's support had again consisted of lip service only—that the administration had not lobbied for the amendment and, by indicating that Bush would sign the bill without vouchers, had undercut support for that feature. Bush, in fact, had persuaded a conservative Republican to refrain from offering his block-grant proposal as a floor amendment, fearing that passage would destroy Democratic support for the bill. So why had many conservative Republicans nevertheless voted for the bill in committee and on the floor? "He had a very narrow win, and we don't want to do anything to jeopardize his No. 1 initiative," one explained. "But that doesn't mean we like it."[16]

In the meantime, Senate education leaders of both parties, Ted Kennedy (D-Mass.) prominent among them, were negotiating with the White House over the Senate bill. The outlines of a deal that included some flexibility provisions, "vouchers" for private tutoring but not private schools, and more funding began to take shape. After six weeks of floor consideration, during which more negotiations took place and the bill was extensively amended to add more funding for a variety of specific education programs, the bill passed 91–8.

Negotiations to resolve House–Senate differences were prolonged but ended in success in December. The compromise was quickly approved in both chambers and Bush signed the bill into law on 8 January 2002, with smiling Democrats and Republicans providing the backdrop. The bill was truly a bipartisan product; it included much more funding than Bush had originally requested and excluded vouchers and the strong flexibility provisions he had asked for. Yet passage was clearly a big win for Bush. He got much of the testing and accountability measures he had asked for. He could—and did—brag that he had delivered on a top priority and had done so in a bipartisan fashion.

The different strategies on the tax and education bills, thus, seem to be explained by issue and procedural differences but also, and preeminently, by the political purposes the bills were intended to serve. Delivering on a solidly conservative and Republican tax bill would solidify Bush's core support; a bipartisan education bill would allow Bush to reach out beyond his core to voters concerned about issues on which Democrats usually have an advantage and to those put off by intense partisanship.

Why, then, did the tax fight rather than the education bill shape Democrats' perceptions of the Bush legislative strategy? In part, the tax fight set the tone because its long-term consequences for policy were so much more far-reaching—the money absorbed by the tax cut would not be available for spending on education or any other domestic programs. In addition, as time went on, the partisan strategy seemed to be the norm, the bipartisan strategy an aberration. Bush would try to govern by passing strongly conservative measures in the House and then attempting to pick off just enough conservative Democrats in the Senate to pass his bills there. He would make little to no attempt to compromise with mainstream Democrats or Democratic party leaders. And the perception of Bush as a partisan leader extended well beyond the politically attentive. Public opinion polls showed that Bush had made little headway in building support among those—half of all voters—who had not voted for him.

Playing Defense: The Jeffords Defection and Its Consequences

On 24 May, in his home state of Vermont, Senator Jim Jeffords announced to a throng of reporters, staff and supporters:

> Increasingly, I find myself in disagreement with my party. . . .
>
> In the past, without the presidency, the various wings of the Republican party in Congress have had some freedom to argue and influence and ultimately shape the party's agenda. The election of President Bush changed that dramatically.
>
> . . . [I]t is only natural to expect that people like myself, who have been honored with positions of leadership, will largely support the president's agenda.

And yet, more and more, I find I cannot. . . .

Looking ahead, I see more and more instances where I'll disagree with the president on very fundamental issues..

In order to best represent my state of Vermont, my own conscience and principles I have stood for my whole life, I will leave the Republican party and become an Independent.

Control of the Senate will be changed by my decision.[17]

Jeffords's decision hit Washington like an earthquake, and recriminations among Republicans began immediately. Majority Leader Trent Lott was blamed for being caught unawares and for not somehow stopping the defection. The Bush administration was blamed for snubbing Jeffords by failing to invite him to a White House ceremony honoring the teacher of the year, a Vermonter, and for otherwise not cultivating Jeffords sufficiently. Almost certainly, however, such gestures would have made no difference, for Jeffords's basic complaint concerned policy differences and Bush's decision to pursue a conservative rather than a moderate line. The moderate-to-liberal Jeffords had become more and more of a misfit as the Republican Party moved farther and farther right.

The Jeffords defection dramatically rearranged the political terrain. Although Jeffords promised President Bush that he would make the switch official only after the tax bill was sent to the president, so that his decision did not affect that bill's fate, Bush's first big triumph was largely eclipsed in the media by the Jeffords story. More important in the long run, Bush had lost the advantage of Republican control of both houses of Congress—Democrats would organize the Senate, chairing and commanding a majority on all committees and at least nominally controlling the Senate floor agenda. Democrats would now find it much easier to bring their issues to the floor and so challenge Bush for agenda control; they might also be able to block some of Bush's initiatives from ever getting to the Senate floor.

Even a cohesive majority party, however, does not exercise the sort of tight control over the floor agenda in the Senate that it does in the House. Well before the Jeffords switch, maverick John McCain (R-Ariz.) and the Democrats had forced campaign finance legislation to the Senate floor. Bush and most congressional Republicans strongly opposed the campaign finance reform bill that McCain and Senator Russell Feingold (D-Wisc.) had pushed for years. Yet, when McCain threatened to add the bill as an amendment to whatever legislation came to the floor, thus complicating and perhaps delaying Bush-supported bills, Lott had little choice but to agree to bring it to the floor. McCain claimed to have the 60 votes needed to cut off a filibuster.

As Lott had agreed, campaign finance reform came to the floor in March. Supporters fended off all killer amendments and, on 2 April, passed the bill on a 59–41 vote; twelve Republicans joined forty-seven of the fifty Democrats in voting in favor. The administration was absent from the fight; Bush had decided that it might well be politically costly to offer high-visibility opposition so early in his presidency to a measure universally identified in the media as reform. That it would be a battle with his primary opponent McCain guaranteed it lavish press coverage. Thus White House officials made no attempt to lobby Senate Republicans, and the word *veto* never passed the president's lips.

This case highlights the extent to which Senate individualism can pose a problem for presidents. Using the immense prerogatives the Senate gives each of its members, John McCain forced onto the agenda an issue well known to be opposed by the newly elected president of his own party; and even though Bush refused to engage publicly, McCain nevertheless received an enormous amount of favorable media attention for his efforts. Of course, the president can be the beneficiary as well as the victim of Senate individualism. When, in late January, Georgia Democrat Zell Miller announced his support for Bush's tax plan without even forewarning Democratic leader Tom Daschle, Bush benefited. The heavy and positive media coverage Miller received as a courageous independent thinker again demonstrates the payoff to senators for maverick behavior.

After Democrats took control of the Senate, the first major bill Majority Leader Daschle brought to the floor was the patients' bill of rights—legislation designed to give patients more rights vis-à-vis their HMOs. Democrats had been trying to enact such legislation for years, and acceptable bills had passed the House but never the Senate. Bush supported a patients' bill of rights, but a very different one from that advocated by Democrats. Democrats and Republicans disagreed most basically about the right of patients to sue their health care providers in state courts, with the Democrats wanting to give patients much broader rights than Republicans did. This was not a high-priority issue for Bush, and, like campaign finance reform, it was one that could put him on the defensive.

On June 19, Daschle brought the McCain-Edwards-Kennedy bill to the Senate floor—McCain had signed on as a sponsor of the Democrats' bill drafted by Senators Kennedy and John Edwards of North Carolina, giving him and the bill even more visibility. Because the bill was very popular with the public, Republican opponents did not want to filibuster it, so they decided on a strategy of amending the bill drastically instead. On 21 June, President Bush issued a threat to veto the bill if the liability provisions were not changed to his liking. Democrats and their small number of Republican allies held together and beat back amendment after amendment. When opponents seemed ready to prolong the process endlessly with amendments, Daschle announced that he would keep the Senate in session—and the senators in Washington—until the bill was finished, even if that cut into the July 4th recess. Having lost on all their important amendments and eager to get home, Republicans gave up. "Why stay here for three more days and end up with the same bill," explained Senator Bill Frist (R-Tenn.), one of the Republican floor managers.[18] On 29 June, the Senate passed the McCain-Edwards-Kennedy bill by a 59–36 vote, with all fifty Democrats and nine Republicans voting in favor. Had control of the Senate not switched, that outcome would have been much less likely.

Bush certainly did not want to be confronted with a choice between vetoing popular patients' bill of rights legislation or signing a bill he strongly opposed. Yet prospects looked somewhat grim. The House in the previous Congress had passed legislation sponsored by Charlie Norwood (R-Ga.) and John Dingell (D-Mich.) that was very similar to the Senate bill. Republican opponents of the bill would have to persuade some Republican supporters of the legislation to reverse course. Because it provides their electoral challengers with an easy target, elected officials hate making such clear reversals. A more promising strategy would provide such members with an acceptable alternative for which to vote, and to make that strategy work, Republicans would have to persuade Charlie Norwood to compromise on a measure that would be acceptable to the president. Norwood's imprimatur would provide the political cover necessary to allow other Republicans to reverse course. Getting Norwood to agree to such a deal, however, would not be easy; House Republican leaders had tried in the past and failed. Only the president had a shot at succeeding. White House officials and Bush himself worked on Norwood for weeks, pressing upon him the importance of such a deal to the success of the Bush presidency. Norwood, conservative on most issues and ordinarily a loyal Republican, found such appeals hard to resist. Few members want to be seen as responsible for inflicting a grievous wound on a president of their own party.

Norwood succumbed to the entreaties and made a deal with Bush; the Bush-Norwood compromise won on the House floor on a 218–213 vote, with all but six Republicans supporting the deal. The bill then passed on a 226–203 vote, with every Republican voting in favor. Thus, Norwood and the House Republicans came through for Bush, protecting him from a potentially politically damaging conundrum.

During the summer of 2001, the House leadership came to Bush's aid on campaign finance legislation as well. In this case, House Republicans had more at stake than did Bush himself. Most believed that the bill would put Republicans at a disadvantage in congressional races. Under intense pressure to bring the bill to the floor, Speaker Dennis Hastert did so but under a rule that campaign reform supporters claimed would doom them to failure: in order to succeed, they would have to win votes on twenty-two amendments in a row. Bill supporters themselves voted down the rule and thus seemed to kill the bill.

The switch in Senate control affected several other Bush legislative priorities adversely. Bush's proposal to make more federal social service funds available to religious groups (the so called faith-based charity initiative) passed the House, though with some difficulty. Moderate Republicans were disturbed about a provision that exempted religious groups from state and local antidiscrimination laws.[19] That provision was totally unacceptable to Democrats in both chambers, and, in any case, this initiative was not a high-priority issue for Senate Democrats. Daschle did not bring it to the floor in 2001.

After aggressive lobbying by the administration, industry, and affected labor unions, the House passed President Bush's energy program. The bill emphasized production over conservation and opened Alaska's Arctic National Wildlife Refuge (ANWR) to oil and gas exploration as Bush had proposed.[20] Lobbying by the Teamsters and the United Auto Workers, both of which saw jobs at stake, yielded the support of a number of House Democrats. Republicans wanted to build on the momentum and get a quick vote in the Senate, as they would have been able to do had they still controlled the chamber. Again, Daschle foiled them by putting the issue off.[21]

The Jeffords defection was followed by a spate of news stories quoting congressional Republicans, often but not always anonymously, criticizing the administration. Bush political adviser Karl Rove and White House liaison Nick Calio are "abrasive," "distrustful," and unwilling to negotiate with legislators, Republican senators and staff told the *Washington Post*.[22] "Overall, I give the White House a C- on communications. And that's being generous," a senior House Republican staffer said.[23] Treasury Secretary Paul O'Neill and OMB Director Mitch Daniels, with their dismissive attitude toward Congress, had made few friends on the Hill on either side of the aisle. Now complaints about them became louder.

Tension between the president and the members of his party in Congress are inevitable, even when his party is in the majority. Many congressional Republicans had never served with a president of their own party, and none had served in the majority with a Republican president. Thus, congressional Republicans were accustomed to setting their own course. In addition, many had somewhat unrealistic expectations about what a unified Republican government could accomplish. And never far from their awareness was the difference in time horizon between president and Congress. As a senior Republican congressional aide explained, "The President has four years, but we have an election next year. . . ."[24] When Bush did not consult them as much as they expected, when he asked them to take tough votes that conflicted with their ideology, when he did not lobby as hard as they wanted him to on issues dear to their hearts, they were disappointed. So long as they and Bush were mostly winning, congressional Republicans muted their complaints, but the shock of losing the Senate and what it portended for future legislative success made Republicans much more willing to speak openly.

The Bush administration reacted quickly. Fearing that they would be seen as grievously weakened by losing control of the Senate, Bush and White House officials aggressively asserted that the switch would not change their agenda or their approach. Bush might now use the bully pulpit more to pressure Democrats to support his program, but anyway they had been working in a bipartisan fashion all along.[25] In July, Bush came to the Hill and gave a thirty-minute "pep talk" to House Republicans. "He reminded our Conference that there is far more that unites us than divides us," reported a spokesman for House Majority Leader Dick Armey (R-Tex.).[26] Efforts to improve communications between the White House and congressional Republicans were redoubled. To encourage the dissemination of a unified message from both ends of the avenue, White House and Republican leadership aides conferred by conference call daily, attempting to come up with a "message of the day."[27] Administration figures were much more engaged in negotiations and lobbying of House members on the patients' bill of rights and on the energy program than they had been on other priorities. Vice President Cheney and cabinet officials blanketed wavering House Republicans with phone calls; Bush and Cheney went up to the Hill, and Bush invited many to the White House. "The administration's appreciation for the House and the House as a critical part of advancing their agenda has grown vastly in the last couple of months," chief deputy whip Roy Blunt (R-Mo.) reported in early August.[28] Bush's enhanced attention to the House was almost certainly crucial to the success of his versions of the patients' bill of rights and the energy legislation in that chamber, and these victories allowed him and congressional Republicans to enter the August recess on a relative high note.

Still, Bush's prospects for further legislative success did not look promising. His public opinion poll numbers were mediocre and sliding, certainly not at a level that would provide him with the ammunition to scare Democrats, who now controlled the Senate, into supporting his programs. Bush's attempts to use the bully pulpit had in any case yielded little success. Although tempered a bit by his House wins just before the recess, the tenor of media evaluations of Bush and his future prospects was largely negative. The president who had received mostly positive reviews for his strategic acumen in the spring was being slammed as a severely wounded political klutz in August.

September 11th and Its Aftermath

The shocking events of September 11th marked a major turning point in the Bush presidency. Whether they would "change everything," as so many commentators claimed, remained to be seen, but they certainly transformed Americans' concerns and so elected officials' priorities. Foreign crises tend to produce a "rally round the flag" effect by both the public and members of Congress.[29] Private citizens and public officials alike responded to the horrendous attacks on U.S. soil by rallying around the president and vowing solidarity. Democratic congressional leaders quickly pledged their support. "We are shoulder to shoulder. We are in complete agreement and we will act together as one. There is no division between the parties, between the Congress and the president," House Minority Leader Dick Gephardt said. "The world should know that the members of both parties in both houses stand united," reiterated Majority Leader Tom Daschle.[30]

For all his talk about changing the tone in Washington and governing in a bipartisan fashion, Bush had, with the one exception of education reform, pursued his primarily conservative objectives through a partisan strategy. By late summer, this strategy had seemed less and less likely to bear further legislative fruit. Now the true change in the tone of American public life and the change in agenda that September 11th brought about called for a change in strategy. Real bipartisanship seemed possible, and it offered Bush the chance for a new and more productive approach to Congress.

The president immediately began to confer with congressional leaders from both parties. After Bush's first flurry of "getting to know you" meetings, Democratic Party leaders had had little contact with Bush. Now, following 9/11, Bush and other high administration officials were in touch almost daily. Once a week, Bush and the four top congressional leaders breakfasted together at the White House.

The sense of crisis, as well as Bush's reaching out, prompted Congress to act with speed and unity. On 14 September both houses approved a resolution authorizing the president to "use all necessary and appropriate force against those nations, organizations or persons he determines planned, authorized, committed or aided the terrorist attacks on September 11, 2001 or harbored such organizations or persons."[31] On the same day both houses passed an emergency supplemental appropriations bill providing $40 billion for recovery and antiterrorism efforts. One vote was cast against the use-of-force resolution; none against the money bill. The Senate by voice vote approved the previously controversial nomination of John Negroponte as U.S. ambassador to the United Nations. House Republicans, who had opposed paying dues the United States owed to the UN, backed down so as to facilitate Bush's efforts to build an antiterrorism coalition. On 25 October, only six weeks after the attack, Congress sent Bush a far-reaching antiterrorism bill that made it easier for law enforcement to track Internet communications, detain suspected terrorists, and obtain nationwide warrants for searches and eavesdropping.[32]

Yet, even under these extreme circumstances, Congress was not willing to hand the president a blank check; concerns about the constitutional separation of powers, about maintaining the prerogatives of the legislative branch, and about threats to civil liberties served as restraints even as members realized that the public wanted them to act swiftly and give the president the tools he needed. The administration originally wanted language in the use-of-force resolution giving the president the authority to use force to "deter and preempt any future acts of terrorism or aggression against the United States."[33] The expansiveness of the language worried many members, especially Democrats with memories of Vietnam, and this wording was dropped. The Bush request for emergency spending included provisions giving the president unprecedented latitude to spend the money as he chose without direction or oversight from Congress. Again Democrats—especially members of the Appropriations Committee, which determines spending—objected, and soon many Republicans—again especially members of the Appropriations Committee—came to agree. Congress gave the president the money but insisted on maintaining some control over how it was to be spent.

When Attorney General John Ashcroft sent Congress a draft of the antiterrorism legislation on 19 September, he asked Congress to pass it in a week. With the House taking the lead, however, Congress insisted on giving the far-reaching proposals more scrutiny. A number of the most conservative House Republicans believed that Ashcroft's proposals went too far in empowering the government to snoop into Americans' affairs, and they joined civil liberties groups and many Democrats in working to water down the proposal. In the end, the U.S.A. Patriot Act included much of what the administration wanted, but the most controversial provisions were dropped or softened and many of the provisions were "sunseted" to expire in 2005. Civil libertarians were still unhappy with a number of provisions, and some members believed that Congress had still acted too quickly and not established a sufficient legislative record; yet Congress had made significant mitigating changes and had not simply given the administration the enormous new powers it requested.

Even as the Bush administration waged war in Afghanistan, partisan differences began to reemerge. The hope that September 11th would somehow purge partisanship from politics forever was never realistic. Democrats continued to support the president faithfully on terrorism and war issues, but as domestic issues that evoked deeply-held ideological beliefs resurfaced, so did partisan debate and jockeying. Not surprisingly, Bush and the Republicans attempted to use the crisis to their legislative advantage on issues far removed from the war on terrorism, trying to sell everything from trade promotion authority to drilling in ANWAR as national security matters. Despite Bush's sky-high popularity, however, polls and visits home showed Democrats that their constituents did not expect them to support Bush on such issues.

Airline security legislation might appear to be an unlikely issue to trigger a partisan battle. September 11th had created a consensus that airline security had to be strengthened significantly and quickly. House Republicans, however, were ideologically opposed to making airport screeners federal employees. The Senate quickly and unanimously passed legislation that did just that, but House conservatives adamantly refused to go along. House Republican leaders pressured Bush to support their version, which gave the president the choice of whether to federalize screeners and, with both a statement and lobbying help from Bush, they narrowly passed their version in the House. However, the administration had already signaled that the president was unlikely to veto a bill that federalized screeners. With public opinion strongly backing their position, Democrats hung tough, and House Republicans were forced to give in. Few were willing to go into the Thanksgiving weekend without having passed such legislation.

Bush also seemed unwilling to expend large amounts of his time and resources on getting an economic stimulus program enacted. The body blow that the terrorist attacks had dealt to an already staggering economy led to calls for measures to stimulate the economy, and on 5 October, Bush set out what he would like to see in such a bill. Arguing that the $40 billion spending bill passed earlier made additional spending unnecessary, Bush advocated more tax cuts. Economic policy lies at the heart of the differences between the parties and, not surprisingly, Democrats and Republicans differed sharply on what the stimulus package should contain. On a narrow, partisan vote House Republicans passed a bill that made significantly more tax cuts than even Bush had advocated. Senate Democrats on the Finance Committee reported a bill with much more spending for displaced workers, but they could not get the sixty votes needed to pass it on the floor. Bush made multiple public appeals, trying to put pressure on Senate Democrats to yield to the Republican approach, but he never became directly involved in negotiations, seemingly unwilling to get into the trenches and make the necessary deals. The jockeying extended well into the new year, but as the economy showed signs of improvement, the pressure to pass a bill declined. In the end, only pared-down legislation that extended unemployment insurance benefits passed and became law.

On trade promotion (previously known as fast-track) authority, in contrast, Bush was deeply engaged. He was determined to regain the president's power—which had lapsed during the Clinton administration—to negotiate foreign-trade pacts that would then be subject only to up-or-down votes in Congress. House passage would present the greatest obstacle; a number of Republicans were leery of foreign-trade deals that might cost jobs in their districts, while even free-trade Democrats would have little incentive to oppose the unions in order to help out an opposition-party president. Republican leaders in the House, lacking the votes, had put off consideration of the bill earlier, but in December they decided to make the attempt. Bush pulled out all the stops, courting undecided members by phone and in person, at special White House meetings, on *Air Force One*, and at a black-tie ball. Cabinet members spread out over the Hill, sweet-talking and pressuring members by turn. Business groups deployed their lobbyists in full force. Bush and his party leadership allies were willing to make deals, promising fixes of various kinds to members concerned with potential harm to their districts. And emotional arguments were not eschewed. In his floor speech, Speaker Hastert called on members to put supporting "our president who is fighting a courageous war on terrorism" above the parochial concerns of their districts.[34] Not all Republicans were persuaded. Mark Foley (R-Fla.) worried about citrus growers, explaining, "I understand and appreciate [Bush's] position. But I came to Congress representing [my] constituents, and their jobs are on the line."[35] However, just enough were swayed to pass the bill on a 215–214 vote. Republicans such as Robin Hayes, from a textile district in North Carolina that was strongly opposed to the bill, and Dana Rohrabacher, a longtime opponent, had switched out of loyalty to the president.

The events of September 11th did alter the relationship between Congress and President Bush. Defense, national security, and foreign policy issues on which presidents have great advantages vis-à-vis Congress were brought to the fore. Issues such as campaign finance and the patients' bill of rights, which advantage Democrats, were eclipsed; Democrats, in fact, had great difficulty getting news coverage except when they were playing the role of extras to the president as star. Bush emerged with greatly enhanced prestige and with phenomenally high popularity. Yet all this did not translate into across-the-board legislative victories for the president. He got much of what he asked for on defense and war-on-terrorism-related issues, but members of Congress were not willing to abdicate their constitutional responsibilities entirely.

Many Republicans argued that Bush should use his new prestige to force Democrats to accept his domestic agenda. A president with 90 percent approval ratings, they contended, should be able to go to the country and create the pressure necessary to scare Democrats into doing so. But the polls showed that the public was still as evenly split on Bush's domestic agenda as it had been before 9/11; all-out efforts to use his popularity to coerce Democrats would certainly bring an end to the fragile bipartisanship that still pertained at the end of 2001 and very likely would not work. In any case, Bush was unwilling to take the risk.

Back toward Normal:
Corporate Scandals, Economic Woes, and Looming Elections

Bush's relations with Congress during his second year were shaped by one completely predictable factor—the upcoming midterm elections—but also by unanticipated events that altered the strategic situation.

Successful politicians consider the effects of their actions on future electoral contests. With the margins of control in both houses of Congress extremely narrow and thus the stakes in the 2002 midterm elections high, political actors could be expected to weigh those consequences carefully and do what they could to affect the elections' outcome. By January 2002, the battle over the stimulus bill had clearly become a public relations fight over who would bear the blame for the failure of the legislation. Republicans had begun to attack Daschle in 2001, hoping to make him into a symbol of Democratic obstructionism. A right-wing group had even run an ad in Daschle's home state of South Dakota comparing him to Saddam Hussein for holding up the energy bill. Attacks accelerated in 2002, certainly not facilitating the prospects for bipartisanship. Daschle opened the year with a tough speech attacking Bush's tax cut for bringing back federal deficits and hurting the economy. (He did not, however, propose rescinding the tax cut, for which a number of his electorally vulnerable members had voted.) The frequency of contact between Democratic congressional leaders and President Bush declined.

Two important policy decisions Bush made in the spring of 2002 can be read as aimed at boosting Republican electoral prospects in the fall and perhaps his own in 2004 as well. Despite his professed commitment to free trade, Bush imposed tariffs on imported steel, and he signed into law a farm bill that was much more expensive that what he had originally wanted. Many of the closest Senate races, the outcomes of which would determine partisan control of the Senate, were in farm states.

The first unanticipated event to shape the legislative struggle in 2002 was the bankruptcy of the Enron Corporation. The failure of this huge company amid allegations of wrongdoing gave new impetus to campaign finance reform. Enron had been a very generous political donor—in fact, the single largest contributor to the Bush campaign. With the Democratic leadership playing a central role, campaign finance reform supporters successfully got the 218 signatures necessary on a discharge petition to force the legislation to the House floor. Despite pleas from House Republican leaders, the Bush administration was unwilling to use its resources to try to stop the legislation; it remained conspicuously absent from the effort to gain support for blocking it from House Republicans worried about the impact an antireform vote might have on their reelection prospects. The bill passed the House and survived an attempt to derail it in the Senate, where many Republicans were also leery of opposing the reform bill too visibly. Bush signed the bill without the signing ceremony that ordinarily accompanies major legislation. The president's unwillingness to help them led to strains between congressional Republicans and the White House, but congressional Republicans knew that Bush's popularity and future legislative success were important to their prospects in November, so they did little more than grumble.

Bush's popularity remained high but did not translate into many legislative victories. If the president lacked the political strength to coerce Democrats to support his domestic priorities, however, Democrats also lacked the political strength to impose their legislative will—with the exception of campaign finance reform—on Bush and the Republicans. By midsummer, gridlock loomed on a number of legislative fronts. Democrats had not even been able to pass a budget resolution in the Senate; but even if they had, an agreement between the House and Senate versions would have been extremely unlikely. The energy legislation that the Senate passed was unacceptable to Bush and very different from the House's bill, and the conference committee seemed stuck. Attempts to work out a compromise on the patients' bill of rights via direct talks between congressional supporters and the administration reached an impasse over the right-to-sue issue. Bush's faith-based initiative seemed stalled. Hoping to inoculate their members from charges of doing nothing about an issue deeply worrying seniors, Republican leaders engineered the passage of a Republican prescription drug–benefit bill through the House. The Senate was unable to muster the necessary sixty votes for any of the bills offered.

Just before the August recess, congressional gridlock was broken on a few important bills. Another rash of corporate accounting scandals gave new life to a corporate accountability bill that had seemed stalled. With the stock market falling precipitously, the House accepted most of the much stronger provisions in the Senate bill; Bush reversed his position and claimed credit for the bill, which he signed with great fanfare. The Senate had passed trade promotion authority, though with much more aid for displaced workers than Bush had wanted; now a deal was worked out that enabled Bush to claim victory on one of his top priorities.

In an effort to regain the legislative initiative, Bush in early June had called on Congress to create a new cabinet-level Department of Homeland Security. In fact, Senate Democrats had already been working on such legislation; coordination problems, which seem to have contributed to the 9/11 debacle, would be alleviated by bringing far-flung agencies into a single department, supporters believed. Again the House passed Bush's plan largely intact. The Senate, however, balked at some of the Bush-requested provisions that would weaken workers' rights.

Reasserting Presidential Prerogatives

The administration's determination to reassert what were, in its view, presidential prerogatives inevitably brought it into conflict with Congress. Both principle and political expediency seemed to motivate the administration's penchant for secrecy and its reluctance to share information with Congress. Thus Vice President Dick Cheney refused to turn over information on whom his energy task force met with in the process of drafting the administration's energy plan. Cheney argued that forcing him to do so would stifle the sort of free-wheeling debate and advice-seeking necessary to the president in formulating policy; the likelihood that those consulted were mostly generous campaign donors may have also played a role. Many Republicans advised the administration that its stance was politically costly—What did the administration have to hide? was the question inevitably raised—and unlikely, in the end, to succeed; still, the administration refused to comply with the General Accounting Office's request, and the GAO filed suit.

The issue took on added importance in the wake of the terrorist attacks. Members complained that administration briefings were a lot less informative than CNN. After some information was leaked, Bush announced he would restrict classified briefings to a few congressional leaders, but he was soon forced to back down. The law required broader briefings, and, in any case, as John Murtha of Pennsylvania, the highly influential ranking Democrat on the House Defense Appropriations subcommittee, expressed it, "When they put it in writing that they're not going to brief the committee that funds them, that's pretty stupid."[36] In response to the sense of crisis engendered by 9/11, Congress did give the administration significant new powers, but as discussed earlier, far from all the administration requested. Under the president's authority as commander in chief and without consulting Congress, Bush authorized military tribunals to try noncitizens accused of terrorism. A few members of Congress and many independent voices argued that such tribunals were an offense against civil liberties, and the Justice Department's rules for the conduct of the tribunals seem to have been affected by the criticism, but the basic decision stood. The administration refused to allow Tom Ridge, director of the Office of Homeland Security, to testify before Congress, arguing that the position was akin to that of the national security adviser, who as simply an adviser to the president, does not testify. The leaders of the Senate Appropriations Committee, Republican Ted Stevens of Alaska and Democrat Robert Byrd of West Virginia, threatened to subpoena Ridge. The Justice Department has largely refused to provide information to the Judiciary Committees on how it is using its new powers under the Patriot Act.[37]

Given its expansive views of executive powers and the continuing worries over terrorism, the Bush administration is likely to continue throughout its tenure to push the envelope. In a time of crisis, members of Congress are loath to seem to second-guess and hinder a popular president who claims he is simply doing what is necessary to safeguard the American people. Yet even in the immediate wake of the 9/11 attacks, Congress did not simply acquiesce. Nor have only Democrats objected to administration claims. Consequently, the tug-of-war between president and Congress is likely to persist and, barring more terrorist attacks, to become more prominent.

Agenda Dominance Is the Name of the Game

In poll after poll, Americans report that they have more confidence in the Republican Party on issues such as defense, foreign policy, and terrorism and more confidence in the Democratic Party on issues such as Social Security, the environment, and education. Therefore, which sort of issues occupy Americans' attention around election time is likely to affect the results. The focus during much of September and October 2002 was on Republican issues. Even before the August break, Bush's proposal for a huge new Department of Homeland Security had absorbed enormous media attention, and Democrats had been ineffective in attracting coverage of the domestic issues they wanted to highlight.

In the fall, Iraq became the dominant issue. The Bush administration had been threatening to use force against Iraq for months; during the late summer of 2002, many in Congress and the foreign policy establishment became increasingly concerned that the administration had not thought through or justified its policy sufficiently. A series of cautionary public statements by high officials from the first Bush administration and claims by the current administration that it required no authorization from Congress to launch an attack on Iraq provoked strong calls by both Democrats and Republicans for Bush to go to Congress for a formal expression of support. On 4 September, Bush announced that he would seek congressional backing but demanded that Congress vote quickly and give him carte blanche. On 19 September, a week after his UN speech, Bush sent his proposed resolution to Congress; it would give the president wide latitude to do whatever "he determines to be appropriate."

The decision on the Iraq resolution presented many members of Congress with a complex calculus. Many believed that the resolution was too open-ended, that the

United States should not go it alone but should work through the UN or at least with a significant coalition of allies, and that the Bush administration had not yet satisfactorily presented a case for preemptive action against Iraq. They also worried, however, that too much hesitancy would undercut U.S. foreign policy and would make support from the UN less likely. Republicans particularly were uncomfortable with providing anything less than strong support for the president and, as negotiations refined and constrained the resolution's language, even the most doubtful fell into line. Democrats also had political concerns—many believed that a vote against the president on this issue right before the elections would be political suicide. In addition, Democrats were desperate to change the agenda to issues more beneficial to their party, and that required disposing of the resolution.

On 2 October, at a Rose Garden ceremony, Bush and House Minority Leader Richard Gephardt announced that they had agreed to a compromise resolution. With Gephardt signing on, Senate Democrats were placed in an untenable position to force more concessions. When the resolution came to a House vote on 10 October, it passed by 296–133; Republicans voted in favor by a margin of 215–6; Democrats, by 81–126. The Senate passed the resolution in the early hours of 11 October by 77–23; all but one Republican supported the resolution, while Democrats split 29–21. Of Democratic senators in close races, only Paul Wellstone of Minnesota voted against the resolution. In the wake of September 11th, the majority of members in both chambers concluded that both political and policy considerations dictated supporting the president.

In mid-October Congress recessed until after the elections. At the last moment and spurred on by another Florida Election-Day disaster (this time in the primary), the House and Senate reached an agreement on an electoral reform bill; but most of the regular appropriations bills and the homeland security legislation were left unfinished. Members went home to campaign, hoping and fearing that the outcome of the elections would break the stalemate that continued to grip the government on domestic issues.

Bush's Gamble and Its Political and Policy Consequences

In the fall of 2002 Bush was faced with a choice: compromise with Senate Democrats on the spending bills, his homeland security bill, and other domestic legislation or gamble on taking control of both chambers in the midterm elections and so gaining a stronger hand to play. Bush decided to put all his chips on the electoral strategy. For a president who had shown himself unwilling to take on domestic battles that might prove politically costly—on campaign finance reform and aid to farmers, for example—this was a bold choice. Yet the administration's experience during much of 2002 had demonstrated Bush's lack of clout on domestic issues; if the elections reinforced the status quo or resulted in a Democratic gain, Bush could anticipate two more years of having to make unpalatable compromises with Democrats and, even so, of achieving limited domestic policy successes to take into his reelection fight in 2004.

Bush and Cheney had been actively fund raising for Republican candidates all year, and after the Iraq resolution passed, Bush took to the campaign trail with an intensity unprecedented for a sitting president at midterm. In total, Bush raised more that $140 million and Cheney more than $40 million. Bush campaigned for dozens of Republican candidates and dispatched Cheney, cabinet officers, and White House officials to do the same. In the week before the election, Bush visited fifteen states.

Bush's gamble paid off, as Republicans gained a majority in the Senate and increased their majority in the House. The president's effort translated his popularity into strong turnout among core Republican voters. Although Iraq does not appear to have been the major issue motivating voters, the media's focus on the issue seems to have prevented domestic issues from becoming highly salient in a way that might have helped the opposition. Commentators and, after the elections, Democrats themselves concluded that Democrats had also failed to present effective policy alternatives that might have made it possible for the party to benefit electorally from the poor economy.

The election results greatly increased Bush's political clout. Bush got the credit for the Republicans' victory, just as he would have gotten the blame had Republicans lost ground. With Republicans controlling both chambers, the prospects of Congress passing Bush's domestic agenda in the form he favored seemed very much enhanced.

Bush did benefit when the big tax cut package he proposed in January 2003 became law, which almost certainly would not have happened had Democrats held the Senate. With the conference committees that work out differences between the chambers' bills now controlled by Republicans, losses in one chamber or the other could be reversed, as happened on the $87 billion for Iraq in fall of 2003. Yet the margins of control remained narrow, and in the Senate, Democrats were still able to impose roadblocks when they stuck together, as they did on a number of Bush's most conservative judicial nominees. And when the aftermath of the war in Iraq went badly and Bush's popularity decreased, he began to have occasional difficulties with Republicans concerned about their own reelection as well. Control of both houses of Congress remains invaluable to Bush, but unanticipated events once more changed the context within which the president acts, and may yet do so once again.

Notes

1. Charles O. Jones, *The Presidency in a Separated System* (Washington, D.C.: Brookings Institution, 1994).
2. Jon Bond and Richard Fleisher, *The President in the Legislative Arena* (Chicago: University of Chicago Press, 1990).

3. Barbara Sinclair, *Majority Leadership in the U.S. House* (Baltimore: Johns Hopkins University Press, 1983); and idem, *Legislators, Leaders and Lawmaking* (Baltimore: Johns Hopkins University Press, 1995).

4. There was one vacancy and two independents, who usually split their votes between the parties.

5. Data are from *Congressional Quarterly Almanac*, various dates.

6. *New York Times*, 6 December 2000.

7. Sinclair, *Majority Leadership* and *Legislators, Leaders and Lawmaking*; and David Rohde, *Parties and Leaders in the Postreform House* (Chicago: University of Chicago Press, 1991).

8. Barbara Sinclair, *The Transformation of the U.S. Senate* (Baltimore: Johns Hopkins University Press, 1989).

9. Barbara Sinclair, *Unorthodox Lawmaking*, 2d ed.(Washington, D.C.: CQ Press, 2000); and idem, "The New World of U.S. Senators," in *Congress Reconsidered*, 7th ed., ed. Lawrence C. Dodd and Bruce I. Oppenheimer (Washington, D.C.: CQ Press, 2001).

10. *Congressional Quarterly Weekly*, 16 December 2000, 2853.

11. *Washington Post*, 7 December 2000.

12. *Congressional Quarterly Weekly*, 3 March 2001, 466.

13. *Congressional Quarterly Weekly*, 10 March 2001, 530.

14. *Congressional Quarterly Weekly*, 28 April 2001, 904.

15. *Congressional Quarterly Weekly*, 26 May 2001, 1251–54.

16. *Congressional Quarterly Weekly*, 5 May 2001, 1010.

17. *Congressional Quarterly Weekly*, 26 May 2001, 1280.

18. *Congressional Quarterly Weekly*, 30 June 2001, 1569.

19. *Congressional Quarterly Weekly*, 21 July 2001, 1774–75.

20. *Congressional Quarterly Weekly*, 4 August 2001, 1915.

21. Among the most problematic consequences for Bush of the switch in Senate control was its effect on judicial nominations. See chapter 6.

22. *Washington Post*, 26 May 2001, A19.

23. *Roll Call*, 21 May 2001, 27.

24. Ibid.

25. *Washington Post*, 26 May 2001.

26. *Roll Call*, 12 July 2001, 3.

27. *Roll Call*, 23 July 2001, 12.

28. *Congressional Quarterly Weekly*, 4 August 2001, 1906.

29. John Mueller, *War, Presidents and Public Opinion* (New York: John Wiley, 1973); and Richard A. Brody, *Assessing the President* (Stanford, Calif.: Stanford University Press, 1991).

30. *Congressional Quarterly Weekly*, 15 September 2001, 2116.

31. *Congressional Quarterly Weekly*, 15 September 2001, 2158.

32. *Congressional Quarterly Weekly*, 27 October 2001, 2533.

33. *Congressional Quarterly Weekly*, 15 September 2001, 2119.

34. *Congressional Quarterly Weekly*, 8 December 2001, 2919.

35. *Los Angeles Times*, 5 December 2001.

36. *Congressional Quarterly Weekly*, 13 October 2001.

37. *New York Times*, 15 August 2002.

CHAPTER 6

Ironies and Disappointments
Bush and Federal Judgeships

David M. O'Brien

THERE IS NO LITTLE IRONY in President George W. Bush's record of appointments to the federal bench. In his 2000 presidential campaign he vowed to appoint conservatives opposed to "judicial activism." Then, although trailing in the national popular vote, a bare majority of the Supreme Court overruled the Florida Supreme Court and stopped a recount of contested ballots in Florida. The state's 25 electoral votes were thereby secured for Bush, giving him more than the required 270 of the 528 votes needed to win in the electoral college. Emboldened and determined, Bush's Department of Justice subsequently put into place a rigorously ideological judicial selection process.

The Bush administration was confident—initially overly confident—that, even though the Senate was evenly split between Republicans and Democrats, Vice President Dick Cheney, presiding as president of the Senate, would cast the deciding vote in battles over the Senate's confirmation of judicial nominees and other matters. However, in mid-May 2001, in the very week in which Bush sent his first judicial nominations to the Senate, Vermont's moderate Republican Senator James Jeffords announced that he was abandoning the party to become an independent and would vote with Democrats, thus giving them control of the Senate. Already fearful of the mark that Bush might make on the federal judiciary, angry over the Republican-controlled Senate's history of thwarting approval of many of Democratic President Bill Clinton's judicial nominees,[1] and bitter over the decision by the conservative bare majority on the Court to stop the Florida recount, Democratic senators considered it political payback time. Consequently, the Bush administration confronted delays and disappointments in filling seats on the federal bench.

The Irony of the 2000 Election

Over the past three decades, federal judgeships have become a key issue in presidential elections. They have always offered presidents opportunities for political patronage and for rewarding faithful party supporters. But, they are also opportunities to influence law and public policy long after presidents leave the Oval Office, because these judges are lifetime appointees, subject to removal only by impeachment for high crimes and misdemeanors. Federal judges also rule on virtually every major political controversy in the land—from abortion and busing, to federalism, homosexual rights, the right to privacy, and to the rights of political, racial, and religious minorities.

During the 1968 election, as part of his "southern strategy" to win over white Democratic voters in the South, Republican presidential candidate Richard M. Nixon campaigned on restoring "law and order" to the country and appointing to the federal bench "strict constructionists" who opposed "judicial activism."[2] He succeeded in turning federal judgeships into symbols of presidential power. More specifically, Nixon vowed to remake the Supreme Court in his own image of "judicial self-restraint" by appointing justices who deferred to the political process.

After his election Nixon had the opportunity to name four justices. In 1969 he appointed Chief Justice Warren E. Burger, who was known as a conservative judge on the Court of Appeals for the District of Columbia Circuit. The following year, after controversies forced the withdrawal of two earlier nominees, he elevated another federal appellate court judge, Harry A. Blackmun. And in 1972 the Senate confirmed his last two appointees: Lewis F. Powell Jr., a former president of the American Bar Association, and William H. Rehnquist, a young conservative assistant attorney general in the Department of Justice.

Nixon's lower court judges and four appointees to the Court nevertheless proved largely disappointing for conservatives. Chief Justice Burger lacked the intellectual wherewithal to lead the Court. Justice Blackmun authored the abortion ruling in *Roe v. Wade*[3] and increasingly voted with liberals, except in the area of criminal procedure. Justice Powell became the swing voter in major controversies but was inclined to abide by liberal precedents. Republican President Gerald R. Ford's appointment of Justice John Paul Stevens in 1975 was to be no less disappointing for conservatives, for he was too independent, a "maverick," and unpredictable. Only Justice Rehnquist toed a conservative line, writing more solo dissents than any other justice and earning him the nickname "the Lone Ranger."

In short, the Burger Court not only failed to forge a "constitutional counterrevolution," but went on to uphold women's right to have abortions, courtordered busing to achieve integrated schools, and most affirmative action programs, as well as to give greater scope to the Fourteenth Amendment's equal protection clause on claims of nonracial discrimination. Those rulings, no less than those of the Warren Court in the 1950s and 1960s, embittered the New

Christian Right, "movement conservatives," pro-life supporters, and others in the coalition that supported the election of Republican President Ronald Reagan. In other words, Nixon made federal judgeships a symbol of presidential power but failed to take the judicial selection process seriously. As a result, the direction of the federal judiciary continued in a moderate-to-liberal direction. The "Reagan revolution," however, aimed to rectify that.

Reagan promised to appoint justices and judges who were opposed to past "judicial activism" and who respected the "original intent" of the founders of the Constitution. Unlike Nixon, he put into place one of the most rigorous and ideological judicial selection processes ever.[4] In his 1980 presidential campaign Reagan also promised to appoint the first woman to the Court, and in 1981 he appointed Justice Sandra Day O'Connor, a conservative Republican judge from an Arizona state appellate court. Subsequently, in 1987, he made a major mark on the Court by elevating Justice Rehnquist to the chief justiceship and filling his seat with Justice Antonin Scalia, a former University of Chicago Law School professor who was known for championing a jurisprudence of original intent and whom Reagan had previously named to the Court of Appeals for the District of Columbia Circuit. The next year, after Justice Powell stepped down, Reagan's nomination of Judge Robert H. Bork—a former solicitor general in the Nixon administration and professor at Yale Law School, who was known for advocating a jurisprudence of original intent and whom Reagan also had earlier placed on the Court of Appeals for the District of Columbia Circuit—became ensnarled in a bitter Senate confirmation battle. The eventual defeat of Judge Bork's nomination deeply embittered conservatives and raised the stakes even higher for the appointment of federal judges. Reagan finally filled the position in 1988 by elevating Judge Anthony Kennedy, a more moderate, less-doctrinaire conservative judge on the Court of Appeals for the Ninth Circuit.

Reagan's successor, President George Bush, then had the opportunity in 1990 and 1991 to fill the seats of the last two leading liberals, Justices William J. Brennan Jr. and Thurgood Marshall. But his appointees proved a mixed bag for conservatives. Justice David H. Souter soon sided with the left of center on the Court, again angering conservatives and renewing their commitment to take judicial selection seriously and to use presidential power to push the federal courts in a more conservative direction. By contrast, Justice Clarence Thomas proved a reliable conservative advocate of adhering to the framers' intent, and he became an icon for attorneys working in the second Bush administration.

During Democratic President Bill Clinton's two terms, New Right movement conservatives, especially interest group organizations such as the Free Congress Foundation, which monitors judicial appointments, and the Institute for Justice, a conservative policy institute in Washington, D.C., sought to preserve their past success in moving the federal judiciary in a more conservative direction and to force the administration to compromise on judicial nominees. The Republican-controlled Senate was thus under pressure to hold up and defeat Clinton's judicial nominees. As a result, Clinton's judges were for the most part moderate centrists, much to the dismay of some of the president's liberal supporters. His two appointees to the Court, for example—Justices Ruth Bader Ginsburg and Stephen Breyer—proved noncontroversial and won easy Senate confirmation.[5]

George W. Bush's supporters, therefore, looked forward to renewing the "Reagan revolution" through his judicial appointments. As the leading and overwhelmingly best-financed candidate in the Republican primaries, Bush was not openly attacked by the Christian Coalition and other conservative organizations, and Bush reassured them that his judicial nominees would be solidly conservative, repeatedly promising to appoint judges like Justices Scalia and Thomas.

Although Bush claimed a broad mandate to govern, his first year in office was overshadowed by the extraordinary circumstances of his election and the ruling in *Bush v. Gore.*[6] On the night of the presidential election, 7 November 2000, Gore was winning the national popular vote but locked in a tight fight for Florida's 25 electoral votes, which would give either candidate the votes needed to win in the electoral college. Based on projections, CNN and other news services declared first Gore and then Bush the winner, before ultimately concluding that the election was too close to call. The next day, the Florida Division of Election reported that Bush had a margin of 1,784 votes. Because that was less than one-half of one percent of the votes cast, an automatic machine recount was conducted, as required by state law. The result diminished Bush's lead to 327 votes, and Gore sought manual recounts in three counties, as allowed under Florida's law for protesting election results. Palm Beach County then announced that it would manually recount all votes, and Bush filed suit to bar that action. In the meantime, a dispute arose over the deadline for canvassing boards to submit their election returns because the Florida secretary of state declined to waive a 14 November deadline for certification, and that decision was challenged in state courts. The Florida Supreme Court then ruled that the manual recounts should be included in the final vote and extended the certification deadline to 26 November, a decision that Bush's attorneys appealed to the U.S. Supreme Court. Before the Court heard oral arguments in that case, *Bush v. Palm Beach County Canvassing Board (Bush I),*[7] the secretary of state certified Bush as the winner by 537 votes. Gore immediately filed a lawsuit, as provided under state law, contesting the election. In *Bush I* the Court unanimously vacated the Florida Supreme Court's decision to extend the certification date and directed it to clarify the basis for its ruling.

Subsequently, on 8 December, the Florida Supreme Court ordered an immediate manual recount of all votes in the state where no vote for president had been machine recorded. Bush's attorneys in turn immediately appealed that decision to the Supreme Court, which granted a stay of the statewide recount and set the case,

Bush v. Gore, for oral arguments the following Monday, 11 December. Bush's attorneys argued that the manual recount was standardless and thus violated the Fourteenth Amendment's equal protection clause. By contrast, Gore's lawyers claimed that every vote should be counted. At 10 P.M. on the following night, 12 December, the Court handed down its decision reversing the state supreme court. Seven members of the Court, with Justices Stevens and Ginsburg dissenting, found that a standardless recount violated the equal protection clause. But by a 5–4 vote the Court held that there was no remedy available. Justices Stevens, Souter, Ginsburg, and Breyer each filed angry dissents, criticizing the majority's decision and protesting its "judicial activism" in intervening into the electoral process.

Needless to say, Democrats were outraged and embittered by the ruling in *Bush v. Gore*. Not only had the Court's most conservative justices—all appointees of Nixon, Reagan, and Bush—handed the election to the Republican candidate, but several of them were rumored to be thinking about retiring and thus giving Bush the opportunity to fill their seats and to move the Court in even more sharply conservative directions. Chief Justice Rehnquist was 76, and Justice O'Connor, at age 70, was entering her twentieth year of service on the high bench. Both appeared likely to step down during Bush's term. Justice Stevens was 80 and also might possibly retire.

Hence, even before Bush came into office it was clear he would have to do battle with Democratic senators over his judicial nominees. As the ranking Democrat on the Senate Judiciary Committee, Vermont's Senator Patrick J. Leahy, put it in January 2001, shortly before Bush's inauguration, "I think the closeness of the election and the ill will engendered by the Supreme Court is going to make it difficult for the new administration to make some clear ideological stamp on the courts."[8]

Reestablishing a Rigorous, Ideological Judicial Selection Process

In spite of the controversy surrounding his election, Bush stood by his campaign promises to pro-life supporters and movement conservatives when staffing the Department of Justice (DoJ). Many in the DoJ and White House are members of the Federalist Society, a legal organization founded in 1982 by then professors Antonin Scalia and Robert Bork, among other conservative legal scholars, to combat what they deemed a liberal bias in law schools and on the federal bench. Through their writings, litigation, and influence over judicial appointments, they aimed to counter that alleged bias. Although very influential during the Reagan administration, they had proved less so during the first Bush's presidency. And they sought to remedy that situation in the second Bush administration.

Virtually everyone in the DoJ and in the White House with responsibility for vetting and selecting judicial nominees is associated with the Federalist Society.

Attorney General John Ashcroft is a member and a darling of pro-life supporters for his outspoken views as Missouri's former governor and senator.[9] While in the Senate, he also sparked controversy by stridently attacking Clinton's nomination of a black Missouri Supreme Court justice, Ronnie White, to the federal bench and led the fight to defeat White's confirmation, claiming that he was soft on criminals. On that and other occasions, Ashcroft appealed to his supporters and angered more moderate Republicans and Democrats.

Bush's nomination of Theodore Olson to be solicitor general, with responsibility for representing the government in cases before the Supreme Court—a position from which new justices are occasionally chosen— reinforced his message to conservatives. Olson had served in the Reagan administration, chaired the D.C. chapter of the Federalist Society, and argued *Bush v. Gore* before the Court. Not surprisingly, both Ashcroft and Olson confronted opposition from liberal groups, such as the People for the American Way, and intense grilling in the Senate Judiciary Committee before winning their confirmations.

Under Attorney General Ashcroft, the Office of Legal Policy (OLP) was reestablished within the DoJ to manage the selection of judicial nominees and to oversee legal policy strategies and programs of the administration. The OLP was created in 1981 under Reagan's attorney general, William French Smith, and credited with that administration's success in appointing more ideological conservatives to the federal bench. It was part of the Reagan administration's reorganizations in order to concentrate power, institutionalize a rigorous judicial selection process, and better position the White House to combat senatorial patronage when filling lower federal court vacancies. An unprecedented screening process for potential judicial nominees was introduced: potential candidates' speeches, articles, and opinions were scrutinized before they were invited for day-long interviews with OLP attorneys. Only then did the OLP make recommendations on whom to nominate, and then a White House Judicial Selection Committee made the ultimate decision on Reagan's nominees. The selection committee, which met weekly in the White House, included the attorney general, the counselor to the president, the assistant attorney for the OLP, and other White House advisers. The OLP, however, was reorganized and its responsibilities shifted in 1989, and subsequently, the Clinton administration abolished the structure and put another assistant attorney general in charge of coordinating judicial nominations.[10] Thus, the Bush administration's reestablishment of the OLP was both symbolic and strategic.

In Bush's DoJ, Assistant Attorney General Viet D. Dinh was put in charge of the OLP. A former professor at Georgetown University Law Center, as well as a graduate of Harvard Law School and clerk for Justice O'Connor, he too is associated with the Federalist Society. Others in the OLP are likewise members of that organization, and, perhaps not surprisingly, no less than six of Bush's first eleven federal court of appeals nominees were also affiliated with the Federalist Society.

Within a couple of months of coming into office, Bush sent another signal to reassure conservatives that he would stand by his word about appointing conservative judges and not make the kind of mistake his father did in appointing Justice Souter. In March 2001, his chief legal counsel, Alberto R. Gonzales, a former justice on the Texas Supreme Court and a potential nominee for any vacancy that opens on the high bench, sent the American Bar Association (ABA) a letter informing it that the administration would no longer submit the names of judicial candidates for evaluation. For a half century, since the administration of Republican President Dwight D. Eisenhower, the ABA had been asked by Republican and Democratic presidents to evaluate the qualifications of potential judicial nominees.[11] But in the 1980s the ABA came under attack because of its opposition to some of Reagan's most conservative judicial nominees—and especially due to its divided recommendation and criticism of the qualifications of Judge Bork in conjunction with his ill-fated nomination to the Supreme Court. Movement conservatives deeply resented the role played by the ABA in the judicial selection process. As Clint Bolick of the Institute for Justice bluntly put it, "It's high time that the White House sent the ABA packing." Gonzales was a bit more tactful, explaining that it was unfair to give the ABA or "any single group such a preferential, quasi-official role."[12] Yet the fact remained that many on Bush's legal team, like those in the Reagan administration, consider the ABA not merely too liberal a body, but also an intrusion on the prerogatives of the president in selecting federal judges.

Predictably, liberal groups such as the Alliance for Justice, which for twenty years has monitored the appointment of federal judges for a coalition of liberal organizations, deemed Gonzales's explanation disingenuous. That was so in light of the prominent role that members of the Federalist Society play in the Bush administration's judicial selection process and of the fact that a large number of judicial nominees have been associated with the society. Nan Aron, president of the Alliance for Justice, for one, charged, "The President's action is an alarming sign that he intends to place ideological purity above all other criteria, including competence."[13] For their part, Democratic senators on the Judiciary Committee vowed to continue to solicit and consider the ABA's evaluations of the qualifications of judicial nominees.

The Irony of Losing Control of the Senate

Even before Bush announced his first judicial nominees, fights broke out between Democratic senators and the White House, as well as within the evenly divided Senate, over the nomination and confirmation process. These disputes centered on the need for consultation with senators when selecting judicial nominees and how much deference—"senatorial courtesy"—would be given to home-state senators when naming judges to the lower federal courts. Article II of the Constitution gives the president the power to appoint federal judges "with the advice and consent" of the Senate. But, like Reagan, Bush considered the selection of judges to be entirely a presidential prerogative, and he aimed to aggressively assert the president's power. And that went against the tradition of consulting with and accommodating senators.

Traditionally, the White House consults with the home-state senators, including those of the opposing party, when filling vacancies in district courts and, in recent years, in federal appellate courts even though their jurisdiction spans several states. The DoJ routinely asks for recommendations from senators of the administration's party, vets their candidates, and almost invariably has their support before making a nomination. During the Clinton administration, Republican senators were consulted and, because they controlled the Senate in his last term, Clinton was forced to make concessions, trading judgeships and nominating some judges recommended by Republicans in order to have the Senate confirm his own judicial nominees.[14]

In its first months in office, the Bush administration refused or failed to consult with senators in selecting judicial candidates, thereby increasing tensions with Democratic senators. This failure appears to have been rooted in the view of the OLP and the White House that it had a mandate to make Bush's mark on the federal judiciary, just as Reagan had. However, next to Democratic President Franklin D. Roosevelt in the 1930s, Reagan was one of the most popular presidents of the twentieth century; unlike Reagan, Bush had not even won the popular vote in the 2000 election. Whether Bush had a mandate to pack the courts thus became a matter of heated debate. Conservatives contended that he had won the election and therefore should vigorously assert the powers of his office, while liberals countered that the Court had robbed the presidential election of its legitimacy and that since Bush was not elected by a popular vote, he could not claim a mandate to pack the courts.

The antagonism flared into the open in late April 2001, when California's Democratic senators Dianne Feinstein and Barbara Boxer learned that the White House was considering naming California's Republican Representative Christopher Cox to a seat on the Court of Appeals for the Ninth Circuit. The Ninth Circuit—the nation's largest circuit, spanning all of the western states, including Alaska and Hawaii—is considered the most liberal but remains sharply divided between appointees of Reagan and Carter. Neither Democratic senator had been consulted, or even informed about the possible choice, and both opposed Cox as too conservative. The administration was forced to back down, withdrawing Cox from consideration. In addition, the administration agreed to a deal with Senator Feinstein, a member of the Senate Judiciary Committee, on the selection of federal district court judges in California. A six-member commission, composed of three members appointed by the administration and three by the senator, now recommends judicial candidates but only if they have the backing of at least four commission members.[15]

During his time in office, President Clinton made similar arrangements and tradeoffs with Republican senators. Yet the Bush administration initially resisted, for it was slow to grasp the realities of an equally divided Senate and of its traditions. Indeed, in several cases it only bothered to consult with Republican home-state senators, drawing anger from the same state's Democratic senators. Senator Leahy blasted the administration, warning, "It sure looks like [the administration and Republican senators] are intent on building an ideologically driven court-packing machine."[16]

In short, the Bush administration initially reinforced Democrats' bitterness left over from eight years of Republican obstructionism and attacks on Clinton's judicial nominees, along with the outcome of the 2000 election. The Senate minority leader, South Dakota Senator Thomas A. Daschle, and all nine Democrats on the Judiciary Committee protested in a letter to White House Counsel Gonzales demanding greater consultation and threatening to prevent votes on judicial nominees if Democratic senators were not consulted. Given the equal division of the Senate at the time, they needed only forty-one votes to block confirmation and legislation in retaliation for the White House's refusal to consult with Democratic home-state senators.

Given that political reality, Gonzales and the White House vowed to "work together constructively." As Gonzales explained, "Although the Constitution entrusts the president alone with the power to propose nominees, we believe that prenomination consultation between the administration and home-state senators, regardless of party, will facilitate this process."[17] Deputy White House Counsel Timothy Flanigan, though, perhaps put it best when conceding, "It doesn't do the president any good to send up nominees who are on suicide missions."[18]

The controversy over consulting with senators continued to escalate. The Bush administration was forced to back off somewhat from its initial hardball stance in asserting presidential power because the tradition of senatorial courtesy is deeply ingrained and reinforced by a practice known as the blue slip. The chair of the judiciary committee sends a blue slip (because of the color of the paper on which the letter is printed) asking home-state senators if they support a judicial nominee. If a senator does not return the blue slip, the committee generally does not hold a hearing or forward the nominee to the full Senate for a vote. Although committee chairs have occasionally broken with that tradition—if, for instance, the president personally goes to bat for a nominee[19]—the blue-slip practice effectively puts controversial judicial nominees on hold and typically forecloses the possibility of their confirmation by the full Senate.

This controversy was further compounded in the early months of Bush's presidency by signals sent to Democratic senators by the chair of the Senate Judiciary

Committee, Utah Senator Orrin G. Hatch. A staunch supporter of the administration and a veteran of the wars fought over the judicial nominees of Presidents Reagan, Bush, and Clinton, Hatch added fuel to the fire of controversy by indicating that he planned to require *both* home-state senators to withhold blue slips before sinking a nomination. And he indicated that he would proceed with confirmation hearings on some nominees even if one senator failed to return the blue slip. In a letter to Democratic senators, Hatch said he "would resist any demand that absolute veto power be granted to any single senator."[20] Although not entirely unprecedented,[21] his plan for moving Bush's nominees through the judiciary committee sent Democratic senators ballistic. They considered it an infringement on their political patronage and an outrage, since during the Clinton administration Senator Hatch himself had enforced the blue-slip practice in order to deny hearings and to defeat some of the president's nominees, particularly during Clinton's last two years in office.

But circumstances changed dramatically before Senator Hatch could proceed with his plans. Senator Jeffords announced he was abandoning the Republican Party to become an independent. The balance of power in the Senate shifted to 50 Democrats and 49 Republicans, giving Democrats control of the Senate. Jeffords had long been at odds with his increasingly conservative party over abortion, gay rights, the environment, and taxes and spending. A moderate with twenty-seven years' experience in Congress—fourteen years in the House of Representatives and thirteen in the Senate—Jeffords still had not risen to key positions. He regretted his lack of influence as well as the direction of the Republican-controlled Congress. When the White House and congressional Republicans stripped $450 billion from an education-spending bill, he decided to leave his party. As he later reflected, "I knew that the unique circumstances of our time would allow one person to walk across the aisle and dramatically change the power structure of the government, to again give moderation and balance to the system."[22]

Jeffords's action was uncommon but not unprecedented, for members of Congress have switched parties before—in fact, seventeen senators have done so since 1893. Still, none had done so at the cost of control over a chamber of Congress. Not surprisingly, having failed to persuade Jeffords to reconsider, Republicans vilified him as "a traitor." Senate Republican Leader Trent Lott called it a "coup of one." And, the Mississippi senator lamented, "The decision of one man has, however else you describe it, trumped the will of the American people."[23]

Democrats, needless to say, did not share Lott's view. They celebrated Jeffords's decision and congratulated him for his courage. Replacing Lott as Senate majority leader, Daschle praised Jeffords for helping "put the balance back in our system of checks and balances."[24] He also boasted that the Democratic majority in the Senate would "put the brakes" on GOP initiatives. As a result, the Senate did defeat the administration's plans for oil drilling in the Arctic wilderness, for example, and passed campaign finance reform, which the Republican majority had previously derailed.

For Democrats, Jeffords's defection changed not only the power structure within the Senate but also the political dynamics between that body and the White House. It appeared supremely ironic—poetic justice for Democrats still outraged over the Rehnquist Court's deciding the 2000 presidential election. The Court had intervened in the national election in an extraordinary way, and Jeffords's defection was no less extraordinary. Both decisions, nevertheless, registered how intensely partisan Congress and the courts have become over the past two decades. They also underscored the critical importance and consequences of who sits on the federal bench, particularly on the Supreme Court, making it plain that the stakes were very high and that if a vacancy were to open up on the Court during Bush's presidency, there was bound to be a major confrontation over any nominee deemed too conservative. The current justices were split 5–4 on a range of issues, including abortion, affirmative action, minority-majority redistricting, congressional power versus states' rights, and vouchers. Thus, Bush became institutionally constrained, just like Clinton after Republicans regained control of the Senate in his second term and like Reagan after Republicans lost control of the Senate in the 1986 midterm elections, which contributed to the defeat of Judge Bork in 1987.

Along with shifting control of the Senate, perhaps the most important consequence of Jeffords's defection was that Democratic senators were now in a position to delay and defeat Bush's judicial nominees, even though they had only the slimmest majority. Taking over the chairmanship of the Judiciary Committee from Senator Hatch, Senator Leahy made it crystal clear that the Senate confirmation process for federal judges had changed, and with it Bush's influence over shaping the federal judiciary. In Leahy's words, "Many around the White House thought they had a mandate to change the federal courts, even though they lost the popular vote. Now, that's impossible."[25]

After control of the Senate changed hands, Senate Majority Leader Daschle promised not to exact revenge for the way Republican senators had stalled and defeated the confirmation of Clinton's judicial nominees. At a news conference on Capitol Hill, he said Bush's judicial nominees would be given "a fair chance." Admitting that "[t]here is ample reason to believe that perhaps payback is something we should entertain," Daschle claimed, "we're not going to do that. I don't believe in it. We have to break the cycle. We want to be fair. We want to set an example. We want to create a level of civility that I don't think has existed for a while."[26]

Republicans in the Senate, however, doubted that the Judiciary Committee, now composed of ten Democrats and nine Republicans, under the leadership of Senator Leahy, could resist giving Bush's nominees a hard time. And a year-and-a-half into his presidency, they and the White House were complaining about the committee's delaying confirmations and rejection of two appellate court nominees. Pennsylvania's Republican Senator Rick Santorum, among others, blasted the Democratic-controlled committee for engaging in "McCarthyism"—referring to Senator Joseph McCarthy's witch hunt for communists during the 1950s. Mimicking Senator McCarthy's standard line, he accused them of asking, "Are you now or have you ever been a conservative or a member of a conservative organization?" and concluded, "That's it; you are disqualified. It's just a different C word."[27]

Senator Santorum, like other Republicans in the Senate and the administration, complained about lengthy delays in the Judiciary Committee's confirmation hearings. In particular, he was angry about the delay in holding a hearing on the nomination of Judge D. Brooks Smith, a federal district court judge from Pennsylvania, for a seat on the Court of Appeals for the Third Circuit. Democratic senators and liberal groups who opposed Judge Smith were raising questions about his judicial ethics in a fraud case and about his voting record and opinions on states' rights, the environment, and civil rights. The Alliance for Justice brought twenty law school professors to Capitol Hill to lobby senators to vote against confirmation. During his confirmation hearing, Delaware's Democratic Senator Joseph R. Biden Jr. warned that if Judge Smith was not forthcoming in answering to the committee's questions, "I will do everything in my power to defeat you, including moving to the Senate floor to take action I've never taken in my life as a United States Senator: a filibuster."[28] Nonetheless, Judge Smith was given a hearing before the committee on 26 February 2002, six months after his nomination, and he was ultimately confirmed by the Senate.

President Bush and Attorney General Ashcroft also criticized the delays in confirming judicial nominees, especially in the months preceding the November 2002 elections. They aimed to make federal judgeships, once again, a campaign issue in their party's effort to regain control of the Senate. On "Law Day," 3 May 2002, for instance, Bush lamented:

> There is a vacancy crisis on our federal courts. Both the president and the United States Senate have constitutional responsibilities to address vacancies on the federal bench. I have nominated 100 outstanding jurists for these posts. But the Senate, thus far, has not done its part to ensure that our federal courts operate at full strength. Justice is at risk in America, and the Senate must act for the good of the country.[29]

In fact, during the past two decades, the length of time between the time of a president's nominations and the Judiciary Committee's hearings on nominees has gradually increased, as has the time elapsed before the Senate votes on confirmation.[30] It took an average of 77 days for an appellate court nominee to receive a hearing during the first Bush administration, for example, and 81 days during Clinton's first term. But the period grew to 231 days during 1997–98 and then, during Clinton's last year in office, to 247 days. A number of Clinton's judicial nominees were *never* given hearings by the Republican-controlled Judiciary Committee under Senator Hatch. A record time lapse of 1,506 days—four years and twenty-six days—was set in the case of Clinton's nomination and the Senate's final confirmation vote on Court of Appeals for the Ninth Circuit Judge Richard A. Paez.

Bush and Republican senators also complained about the number of appellate court nominees confirmed. In his first twenty-two months in office, Bush nominated thirty-two court of appeals judges, but only seventeen were ultimately confirmed. By comparison, in their first two years in office, President Clinton nominated twenty-two circuit judges, of whom nineteen were confirmed; the first President Bush nominated twenty-three, of whom twenty-two were confirmed; and President Reagan named twenty, of whom nineteen were confirmed.

There is no denying that Senate Democrats and liberal groups targeted and stalled hearings and confirmation votes on Bush's most conservative appellate court nominees. That was strategic and not particularly surprising in light of the Republican-controlled Senate's handling of Clinton's court of appeals nominees. Moreover, in the past thirty years every appointee to the Supreme Court, with the exceptions of Rehnquist and O'Connor, has been elevated from a federal appellate court. Furthermore, given rising caseloads and having few of their decisions reviewed by the Supreme Court, federal appellate courts increasingly play the role of "mini-supreme courts." Democratic senators and liberal interest groups therefore aimed to send the White House a strong message about naming a candidate like Justices Scalia and Thomas to the Court should a vacancy become available.

The delays and the hotly contested confirmation hearings and votes in the Senate inexorably reflect how the confirmation process for judicial nominees has been transformed over the past few decades as presidents have made federal judgeships both symbols and instruments of their own power. These phenomena are also the result of an increasingly polarized Congress and the greater role played by conservative and liberal interest groups in screening and then pushing or fighting judicial nominees.

Lower Federal Court Appointments

As of 1 January 2003, the Senate had confirmed 101 of Bush's 131 judicial nominees, but almost 20 percent of them were confirmed after the November 2002 election, in which the Democrats again lost control of the Senate.[31] Of these, 17 were court of appeals judges and the remaining 84 were district court judges. As with most presidents, Bush named judges who were overwhelmingly faithful party supporters (see table 6.1). Bush also proved sensitive to arguments about diversity on the bench—appointing twenty-one women, seven Hispanics, three African Americans, and one Asian American (a Hawaiian)—although this consideration was not as high a priority as it had been in the Carter and Clinton administrations (see table 6.2).

The story of Bush's priorities and strategy in nominating judges, along with his battles with the Democratic-controlled Senate Judiciary Committee, is illuminated by the fate of his first eleven appellate court nominees and the committee's defeat of two appellate court nominees. Bush's appellate court nominees became a battleground between the White House and the Senate because of their role in legal policymaking, as discussed earlier, and because Democrats aimed to send a clear message about any nominee to the Supreme Court.

At first blush, Bush's initial nominees aimed to bring diversity to the bench, appeared conciliatory to Democrats, and on the whole were designed to deflect political opposition. Among the eleven were two African Americans, one Hispanic, one man born in the Middle East, and three women. Four were sitting district court judges and two were state supreme court justices. Clinton had appointed the two African Americans, though one was a recess appointee because Republicans had blocked a vote on his confirmation; one was a Reagan appointee; and the first President Bush had appointed two others and had nominated two more who had failed to win confirmation.

Moreover, Bush decided against nominating two other potential candidates because of opposition from their home-state senators and liberal groups. In addition to declining to nominate Representative Cox to the Ninth Circuit, the administration backed down from naming Paul Keisler to the Fourth Circuit. Keisler, an attorney who had clerked for both Judge Bork and Justice Kennedy, was opposed by Democratic senators Paul Sarbanes and Barbara Mikulski of Maryland. The Fourth Circuit, one of the most conservative, has been for years a battleground when it comes to filling vacancies there.

In spite of the strategy of choosing candidates who would bring diversity to the bench, several of Bush's initial appellate court nominees were immediately targeted by liberal groups as too conservative. Given that Democrats now controlled the Senate, those nominees were certain to face "an obstructionist campaign," in the words of Tom Jipping, head of the conservative Free Congress's judicial selection project. Bush's final pick of his initial appellate court nominees, thus, appeared a "strategic decision for the time being."[32] Over a year after their nominations, the Senate had confirmed only three of the eleven. The Judiciary Committee held hearings on four more, but they and the others not given hearings were put on hold, stalled by the committee, until after the 2002 midterm elections. And one was rejected. The Judiciary Committee also defeated the nomination of Judge Charles W. Pickering for the Fifth Circuit.

TABLE 6.1   Party Affiliation of Judicial Appointees

President	Party	Appointees from Same Party
Roosevelt	Democratic	97%
Truman	Democratic	92
Eisenhower	Republican	95
Kennedy	Democratic	92
Johnson	Democratic	96
Nixon	Republican	93
Ford	Republican	81
Carter	Democratic	90
Reagan	Republican	94
Bush	Republican	89
Clinton	Democratic	88
Bush	Republican	93

Sources: Updated from the Federal Judicial Center at
http://air.fjc.gov/history_judges_frm.html (as of 1 November 2002).

TABLE 6.2   Diversity in Federal Judicial Appointments

	Carter	Reagan	Bush I	Clinton	Bush II
Women	40 (15.5%)	29 (7.7%)	36 (19.4%)	108 (29.3%)	21 (20.7%)
African American	37 (14.3%)	7 (1.8%)	12 (6.4%)	61 (16.5%)	3 (2.9%)
Hispanic	16 (6.2%)	15 (4.0%)	8 (4.3%)	25 (6.7%)	7 (6.9%)
Asian American	2 (0.7%)	2 (0.5%)		11 (2.9%)	1 (1.5%)
Native American				1 (0.2%)	
Totals:	95	53	56	206	32 (31.6%)
Total judges appointed:	258	372	185	368	101

Source: Sheldon Goldman, Elliot Slotnick, Gerard Gryski, and Gary Zuk, "Clinton's
Judges," *Judicature* 84 (March–April 2001), 228–58; and Department of Justice, Office of
Legal Policy at www.usdoj.gov/olp/confirmed.htm (as of 1 January 2003).

The fates of the initial appellate court nominees illustrate, on the one hand, Bush's agenda of not merely rewarding faithful GOP supporters but of nominating proven ideological conservatives aligned with the New Right movement, the Reagan administration, and the Federalist Society. On the other hand, their experiences also reflect the intensity of opposition by Democratic senators and liberal groups, as well as the strategy of the Judiciary Committee to move promptly on acceptable nominees but stall indefinitely, or at least until after the November 2002 elections, those deemed too ideologically conservative. In addition, their fates underscore the significance of Senator Jeffords's defection and how even such a slim Democratic majority in the Senate effectively checked and institutionally constrained Bush.

The three appellate court judges confirmed by the Senate included two of President Clinton's African American appointees to district courts and one female district judge appointed by the first President Bush. Notably, the very first to receive a hearing was Judge Roger L. Gregory, a recess appointee named by Clinton in his final days in the Oval Office. The committee's decision to move quickly on his nomination, like Clinton's decision to give him a recess appointment, was symbolic—a payback for past obstructionism by the Republican-controlled Senate.

Judge Gregory had been named by Clinton to the Fourth Circuit in December 2000 after Senator Hatch, as chair of the Judiciary Committee, refused to hold a hearing on his nomination. He thus became the first African American to sit on the Fourth Circuit, whose jurisdiction spans the states of Maryland, Virginia, and North and South Carolina, and includes a higher percentage of minorities than any other circuit. Although Judge Gregory had had the support of his home-state senators—Republican Senator John W. Warner and then-Democratic Senator Charles S. Robb, as well as the latter's successor, Republican Senator George Allen[33]—Hatch had permitted North Carolina Republican Senator Jesse Helms to put a hold on the nomination. Helms had for years successfully halted the confirmation of any African American considered for a seat on the Fourth Circuit, contending that the circuit did not need any more judges and that its caseload did not warrant filling vacancies. Both because Judge Gregory had a one-year temporary appointment that had angered Republicans, the Democratic-controlled Judiciary Committee moved expeditiously, sending his nomination to the full Senate barely two months after Bush renominated him.

The next nominee to receive a hearing was the other African American district court judge appointed by Clinton—Judge Barrington D. Parker Jr., who was confirmed for a seat on the Court of Appeals for the Second Circuit. The son of a renowned federal district court judge in the District of Columbia, he had graduated from Yale Law School and practiced commercial law for over twenty years before his appointment to the district court in 1994.

The third Bush nominee confirmed was Judge Edith Brown Clement, a district court judge appointed by President George H.W. Bush in 1991 and elevated to the Fifth Circuit. Judge Clement, an expert in admiralty and maritime law, had the strong support of both home-state senators and generally won high praise from the bar for her work on the bench.

More controversial were Bush's remaining initial appellate court nominees. Only Judges Dennis W. Shedd, Michael McConnell, Miguel Estrada, and Texas Supreme Court Justice Priscilla R. Owen were given hearings before the Judiciary Committee. Judges Shedd, McConnell, and Estrada, nonetheless, remained on hold, and Justice Owen was eventually rejected by the committee, which split along party lines. Bush's two other nominees for the Fourth Circuit were opposed by Democratic senators and liberal groups both because of their views and because they had worked for two of the most conservative senators— Helms and South Carolina Republican Senator Strom Thurmond, both of whom had previously held up Democratic appointments to the Fourth Circuit. Judge Terrence W. Boyle was named to the district court in 1984 and later nominated by the first President Bush to a seat on the Fourth Circuit but not confirmed by the Senate. Prior to his appointment he had been an aide to Senator Helms, and his renomination to the Fourth Circuit rekindled old fires of opposition. The other Fourth Circuit nominee, Judge Shedd, had been named to a district court by Bush's father in 1990. Prior to that, Shedd had been a legislative aide to Senator Thurmond; indeed, in the mid–1980s, when Senator Thurmond chaired the Judiciary Committee, he had served as chief counsel and staff director for the committee. Hence, Judge Shedd was not unfamiliar with how unforgiving the politics of Senate confirmation of judicial nominees has become over the past two decades.

Although Judge Shedd had the support of South Carolina's other senator, Democrat Ernest F. Hollings, he drew immediate opposition from the National Association for the Advancement of Colored People (NAACP). Dwight James, director of South Carolina's NAACP chapter, attacked Shedd's eleven-year record on the federal bench for exhibiting "a deep and abiding hostility to civil rights cases."[34] As with several other nominees, Judge Shedd also invited criticism for his rulings defending states' rights and limiting congressional power. In particular, he had struck down the federal Driver's Privacy Protection Act, which mandated that personal information, such as home address and telephone number, that had been collected by departments of motor vehicles be kept confidential and not sold by state agencies to insurance companies and law firms. In Shedd's view, the act infringed on the Tenth Amendment and exceeded Congress's power over the regulation of interstate commerce, but his decision went too far even for the Rehnquist Court, which reversed it and upheld the act in an opinion delivered by none other than Chief Justice Rehnquist himself.[35]

Likewise, Bush's two nominees to the Sixth Circuit provoked opposition. Ohio Supreme Court Justice Deborah L. Cook was twice elected, in 1994 and 2000, to the state bench, but she now came under attack for being too probusiness and anti–consumer protection. The other, Jeffrey S. Sutton, an attorney in the well-regarded firm of Jones, Day, Reavis & Pogue, had been born in Saudi Arabia and, after graduating from law school, had clerked for Justices Powell and Scalia. An officer in the Federalist Society's Separation of Powers and Federalism practice group, he had previously been nominated by the first President Bush, but his nomination never reached the Senate floor for a vote. Within legal circles, Sutton is well known for championing the Eleventh Amendment guarantee of states' sovereign immunity as a limitation on congressional legislation authorizing private lawsuits to force states to comply with federal law. His position, to be sure, was eventually embraced by a majority of the Rehnquist Court but split the justices 5–4, again along conservative versus liberal lines.[36] Not surprisingly, perhaps, the People for the American Way and other liberal groups criticized his appellate court work for seeking to curtail congressional power and for limiting federal protections against discrimination based on age, disabilities, gender, race, and religion. In the two months following his nomination, more than 50 national organizations and over 220 state and local groups came out against his confirmation.[37]

Even more controversial was Bush's nomination of University of Utah Law School professor Michael W. McConnell for a seat on the Court of Appeals for the Tenth Circuit. Based on academic accomplishments, McConnell appeared exceptionally well suited, but he was not given a hearing until 18 September 2002, sixteen months after his nomination. After receiving his law degree from the University of Chicago, where he was an editor on the law review, he had clerked for Justice Brennan and had subsequently served in the Reagan administration for two years as an assistant solicitor general before returning as a professor to the University of Chicago, where he taught for twelve years prior to moving to Utah in 1997.

Also a member of the Federalist Society, McConnell sparked immediate and significant criticism from liberal groups. Although a staunch defender of religious freedom under the First Amendment free exercise clause, he had a reputation for challenging the "high wall of separation" of church and state and for championing vouchers for religious schools, which a bare majority of the Rehnquist Court had upheld in its 2002 ruling in *Zelman v. Simmons-Harris*,[38] with the justices again dividing 5–4 along conservative versus liberal lines. No less controversially, McConnell had spoken out on the "third-rail" of American politics, abortion, dismissing the landmark ruling in *Roe v. Wade* as "illegitimate" and "an embarrassment." Moreover, he had endorsed a 1996 "pro-life" statement asserting that abortion "kills 1.5 million innocent human beings in America every year" and calling for a constitutional amendment to outlaw the practice. Women's organizations and liberal groups therefore staunchly opposed McConnell's nomination.

Just as controversial were Bush's two nominees to the Court of Appeals for the District of Columbia Circuit— both because of their conservative views and because that circuit is widely considered the second most powerful court in the country, next to the Supreme Court, because Congress has designated it to hear appeals from federal agencies. The D.C. Circuit, therefore, has a major impact on the implementation of federal regulations and public policies. Moreover, John G. Roberts Jr. was nominated to fill the seat of Judge James L. Buckley, a conservative Reagan appointee, whereas Miguel A. Estrada would fill the seat of Judge Patricia M. Wald, a liberal Carter appointee, and if confirmed, these two conservatives would solidify the Republican balance on the D.C. Circuit, where five of the nine active judges are Republican appointees. In addition, as earlier noted, the D.C. Circuit is regarded as a stepping-stone to the Supreme Court. Three current justices—Scalia, Thomas, and Ginsburg—were elevated from there, as would have been Reagan's ill-fated nominees, Judges Bork and Douglas Ginsberg. In sum, Roberts and Estrada would not only reinforce the conservatism of the D.C. Circuit but also would be positioned for the fast track to the Supreme Court.

Roberts and Estrada also had much in common. Besides being identified as "movement conservatives," both were in their early forties, graduates of Harvard Law School, where they were editors on the law review, and had clerked at the Supreme Court, Roberts for Chief Justice Rehnquist and Estrada for Justice Kennedy. Both had subsequently worked in the Reagan administration, before joining prominent D.C. law firms. After his clerkship, Roberts became a special assistant to Attorney General Smith and then spent four years as associate White House counsel for Reagan. From 1989 to 1993 Roberts had served as principal deputy solicitor general and then joined the firm of Hogan & Hartson. After his clerkship Estrada, who was born in Honduras, had also joined the office of the solicitor general, under Kenneth W. Starr, and remained there through much of Clinton's administration, until 1997, when Theodore Olson recruited him to join his firm, Gibson, Dunn & Crutcher. During that time, he won two-thirds of the fifteen cases he argued before the Supreme Court.

Estrada was finally given a hearing by the Senate Judiciary Committee over a year after his nomination, on 26 September 2002. It was highly contentious, dividing even Hispanic groups. Estrada's sharply conservative views and upper-middle-class background set him apart from the larger Hispanic community, according to the Congressional Hispanic Caucus and the Puerto Rican Legal Defense and Education Fund, which opposed his confirmation. By contrast, the League of United Latin American Citizens, the Hispanic National Bar Association, and the Cuban-American National Foundation supported his confirmation; they and the White House praised Estrada's impressive professional achievements and immigrant background. But, liberal Democratic senators and interest groups worried that Estrada, who would become the first Hispanic on the D.C. Circuit, would then be on the fast track to the Supreme Court—they recalled that the first President Bush had named Clarence Thomas to that court just a year before elevating him to the Supreme Court. Democratic opponents to Estrada, as Senator Hatch bluntly put it, were "afraid Bush will nominate him to the Supreme Court where he won't toe their left-of-center line."[39] In short, both Roberts and Estrada have impressive academic and professional qualifications, along with well-established connections to the D.C. conservative legal community. And that is precisely why Bush nominated them and why liberals vigorously opposed holding hearings on their nominations and Senate confirmation.

In addition to stalling hearings on Bush's most conservative nominees, the Democratic majority on the Senate Judiciary Committee underscored its message to the president by rejecting two nominees to the Fifth Circuit, Judge Pickering and Texas Supreme Court Justice Owen. Both were defeated in the committee, with the ten Democratic senators voting against the nine Republicans to reject sending their nominations to the full Senate for a vote. Notably, if the Judiciary Committee had reported their nominations, both would in all likelihood have been confirmed, though by very narrow margins, by the full Senate; conservative Georgia Democratic Senator Zell Miller and Senator Hollings, for instance, said they would vote to confirm Owens if her nomination went to the floor of the Senate. Therefore, Democratic senators on the Judiciary Committee killed their nominations by not reporting them out of committee—a tactic not used since 1991 to defeat an appellate court nominee. Their message was unambiguous: in the words of New York's Democratic Senator Charles E. Schumer, "There's clearly no mandate from the American people to stack the courts with conservative ideologues. So if the White House persists in sending us nominees who threaten to throw the courts out of whack with the country, we have no choice but to vote 'no.'"[40]

The Fifth Circuit, which includes Mississippi, Louisiana, and Texas, was considered already too conservative in the view of Democrats, and Judge Pickering and Justice Owen were opposed as too conservative, based on their voting records and opinions on such red-hot issues as abortion and racial discrimination. Judge Pickering, a 64-year-old federal district court judge in Mississippi who had been appointed in 1990 by Bush's father, was challenged for ethical lapses, for his opposition to abortion, and for demonstrating during his twelve years on the bench an "insensitivity to civil rights concerns."[41]

Likewise, Justice Owen's record sparked heated opposition from liberal groups. After graduating first in her class at Baylor Law School, she became the second woman to serve on the Texas Supreme Court. However, Justice Owen, an adviser to the Austin chapter of the Federalist Society, immediately came in for criticism on grounds that her rulings placed her on "the far right wing" of the state supreme court, even farther to the right than then-Governor George W. Bush's appointees. In particular, Justice Owen had dissented from a decision invalidating Texas's parental consent law for minors seeking to obtain abortions. Notably, in that case, then-Texas Supreme Court Justice Alberto Gonzalez, voting with the majority, had criticized Owen's dissent as "an unconscionable act of judicial activism."[42] And Democratic senators repeatedly reminded their colleagues of that remark when voting against sending her nomination to the full Senate for a vote.

Conclusion

Much thus turned on the outcome of the November 2002 Senate elections. Not surprisingly, President Bush drew attention to the importance of regaining Republican control of the Senate by emphasizing the need for confirmation of his judicial nominees. Less than a week before the 5 November 2002 election, Bush claimed that there was a "vacancy crisis" on the federal bench and proposed four major but highly problematic changes in the process for selecting and confirming federal judges. First, he proposed that federal judges notify the White House a year in advance of their intention to retire, in order for the Department of Justice to begin earlier searches to fill forthcoming vacancies. For a variety of reasons, however, federal judges may not plan or want their retirement plans known that far in advance. Second, Bush proposed sending nominations to the Senate within 180 days of notification of a pending vacancy. While this proposal aimed to expedite the judicial selection process, based on past practice it did not appear likely that home-state senators would move that expeditiously.[43] Third, Bush called on the Senate Judiciary Committee to hold hearings on judicial nominees within 90 days of receiving their nominations. And fourth, he called on the full Senate to hold a floor vote within 180 days of receiving a judicial nomination.[44] Both of these two latter proposals appeared unrealistic, and both Democratic and some Republican senators took sharp exception to Bush's attempt to intrude on how the Senate operates and attempt to influence its practices and traditions.

The chair of the Senate Judiciary Committee, Senator Leahy, immediately responded by pointing out that seventy-six of Bush's judicial nominees had been nominated more than 180 days after the position became available. There were also fourteen judgeships that remained vacant for more than 180 days without Bush nominating a candidate, and Bush had not forwarded nominees for twenty-six of the seventy-seven current vacancies on the federal bench. Leahy also laid the blame for delays in the confirmation process on the president's ideological judicial selection process. In his words,

> President Bush said he wanted to be a uniter and not a divider, but he has nominated several appellate court nominees who divide the American people and who divide the Senate, and controversial nominations always take longer. The President can help by choosing nominees not primarily for their ideology but for their fairness. The Senate has clearly shown that consensus nominees are acted on promptly.[45]

With the victories in the 2002 midterm elections, Republicans regained control of the Senate and the Judiciary Committee. Consequently, several of the circuit court nominees that the Democratic-controlled Judiciary Committee had stalled were subsequently confirmed, most notably Judges Shedd and Rogers for the Fourth and Fifth Circuits, as well as Michael McConnell for the Tenth Circuit. But Democrats dug in for bitter fights against Bush's most conservative and controversial appellate court nominees. They filibustered to deny confirmation votes on the Senate floor for several, including Fifth Circuit court nominees Judge Pickering and Priscilla R. Owen, whom Bush renominated in defiance after his party regained control of the Senate. The Democrats' tactic of filibustering also resulted in Miguel A. Estrada's withdrawing his nomination for a seat on the Court of Appeals for the District of Columbia. Estrada was thereby denied a seat and experience on a prestigious appellate court from which several justices—Antonin Scalia, Clarence Thomas, and Ruth Bader Ginsburg—had been elevated and on which sat Reagan's two unsuccessful Supreme Court nominees, Robert H. Bork and Douglas H. Ginsburg. In retaliation Bush nominated to that court a no less controversial conservative, Janice Rogers Brown. An African American woman and California state court justice, Brown was immediately opposed by the Congressional Black Caucus and confronted a possible Democratic filibuster. With Senate Republicans unable to muster the sixty votes needed for cloture and defeating filibusters, the war over judgeships only intensified.

Still, only Bush's most controversial nominees were delayed, and only a few defeated or forced to withdraw. In Bush's first two years in office, the Democratic-controlled Senate confirmed 17 of 32 circuit court nominees (53 percent), and 83 of his 99 nominees for district courts (83 percent), for a total of 100 judges out of 131 nominations (76 percent).[46] And, ironically, in 2003 the Republican-controlled Senate confirmed another 12 of 19 appellate court nominees (41 percent), and 54 of 74 district court nominations (72 percent), or 66 judges from his 104 additional nominations (63 percent).[47] In sum, roughly 70 percent of Bush's judicial nominations were confirmed during his first three years in office.

Federal judgeships were certain to loom even larger in the 2004 election. In anticipation, Senate Majority Leader Bill Frist (R-Tenn.) considered raising their visibility by forcing cloture votes on nominations that Democrats had stopped, thereby establishing a record of obstructionism and a basis for proposing the so-called nuclear option of reducing the number of votes needed for cloture and forcing Senate votes on judicial nominees. For his part, at virtually every fund-raising event for the presidential election Bush underscored the importance of his naming conservative judges to the federal bench. Both sides in the escalating war over federal judgeships understood that the stakes were higher in 2004 than in the midterm elections. The 2004 presidential election held out the ultimate prize that had eluded Bush even after the midterm elections, namely, the prospect of filling vacancies on the Supreme Court in the likely event that two or more justices retired after the election due to their ages, and thus reinforcing the conservative direction of the bare majority on the Court that decided the 2000 presidential election.

Notes

1. For further discussion, see David M. O'Brien, "Judicial Legacies: The Clinton Presidency and the Courts," in Colin Campbell and Bert A. Rockman, eds., *The Clinton Legacy* (New York: Chatham House, 2000), 96–117.
2. For further discussion of appointments to the Court, see David M. O'Brien, *Storm Center: The Supreme Court in American Politics*, 6th ed. (New York: Norton, 2003), 32–104; and Henry J. Abraham, *Justices, Presidents, and Senators: A History of the U.S. Supreme Court Appointments from Washington to Clinton* (Lanham, Md.: Rowman & Littlefield, 1999).
3. *Roe v. Wade*, 410 U.S. 113 (1973).
4. For further discussion, see David M. O'Brien, "Federal Judgeships in Retrospect," in W. Elliot Brownlee and Hugh Davis Graham, eds., *The Reagan Presidency: Pragmatic Conservatism and Its Legacies* (Lawrence: University Press of Kansas, 2003), 327–354. See, generally, Sheldon Goldman, *Picking Federal Judges: Lower Court Selection From Roosevelt Through Reagan* (New Haven: Yale University Press, 1997); and Elliot E. Slotnick, "A Historical Perspective on Federal Judicial Selection," *Judicature* 86 (July–August 2002), 13–16.
5. See Sheldon Goldman, Elliot Slotnick, Gerard Gryski, and Gary Zuk, "Clinton's Judges: Summing Up the Legacy," *Judicature* 84 (2001): 228–53; and O'Brien, "Judicial Legacies."
6. *Bush v. Gore*, 531 U.S. 98 (2000). For critical assessments of the ruling, see Vincent Bugliosi, *The Betrayal of America: How the Supreme Court Undermined the Constitution and Chose Our President* (New York: Thunder's Mouth Press, 2001); and Alan Dershowitz, *Supreme Injustice: How the High Court Hijacked the Election 2000* (New York: Oxford University Press, 2001). For a pragmatic defense of the decision, see Richard A. Posner, *Breaking the Deadlock: The 2000 Election, the Constitution, and the Courts* (Princeton: Princeton University Press, 2001). See also Howard Gillman, *The Votes That Counted: How the Court Decided the 2000 Presidential Election* (Chicago: University of Chicago Press, 2001).
7. *Bush v. Palm Beach County Canvassing Board*, 531 U.S. 70 (2000).
8. Quoted by Neil A. Lewis, "Bush May Face Hurdles in Shaping Courts," *Chattanooga Times/Chattanooga Free Press*, 2 January 2001, A1.
9. See, e.g., *Planned Parenthood Association of Kansas City v. Ashcroft*, 462 U.S. 476 (1983).
10. See O'Brien, "Judicial Legacies"and "Reagan Judges," as well as the Office of Legal Policy's web site at www.usdoj.gov/olp/history.htm.
11. For further discussion, see David M. O'Brien, *Judicial Roulette* (New York: Twentieth Century Foundation/Priority Press Publications, 1988), 81–95.
12. Quoted in Amy Goldstein, "Bush Curtails ABA Role in Selecting U.S. Judges," *Washington Post*, 23 March 2001, A1.

13. Press Release, 22 March 2001, available at www.afj.org/jsp/newsabarelease.html.

14. For further discussion, see O'Brien, "Judicial Legacies."

15. See Thomas B. Edsall, "Democrats Push Bush for Input on Judges," *Washington Post*, 28 April 2001, A4; and Jonathan Ringel, "Bush Staff Learning Pitfalls of Getting Judicial Picks through the Senate," *American Lawyer*, 1 May 2001 (available on Lexis-Nexis).

16. Quoted in ibid.

17. Quoted in Helen Dewar, "Daschle Warns GOP on Judicial Confirmations," *Washington Post*, 3 May 2001, A19.

18. Quoted by George Lardner Jr., "'Careful' Judicial Vetting Process," *Washington Post*, 19 April 2001, A13.

19. For a good history and analysis of the "blue-slip" process, see Brannon P. Denning, "The Judicial Confirmation Process and the Blue Slip," *Judicature* 85 (March–April 2002), 218–26. See also Stephen B. Burbank, "Politics, Privilege & Power: The Senate's Role in the Appointment of Federal Judges," *Judicature* 86 (July–August 2002), 24–27.

20. Quoted by Mary Alice Robbins and Jonathan Ringel, "Bush Nominates Owen, Clement to Vacant 5th Circuit Slots," *Texas Lawyer*, 14 May 2001, 1.

21. See Id.

22. Quoted by Scott Shepard, "Senator's Declaration of Independence Still Reverberating in D.C.," *Austin American Statesman*, 26 May 2002, A19.

23. Quoted in Associated Press, "Demos Celebrate Jeffords' Defection," *Desert News*, 26 May 2002, A13.

24. Quoted in Shepard, "Senator's Declaration of Independence."

25. Quoted in Gail Russell Chaddock, "What Jeffords Got, A Year after Switch," *Christian Science Monitor*, 24 May 2002, 1.

26. Quoted in Alison Mitchell, "Daschle Says Most Nominees Will Get a Senate Vote," *New York Times*, 9 June 2001, A1.

27. Quoted in Audrey Hudson, "GOP: Bush Nominees Treated Unfairly; Have Relatively Low Confirmation Rate," *Washington Times*, 2 April 2002, A4.

28. Quoted in ibid.

29. CNN Live Event, 3 May 2002, transcript 050301CN.V54, available on Lexis-Nexis.

30. See White Burkett Miller Center of Public Affairs, *Improving the Process of Appointing Federal Judges* (Charlottesville: Miller Center, University of Virginia, 1996); and The Century Foundation, *Justice Held Hostage: Politics and Selecting Federal Judges* (New York: Century Foundation, 2000).

31. As of 1 January 2003. Excluded are appointees to the federal court of claims.

32. Robbins and Ringel, "Bush Nominates Owen, Clement."

33. See Dan Eggen, "Clinton Names Black Judge to Appeals Court; Recess Choice for Richmond Is Challenge to GOP," *Washington Post*, 8 December 2000, A1.

34. Quoted in Tom Jackson, "Judicial Nomination Alarms Rights Groups," *Washington Post*, 25 June 2002, A5.

35. *Reno v. Condon*, 528 U.S. 141 (2000).

36. See, for example, *Seminole Tribe of Florida v. Florida*, 517 U.S. 44 (1996); *Alden v. Maine*, 527 U.S. 706 (1999); *Florida Prepaid Postsecondary Education Expense Board v. College Savings Bank*, 527 U.S. 627 (1999); *Kimel v. Florida Board of Regents*, 527 U.S. 62 (2000); and *Board of Trustees of the University of Alabama v. Garrett*, 531 U.S. 356 (2001).

37. See www.pfaw.org/issues/judiciary/reports/judicialreport/bushadmin.html.

38. *Zelman v. Simmons-Harris*, 122 S.Ct. 2460 (2002).

39. Quoted in Charles Lane, "Nominee for Court Faces Two Battles," *Washington Post*, 24 September 2002, A1, A10.

40. Quoted by Helen Dewar and Amy Goldstein, "Appeals Court Choice Rejected," *Washington Post*, 15 March 2002, A1.

41. See, e.g., "Blacks' Protests Doom Pickering's Appeals Court Confirmation," *Jet*, 1 April 2002, 4; and compare Terry Eastland, "A Nomination Worth Fighting For," *Weekly Standard* 13 (4 March 2002).

42. Quoted by Neil A. Lewis, "Democrats Reject Bush Pick in Battle over Court Balance," *New York Times*, 6 September 2002, A1. See also the reports on the web site of Texans for Public Justice at www.tpj.org.

43. See, e.g., Century Foundation, *Justice Held Hostage*.

44. See "President Announces Plan for Timely Consideration of Judicial Nominees," 30 October 2002, at www.whitehouse.gov/news/releases/2002/10/print/20021030-4.html.

45. "Comments of Judiciary Committee Chairman Patrick Leahy on the White House Proposal On Judicial Nominations, Wednesday, Oct. 30, 2002," press release, available at http://leahy.senate.gov/press/200210/103002.html.

46. For further discussion, see Sheldon Goldman, Elliot Slotnick, Gerard Gryski, Gary Zuk, and Sara Schiavoni, "George W. Bush Remaking the Judiciary: Like Father Like Son? 86 *Jucidature* 282–309 (May–June, 2003); and Lisa Holmes and Elisha Savchak, "Judicial Appointment Politics in the 107th Congress," 86 *Judicature* 232–257 (March–April, 2003).

47. As of October 28, 2003, and based on www.usdoj.gov/olp/judicialnominations.htm.

CHAPTER 7

Deliberations of a "Compassionate Conservative"

George W. Bush's Domestic Presidency

Gary Mucciaroni and Paul J. Quirk

IN A CENTRAL THEME of his 2000 election campaign, George W. Bush promised to produce results in domestic policy. As he said in one of the televised debates, "I can get something positive done on behalf of the people. That's what the question in this campaign is about. It's not only what's your philosophy and what's your position on issues, but can you get things done? And I believe I can."[1] In elaborating such claims, he referred to domestic issues—cutting taxes, improving education, reforming Social Security, and others.

Bush's emphasis on domestic policy was partly a reaction to the experience of his father, George H.W. Bush, whose inadequate domestic efforts contributed to his failure to be reelected president in 1992. Indeed, the elder Bush's defeat bore several lessons about presidential domestic policy: the need for a paramount commitment to economic growth and high employment, which he had overlooked in trying to ride out the 1990–91 recession; the value of a coherent general conception of public policy, which he had dismissed as "the vision thing"; and the importance of keeping faith with core constituencies, whom he had alienated by reneging on a "read-my-lips" campaign pledge to oppose new taxes. Notwithstanding the redirection of national priorities to the war on terrorism after the September 11th attacks, George W. Bush and his advisers remained mindful that a lack of attention to the economy and other domestic issues could sink his presidency.

Bush's concern with producing results, as opposed to merely trading in philosophy and positions, also reflected the particular philosophy that Bush proclaimed in his campaign—a moderate, pragmatic approach that he called "compassionate conservatism." To be sure, Bush embraced conservative Republican principles of individual responsibility, private enterprise, and resistance to government spending, taxes, and regulation. But he also purported to marry these principles to sincere compassion for the disadvantaged, and he accepted some modifications of Republican orthodoxy. He granted the necessity of the federal government's playing an active role in solving problems in education, health care, and other areas and in enabling private and nonprofit organizations to assist those in need. Bush's "compassionate conservative" stance mirrored the moderate "New Democrat" stance that Bill Clinton had employed in two successful presidential campaigns. It was an appealing posture for swing voters, such as many Catholics, who were conservative on moral issues but supported helping the disadvantaged. And it called for identifying conservative forms of government intervention that would make a genuine difference in Americans' lives.

In what follows, we review Bush's efforts and performance on several leading domestic issues. On the whole, the results fell short of these aspirations. Bush had two significant political successes in domestic policy—on tax cuts and education—before the 2002 midterm election, and a third—creating a Homeland Security Department—in the lame-duck session after the election. His faith-based initiative was blocked, although some Republicans held out hope of reviving it in the 108th Congress. In all of these cases, however, Bush and his domestic advisers apparently overlooked important questions about the feasibility of his proposals or their likely consequences. As a result, his substantive achievements were, if anything, less impressive than his political successes.

Bush's domestic presidency also was beset by economic misfortune. Despite the lessons of his father, Bush was unable to escape a long economic downturn that sent unemployment to 6 percent, the highest level in eight years, by the fall of 2002. A year later the jobless rate remained stubbornly at the same level, despite robust economic growth in the third quarter of 2003.[2] The Republicans achieved major gains in the midterm elections—an historic political victory for President Bush. But these gains reflected the salience to voters of international affairs and the war on terrorism, and their satisfaction with Bush's performance in these areas, far more than approval of his domestic leadership.

Coalitions and Deliberation

What President Bush set out to do, according to his campaign rhetoric, was not easy. In general, he faced two kinds of obstacles to realizing his aspirations for domestic policy. First, a president who seeks to pursue a centrist agenda—"compassionate conservative" or "New Democrat"—faces increasingly difficult problems of coalition-building in Congress. For more than a decade, the number of moderates in Congress has been declining, as the congressional parties have become increasingly polarized.[3] Thus the natural base of support for a moderate presidential agenda has shrunk, and the opposition base—liberal Democrats and conservative Republicans—has grown. It has become easier for hard-line liberals and conservatives to join forces to defeat a moderate proposal.

These difficulties create strong temptations for a centrist president who wants to build a domestic record. One tendency, reflected in the first two years of the Clinton presidency, is to revert to hard-line ideological positions and exploit the reliable support from the president's own party.[4] This approach is simply to abandon the centrist position, perhaps maintaining it as a rhetorical posture. A second tendency for a centrist president, often reflected in the later Clinton years, is ad hoc opportunism—to adopt whatever policies, liberal or conservative, have the most powerful mass-public or interest-group support.[5] This results in a record that is centrist, on average, but may include individual measures that are ideologically divisive, as when Clinton signed the welfare reform bill in 1996. This approach sacrifices substantive merit and the concern for genuinely effective policies to the pursuit of political convenience. Finally, a third tendency is to settle for lowest-common denominator agreements to achieve bipartisan consensus. Such agreements are those that minimize the importance and political difficulty of the concessions that each side is required to make, rather than maximizing the effectiveness and substantive payoffs of the resulting policy. The hallmark of such agreements is the avoidance of fundamental policy change that could produce major benefits.

Second, a president who aspires to achieve substantive results and make a real difference to Americans' lives must overcome several threats to sound deliberation. To make good decisions on public policy, presidents, with the help of their advisers, must gather information about policies and their effects, and must weigh that information thoughtfully and intelligently.[6] In particular, they must form expectations for the effects of policies that are more-or-less realistic—given what we know, and what we don't know, about how the policies are likely to work. Effective deliberation will of course give considerable weight to the president's general beliefs about government and society, such as a conservative president's general trust in free markets or a liberal's faith in government programs. But such beliefs will be tempered by facts, and by bona fide specialized knowledge. A careful decision maker, for example, will take into account the available evidence on the success or failure of particular programs.

Presidents must also balance substantive considerations—what will work—with political ones—what will pass, and what will enhance the president's political support.[7] This requires balancing advice from the *policy* side of the White House—especially the Council of Economic Advisers and the Domestic Policy Staff—with that from the *political* side—especially the communications director, the congressional relations staff, and other senior political advisers.

Unfortunately, certain tendencies in presidential politics can easily undermine such deliberation.[8] Presidents may placate key ideological constituencies at the expense of sacrificing broader interests or ignoring evidence about the effects of policies. They may pander to an uninformed general public. They may prefer bold, even if substantively dubious solutions. They may form and promote grossly exaggerated expectations about policy benefits. And they may overlook warnings about the costs and risks of their proposals. Indeed, presidents are often prone toward wishful thinking about their policies. In the competitive environment of the White House, their advisers often shrink from the dangerous task of giving them bad news.

Two specific threats to intelligent presidential deliberation are worth mentioning. Presidents, like the public, may over-learn the apparent lessons of the recent past. For many years after the Vietnam War, for example, presidents were extraordinarily reluctant to contemplate even minimal forms of military intervention. They also may ignore political constraints that will affect implementation of their plans. In considering the budgetary effects of a tax cut or a spending initiative, for example, a president may forget that Congress will continue to face new pressures to cut taxes and raise spending. For any of these reasons, presidents may ignore critical information that does not fit their assumptions or hopes. When they do so, they will make decisions whose foreseeable effects they do not intend.

As we will see, President Bush's ability to deliver on his promises of compassionate conservatism and domestic accomplishment was severely hampered by these difficulties of coalition building and of deliberation.

Staffing for Domestic Policy

How a president performs in policymaking depends in large part on the policy inclinations and the decision-making and organizational skills of the people he selects for high-level positions in the White House and the executive branch. Bush's domestic team—Cabinet members and White House staff, along with Vice President Dick Cheney—had some strengths for implementing a pragmatic compassionate-conservative agenda. But it also had serious weaknesses with respect to maintaining a centrist approach based on sound deliberation.

The Bush domestic policy team was prone to capture by the ideological right. For the most part, Bush's appointments to the Cabinet stressed moderation over ideology, and managerial competence over policy expertise. As the *New York Times* described it prior to the inauguration, "Mr. Bush has shunned champions of conservative causes. Instead, he has favored can-do managers with low-key styles. . . . It is a lineup for an administration that intends to submerge ideology in the name of efficiency. By and large, Mr. Bush's choices are pragmatic conservatives."[9] In fact, however, the *Times's* inference that ideology was to be submerged in favor of efficiency proved erroneous.

Appointments to the White House staff were divided between pragmatic, policy-oriented advisers and more ideological and politically-minded ones. During 2001, the staff reflected some degree of balance. According to Chief of Staff Andrew Card, there was an ongoing tug-of-war between two long-time, trusted associates of Bush—the moderate and pragmatic communications director, Karen Hughes, and the partisan, Christian-conservative senior adviser to the president for strategic initiatives, Karl Rove.[10]

But even then, hard-line conservatives generally had the upper hand in administration policies. Vice President Cheney, formerly one of the most conservative members of the House of Representatives, played an influential role in the administration's decisions. Cheney was so powerful that Bush sometimes went out of his way to counter the impression that Cheney, and not he, was making the important policy decisions. Two of Bush's major cabinet appointees were champions of conservative causes—Interior Secretary Gale Norton, a militant advocate of placing economic development above environmental concerns, and Attorney General John Ashcroft, a hard-line Christian conservative. And Bush relied heavily on corporate executives for top positions concerned with economic, environmental, and regulatory issues. Bush and Cheney had been executives in the energy industry. Harvey Pitt, Bush's selection as chairman of the Securities and Exchange Commission, had been one of the leading Wall Street opponents of proposals to strengthen regulation of corporate accounting.[11]

In Bush's second year, the ideological tug-of-war essentially ended, with the moderates vanquished. When Hughes departed the White House for family reasons in the spring of 2002, Card told *Esquire* reporter Ron Suskind that he feared Rove would dominate the White House and Bush would get imbalanced advice.[12] The premonition was evidently accurate. In late spring, Rove was the first person Card briefed on the plan to create a Department of Homeland Security.[13] By the end of the year, a senior White House official, speaking anonymously to Suskind, said that after Hughes' departure, "Karl went from prime minister to King. Amazing. . . and a little scary. Now no one will speak candidly about him or take him on or contradict him. Pure power, no real accountability. It's just 'listen to Karl and everything will work out.'"[14] Much as the Clinton White House was dominated by liberal ideologues in 1993 and 1994, the configuration of Bush's domestic team created the hazard that his agenda, or parts of it, would be hijacked by the right.

According to insider accounts given to Suskind, moreover, the Bush domestic team gave short shrift to substantive deliberation—indeed, they hardly even attempted it. John DiIulio, an academic policy expert who worked in the Bush White House as codirector of the Faith-Based Initiatives program until the late summer of 2001, told Suskind,

I heard many, many staff discussions but not three meaningful, substantive policy discussions. . . . There were no actual policy white papers on domestic issues. . . .[O]n social policy and related issues, the lack of even basic policy knowledge, and the only casual interest in knowing more, was somewhat breathtaking: discussions by fairly senior people who meant *Medicaid* but were talking *Medicare*; near-instant shifts from discussing any actual policy pros and cons to discussing political communications, media strategy, et cetera.[15]

Domestic policymaking was dominated by Rove and the political side of the White House. "This approach to policymaking," wrote Suskind, "[was] a fairly radical departure from the customary relationship between White House political directors and policy professionals. Each has always influenced the other, of course; but the political office has rarely been so central to guiding policy in virtually every area, deciding what is promoted and what is tabled."[16] We cannot take these accounts, all reported by a single (though well-regarded) journalist, entirely at face value. What they suggest, however, is a presidential domestic policymaking process that has been seriously lacking in deliberative capacity or even intent.[17]

Four Cases of Policymaking

Domestic policymaking in the Bush presidency has centered largely on four issues. Three of them—tax cuts, education reform, and faith-based social-services delivery—were planned elements of Bush's agenda. Bush had been politically successful with each of these issues as governor of Texas. The 2000 Republican platform had listed them as central items in the party's plan for governing.[18] And Bush had given them top priority in his election campaign. The fourth domestic issue of great importance was not anticipated: Bush devoted enormous time and energy dealing with "homeland security" in response to the terrorist attacks of September 2001.

In each case, we first tell the story of President Bush's proposals, the debates concerning them, and the political outcome. We then assess the president's decisions and the quality of the administration's deliberations, and briefly consider likely consequences.[19]

Taxes and the Economy: Faith-Based Economics

George W. Bush's single most important campaign promise was a $1.3 trillion reduction in federal taxes over ten years. Most of the reductions, he said, would come in lower income-tax rates for all taxpayers. The plan called, for example, for lowering the rate on the first $12,000 of income from 15 to 12 percent, and that on incomes above $200,000 from 39.5 to 33 percent. He also called for repealing the estate tax, eliminating the "marriage penalty," doubling the child credit, and increasing the deductibility of charitable contributions. Because the tax cut would also add $300 billion in interest costs, its total estimated cost was $1.6 trillion. In the end, Bush got most of what he sought, as Congress approved cuts costing $1.35 trillion over ten years, a reduction of about 9 percent in federal revenue.[20] In 2003 Congress approved another round of tax cuts, which totaled $350 billion. Those cuts dropped the top tax bracket from 38.6 to 35 percent and increased the child care tax credit from $600 to $1,000 per child.[21]

The rationale that Bush offered for the tax cut varied considerably with changing circumstances. "I want to give some of your money back," he declared during the campaign. "See, I don't think the surplus is the government's money. I think it's the people's money."[22] In addition, with the economy apparently healthy, the Congressional Budget Office (CBO) estimated the budget surplus at $2.1 trillion over ten years. Bush took the estimate at face value and projected that the proposed tax cut would leave $500 billion for debt reduction and increased spending on education and other domestic programs. In addition, he promised to save $200 billion by "improving the way government works."[23]

When signs of recession appeared after the election, however, the president shifted ground and argued that the tax cut was needed to boost the economy. Then, when Senate Democrats proposed a small, temporary tax cut for that purpose, he shifted, once more, to the supply-side argument that a permanent, multi-year cut was necessary for long-term economic health. He argued that it would give businesses and investors the necessary certainty about future cash flows to "expand their job base and make new capital purchases."[24] Finally, when energy prices increased sharply in the spring of 2001, he added yet another rationale: tax cuts would provide relief to hard-pressed consumers.[25]

In fact, there was no debate over the basic question of whether to cut taxes. Democratic presidential candidate Al Gore had also proposed tax cuts during the campaign, and congressional Democrats continued to support them after the election. All the disagreement was about the structure and magnitude of the cuts. By contrast with Bush's proposals, Democratic plans called for more modest cuts, targeted more specific purposes, and favored lower-income taxpayers.

Critics of the Bush plan, including many economists and financial experts as well as Democrats, had three major areas of concern: affordability, economic soundness, and fairness.[26] The affordability of the Bush plan was much in doubt. The case for the plan assumed that the economic trends producing surpluses would continue ten years into the future—a remarkable assumption, considering the vagaries of the business cycle and the uncertainties of long-range economic forecasting. It also counted surpluses in the Medicare and government-retirement programs that could not be used for other purposes. And it overlooked the likelihood of increased spending in several areas: education, the military, prescription-drug benefits for the elderly, and Social Security private investment accounts.[27]

There were strong objections to the economics of the tax cut—its value both for short-term economic stimulation and for long-term economic growth. In view of the need for debate and action in Congress, the tax cut likely would come too late to do much good in speeding recovery. Instead, the stimulus could easily kick in at the beginning of a new boom, when it might overheat the economy. In any case, most of the tax cut was "backloaded" up to ten years into the future, far too late to affect the current recession. With respect to the long term, critics argued that the tax cut would impede economic growth by slowing progress in paying down the national debt.[28]

Finally, liberals argued that the Bush tax cut was too sharply tilted toward upper-income groups. They noted that the richest 1 percent of taxpayers would get up to 45 percent of the benefits while the poorest 60 percent, with incomes below $44,000, would receive less than 13 percent of them.[29]

The Bush administration answered some of the criticisms. The Council of Economic Advisers pointed out that there was a shortage of evidence that budget deficits significantly affect long-term interest rates or economic growth.[30] To support claims of a near-term stimulus effect, it made part of the cut retroactive to January 2001 and argued that even the promise of a tax cut would buoy consumer spirits.[31] With regard to equity, the administration argued that higher-income taxpayers received greater benefits in absolute dollars simply because they paid more in taxes; as a proportion of their incomes, lower income taxpayers would benefit more.[32]

Just two years after the end of a fifteen-year period of constant concern about budget deficits, public support for the Bush tax cut was weak.[33] According to polls, 60 percent favored using the surplus "to help make the Social Security and Medicare programs financially sound" or "for increased spending on domestic programs such as health, education and the environment." Only 19 percent preferred using the money for a tax cut, about the same number that wanted it used for debt reduction.[34] And a majority preferred a smaller tax cut than Bush proposed.[35]

The problems of affordability and economics, tepid public support, and Democratic resistance did not induce Bush to trim his proposal. Rather, he pressed Congress hard to enact the plan largely intact. Ever mindful of his father's experience, Bush was determined to prove his allegiance to economic conservatives in the Republican Party. The *New York Times* found "something almost Oedipal in Mr. Bush's revitalization of Republican stereotypes, as if by invoking them he can avoid the conservative revolt on taxes that upended his father's presidency."[36] In addition, the tax cut had been the major domestic proposal of Bush's campaign.

To abandon it during the honeymoon period would have been an embarrassment to his presidency.[37]

Because Republicans controlled the Senate by only a single vote, they could not pass the bill simply by relying on party support. They were able, however, to use their control of the agenda to consider the tax cut apart from the regular budget process. Doing so allowed for rapid action. More important, it avoided discussion of multiyear budget projections and explicit tradeoffs among tax cuts, spending needs, and debt reduction.[38]

Two developments facilitated adoption of the tax cut. First, even though the economy was clearly in a slowdown, the CBO's projections for the ten-year budget surplus continued to rise—from \$4.6 trillion in October to \$5.6 trillion in January, when the new administration took office.[39] The recession lent a sense of urgency to the enactment of the tax cut; and the large surplus projections gave it apparent feasibility.[40] By February, even liberal Democrats in Congress unveiled their own plan to cut taxes by \$800–900 billion, a huge jump from what Gore had advocated in the campaign.[41] Second, just after Bush's inauguration in January, Federal Reserve chairman Alan Greenspan announced his support for the tax cut in testimony before Congress. [42] Although his endorsement caught many off guard and was criticized by respected economists as reflecting ideology more than economic analysis, it undermined the Democrats' claim that the Bush plan was fiscally irresponsible.[43]

In late March, with all the Republicans and sixty-four Democrats voting in favor, the Bush plan passed the House of Representatives, 282–144. A few days later, Vice President Cheney cast his first tie-breaking vote in the Senate to defeat a much smaller Democratic alternative proposal, after which the Bush plan passed with twelve Democrats voting in favor and a comfortable 56–44 margin of victory.

The other major economic issue that Bush dealt with was corporate misconduct. The issue emerged from a series of business scandals and collapses involving Enron, Tyco, WorldCom, and other firms. The companies reported inflated profits or hid the risks and long-term costs associated with investments intended to produce quick profits. Rather than lose money personally when the investments failed, the executives responsible for these decisions sold their own shares, profiting immensely, before the firms collapsed. Others engaged in more basic and egregious dishonesty by misstating costs and using artificial, paper transactions to create fictitious assets. Auditors from independent accounting firms, whose job was to ensure that investors received accurate information, were often accomplices in the deception. Investors lost billions of dollars and many employees lost their pensions. By undermining the trust of investors, the scandals further depressed a declining stock market and may have impeded the economy's recovery from recession.[44]

Bush resisted enacting a strong corporate reform bill but eventually was compelled to go along. Defining the misconduct as the work of "a few bad apples," rather than a sign of more serious deficiencies in accounting standards and the regulation of accounting firms and their corporate clients, the president attempted a minimal response. He proposed a bill providing for longer prison sentences and giving more resources to the Securities and Exchange Commission (SEC) to detect fraud, with only minor substantive changes in regulations governing corporate conduct. Democrats and many Republicans, however, were inclined to respond far more vigorously. Senator Paul Sarbanes (D-Md.) introduced a more ambitious proposal to tighten the oversight of auditors and reduce conflicts of interest in the accounting profession and among securities analysts.[45] As the magnitude of the scandals grew, so did momentum in Congress in favor of the Sarbanes bill. Nevertheless, the White House contended that the bill's ban on the practice of accounting firms offering consulting services to corporate clients that they also audited was too rigid, the barriers to future corporate employment for executives who engaged in misdeeds were too severe, and the new regulatory board designed to oversee the accounting industry was given too much power.[46]

Only after the collapse of more and more companies, a continued slide in the stock market, and the coalescence of large bipartisan majorities in Congress in favor of Sarbanes's bill did Bush decide to support the legislation.[47] The administration undoubtedly recognized the political peril posed by the issue, particularly given an anemic economic recovery, shrinking stock portfolios, and a rising poverty rate.[48] Opinion polls in the summer of 2002 revealed that the public perceived Bush and his administration as "too heavily influenced by big business," that it feared that Bush was "hiding something about his own corporate past," and that it judged the economy to be "in its worst shape since 1994."[49]

By the time attention shifted to the implementation of the new law, with expectations of vigorous enforcement by the SEC, several congressional Democrats and Republicans had called for the resignation of Harvey Pitt, the agency's chairman. Pitt, a former lawyer for the accounting industry and an opponent of stronger regulation, was accused of reacting too slowly and timidly to the accounting crisis, failing to distance himself sufficiently from former clients, and committing a series of political blunders.[50] After appointing as head of the new accounting oversight board an individual who was being investigated for his role in one company's accounting irregularities, Pitt was forced to resign.[51]

Assessment. The Bush administration's conduct of deliberation over the tax cut was deficient in several respects. First, the abbreviated decision process, separated from normal budgeting, precluded explicit weighing of competing priorities. Second, the administration relied on dubious assessments of budget options. The CBO stressed the huge uncertainties in forecasts of the surplus, devoting a chapter to the problem in the January 2001 report that revised the forecast upwards. CBO's five-year estimates have been off the mark, on average, by the equivalent of about $400 billion in 2006; and two-thirds of the Bush plan's costs would come even later, in the last five years of the plan.[52] In any case, CBO estimates employ the fictitious assumption that Congress will not create new spending programs or expand existing ones.

Third, the administration and Congress both suppressed information about the distribution of the benefits. The Treasury Department and Congress's Joint Tax Committee have usually prepared distributional tables during discussion of major tax legislation, although Republicans have complained that these analyses fueled "class warfare." With Republicans in charge, however, neither Treasury nor Congress chose to present these facts. Their omission left the calculation of burdens and benefits to a liberal advocacy group, Citizens for Tax Justice, whose analyses, although reliable, could be challenged or dismissed more readily than official government figures.[53]

Finally, discussion of the plan featured extravagant resort to budget gimmicks.[54] Bush, for example, claimed his budget would produce "the second-largest surplus in history"—an accurate statement only with the inclusion of the Social Security surplus, which both parties had agreed to set aside.[55] The theory that tax cuts would serve as a bulwark against spending may work to some degree, but at the cost of displacing thoughtful deliberation and democratic choices about priorities. If it fails to work, it leads to deeper budget deficits.

As one would expect from such decision making, the tax cut created several risks. The most obvious is the potential return of chronic massive deficits and the budget stalemate of the 1980s—in which Republican presidents repeatedly blocked tax increases, congressional Democrats blocked spending cuts, and deficits persisted at levels that both parties and most economists considered excessive. In August 2001, the CBO announced that the budget surplus had dropped to $153 billion, down $122 billion from three months earlier, and attributed two-thirds of the reduction to the tax cut.[56] The worsening fiscal picture ensured that either Bush's proposed military buildup would have to be deferred or the federal government would have to return to borrowing from the Medicare and Social Security trust funds.[57] The September 11th attacks and the war on terrorism would only add to the fiscal pressure[58]—when the administration proposed the largest increase in military spending in two decades, it guaranteed the return of federal budget deficits for at least two years.[59] Indeed, by summer 2003 the White House projected a record deficit of $455 billion for the fiscal year and $475 billion for the following year, and massive deficits extending many years into the future were no longer in doubt.[60]

A second risk is a political one, involving a potential loss of support if the economy should fail to return reasonably quickly to robust growth. Because Bush claimed that his tax cut would cure a variety of economic ills, he will bear the blame even more than otherwise if economic performance is disappointing.[61] As conservative scholar Marshall Wittmann said, "If the tax cuts don't lead to a brighter economic future, then all the broken promises come back to haunt them."[62]

Finally, the tax cut will make it difficult, if not impossible, for the president to fulfill his other promises—to give more to education, launch a prescription drug program, leave the Social Security trust fund untouched, and fight terrorism at home and abroad.[63] In fact, indications of other successes in domestic policy were minimal. The *New York Times* reported in mid–2002 that "after a quick victory last year with passage of its tax cut, the administration has had little success advancing the rest of its economic agenda and faces questions on the strength of its economic team."[64]

Soon after the midterm elections, Bush responded to the lack of progress in ending the economic slump by firing both of his top economic advisers. Yet he gave no indication of a change in policies.[65] Rather, he proposed speeding up reductions in personal tax rates and other individual tax cuts, providing rebates for those with children, ending the taxation of dividends, and providing incentives for small businesses to purchase equipment. The new tax cuts were estimated to cost $670 billion over ten years.[66]

In resisting the new law to police corporate misconduct, the administration presumed that the scandals reflected only the misdeeds of a handful of miscreants. It overlooked systemic causes of corporate corruption. A study of the savings and loan bankruptcies of the 1980s, for example, showed that when rules on accounting practices were relaxed, "it was rational for executives to 'loot' their companies."[67] Bush refused to break ranks with his friends and constituents in the business community until Republicans in Congress bowed to the political realities.

Faith-Based Social Policy: Without a Prayer

Whereas the tax cut represented Republican orthodoxy, Bush's agenda in social policy broke with that orthodoxy in accepting the existence of the welfare state and seeking to improve it by incorporating conservative principles. This approach represented both a political strategy and a new strand of conservative thinking about social problems and the poor. Politically, unvarnished economic conservatism left Republicans vulnerable to criticism that the party cared only about business and the well-to-do, and was indifferent to the plight of the less fortunate. Many voters, especially Catholics, favored Republican positions on issues such as abortion and school prayer but disapproved of such indifference. Bush's "compassionate conservative" rhetoric was partly a response to this political problem.[68]

At the same time, some conservative policy intellectuals were developing a new perspective on social programs.[69] Both Bush and political adviser Karl Rove had read the works of Myron Magnet, author of *The Dream and the Nightmare*, and Marvin Olasky, author of *The Tragedy of American Compassion*.[70] Government policies, these authors argued, teach lessons about the obligations of citizenship and instill values that influence behavior. Unfortunately, the policies of the modern welfare state have taught lessons that perpetuate urban poverty—such as acceptance of childbearing outside of wedlock and dependence on government benefits rather than individual responsibility. To improve their condition, the poor need more than material assistance; they need to transform their lives.

The central idea of the faith-based initiative was to facilitate the involvement of religious organizations in the delivery of government-funded social services. Advocates such as Olasky held that religious faith and character-building were central to transforming lives and were the missing elements in existing programs to help the jobless, the homeless, prisoners, alcohol and drug abusers, and other needy persons. Faith-based service deliverers would teach these people that they are partly to blame for their own condition and help them to change their behavior and beliefs.

Apart from the seeming political advantages, the notion of faith-based social services also resonated with Bush's personal beliefs. Bush himself had undergone a religious awakening in the 1980s, overcoming his abuse of alcohol. He identified with the less fortunate who sought redemption and succor in the religious faith and self-help that many inner-city organizations relied upon.[71] In a remarkable manner for a president, Bush spoke with conviction about the importance of religion in his life, and he advocated faith-based programs with religious fervor: "Government can write checks, but it can't put hope in people's hearts, or a sense of purpose in people's lives. That is done by people who have heard a call and who act on faith and are willing to share in that faith. . . . We ought to recognize the healing power of faith in our society."[72]

The administration launched the initiative by creating an Office of Faith-Based and Community Initiatives (OFBCI) in the White House—appointing John DiIulio, a conservative Democratic policy academic, and Stephen Goldsmith, a Republican former mayor of Indianapolis, to lead it. They were dispatched to lift bureaucratic barriers to contracting with religious groups, to identify exemplary faith-based programs, and to draft legislation that would encourage charitable contributions to such groups and establish a grant program to support them.

Within months, however, what should have been easily foreseeable difficulties with the initiative had stirred up enough controversy to kill it, at least for the 107th Congress. Few doubted that many religious organizations performed valuable social services, from running food pantries and soup kitchens, to finding shelter for the homeless and jobs for the jobless, to providing transitional homes for recovering addicts and convicts on parole. But there was virtually no evidence indicating that religious organizations were in fact superior to secular ones in ameliorating social problems, or showing which such programs had the best results. Byron Johnson, one of the few researchers who had studied the effectiveness of faith-based programs, said that empirical evidence that they work was "pretty much nonexistent. We've created a [White House] Office out of anecdotes."[73] DiIulio himself admitted in a *Wall Street Journal* article that there were "no suitably scientific studies that 'prove' the efficacy or cost-effectiveness of faith-based approaches to social ills."[74]

The faith-based initiative faced even greater difficulties in its implications for religious freedom. There were problems both of government sponsorship of religion and of government intrusion in religious affairs. The proposal was attacked, predictably, by civil libertarians, who argued that the use of government funds by religious organizations would violate the First Amendment's establishment clause. But it also met with a cool reception or even outright hostility from many religious leaders. The Southern Baptist Convention warned of a tendency "for the government to attempt to control that which it subsidizes." Conservative Christian leaders and staunch Bush supporters such as Pat Robertson, as well as compassionate conservative advocates such as Marvin Olasky, opposed the measure.[75] Some feared that Bush and DiIulio would refuse to fund evangelical religious organizations or would muzzle their religious message. Others were concerned that government financing might lead to interference in the ministries or make them dependent on federal money. They also worried that grants would be funneled to the most well-connected ministers and churches, and that religious providers would be swamped by bureaucratic rules, regulations, and reporting requirements. Some church leaders echoed the civil libertarians' concern that the initiative would finance proselytizing and favor some religions over others.[76]

The administration found itself the victim of two fairly obvious, yet serious traps. One concerned the scope of participation. On the one hand, if all religions would be eligible to participate, it would raise fears that controversial sects such as the Nation of Islam or the Church of Scientology would receive funds. On the other hand, if certain religions were to be excluded, it would raise objections about discrimination.[77] The other trap had to do with religious indoctrination. Allowing religious organizations that received funds to proselytize clients would raise concerns about forcing people to subject themselves to religious teaching as a condition for assistance. But requiring the organizations to refrain from proselytizing would undermine the whole rationale for the initiative—to improve clients' behavior by using religion to build character.[78]

As DiIulio and other administration spokespersons presented their ideas to interested groups and testified before Congress, skepticism and challenges mounted from a wide variety of religious organizations, civil rights and civil liberties groups, women's groups, labor unions, and lawmakers.[79] DiIulio tried to allay the various concerns. He argued that clients would always be afforded the opportunity to enroll in programs run by nonreligious organizations and that religious organizations rarely made religious participation a condition for aid. He said that the only criterion for funding would be performance in helping the needy.[80] But opponents pointed out that when Bush was governor of Texas, the state had funded a job-training program that required students to study the Bible and accept Jesus as their savior; meanwhile, it provided no secular alternative program in the same county. If performance were to be the only criterion for funding, religious organizations with offensive teachings would be eligible—and if not, who was to judge which teachings were offensive?[81]

The initiative ran into even more controversy when the bill passed by the House, on a party-line vote, included a "charitable-choice" provision, permitting faith-based service providers to discriminate on religious grounds in their hiring. The provision prompted opposition from civil rights groups and labor unions,[82] and an opinion poll found that the prospect of such discrimination was the public's greatest reservation about the proposal.[83] When the administration refused to work with Democrats to bar such discrimination, it undermined the effort to portray the plan as bipartisan.[84]

The faith-based initiative received a further blow when DiIulio resigned as head of OFBCI in August 2001. Although he denied leaving in frustration or under pressure, the faith-based initiative had been far more contentious than he or the administration had expected, and DiIulio had offended conservatives by warning that evangelical Christian groups would be ineligible for funding if they insisted on proselytizing clients.[85]

The September 11th attacks and the war on terrorism left little time for the White House to invest in what was now clearly a lost cause. In his 2002 State of the Union address, the president made only a brief mention of the importance of faith-based groups. Shortly afterward, the White House and Senate reached a compromise that removed the most controversial provisions from the House bill. But by the midterm elections, only a pale imitation of Bush's original proposal—with no new federal money—was under active consideration in Congress.[86]

Assessment.   The central problem of the faith-based initiative, in the end, was simple: In a society that protects religious freedom, government cannot use religion, directly and explicitly, as a tool of policy. Nor can it directly promote religious belief as a means to improve behavior. Workable public policies to encourage religious belief and practice, if possible at all, must be more indirect.[87] Yet the Bush administration appeared not to recognize the thicket of difficulties it was getting into with this initiative. In addition, Bush made extravagant claims for the performance of faith-based organizations on the basis of nothing more than anecdotal evidence. In both respects, the Bush administration's conduct of deliberation was deficient.

A more promising approach would have been to undertake modest legislative and administrative efforts to facilitate religious organizations' participation in social programs.[88] In fact, beginning with welfare reform in 1996, such provisions had been written into four federal laws with minimal controversy. The ambitious yet ill-considered Bush initiative, in contrast, may come to virtually nothing.

Education Reform: Empty Consensus

If the failure of the faith-based initiative was compassionate conservatism's greatest disappointment, education reform was its most visible political success, at least initially. The Leave No Child Behind Act, signed into law by President Bush in January 2002, ushered in the most sweeping changes in federal education policy since the Elementary and Secondary Education Act (ESEA) of 1965. It also helped fulfill the president's campaign promise to build bipartisan coalitions. Leading liberals and conservatives on the education committees in Congress worked with the administration for nearly a year on the measure, and large majorities of Democrats and Republicans voted to pass it.[89]

There were compelling political grounds for Bush to latch on to education reform. Strengthening education has strong appeal for many Americans, especially suburban swing voters, who have regularly placed education at the top of their priorities.[90] Although these voters are generally satisfied with schools in their own communities, they are distressed about the serious problems of schools in the inner cities.[91] As governor, Bush shepherded a bipartisan education bill through the Texas legislature and claimed credit, although dubiously, for improved test scores in the state.[92] With strong support in Republican polling, he made improving education one of his key campaign promises in the race against Gore.[93]

In pursuing a bipartisan approach, however, Bush demonstrated both the ideological opportunism and the willingness to settle for a lowest-common-denominator agreement that often affect centrist strategies. In opportunist fashion, he deferred to the popularity of and interest-group support for liberal policies on education. And he bypassed any effort to adopt the potentially effective but politically difficult measures favored by either side.

From the outset of his administration, Bush opted for a bipartisan strategy on education. There were increasingly significant areas of agreement on education policy between the two parties. Moving toward the Democrats, many Republicans had come to accept a federal role in education and believed that federal efforts should focus on improving schooling for the poor. Moving toward the Republicans, many Democrats were more willing to impose accountability and performance standards on schools, to mandate testing to measure results, and to allow increased local control—provided that Washington provided the resources to make improvements.[94]

To build on this potential for bipartisan support, Bush met with leading congressional liberals on education, including Representative George Miller (D-Calif.) and Senator Ted Kennedy (D-Mass.), to forge working relationships.[95] He hired a centrist Democrat, Sandy Kress, as a key education adviser. Kress brought in ideas from the Progressive Policy Institute, a centrist think tank, such as making federal grants conditional on schools' achieving academic goals and consolidating categorical grant programs to give state and local officials more control of spending.[96] Bush portrayed those in either party who resisted compromise as obstructionists.

He soon concluded that the compromises needed would be substantial. The bill negotiated with congressional leaders omitted the main distinctly conservative element of Bush's original plan and the one most likely to produce significant change in educational performance—giving students in failing public schools vouchers to help pay for private-school tuition. Most Democrats and their allies in the teachers' unions adamantly opposed vouchers, and most of the public did not want to divert resources from public schools. Accordingly, Bush abandoned that plan.[97] Acknowledging the situation, Bush explained, "There are people that are afraid of choice. I'm a realist. I understand that. It doesn't change my opinion, but [my position] isn't going to change the votes, either."[98] Moreover, although the bill gave the states greater flexibility in the use of federal money, it gave much less of it than the extensive consolidation of categorical programs that Bush initially proposed.[99]

He chose a title for the bill—Leave No Child Behind—that echoed language of President Bill Clinton and the liberal Children's Defense Fund and highlighted the focus on the plight of poor children.[100] In a major expansion of the federal role in education, the bill mandated that the states test children annually in grades 4 through 8 using, in part, a uniform national test. It required that children in chronically failing schools be moved to successful ones, set a timetable for closing gaps in student achievement, and authorized a 20 percent increase in funding for Title I of the ESEA, targeted to the poorest inner-city schools.[101] Explaining the measure, the assistant secretary for elementary and secondary education expressed the sentiment, uncharacteristic for a Republican official, that she wanted "to change the face of reading instruction across the United States."[102]

At the same time, Bush and the Republicans rejected the most significant liberal prescriptions for improving education. The bill provided no funds for school construction or rehabilitation, for expanding compensatory education, or for reducing class sizes. More important, nothing in the bill guaranteed the planned 20 percent increase in Title I funds, or indeed any increase.

As the bill neared passage, liberal organizations such as the National Education Association were generally satisfied with the outcome; conservative ones, such as the Heritage Foundation, were unenthusiastic. Conservative commentators

William Bennett and Chester Finn decried Bush's compromises and urged him to insist on a measure closer to his original plan.[103] Bush, however, demonstrated that he had the courage of his opportunism. He made it "absolutely clear" to conservative Republicans that he would insist on passing education reform, and that they would have to live with the increased federal role in education.[104] The final legislation passed both chambers of Congress with support from large majorities of both Democrats and Republicans.[105]

Assessment. The Leave No Child Behind Act of 2001 is a large and complex piece of legislation. From a public relations standpoint, it has been a major accomplishment for the Bush presidency. But despite all of the hard work and bipartisan cooperation in crafting the measure, it is far from clear that it will actually accomplish anything of importance for education. Indeed, there are sufficient doubts about the theory underlying the policy and enough obstacles to its effective implementation to raise questions about how carefully policymakers thought about what they were doing.

First, it is doubtful that the simple strategy for educational improvement at the heart of the legislation actually works. A recent study by RAND, a highly regarded independent think tank, notes that many education policymakers have embraced test-based accountability as the most promising strategy for improving educational performance. Unfortunately, the study concludes, "the evidence has yet to justify the expectations."[106] In states that have used "high-stakes testing," scores have indeed risen, but the gains appear to reflect largely the schools' coaching the students to do well on a particular test.[107] And because such practices leave fewer resources for social studies, science, art, and health and fitness, they have produced "a growing middle-class backlash against schools' stripping their curriculums and resembling test-prep factories."[108] Another major study concluded that high-stakes testing may reduce academic achievement and worsen dropout rates.[109]

Second, the law's promise to move children out of thousands of chronically failing schools and into alternative, successful schools appears to be largely empty. School officials around the country say that no such alternative schools are available because the good schools, and even many poor ones, are overcrowded.[110] During the first year of implementation of the legislation, it was clear that children in failing schools were not being transferred to successful schools. Personnel from successful school districts cited a lack of space, wanting to avoid enlarging their classes and incurring the added costs of educating students with special needs, and the potential for lowering the schools' standardized test scores.[111] Third, a key element of the plan was the authorizing of additional funds to help improve schools serving poor children. According to many experts, real improvement in such schools will require reducing class sizes in early grades, making prekindergarten classes widely available, and creating better classroom working conditions for teachers—all of which cost money.[112] But, as Democrats complained, the president's budget, submitted a month after passage of the bill, actually included far less money than had been authorized for such purposes.[113] By fall 2003 criticism of the law among educators was widespread, and evidence was emerging that it was becoming a political liability for Bush in the 2004 reelection campaign.[114]

Stated simply, conservatives want to improve education by using vouchers and choice to reshape the incentives that govern schools. Liberals want to do so by providing funds to expand and improve educational services. Both solutions are credible, but both are politically difficult. In the rush to pass the Leave No Child Behind Act, Bush left the credible solutions behind.

Homeland Security: Improvising Institutional Change

The terrorist attacks of September 2001 created, unexpectedly, a massively complex and difficult domestic policy issue for the Bush administration. In short order, federal agencies sprang into action, assisting the recovery and the rebuilding of the Pentagon and New York City. The administration moved to strengthen airport security by creating a new Transportation Security Administration and eventually agreed to make guards and baggage screeners federal employees. But the more fundamental issues were long-term: policymakers saw the need for a comprehensive reexamination of the nation's capabilities for fighting terrorism, for development of a long-term strategy for safeguarding the country, and for designing new institutional mechanisms to facilitate these efforts. No approach to dealing with such complex issues would have escaped criticism. Even so, the Bush administration appears to have used a superficial, ad hoc style of decision making— improvising responses for short-term convenience, rather than undertaking careful, systematic deliberation.

Prior to September 11th, studies of the nation's vulnerability to terrorist attack had been conducted by the General Accounting Office, the National Intelligence Council, and, most recently, by the U.S. Commission on National Security—a blue-ribbon panel cochaired by former Senators Gary Hart and Warren Rudman. All the reports said the same things: that the nation was severely unprepared for terrorist strikes, and that improving security would require a new administrative apparatus to coordinate the activities of numerous relevant government agencies. The Hart-Rudman Commission called for a large-scale reorganization to bring together the Border Patrol, the Coast Guard, the Customs Service, and the Federal Emergency Management Agency in a new National Homeland Security Agency.[115]

Even in the aftermath of the attacks, however, President Bush decided to forego the difficult and potentially prolonged process of establishing a new cabinet department. Instead, he appointed Tom Ridge, a longtime friend and former governor of Pennsylvania, as director of an Office of Homeland Security located in the White House. Despite a lack of cabinet-level status, Ridge was permitted to report directly to the president and given a broad mandate to "lead, oversee and coordinate a comprehensive national strategy to safeguard our country against terrorism."[116]

Ridge's task was, in a word, implausible. At least forty federal agencies were involved in efforts to prevent or respond to terrorist attacks. Not one of them claimed countering terrorism as its primary mission or had authority to impose decisions on other agencies.[117] Many had overlapping jurisdictions, long-time rivalries, and histories of a lack of cooperation. For example, four separate agencies policed the nation's borders: the Immigration and Naturalization Service, the Customs Service, the Agriculture Department's inspection office, and the Coast Guard.

Critics charged persuasively that Ridge lacked the means to carry out his mandate. He had no budgetary authority, a small staff, and little legal authority to induce compliance with his decisions.[118] House Intelligence Committee ranking member Jane Harman (D-Calif.) remarked, "Never has a person been given so much responsibility with so little authority."[119]

For eight months after September 11th, the administration resisted calls for creating an agency with more authority and resources. It insisted that Ridge's close relationship with the president was sufficient authority for his mission. In an effort to prove that reorganizing the government would pose many difficulties, the White House unveiled a chart showing the numerous agencies that would have to be merged into a new department for homeland security. But some observers drew the opposite conclusion from the same chart—that it was impossible to coordinate such a hodge-podge of agencies without extensive resources and authority.[120]

In fact, Ridge appeared to do less mapping of strategy or coordinating of agencies than he did managing the anthrax crisis and issuing much-ridiculed color-coded threat alerts.[121] In the view of congressional and media critics, Ridge "bumped from one humiliation to another as various cabinet departments have openly flouted his advice and failed to address security problems identified by their own inspectors general."[122]

Tensions between the administration and Congress heightened when the White House refused to let Ridge testify before Congress and opposed legislative efforts to provide more funding for homeland security.[123] The administration argued that Ridge was not the head of an executive-branch agency, but a presidential adviser shielded by executive privilege. The administration's model for the Office of Homeland Security was the National Security Council (NSC), created at the start of the Cold War to advise the president on national security and foreign affairs. But opponents of the plan argued that the NSC was the wrong model for homeland security. Ridge needed to go beyond synthesizing information and planning strategy for the president. He needed to secure cooperation from other agencies, reorient their priorities, or even take operational control of certain activities. Unlike the NSC adviser, he also needed to work closely with Congress and communicate with the public and local officials. They warned that Ridge would end up like the feckless "drug czars" of past administrations, White House coordinators who lacked the means to carry out an effective policy.[124]

In his 2002 State of the Union message, Bush announced plans to double funding for homeland security and promised initiatives to deal with bioterrorism, airport and border security, improved intelligence, and emergency response.[125] But the announcements did not quiet the drumbeat of demands for a stronger role for the director of Homeland Security, and for more congressional oversight of his office.[126]

Events soon intensified the pressure on Bush to change his mind. In March news reports revealed that the Immigration and Naturalization Service (INS) had approved visas for two of the hijackers months after the September 11th attacks had brought their names to national attention (and ended their lives).[127] A bipartisan group of legislators from the House and Senate soon introduced a bill to create a Department of Homeland Security.[128] And further reports revealed that the intelligence agencies had received information, prior to September 11th, that might have exposed the planning for the terrorist attacks. Either the information had never reached responsible officials at the highest levels of government, or else they had overlooked it. In addition, lack of coordination among federal agencies had permitted terrorists who were already on the FBI's "watch list" to enter the country and carry out the attacks.

Just as Congress launched public hearings on the bill, the president, without having signaled an impending change, dramatically reversed his position and proposed creating a cabinet-level Department of Homeland Security (DHS). In the largest reorganization of federal agencies since 1947, the new department would incorporate the INS, FEMA, Customs Service, Secret Service, Coast Guard, Animal and Plant Health Inspection Service, and the new Transportation Service Administration. It would have a workforce of nearly 170,000, drawn from twenty-two existing agencies, and a total budget of $37.5 billion. To avoid the kinds of miscues that had led to the failure to anticipate the September 11th attacks, there would be a division within the DHS devoted to "information analysis and infrastructure security." Rather than collect intelligence, the division would act as a clearinghouse and "customer" for information on terrorist threats gathered by the CIA, FBI, and other intelligence agencies, which would have an "affirmative obligation" to report such information.[129]

Other divisions of the proposed department would be responsible for controlling U.S. borders to prevent terrorists and weapons from entering the country, defending against biological and chemical weapons, and controlling the damage from any terrorist attacks that might occur.[130] Bush considered but decided against including the FBI, the National Guard, and the State Department's consular division.[131] Coming from an administration that had steadfastly denied the need for a new department, the proposal was remarkable in its scope, as well as puzzling in its origins. In particular, considering the sudden reversal of Bush's position and the unusual secrecy of the administration's decision process, it was unclear how much deliberation had gone into the proposal.[132]

As with any major reorganization, the DHS proposal encountered considerable opposition in Congress. The potential merger of so many agencies elicited resistance from about a dozen House committees with jurisdiction over the Coast Guard, the Secret Service, FEMA, or other affected agencies. While avoiding open disagreement with the president, agencies slated to lose responsibilities to the new department "worked behind the scenes to preserve some of their turf."[133] Fortunately for Bush, House Speaker Dennis Hastert (R-Ill.) referred the standing committees' objections to a special committee designed to overcome parochial motivations and draft a plan to be voted on by the House. Under pressure from the White House, Republican leaders gave assurances that the committee would include in the new department most of the agencies proposed by the administration.[134]

Reinforcing the questions about the depth of the administration's deliberations, a team of researchers that had been studying the organization of homeland security functions for the Brookings Institution strongly criticized the president's proposal.[135] They argued that it attempted to bring under one roof too many agencies with diverse functions. The agencies proposed for inclusion in the merger performed a wide range of important functions not related to terrorism. FEMA, for example, responded to natural disasters, and the Animal and Plant Health Inspection Service set regulations for the humane treatment of animals.[136] Such functions were likely to be diminished or disrupted as a result of a merger; and managing them within the DHS would distract attention from its central mission of preventing terrorism.

The Brookings team recommended excluding FEMA as well as agencies and research centers dealing with chemical, biological, radiological, and nuclear contamination. It called for a more focused homeland security department, whose functions would center on "border and transportation security, infrastructure protection, and domestic terrorism assessment and analysis."[137] The team also criticized the Bush administration as putting the reorganization cart before the strategy horse. Until Bush had a coherent plan for battling terrorism, they argued, it was difficult to evaluate the reorganization.

The Democratic Senate challenged the House legislation and the administration's plan on several points. Several senators pressed the Brookings critique and opposed bringing the Coast Guard, FEMA, and other agencies under the DHS. Joseph Lieberman (D-Conn.), the chief drafter of the Senate bill, argued that the Bush proposal did little to overcome the past failures of the FBI and CIA to share information and cooperate with other agencies.[138]

Most important politically, labor unions and Senate Democrats sought to defeat an administration-sponsored provision to relax civil service protections for DHS employees—permitting them to be dismissed or reassigned largely at the discretion of agency managers. Bush argued that DHS managers would need enhanced flexibility in deploying personnel because of the crucial importance of the department's mission and the need for rapid response to new threats. Democrats countered that government employees with regular civil service protections performed effectively in many other critical functions. Rejecting the administration's rationale, they portrayed the Bush civil service provisions as merely part of a Republican agenda of diminishing employees' rights.

Mostly as a result of the dispute over civil service protection, Congress adjourned for the 2002 midterm elections without completing action on the homeland security reorganization. When the election gave control of the Senate to the Republicans, however, the balance of power immediately changed. Senate Democrats negotiated an agreement with the White House during the lame-duck session, and Congress passed the law creating the Homeland Security Department largely on Bush's terms.[139]

Assessment.   Bush's decisions on homeland security again show evidence of inadequate deliberation in several respects. First, despite multiple warnings from credible authorities, the Bush administration—like the Clinton administration and recent Congresses—failed to address the nation's demonstrable vulnerability to catastrophic terrorist attack until such an attack had actually occurred. Seven months before September 11th, the Hart-Rudman commission had thoroughly documented that vulnerability and recommended creating a new department of homeland security.[140] But until September 11th, its report had been gathering dust. The episode demonstrates the unfortunate tendency of elected officials to ignore hazards until the public or other constituencies become concerned.

Second, for eight months after the terrorist attacks, the Bush administration ignored a preponderance of expert and congressional opinion, which it later acknowledged was correct, that the National Security Council organizational model was not appropriate for homeland security. This resistance may have reflected an ideological aversion to creating a new bureaucracy. It certainly overlooked obvious shortcomings in the capabilities and performance of Ridge's office. And it cost the nation valuable time in developing effective defenses against terrorist attack.

Third, when the administration finally gave up on the White House–coordinator approach and opted for a new homeland security department, it devised a reorganization plan in secrecy and, quite likely, in haste.[141] The White House claimed that it had been planning the reorganization for weeks. But the timing of the announcement was obviously intended to take the wind out of the impending congressional investigation. At best, the Bush administration's decision process on the DHS truncated the usual opportunities for information gathering, discussion, and criticism in the development of a major presidential policy initiative. A secret decision process does not allow for many participants, even within the executive branch. At worst, the process also was badly hurried. As a result, the administration tied its prestige to a sweeping reorganization that arguably had serious problems. It then demanded rapid action and essentially complete ratification by Congress.[142] During the legislative phase, the *New York Times* reported that "several legislative staff members and outside experts have begun to worry that a major new cabinet department cannot be created so quickly without the risk of mistakes and haphazard planning."[143] It was created that quickly anyway, and it poses precisely those risks.

Conclusion

The events of domestic policy in the Bush presidency were overshadowed in media coverage and public awareness by the September 11th attacks, the early stages of a war on terrorism, and the wars with Afghanistan and Iraq. By the time of the 2002 midterm elections, Bush's approval ratings still reflected about half of the 40-point boost he had received in the immediate aftermath of the attacks. In fact, many citizens will probably continue to judge Bush's performance primarily on his response to terrorism, including his handling of the Iraq crisis, for the remainder of his term. Nevertheless, like any president's, Bush's performance on domestic issues will affect Americans' lives long after he leaves office. That performance is revealing of Bush's characteristic responses as a decision maker and, more generally, of the obstacles to moderate, deliberative presidential leadership.

From the standpoint of typical media commentary, Bush had a fairly weak domestic record. On the positive side, he had achieved major political successes on tax cuts and education reform. He also touted an historic campaign-finance reform law as an accomplishment, even though he had actually opposed its passage and signed it into law only reluctantly. On the negative side, he had suffered defeat or encountered stalemate on faith-based initiatives, Medicare prescription drug coverage, Social Security reform, the reauthorization of welfare reform, and the Homeland Security reorganization—of which the last defeat was reversed after the midterm congressional elections. In addition, his administration witnessed corporate financial scandals, a collapse of the stock market, and an economic slump that was entering a third year.

For the most part, these weaknesses of Bush's record reflected constraints that were beyond his control. With Democrats in control of the Senate after May 2001, he had had no realistic opportunity to implement a broad agenda of major initiatives. And few serious commentators held Bush or his policies responsible, more than marginally, for the economic troubles. The recession had begun before his inauguration, and the corporate abuses and their financial impacts had been accumulating since the early 1990s. Nevertheless, if the public had focused attention primarily on domestic issues and the economy—and had held Bush accountable for economic conditions in the usual way—his approval ratings would likely have sunk dramatically by the midterm elections.

Bush's domestic record was also disappointing, however, from the standpoint of substantive accomplishment and the implementation of a compassionate-conservative agenda. Judging from their decisions, Bush and his advisers did not deliberate carefully about the actual consequences of their policies. And they succumbed to several of the threats to effective presidential deliberation. Indeed, we found significant problems with the deliberations on each of the four issues that we examined in detail. The tax cut relied upon patently chancy long-term revenue estimates that proved far off the mark almost as soon as the bill was passed. It brought a return to the huge federal budget deficits of the 1980s, a result that the Bush White House vigorously denied while the bill was being debated. It also constrained funding for important objectives, including antiterrorism security, where the administration resisted congressional Democrats' calls for increased spending.

The much-celebrated education reform law is likely to prove little more than a symbolic gesture. It established mandatory national testing—a controversial step, but not in itself a strong basis for expecting improvement. It then simply declared that the states would give students in low-performing schools access to alternative schools. The law did nothing, however, to bring about the unlikely circumstance that the good alternative schools would actually exist. Nor did it provide for any direct means of improving educational performance. In particular, it provided no funding for preschool programs, smaller classrooms, better qualified teachers—or anything else that could make a direct difference in education outcomes.

There were similar difficulties with decision making on the unsuccessful faith-based initiative. Bush and his advisers failed to confront the obvious conflicts between using religious faith as an instrument of policy and protecting religious freedom for the clients of social-service agencies, and between holding religious organizations accountable for their use of federal funds and protecting religious freedom for the organizations. The result was an embarrassing defeat for Bush, as well as a squandering of time and political resources that might have been used to produce genuine progress on a compassionate conservative agenda.

Finally, on homeland security, the administration lurched from one organizational scheme, with only a small coordinating office in the White House, to a radically different one, establishing a sprawling cabinet-level department. It appeared to respond to short-term political pressures and showed no sign of careful analysis at either stage. The administration wasted almost a year in constructing a new structure to deal with the extraordinary challenges of combating terrorism. More important, the structure that it is now building, in the new Department of Homeland Security, has been subject to trenchant criticism. If the critics are correct, the DHS may be swamped by activities having nothing to do with fighting terrorism and, at the same time, may be unable to address the calamitous intelligence failures of the FBI and the CIA.

Early in this chapter, we took notice of insider accounts of decision making in the Bush White House that alleged the domination of its decisions by political advisers and portrayed a virtual indifference to substantive information about public policy. These accounts were clear-cut and dramatic. We suspect they were overdrawn. Nevertheless, our brief analyses of Bush's decisions in four areas of domestic policy tend to support their central message. In each of our cases and in a variety of ways, President Bush and his administration appear to have given less than adequate attention to issues and information about the real-world consequences of their policies. The events of Bush's domestic policy have striking parallels to the evidence of the administration's overlooking and distorting evidence about Iraq's alleged possession of weapons of mass destruction in the months leading up to the war. Parallels aside, the deficiencies in Bush's conduct of domestic policy deliberations have diminished his presidency.

Notes

The authors wish to thank Justin Gollob for his assistance with the research for this chapter.

1. "The 2000 Campaign: Exchanges between the Candidates in the Third Presidential Debate," *New York Times*, 18 October 2000, A26.
2. Bob Herbert, "There's A Catch: Jobs," *New York Times,* 27 Ocober 2003, A21; Paul Krugman, "A Big Quarter," *New York Times,* 31 October 2003, A23.
3. Jon R. Bond and Richard Fleisher, eds., *Polarized Politics: Congress and the President in a Partisan Era* (Washington, D.C.: CQ Press, 2000).
4. Paul J. Quirk and Joseph Hinchliffe, "Domestic Policy: The Trials of a New Democrat," in *The Clinton Presidency: First Appraisals*, ed. Colin Campbell and Bert A. Rockman (Chatham, N.J.: Chatham House, 1995), 262–89.
5. Paul J. Quirk and William Cunion, "Clinton's Domestic Policy: The Lessons of a 'New Democrat'" in *The Clinton Legacy*, ed. Colin Campbell and Bert Rockman (New York: Chatham House, 1999), 200–25.

6. Paul J. Quirk, "Presidential Competence," in *The Presidency and the Political System*, 7th ed., ed. Michael Nelson (Washington, D.C.: CQ Press, 2003), 158–89; Colin Campbell, *Managing the Presidency: Carter, Reagan, and the Search for Executive Harmony* (Pittsburgh: University of Pittsburgh Press, 1986); and Bert Rockman, *The Leadership Question: The Presidency and the American System* (New York: Praeger, 1984).

7. Roger Porter, *Presidential Decision Making: The Economic Policy Board* (Cambridge: Cambridge University Press, 1982); and Daniel E. Ponder, *Good Advice: Information and Policymaking in the White House* (College Station: Texas A&M University Press, 2000).

8. Alexander George, *Presidential Decision Making in Foreign Policy: The Effective Use of Advice and Information* (Boulder, Colo.: Westview Press, 1979); and Fred Greenstein, *How Presidents Test Reality: Decisions on Vietnam, 1964 & 1965* (New York: Russell Sage, 1989).

9. Joseph Kahn, "Bush's Selections Signal a Widening of Cabinet's Role," *New York Times*, 31 December 2000, 1.

10. Ron Suskind, "Mrs. Hughes Takes Her Leave," *Esquire*, July 2002, 100–107.

11. Stephen Labaton, "In Stormy Time, S.E.C. Is Facing Deeper Trouble," *New York Times*, 1 December 2002, sec. 1, p. 1.

12. Suskind, "Mrs. Hughes Takes Her Leave."

13. David E. Sanger, "In Big Shuffle, Bush Considered Putting F.B.I. in His New Department," *New York Times*, 9 June 2002, sect. 1, 35.

14. Ron Suskind, "Why Are These Men Laughing?" *Esquire*, January 2003, 96–105 (quote on 98).

15. Ibid. 99.

16. Ibid.

17. The reliability of Suskind's January article is in some doubt. It is based largely on interviews with and a seven-page letter from DiIulio. After White House spokesperson Ari Fleischer attacked DiIulio's remarks as "groundless and baseless," DiIulio, in an extraordinary episode, issued an unqualified apology and retraction. Yet he did not deny making the remarks, and he gave no explanation of why he had made allegedly groundless and baseless claims. In the article, Suskind, a Pulitzer Prize–winning reporter, also attributes similar views to a few other senior White House officials, without naming them. In our view, there is probably a good deal of substance to Suskind's story, which is compatible with our own findings on Bush's decisions.

18. "The Republicans: Excerpts from Platform Approved by Republican National Convention," *New York Times*, 1 August 2000, A16. The platform cited a fourth major item, Social Security reform, which we do not address because it has been off the agenda during the first two years of the Bush presidency.

19. Without in-depth interviewing and documentary research, we cannot assess the quality of deliberation directly. We are limited to inferences based on the information that was publicly available, the administration's presumed goals, and their decisions.

20. Alison Mitchell, "Democrats Struggle to Find a Stance on Tax Cut," *New York Times*, 11 February 2001.

21. Jan M. Rosen, "Who Wins, and Who Is Skipped, in the Tax Cut," *New York Times*, 8 June 2003, 9.

22. "The 2000 Campaign: Exchanges between the Candidates in the Third Presidential Debate," 26.

23. Richard W. Stevenson, "Bush Tax Plan: The Debate Takes Shape," *New York Times,* 26 August 26 2000, A1; and Richard W. Stevenson, "Sorting It Out: Tax Cuts and Spending, *New York Times,* 6 October 2000, A26.

24. Frank Bruni, "Bush Says Rebate Isn't a Substitute for His Tax Plan," *New York Times,* 28 March 2001, A1; and David E. Rosenbaum, "House Passes Bill for 2 More Pieces of Bush's Tax Cut," *New York Times,* 29 March 2001.

25. Paul Krugman, "Reckonings: Another Useful Crisis," *New York Times,* 11 November 2001.

26. "What They're Saying about the Bush Tax Cut Proposal," *New York Times,* 26 August 2000, A8; Richard Freeman and Eileen Appelbaum, "Instead of a Tax Cut, Send Out Dividends," *New York Times,* 1 February 2001, A23; Alice M. Rivlin, "Why Fight the Surplus?" *New York Times,* 30 January 2001, A23; and "A Faster, Fairer, Smaller Tax Cut," *New York Times,* 18 March 2001, 12.

27. Stevenson, "Bush Tax Plan." The administration had campaigned promising less military spending, but by July 2001, it had proposed a military budget $33 billion higher than the last Clinton military budget—the largest increase since the 1980s. See James Dao, "Democrats Say Bush's Tax Cuts Jeopardize Military Spending," *New York Times,* 11 July 2001, A14.

28. See Jeff Madrick, "Plans to Cut Taxes May Be Clever Politics, But They're Not Wise Fiscal Policy," *New York Times,* 15 February 2001, 12.

29. David E. Rosenbaum, "Doing the Math on Bush's Tax Cut," *New York Times,* 4 March 2001, 22.

30. Richard W. Stevenson, "On Tax Cuts and Deficits, A Battle of Believers," *New York Times,* 10 February 2002, sect. 3, 4.

31. Richard W. Stevenson, "Bush Wants Tax Cut Sooner to Aid Economy This Year," *New York Times,* 5 February 2001; and David E. Rosenbaum, "On Party Lines, Panel Approves Lower Tax Rate," *New York Times,* 2 March 2001, A1.

32. Rosenbaum, "Doing the Math," 22. The administration calculated that taxpayers with incomes between $30,000 and $50,000 would see their tax burden fall by 19 percent; those with incomes above $200,000 would see theirs fall by 7 percent.

33. Frank Bruni, "Bush's Tax Cut Triumph Is a Political Bouquet, Complete With Thorns," *New York Times,* 27 May 2001, 27.

34. Roper Center, http://web.lexis-nexis.com/universe/ Accession Number 0379277, 2 March 2001; and "The Great Exploding Tax Cut," *The Economist,* 3 March 2001, 27–28.

35. Roper Center, http://web.lexis-nexis.com/universe/ Accession Number 0382175, 15 May 2001; and Accession Number 0378443, 13 February 2001.

36. "Mr. Bush's Beginning," *New York Times,* 29 April 2001, sect. 4, 16.

37. "The Evolving Presidency: A Defining Test on Taxes," *New York Times,* 1 April 2001; and Bruni, "Bush's Tax Cut Triumph."

38. Mitchell, "Democrats Struggle."

39. Stevenson, "Sorting It Out"; and Richard W. Stevenson, "This, It Appears Sure, Is the Year of the Tax Cut," *New York Times,* 1 February 2001, A19.

40. Richard W. Stevenson, "House GOP Leader Calls for Hastening Bush's Tax Cut," *New York Times,* 10 January 2001, A15.

41. Mitchell, "Democrats Struggle."

42. Richard W. Stevenson, "In Policy Change, Greenspan Backs a Broad Tax Cut," *New York Times*, 26 January 2001, A1.

43. Rivlin, "Why Fight the Surplus?"; Stevenson, "This, It Appears Sure"; and Richard W. Stevenson, "Down Into the Fray," *New York Times,* 27 January 2001, A1.

44. Jeff Madrick, "Bush is Talking Tough on Corporate Ethics, But Where Is the Regulatory Bite?" *New York Times*, 11 July 2002, C2.

45. Richard A. Oppel Jr., "G.O.P. in Congress Moving Past Bush on Business Fraud," *New York Times*, 11 July 2002, A1; and David E. Sanger and Richard A. Oppel Jr., "Senate Approves a Broad Overhaul of Business Laws," *New York Times,* 16 July 2002, 1.

46. Richard A. Oppel Jr., "Bush and Democrats Still Deeply Split on What Needs to Be Done," *New York Times*, 10 July 2002, C5.

47. Richard A. Oppel Jr., "In a Shift, Republicans Pledge to Pass Accounting Bill," *New York Times*, 18 July 2002, C1; and idem, "Negotiators Agree on Broad Changes in Business Laws," *New York Times,* 25 July 2002, A1.

48. David Leonhardt, "Payrolls Drop as Economy Seems to Be at a Standstill," *New York Times,* 5 October 2002, C1; and Robert Pear, "Number of People Living in Poverty Increases in U.S.," *New York Times,* 25 September 2002, A1.

49. Richard W. Stevenson and Janet Elder, "Poll Finds Concerns that Bush Is Overly Influenced by Business," *New York Times,* 18 July 2002, A1.

50. John McCain, "The Free Market Needs New Rules," *New York Times*, 8 July 2002, A19; and Stephen Labaton, "Senior Republican Joins in Criticism of S.E.C. Chairman," *New York Times,* 2 November 2002, A1.

51. Stephen Labaton, "Three Inquiries Begun into S.E.C.'s Choice of Audit Overseer," *New York Times,* 1 November 2002, A1; and Floyd Norris, "Bush Facing Two Challenges: S.E.C. Choice and Economy," *New York Times,* 7 November 2002, C1.

52. Julie Kosterlitz, David Baumann, and John Maggs, "Colored by Numbers," *National Journal*, 31 March 2001, 932–39.

53. Rosenbaum, "Doing the Math."

54. David Baumann, "An Easy Out?" *National Journal*, 30 June 2001, 2086–90.

55. William Schneider, "It's Still the Economy, Stupid," *National Journal*, 1 September 2001, 2702.

56. Philip Shenon, "Study in Congress Sees Need to Tap Social Security," *New York Times*, 28 August 2001, A1.

57. Dao, "Democrats Say," A14.

58. Richard W. Stevenson, "Deficit Ahead, Many Forks in the Road," *New York Times*, 11 November 2001, sect. 3, 4.

59. David E. Sanger, "Domestic Security Spending to Double under Bush Plan," *New York Times*, 25 January 2002, A11.

60. Reuters, "Bush Predicts That His Tax Cuts Will Soon Produce More Jobs," *New York Times,* 20 July 2003, 20.

61. Bruni, "Bush's Tax Cut Triumph."

62. Quoted in Richard W. Stevenson, "A New Threat to the President's Agenda: The Tax Cut," *New York Times*, 12 August 2001, sect. 4, 1.

63. Stevenson, "A New Threat," sect. 4, 1; "Citing Drop in Surplus, Democrats Plan to Portray Bush as Reckless," *New York Times*, 21 August 2001, A1; and Carl M. Cannon, "The Deficit Difference," *National Journal*, 9 February 2002, 382–87.

64. Richard W. Stevenson, "Bush Facing Test in House as Economic Agenda Stalls, *New York Times*, 24 June 2002, A1.

65. Elizabeth Bumiller, "The President's Team Changes Some Players But Not Its Game Plan," *New York Times*, 5 January 2003, 14.

66. Richard W. Stevenson, "Bush Unveils Plan to Cut Tax Rates and Spur Economy," *New York Times*, 8 January 2003, A1. According to Robert D. Reischauer, a former director of the Congressional Budget Office and head of the Urban Institute, "It's breathtakingly large, considering the deficits and the political pressure to spend more on defense, security and prescription drugs for the elderly." Quoted in Elizabeth Bumiller, "A Bold Plan with Risks," *New York Times*, 8 January 2003, A1.

67. Madrick, "Bush Is Talking Tough," C2. The study was done by Nobel Prize winner George A. Akerlof, coauthored with Paul M. Romer, "Looting: The Economic Underworld of Bankruptcy for Profit," *Brookings Papers on Economic Activity*, 1993, no. 2, 1–60.

68. Adam Clymer, "Bush Aggressively Courts Catholic Voters for 2004," *New York Times*, 1 June 2001, A14.

69. Burt Solomon, "Militant Moderates," *National Journal*, 7 October 2000, 3144–49.

70. Marvin Olasky, *The Tragedy of American Compassion* (Washington, D.C.: Regnery Gateway, 1992); Myron Magnet, *The Dream and the Nightmare: The Sixties' Legacy to the Underclass* (New York: Morrow, 1993); and Alison Mitchell, "Bush Draws Campaign Theme from More Than the Heart," *New York Times*, 11 June 2000, A1.

71. Mitchell, "Bush Draws Campaign Theme."

72. Elizabeth Bumiller, "Talk of Religion Provokes Amens as Well as Anxiety," *New York Times*, 22 April 2002, A19; and Frank Bruni and Laurie Goodstein, "Bush to Focus on a Favorite Project: Helping Religious Groups Help the Needy," *New York Times*, 26 January 2001, A17. See also George W. Bush, *A Charge To Keep* (New York: Morrow, 1999), chap. 16.

73. Laurie Goodstein, "Church-Based Projects Lack Data on Results," *New York Times*, 24 April 2001, A12.

74. Martha Davis, "Faith, Hope and Charity," *National Journal*, 28 April 2001, 1228–35.

75. Laurie Goodstein, "Bush's Charity Plan Is Raising Concerns for Religious Right," *New York Times*, 3 March 2001, A1.

76. Elizabeth Becker, "Practical Questions Greet Bush Plan to Aid Religious Groups," *New York Times*, 5 February 2001, A11; and Stuart Taylor Jr., "The Risk Is Not Establishing Religion, But Degrading It," *National Journal*, 3 February 2001, 320–21.

77. Richard A. Oppel Jr., with Gustav Niebuhr, "Bush Meeting Focuses on Role of Religion," *New York Times*, 21 December 2000, A37; and Laurie Goodstein, "Bush's Call to Church Groups to Get Untraditional Replies," *New York Times*, 20 February 2001, A1.

78. Peter Steinfels, "So Sue Me, Suggests the Chief of the White House Office of Faith-Based and Community Initiatives," *New York Times*, 10 February 2001, B6; Goodstein, "Bush's Charity Plan"; Elizabeth Becker, "Aid on Track to Religious Charities, Official

Says," *New York Times,* 14 March 2001, A16; and David E. Sanger, "Bush Asks Mayors to Lobby for Faith-Based Social Aid," *New York Times,* 26 June 2001, A17.

79. Goodstein, "Bush's Charity Plan"; idem, "Battle Lines Grow on Plan to Assist Religious Groups," *New York Times,* 12 April 2001, A26; and Elizabeth Becker, "Bush's Plan to Aid Religious Groups Is Faulted," *New York Times,* 26 April 2001, A21.

80. Steinfels, "So Sue Me"; Becker, "Aid on Track."

81. Laurie Goodstein, "In God We Trust, In Government We Hope for the Best," *New York Times,* 4 February 2001, sect. 4, 3; and Becker, "Bush's Plan to Aid Religious Groups."

82. Goodstein, "Battle Lines Grow."

83. Peter Steinfels, "Hiring for Faith-Based Programs: Issues May Be Complicated, but the Public Has an Emphatic View," *New York Times,* 9 June 2001, B6.

84. "Church, State and Joe Lieberman," *New York Times,* 1 September 2001, A14.

85. Elizabeth Becker, " Head of Religion-Based Initiative Resigns," *New York Times,* 18 August 2001, A11.

86. Elizabeth Bumiller, "Bush Backs Religious Charity and a Shaky Incumbent," *New York Times,* 3 July 2002, A20.

87. For a sympathetic discussion of public policies intended to support religion, see A. James Reichley, *The Values Connection* (Lanham, Md.: Rowman & Littlefield, 2001).

88. See Megan Twohey, "Limelight Scorching 'Charitable Choice'?" *National Journal,* 28 April 2001, 1236–37; and Martha Davis, "Keeping the Faith, Quietly," *National Journal,* 1 September 2001, 2678.

89. Adam Clymer and Lizette Alvarez, "Congress Reaches Compromise on Education Bill," *New York Times,* 12 December 2001, A1.

90. Siobhan Gorman, "Behind Bipartisanship," *National Journal,* 14 July 2001, 2228–33; and "Schooled in Survival," *National Journal,* 15 December 2001, 3854–55.

91. Jodi Wilgoren, "Education Plan by Bush Shows New Consensus," *New York Times,* 23 January 2001, A1.

92. According to a RAND study, Bush does not deserve most of the credit for education gains in Texas, which should go to reforms and spending initiated by his predecessors and H. Ross Perot, who inspired them. See Bob Herbert, "Bush's Education Record," *New York Times,* 7 August 2000, A19.

93. William Schneider, "Mommies, Daddies, and Education," *National Journal,* 18 May 2002, 1514.

94. Wilgoren, "Education Plan."

95. Gorman, "Behind Bipartisanship."

96. Ibid.

97. Lizette Alvarez, "House Democrats Block Voucher Plan," *New York Times,* 3 May 2001, A18.

98. Quoted in Alvarez, "House Democrats Block."

99. Diana Jean Schemo, "Bush-Backed School Bill Advances in Senate," *New York Times,* 9 March 2001, A13.

100. Wilgoren, "Education Plan."

101. Diana Jean Schemo, "Senate Approves a Bill to Expand the Federal Role in Pubic Education," *New York Times,* 19 December 2001, A32.

102. Quoted in Diana Jean Schemo, "Education Bill Urges New Emphasis on Phonics as Method for Teaching Reading," *New York Times,* 9 January 2002, A16.

103. Clymer and Alvarez, "Congress Reaches Compromise."

104. Ibid.

105. The vote on final passage in the House was 381–41, and 87–10 in the Senate. Adam Clymer, "House Passes Education Bill," *New York Times,* 14 December 2001, A36; and Schemo, "Senate Approves a Bill."

106. Brian M. Stecher and Laura S. Hamilton, "Putting Theory to the Test," *RAND Review,* Spring 2002, 17.

107. "Test-Based Accountability Systems: Lessons of Kentucky's Experiment," RAND/RB–8017, 1999; and Stephen Klein et al., "What Do Test Scores in Texas Tell Us?" RAND/IP202, 2000.

108. Wilgoren, "Education Plan."

109. Greg Winter, "Make-or-Break Exams Grow, but Big Study Doubts Value," *New York Times,* 28 December 2002, A1.

110. Diana Jean Schemo, "Officials Say School Choice Often Just Isn't an Option," *New York Times*, 22 December 2001, A13.

111. Susan Snyder, " 'No Child Left Behind' Law Bumps Into Hard Reality," *Philadelphia Inquirer,* 12 October 2003, 10.

112. Herbert, "Bush's Education Record."

113. Robert Pear, "Democrats Criticizing Bush Budget on Education," *New York Times*, 13 February 2002, A28.

114. Jim VandeHei, "Education Law May Hurt Bush; No Child Left Behind's Funding Problems Could Be '04 Liability," *Washington Post,* 13 October, 2003, A1.

115. "Tom Ridge's Task," *New York Times,* 23 September 2001, sect. 4, 16; Joseph S. Nye, "How to Protect the Homeland," *New York Times*, 25 September 2001, A29; and Alison Mitchell, "Security Issues Called a Focus of Next Budget," *New York Times,* 27 December 2001, B1.

116. Quoted in "Tom Ridge's Task"; Elizabeth Becker, "Bush Is Said to Consider a New Security Department," *New York Times,* 12 April 2002, A16; Alison Mitchell, "Disputes Erupt on Ridge's Needs for His Job," *New York Times,* 4 November 2001, sect. 1B, 7; and Ernest R. May, "Small Office, Wide Authority," *New York Times*, 20 October 2001, A17.

117. Sydney J. Freedberg Jr., "Shoring Up America," *National Journal,* 20 October 2001, 3238–45.

118. Mitchell, "Disputes Erupt," sect. 1B, 7; Elizabeth Becker and Elaine Scolino, "A New Federal Office Opens amid Concern That Its Head Won't Have Enough Power," *New York Times*, 9 October 2001, B11.

119. Quoted in Elizabeth Becker, "Big Visions for Security Post Shrink amid Political Drama," *New York Times,* 2 May 2002, A1.

120. Mitchell, "Disputes Erupt."

121. Alison Mitchell, "Ridge to Request Billions to Spend on Home Security," *New York Times,* 22 November 2001, A1; Philip Shenon, "Color-Coded System Created to Rate Threat of Terrorism," *New York Times,* 13 March 2002, A16; Sydney J. Freedberg Jr. and Marilyn Werber Serafini, "Contagious Confusion," *National Journal,* 10 November 2001, 3492–97.

122. "Faltering on the Home Front," *New York Times,* 12 May 2002, sect. 4, 14; and Becker, "Big Visions."

123. Adam Clymer, "Democrats Renew Bid to Increase Security Financing," *New York Times,* 3 December 2001, B6.

124. Mitchell, "Disputes Erupt" and "Revisiting Homeland Security," *New York Times,* 7 February 2002, A28.

125. "President Bush's State of the Union Address to Congress and the Nation," *New York Times,* 30 January 2002, A22.

126. "Revisiting Homeland Security"; Alison Mitchell, "Letter to Ridge is Latest Jab in Fight over Balance of Powers," *New York Times,* 5 March 2002, A8.

127. "Tom Ridge's Homeland Silences," *New York Times,* 17 March 2002, sect. 4, 14.

128. Becker, "Big Visions for Security Post."

129. David Firestone and Alison Mitchell, "Congress Gets Bill Setting Up Security Department," *New York Times,* 19 June 2002, http://www.nytimes.com/2002/06/09/politics.

130. Elizabeth Bumiller and David E. Sanger, "Bush, as Terror Inquiry Swirls, Seeks Cabinet Post on Security," *New York Times,* 7 June 2002, A1.

131. David E. Sanger, "In Big Shuffle, Bush Considered Putting F.B.I. in His New Department," *New York Times,* 9 June 2002, 35; and David Firestone, "Support for a New Agency but Concern about the Details," *New York Times,* 13 June 2002, A33.

132. Mitchell, "New Antiterrorism Agency Faces Competing Visions," *New York Times,* 14 June 2002, A27.

133. David Firestone and Elizabeth Becker, "House Leadership Bows to President on Security Dept.," *New York Times,* 19 July 2002, A1.

134. David Firestone, "Congress to Begin Debating a Domestic Security Agency," *New York Times,* 8 July 2002, A1; and Firestone and Becker, "House Leadership Bows to President."

135. Ivo H. Daalder et al., "Assessing the Department of Homeland Security," Washington, D.C.: Brookings Institution, July 2002.

136. Robert Pear, "Lawmakers Asking if Plan on Terror Goes Far Enough," *New York Times,* 8 June 2002, A1.

137. Daalder et al., "Assessing the Department of Homeland Security," viii.

138. Alison Mitchell, "New Antiterrorism Agency," A27; and Warren Rudman and Gary Hart, "Restructuring for Security," *New York Times,* 13 June 2002, A39.

139. David Firestone and Elisabeth Bumiller, "Stalemate Ends in Bush Victory on Terror Bill," *New York Times,* 13 November 13, 2002, A1.

140. Rudman and Hart, "Restructuring."

141. Mitchell, "New Antiterrorism Agency."

142. Ibid.

143. Firestone, "Congress to Begin Debating."

CHAPTER 8

George W. Bush's Foreign Policy

Richard K. Herrmann
with
Michael J. Reese

GEORGE W. BUSH entered the White House emphasizing the importance of U.S. interests close to home and the primacy of a domestic agenda. During the campaign he endorsed an active international role for the United States but emphasized the limits of American power and interests.[1] For instance, he was skeptical that U.S. efforts to solve the internal problems in foreign lands—nation-building, as it was called—made good sense. Rather than concentrating as heavily as the Clinton administration had on global problems and ethnic struggles elsewhere, including the Middle East, Bush gave priority to relations with the great powers, American neighbors, and his domestic agenda. This changed with the attacks of 11 September 2001. The war on terrorism that followed, the president said, would define his presidency.[2] National security would drive a domestic agenda topped by homeland security. Conflict in the Middle East would constitute the central threat around which U.S. foreign policy would revolve.

With America at war, the internal divisions on foreign policy that had been evident from the beginning of the Bush administration became far more visible and consequential. The issues on which top Bush foreign policy advisers most disagreed were now front and center, and the whole world was watching. Moreover, because the American public was shocked by the horror of 9/11 and ready to be mobilized for action, policy options that had appeared to be nonviable due to a lack of public support before the attacks were now on the table. This sharpened the debate and lent it a sense of urgency rooted in substantial public fear of foreign attack that had not been evident in the United States in years. The uncertainty over how long this rise in public attentiveness would last further fueled debate. Some advisers were keen to strike quickly, while public support was high; others argued that military conflicts would be easier to enter than to exit and that the uncertainty about public support over the long haul put U.S. staying power into question. It was this staying power, this group argued, that ultimately translated military victory into strategic success.

The foreign policy team assembled by President Bush included leaders with substantial prior experience. Many of them had worked together in the previous Bush administration and the Reagan administration as well, and the team reflected the cleavage between conservatives and neoconservatives that had been especially evident under Reagan. The Bush team also faced a continuing liberal mindset in a good part of the Congress. The first part of this chapter describes these competing perspectives and identifies the leaders in the Bush administration who advanced them. This sets the scene for the second part of the chapter, which turns to the administration's reaction to the September 11th attacks, concentrating primarily on the decision to use force in Afghanistan and the debate over whether to change U.S. policy toward the Israeli-Palestinian conflict. The third part of the chapter examines the question of attacking Iraq, which dominated the foreign policy agenda in the second half of 2002. It also considers the broader strategic agenda outlined in President Bush's National Security Strategy, which was released from the White House on 17 September 2002.

The Foreign Policy Team and the Agenda before 9/11

Domestic Policy Comes First: Some Fear a Neoisolationism

The second Bush administration entered office recognizing that the Cold War was over and that neither Russia nor China presented the sort of global threat that had driven Washington's previous containment strategy. This recognition allowed prominent attention to be given to issues that had previously been relegated to a secondary status behind national security. The president, for example, emphasized the importance of Mexico and declared a Partnership for Prosperity when he received at the White House Mexican President Vicente Fox as his first visiting foreign head of state.[3] At the same time, top advisers were calling for a change in some of the basic agreements reached with Moscow during the Cold War, arguing that they no longer made sense. The anti–ballistic missile treaty, which had originally been part of agreements designed to limit offensive missile deployments, was said to be no longer needed. Neither Moscow nor Washington was engaged in an arms race of this type any longer, and, further, the ABM treaty constrained efforts to meet new threats, particularly those from third parties seen in Washington as irresponsible rogues.

Although these "rogue states" and nonstate terrorists, along with a host of global problems such as the mounting AIDS epidemic, were seen as real threats, they did not command anywhere near the priority Cold War security concerns had. The administration's legislative agenda in 2001 concentrated on education reform, faith-based initiatives in social services, tax cuts and budget discipline, campaign finance reform (largely to fend off Arizona senator John McCain's initiatives in this direction), and a patients' bill of rights. In this environment of low public concern about external threats, foreign policy debates did not command center stage. Moreover, in some issue areas where nearly everyone agreed that vital U.S. interests were at stake, such as relations with Russia, there were only tactical disagreements; nearly everyone was in favor of building new positive relations with Moscow. Debate in Washington about policy toward areas of the Third World were also muted. Regardless of what experts and special interests felt the United States ought to do in these cases, there was widespread agreement that the public would not accept the high costs for this involvement. President Bush reflected this sentiment often in his skepticism about the wisdom of America's engaging in nation-building abroad.[4]

Its secondary status in the early days of the Bush administration relegated debates about foreign policy to the realm of experts and limited the resources that special interest groups could mobilize. Nevertheless, the differences among top advisers were important, and when foreign policy was thrust into the limelight after 9/11, these divisions were revealed to be as deep and fundamental as in any administration since the end of the Vietnam War. These differences revolved around (1) priorities placed on particular U.S. interests abroad, (2) evaluations of the role and limits of U.S. power, and (3) perceptions of the situation in the Middle East. Four perspectives were evident in the body politic on these matters; to simplify, they can be labeled conservative, neoconservative, liberal, and left. Only the conservative and neoconservative perspectives were prominently represented in the Bush administration. Liberals were influential in Congress. The left had marginal impact, and due to limits of space, will not be considered here.

Competing Perspectives: Conservatives, Neoconservatives, Liberals

The distinction between conservatives and neoconservatives took hold in the mid–1970s and was evident in the Republican Party thereafter. During the Cold War both perspectives put a high priority on national security and saw the Soviet Union and communism as a threat calling for a global strategy. As the Cold War wound down, however, differences in these two perspectives became clear. This was most evident in regard to the Middle East and in Washington's policy of détente toward Moscow. Conservatives tended to concentrate on interests in places that had inherent material importance to the United States, such as Europe and North Asia. They were ready to defend countries that had little intrinsic value to U.S. material concerns but which played critical instrumental roles in a containment strategy, such as Pakistan. Likewise, they were ready to promote human rights as long as this did not undermine the stability of U.S. geostrategic allies. They typically were not prepared to run high risks or pay high costs to export American moral values in any missionary way, nor to protect the special interests of regional allies.

As the Cold War ended, conservatives saw an opportunity to withdraw from peripheral commitments that had mostly instrumental value within the context of containment. They also saw a chance to establish positive relations with potential great-power adversaries, even though there would not be complete ideological agreement. Neoconservatives were less comfortable with these inclinations, fearing that they revealed an isolationist streak that would put some U.S. allies in jeopardy and forfeit America's opportunity to reshape the norms governing world affairs. The 1973 war in the Middle East, coming on the heels of America's exit from Vietnam, especially alarmed neoconservatives. They feared that the "Come Home America" theme popular among liberals at the time and the conservative inclination to concentrate on oil interests and détente with Moscow would undermine Washington's commitment to Israel. Neoconservatives tend to identify Israel's security as a top U.S. priority and to lean heavily toward hawkish Israeli preferences when dealing with the Palestinian issue. They did not endorse the détente policy of Nixon and later Reagan, arguing that it was amoral, and they insisted that great power relations should not be based on geopolitical expediency alone. They emphasized moral concerns as well, such as the right of Jews to leave the Soviet Union and the promotion of human rights in communist states more generally.

The differences between conservatives and neoconservatives became evident during the Reagan administration, and it was in the Middle East that the distinction was clearest. With an anti-American Islamic revolutionary regime in power in Iran, conservatives feared that stable Western access to oil was threatened. To meet this threat, they emphasized the importance of U.S. relations with Arab oil-exporting states and the need to make these relations easier to sustain by accommodating Palestinian, and, in turn, Arab nationalist sentiments. When Israel's hard-line defense Minister Ariel Sharon led Israel into Lebanon and occupied Beirut, conservatives in the Reagan administration were concerned that Washington needed to reaffirm its commitment to the Camp David process, which called for the resolution of the Palestinian refugee problem.[5] Conservatives were also keen to keep U.S. military involvement in this occupation limited and even-handed, as was clear in the doctrine laid out by Secretary of Defense Caspar Weinberger.[6]

Leaders closer to neoconservative views, such as Secretary of State Alexander Haig and Ambassador to the United Nations Jeane Kirkpatrick, on the other hand, were ready to support Israel's move and to carry the conflict into Syria if necessary. They saw a chance to deliver a blow against Moscow's allies in Damascus and to insure that a Lebanese Christian government would stay in office and make peace with Israel.[7] They were less worried than conservatives about the negative effect these actions might have on U.S. relations with oil-exporting Arab states. Neoconservatives tended to believe that Arab oil-exporting states were not reliable U.S. allies and were potential enemies of Israel. Worrying that American dependency on imported oil made the United States more vulnerable to blackmail, they favored reducing this dependency. Failing that, they were ready to project unilateral U.S. power into the region rather than placate Arab regimes they saw as corrupt and hostile to Israel.

Although oil was the obvious reason that American leaders attached strategic importance to the Persian Gulf, conservatives and neoconservatives differed in the implications they drew for U.S. foreign policy. Conservatives, following the lead of many U.S. oil companies and their Middle Eastern partners, favored aligning with conservative anticommunist oil-exporting regimes to secure access to oil. These regimes provided access to military bases and recycled their petrodollars into the U.S. economy. Conservatives, and liberals for that matter, had little doubt that the United States could protect oil-exporting friends and contain potential regional hegemons such as Iraq and Iran. Even if these states had weapons of mass destruction, they could be deterred, conservatives argued—Washington had deterred far more powerful adversaries in the past and kept Western Europe and North Asia free of intimidation. Iraq and Iran, weak states by comparison, also needed to sell oil under all conditions if they wanted to sustain any military power, economic growth, or social stability. Moreover, even commercial blackmail scenarios would be limited by these nations' dependence on imports, which would feed back inflation caused by high oil prices to these oil exporters in the form of higher prices on everything they needed, from food stocks to manufactured goods.

The oil-exporting Arab states that conservatives were ready to protect and align with, of course, were not democratic and thus had some insulation from popular Arab nationalist sentiments. They, nevertheless, found governance easier and more stable when they reflected the concerns of their citizens. This meant supporting Arab causes such as the Palestinians. For conservatives, consequently, to protect access to oil, U.S. policy not only needed to project U.S. military power into the Gulf to defend oil-exporting states from Iraq and Iran but also needed to strike an even-handed position in the Israeli-Palestinian conflict.

This inclination to appease Arab nationalist sentiments and authoritarian regimes upset neoconservatives, who preferred to rely on unilateral U.S. military strength projected directly into the region to secure oil if necessary. They did not want to rely on what they considered to be unreliable and unsavory Arab allies or to be blackmailed by these Arab exporters into putting pressure on Israel to accommodate Palestinian demands. They rarely put this position in terms of defending stable access to low-priced oil, instead calling on America to cut back its oil dependence. Like conservatives, they recognized that it made little commercial sense to try to control oil-producing territories by force. The argument for American involvement typically emphasized a moral mission and the defense of Israel, although this later consideration was usually downplayed and left implicit.

By the end of the Reagan administration, conservatives such as George Shultz came to dominate and neoconservatives were less influential.[8] During the first Bush administration, few neoconservatives held much sway. The forty-first president of the United States, a conservative himself, assembled a foreign policy team led by Secretary of State James Baker and National Security Adviser Brent Scowcroft, who both shared the conservative perspective. Although initially skeptical of Soviet leader Mikhail Gorbachev's New Thinking, they engaged Moscow by putting top priority on geopolitical gains rather than normative determination to bring down communism. In the Middle East, they worked initially with Saddam Hussein's Iraq to protect the Gulf from Iran and put pressure on the Likud government in Israel to return to the Camp David formula of land-for-peace.[9] Although some neoconservatives were also willing to work with Iraq to contain Iran,[10] after U.S.-Iraqi relations had collapsed and war over Kuwait ensued, they were unhappy both that "No. 41" did not bring down the Iraqi dictator and that he opened a new round of Israeli-Palestinian negotiations, pressing the land-for-peace formula. Neoconservatives felt that this rewarded Arabs and pandered to oil interests.

With the Cold War over, conservatives were reluctant to engage in Third World contests. Conservatives among top-level uniformed military officers were reluctant to engage militarily in the Balkans as well.[11] In the 1990s, liberals who had once criticized conservatives for being too ready to intervene with force now found themselves in opposition to conservatives who they felt were too reluctant to intervene. During the war in Vietnam, liberals had come to doubt the global nature of the Soviet threat and had stopped framing regional conflicts in East-versus-West terms.[12] Once the Cold War was over, conservatives followed suit and saw no other compelling reasons to intervene in most places.[13] Liberals, on the other hand, like neoconservatives, believed there were normative reasons to intervene in regional conflicts, and they were ready to promote humanitarian concerns as well as U.S. material interests. Unlike neoconservatives, however, liberals did not want to engage in such intervention in a unilateral fashion, nor did they focus exclusively on cases of moral intervention that also served U.S. material interests or the interests of its allies.

Besides disagreeing over the priority Washington should attach to certain interests abroad, conservatives, neoconservatives, and liberals had different ideas about the utility of Washington's post–Cold War power advantage. All agreed the

United States was the lone superpower, but they disagreed on where the limits of this power lay, what political ends it could achieve, and the tactical instruments that would best produce desired political outcomes. The differences were not so much over the battlefield effectiveness of weapon systems—there was consensus that the U.S. armed forces had substantial superiority over any likely adversary—as over the political impact battlefield victories were likely to produce. Conservatives and liberals were skeptical that military success in Third World conflicts would translate into political gains. Often drawing on analogies with Vietnam, people with conservative and liberal perspectives often attributed substantial importance to indigenous nationalism and worried about getting embroiled in complex social-political quagmires. They also felt that intervention risked producing anti-Americanism that could otherwise be avoided. Somewhat oddly given their different views during the Cold War, by the time "Bush 43" came into office, conservatives and liberals found themselves agreeing that Washington would be wiser to share more and care more about economic and social development in the Third World and to use military force less. Where they disagreed was over how much to share and whether to do so in the context of international organizations. Liberals favored larger budgets and more international institutions, while conservatives worried more about budget discipline and freedom of maneuver.

The neoconservatives' perspective was quite different from that of conservatives or liberals. They often feared that rogue elements in the Third World, and especially in the Muslim world, had come to doubt U.S. resolve. They felt that demonstrations of U.S. military superiority instilled awe and respect and that these feelings among the people of the Middle East, in turn, produced positive political payoffs for Washington and its allies. They were optimistic that Washington's military and economic superiority could be translated into political change that would not only serve U.S. and allied material interests but also advance positive normative aims. They were less concerned that heavy-handed intervention would produce otherwise avoidable anti-Americanism and more determined to meet with superior force what they saw as inherently anti-American and anti-Western leaders and movements. Neoconservatives often described the political change they hoped to compel in terms not unfamiliar to Wilsonian liberals, but they outlined a strategy for producing this democratization and individual freedom that seemed closer to those advanced by hard-liners at the height of nineteenth-century British imperialism than to the tactics of advocates of self-determination such as Woodrow Wilson.

Conservatives, neoconservatives, and liberals all agreed that fighting terrorism was important. The Clinton administration had struck at al-Qaeda several times, although without much success. As the second Bush administration took office, combating terrorists remained a high priority, although it was not the defining issue that it would become after 9/11. It also was not an issue that provoked deep divisions within the administration—everyone agreed that terrorists who attacked Americans were enemies who needed to be defeated. Al-Qaeda was known to the intelligence community, and plans were underway for responding to it; there was mostly continuity between the Clinton and Bush administrations in this regard. Within this broad agreement about the threat, where there may have been a difference in emphasis was between conservatives and neoconservatives, with conservatives focusing on al-Qaeda as a direct threat to the United States and its oil-exporting allies and neoconservatives focusing on Hamas and Hezbollah, which threaten Israel, as well as al-Qaeda, which some neoconservatives before 9/11 felt was not particularly interested in Palestinian affairs. After 9/11, the connections between al-Qaeda and other anti-Israeli political movements and between al-Qaeda and Iraq became matters of considerable debate. Before we turn to these tactical issues, however, we should introduce the personnel who gave life to these various ideological perspectives within the Bush administration.

The Bush Team, First String Players

Of course, the conservative, neoconservative, and liberal labels refer only to ideal-typical perspectives. President Bush filled top positions in his administration with real people whose views only partially resembled any one of these ideal-types. Just the same, powerful leaders with substantial experience and strong conservative and neoconservative leanings were brought together in the Bush 43 team.[14] Colin Powell, the secretary of state, reflected mostly conservative views. His deputy secretary of state, Richard Armitage, was a bit more hawkish but basically conservative as well. Anthony Zinni, Bush's special envoy to the Middle East was, like Powell, a retired four-star general, who reflected conservative attitudes as well. So did most of the uniformed chiefs of staff at the Pentagon.[15]

At the top of the civilian side of the Pentagon, on the other hand, neoconservatives held sway.[16] Deputy Secretary of Defense Paul Wolfowitz was a powerful intellectual voice for this basic perspective and a very experienced bureaucratic player. His former boss in the Bush 41 administration, Richard Cheney, was now vice president. Whereas Brent Scowcroft, the former President Bush's national security adviser, recalled that in the Bush 41 team Cheney had been an outlier—more hawkish in a neoconservative direction than the rest—Cheney reportedly used his influence with the younger President Bush to see that neoconservative concerns were well represented in the Bush 43 team. He is reported to have successfully lobbied for the appointment of Donald Rumsfeld to be secretary of defense over Powell's preferred candidate, Pennsylvania governor Tom Ridge.[17] Douglas Feith was named undersecretary for policy at the Pentagon, supporting Wolfowitz. Richard Perle, one of the best-known neoconservative voices from the Reagan administration, was put in charge of the Pentagon's intelligence advisory board. Lewis "Scooter" Libby, with strong neoconservative views, served as Cheney's chief of staff. At the State Department, John Bolton was named undersecretary for arms control and international security, an appointment Powell was said to be somewhat uncomfortable with. Vice President Cheney's daughter, Elizabeth Cheney, was named deputy assistant secretary of state for Near East affairs, serving under William Burns, Powell's choice to be assistant secretary for Near East affairs. Burns had served as deputy director of Secretary of State Baker's Policy Planning Staff in the Bush 41 administration.

Given the distribution of quite different views and powerful personalities, Bush 43 had assembled a foreign policy team quite likely to clash over priorities should foreign affairs in the Middle East come to center stage. Condoleezza Rice, Bush 43's national security adviser, had worked with Secretary Powell in the past, but she also had good relationships with neoconservatives. Not known for taking strong positions on the central issues that divided conservatives from neoconservatives, or for having strong views on Middle East and Third World affairs, Rice was an expert on Russia and the great-power relations the administration had taken office determined to emphasize.[18] She had her hands full managing the cast of experienced and powerful leaders on the Bush 43 team, who as a group reflected important differences that had not been fully aired since the end of the Cold War.

Of course, ultimately it was not Rice who would decide how to balance the conflicting perspectives in the advisory circle, but President Bush. Because he lacked the track record on foreign policy that his father had brought to office, it was not easy to identify George W. Bush's world view early on in his presidency. During the electoral campaign and then in office prior to 9/11, he appeared to promote a mostly conservative agenda and expressed his appreciation for the love-hate relationship with America reflected in popular opinion in many Third World countries. He argued that an arrogant and overbearing U.S. interventionism would generate resentment and only complicate U.S. foreign relations; this was one of the reasons for his contention that less emphasis should be put on nation-building in far-off places. At the same time, Bush emoted to nationalist themes and to the superiority of U.S. military power, and he appeared to be affected by a moral, even religious, streak that fueled both compassion, as he called it, and self-righteousness, as his critics complained. Some pundits attributed this pious attitude to his Bible-belt constituencies, others to Bush's own religious beliefs and personal predisposition.

Appearance of Consensus during Warm-ups

The different world views in the Bush administration, although noticeable, did not affect major policy decisions prior to the attacks of 9/11. The first substantial foreign policy crisis occurred in April 2000, when an American reconnaissance plane on an observation mission in the Taiwan Strait collided with a Chinese fighter and made an emergency landing on Hainan Island. With the U.S. plane and crew on Chinese territory, officials in Beijing demanded an apology from Washington and insisted that the United States accept blame for the accident. President Bush, who had described China as a potential strategic competitor during the election campaign, insisted that China release the crew and plane immediately.[19] His initial instincts and advice from neoconservatives appeared to lead him to take a tough and angry early position, demanding that China back down. Secretary Powell also defended the justice of the U.S. cause but opened the door for diplomacy. The president then chose to pursue this course, and after a few days of angry posturing on both sides, the administration worked out a compromise deal that defused the tension. Although this incident provoked a brief display of different instincts on the part of neoconservatives and Secretary of State Powell—with the president going with both perspectives sequentially—the differences appeared mostly tactical and stylistic. Despite some difference in tone early on in the conflict, the stark realities of the power and interests involved seemed to produce a consensus within the Bush team. This consensus on how to deal with the great powers was also evident in Bush's meeting with Russian President Vladimir Putin in June 2001.

The conflict between conservatives and neoconservatives was hard to detect in regard to policy toward Afghanistan as well. At the time, both groups regarded that country as quite peripheral to American interests. When, during the first few months of Bush's presidency, the ruling Taliban regime decided to destroy the Bamiyan Buddhas, which it saw as an affront to the Islamic state it was building in Afghanistan, UN Secretary General Kofi Annan intervened to save the ancient monuments, but to no avail. After the destruction of the statues, officials in the Bush administration expressed regret but made no substantive change in policy. The administration did, however, subsequently donate $2.8 million to remove land-mines in Afghanistan,[20] and it also sent drug control officers to help the Taliban stem the cultivation of poppies and the production of heroin.[21] Despite Bush campaign criticisms of the Clinton administration for being too soft vis-à-vis al-Qaeda and terrorism more generally, the Bush administration did not change much in this regard prior to 9/11. Officials were reportedly working on a new plan for attacking al-Qaeda, but no such plan reached the president's desk before 9/11.[22] Nor did it appear that Bush felt this matter deserved higher priority than it had traditionally received.

The inclination to reassert U.S. independence vis-à-vis international organizations also seemed to be shared widely in the administration. During the campaign Condoleezza Rice had written that "multilateral agreements and institutions should not be ends in themselves."[23] She argued that the United States should pursue its own interests and use multilateral options if they advanced those interests in concrete and not just symbolic ways. She argued that signing symbolic agreements was, in fact, a mistake that the Clinton administration had made too often. Once elected, President Bush declined to push the Senate to reconsider the Comprehensive Nuclear Test Ban Treaty (CTBT) and decided to withdraw America's agreement to meet guidelines for limiting carbon emissions set in the 1999 Kyoto Protocol. The administration also declined to endorse the International Criminal Court when it could not persuade other signatories to grant special status to U.S. soldiers.

Although all of these decisions to forego international institutions upset liberals, they did not generate substantial divisions within the top echelon of the Bush foreign policy team. There were technical reasons to stand aside in each case, and none of the first-string Bush players felt strongly about these matters. Most shared the president's conservative skepticism that these international institutions contributed in critical ways to material U.S. interests. One international institution that was seen by most Bush players as playing an important role in that regard was the World Trade Organization—on membership and participation there, consensus seemed clear.

Even on the Israeli-Palestinian conflict, the divisions between conservatives and neoconservatives did not figure very prominently prior to 9/11. During the 2000 campaign, Bush's desire to avoid Clinton-style activism in the conflict was clear. In the first several months of his presidency there were no real prospects for resuming talks anyway. Israel was in the midst of elections called primarily because the previous Israeli government had been ineffective in dealing with the mounting violence. Ariel Sharon was sworn in as Israel's prime minister on 8 March 2001, and he emphasized a security agenda. On 19 March, Secretary of State Powell outlined American policy toward the conflict, declaring that America would "assist, not insist" on a negotiated settlement.[24] He also made it clear that the Bush administration was not keen to devote as much attention to this conflict as the Clinton administration had unless the parties to the conflict demonstrated some serious readiness to implement the accords already agreed to. The United States would neither impose a settlement nor let this issue dominate its foreign policy; other issues related to the great powers and the new issues of globalization demanded attention and promised to affect more fundamental U.S. interests. Very shortly after this, in April, the U.S. plane was downed on Hainan Island, and the crisis with China took center stage for a few weeks.

In May 2001, a commission led by former Senator George Mitchell released a report on violence in the Palestinian-Israeli conflict and created an occasion for top Bush team members to express an opinion. The report called on both sides to stop the fighting and return to the basic elements of the land-for-peace deal embodied in what was called the Oslo process. Conservatives such as Powell expressed sympathy with the report and the call for restraint on both sides. President Bush also endorsed the report on 26 June, when he hosted the new Israeli prime minister at the White House.[25] The president also said that Israel had no better friend than the United States. At this point, the administration gave high priority to its relationship with Israel but not necessarily to its role as a mediator between the Israelis and Palestinians.

Neoconservatives were not eager for Washington to engage as an active mediator. They felt that the Palestinians had resorted to terrorism as a bargaining tactic and that Israel should not be compelled to tolerate this strategy. Rather than intervening to discuss peace, the United States, they argued, should simply insist that the Palestinians stop using terror. Disagreeing with the more even-handed language of the Mitchell Report, they were concerned that U.S. involvement could only strengthen the hand of the Palestinians. Even recognizing the Palestinian Authority as a legitimate partner while terror was ongoing would have this effect.

Of course, Arabs regarded Washington's reluctance to engage as a "green light" for Israel's use of force against the Palestinians, and this led to mounting anger in the Arab world. Feedback to Secretary of State Powell indicated that U.S. ambassadors in the region worried that escalating violence and Washington's passive policy would seriously damage America's standing with its Arab allies and perhaps endanger the domestic stability of these allies should they remain closely identified with the United States. This conservative argument, coupled with continuing suicide bombings in Israel, led Secretary Powell to visit the region in July in an attempt to salvage some part of the previous peace process.[26] Neoconservatives were not supportive of Powell's meeting with Yasir Arafat or pressing Israel to focus on the land issue; instead, they felt Powell should concentrate on pressing the Palestinians to stop the terror. The trip was not successful, and it had little impact on either the negotiations or the violence, which suited the neoconservatives fine but was unwelcome news to conservatives and liberals alike.

At this point, it was not exactly clear where President Bush stood on the debates between conservatives and neoconservatives. It was clear, however, that he felt deep affinity for Israel, and he expressed this sentiment during Sharon's visit. Bush did not evidence much sympathy for Arab anti-imperialist sensibilities, and he saw terrorism as a much bigger problem than satisfying Palestinian nationalist demands. Although he had appeared to appreciate Latin American concerns about an imperial United States during the Vicente Fox visit and had placed an early priority on regional development, he carried little of this sensitivity into the Middle East. There he appeared to side with the Israelis and failed to express the optimism about working with Arab allies that often characterized the oil community in the United States. This struck some as odd given his own background in Texas and Vice President Cheney's experience in the oil business, but it certainly squared easily with traditional U.S. policy, neoconservative inclinations, and even his determination to win Florida more decisively in the next election.

Signs of Disagreement, Smart Sanctions, and Iraq

How to deal with Iraq was the question over which the division between conservatives and neoconservatives was most visible in the early days of the Bush administration.[27] Ten years after the close of the Gulf War, Saddam Hussein was still in power. The sanctions regime that had been put in place to insure that Iraq not be able to reconstitute its military status was still in place but failing. The UN inspection program designed to insure that Iraq did not have weapons of mass destruction had not been functioning since 1998, when Iraq expelled the inspectors. Before Bush even took office, prominent neoconservatives had identified Iraq as a number one priority issue.

When Richard Cheney was secretary of defense in the Bush 41 administration, he had wanted to disarm Iraq and change the regime. In the late 1990s Paul Wolfowitz had written that overthrowing the regime in Iraq should be a high national priority.[28] Condoleezza Rice, in a *Foreign Affairs* article published during the campaign, included this neoconservative item, writing that "nothing will change until Saddam is gone, so the United States must mobilize whatever resources it can, including support from his opposition, to remove him."[29] The argument for overthrowing Saddam Hussein emphasized the inadequacy and nonviability of the sanctions regime over time: Iraq was already in defiance of the inspections portion of the regime, the economic hardship imposed by sanctions hurt innocent Iraqis more than Saddam's clique, and eventually the commercial opportunities Iraq presented would lead other countries to abandon the sanctions—indeed, they already were honoring them less and less. As time went by, Saddam Hussein was regaining strength and developing weapons of mass destruction. He had started two wars, committed crimes against humanity, and posed a threat to Israel and Saudi Arabia, to say nothing of Kuwait. If Slobodan Milosevic deserved to be overthrown and put on trial, then certainly Saddam Hussein deserved no less.

Secretary Powell and other conservatives disliked Saddam Hussein as well, and they too were anxious to see him leave. They were not ready, however, to use force to make this happen. Instead, Secretary Powell advanced the idea that a new, "smarter" sanctions regime could be constructed that would garner international support and contain Iraq. Powell argued that U.S. policies vis-à-vis Iraq had worked and that the United States faced only a weak regime in Baghdad—"strong only in the sense that they can keep this one rather horrible person in power." The secretary of state described Saddam as "an annoyance, a terrible annoyance. He is a potential threat to the region. But at the same time, the world is leaving him behind. He can show up once a year with a hat on the head and shoot rifle rounds in the air, but for the most part, he has been contained while other nations in the world have moved forward leaving him behind."[30]

Powell worked throughout the spring of 2001 to spell out the details of smart sanctions and to enlist international support. Criticized by neoconservatives for taking too soft a position on Iraq, he was said to argue the point against both Secretary Rumsfeld and Paul Wolfowitz, who favored making Saddam Hussein's overthrow a priority. While Powell developed smart sanctions, the Pentagon cultivated contacts with anti-regime Iraqis in exile and planned for a post-Saddam Iraq. President Bush may have felt closer to neoconservatives than to his secretary of state, but Powell seemed determined to establish greater personal rapport with the president by setting up regular private meetings with him. Bush may have doubted that smart sanctions would work, but he endorsed Powell's policy initiative at least as an initial foray on the Iraq issue. He did not mince words in describing his dislike for Saddam Hussein and his desire to see the regime changed, but, at the same time, he did not call for the use of force to bring this about. Before 9/11, changing the regime in Iraq seemed to be an administration goal that might have to wait or at least be pursued by diplomatic and covert means. Domestic matters commanded priority, and the likelihood that the public could be mobilized for another war against Iraq seemed doubtful. That situation changed after September 11th.

The War on Terrorism

Responding to 9/11

The terrorist attacks on New York and Washington put national security into the spotlight, driving other issues into a distant second-priority status. An external threat was now perceived by most Americans, and the demand for defense was clear. Declaring war on terrorism, President Bush vowed that this fight would define his presidency.[31] It would also be a war, he said, that was long and difficult and unlike other wars America had fought. The enemy this time was not a clearly defined state but rather a phenomenon involving multiple perpetrators. This enemy would also strike at America's homeland, making this not just a foreign war but a war that might touch many Americans. Within days of the attack, the United States was leaning on Pakistan to place its airspace at U.S. disposal and naming al-Qaeda as the number one enemy in what might be a long list of terrorist adversaries.

President Bush defined the war in stark, emotionally charged black-and-white terms.[32] Other countries, he said, were either with the United States or with the terrorists; there would be no neutrals. States that allowed terrorist organizations to operate on their territory would be treated by the United States as terrorists themselves. On 20 September, in a joint session of Congress, Bush called on the Taliban government in Afghanistan to hand over Osama bin Laden and close down all al-Qaeda operations. By the first few days of October, NATO's Lord Robinson announced that the United States had provided clear proof that al-Qaeda was guilty in the September 11th attacks.[33] The administration had already approved $100 million in aid for anti-Taliban forces in Afghanistan, concluding that the government in Kabul needed to go. Secretary of Defense Rumsfeld visited five of Afghanistan's neighbors in the first week of October to prepare for military action, and Secretary of State Powell was in Pakistan by the middle of the month, opening high-level contact with the Musharraf government that had been shunned by Washington since it had seized power in October 1999.

There was some disagreement over how quickly to strike back and whether to confine the initial war to Afghanistan. Deputy Secretary of Defense Paul Wolfowitz, for example, called for attacking Iraq as part of Washington's initial campaign. Neither the president nor the most senior players on the Bush team supported this position, however. They identified defeating al-Qaeda—and the Taliban if they should defend al-Qaeda—as the highest priority.[34] Even relations with great powers would be shaped by the war on terrorism. Progress was made on strategic arms talks with Moscow in mid-October once President Putin signed on to the campaign against the Taliban. Later in October, Bush went ahead with his first trip to China, brushing aside any residual fallout from the incident at Hainan Island. He concentrated on building widespread support in Asia for the U.S.–led war on terrorism. At the end of the month, Secretary Rumsfeld was in Moscow and Central Asia to secure the use of airspace and the positioning of forces on the ground. President Bush addressed the UN General Assembly on 11 November 2001, emphasizing that the war on terrorism would be a global campaign that would define U.S. foreign policy.

The tactical plans for the operation in Afghanistan were designed by General Tommy Franks, commander-in-chief of Central Command. When the initial phases of the campaign seemed to be moving slowly, the media described political consternation in Washington. Secretary Rumsfeld had become a popular figure with the media because of his frequent press conferences, but there were persistent rumors that he was unpopular among the uniformed services, especially in the army.[35] The military campaign proceeded fairly quickly, however, and by 15 November the Taliban regime had collapsed and was being routed from Afghan cities. It surrendered its final stronghold in Kandahar on 8 December 2001, two months after the U.S. campaign had begun. By the end of the month, Hamid Karzai had been sworn in as Afghanistan's interim leader, Secretary Rumsfeld had visited Afghanistan, and the U.S. embassy in Kabul had been reopened.

Throughout the campaign in Afghanistan, President Bush made it clear that in his mind this was just the beginning of a wider war on terrorism. Although the war in Afghanistan and the destruction of al-Qaeda did not generate much debate within the Bush team or in Congress, this was not to be the case on the matter of how the wider war on terrorism would be fought. Disagreements became evident almost immediately after the attacks on September 11th, even as the Bush team planned the campaign against the Taliban and al-Qaeda in Afghanistan.

The discussion was not about the priority to place on the war; everyone was ready at least tactically to give this issue top billing and to revisit other issues such as relations with China and Russia and even NATO in terms of how these actors might play an instrumental role in the war on terrorism. Instead, the disagreements were over how far to go in shifting away from a military strategy of deterrence and toward a strategy of preemption, whether to extend the initial war to Iraq, and how much if at all the war on terrorism should affect Washington's policy on the Israeli-Palestinian conflict.

Preemption

The threats posed by terrorism and by anti-American regimes acquiring weapons of mass destruction had been central to U.S. defense planning prior to 9/11. The *Quadrennial Defense Review* released 30 September 2001 by the Pentagon was largely complete before the terrorist attacks, and although it was hastily adjusted in their aftermath to reflect the new urgency of fighting terrorism, it reflected the evolving consensus in the Bush team that the security environment had changed.[36] The United States did not face a clear threat from another great power, nor was it clear that it needed to be ready to fight two regional wars at the same time. Rather than identifying a particular enemy, the *Quadrennial Defense Review* stressed the importance of a "capabilities-based" approach and flexibility. It spoke of a paradigm shift in force planning that included defending the United States and "deterring forward."

Of course, the U.S. armed forces have always had the mission of defending the United States, but because in the nuclear era there was no practical way to defend physically against nuclear weapons, deterrence rather than actual defense dominated strategic thinking. Instead, Washington would protect the United States by making it clear to all potential adversaries that an attack on the United States would lead to the adversary's certain annihilation. In the new security environment, however, confidence in deterrence waned because the adversaries most likely to attack—potentially even with weapons of mass destruction—were not necessarily or even most likely to be states. Terrorists without clear homelands and "rogue" leaders who did not care about the survival of their own countrymen might not be deterred. Al-Qaeda had not been. In this context, attention turned to defense—that is the actual protection of the homeland.

Reliance on deterrence had not been popular with conservatives or neoconservatives for some time. Recognizing the public's desire to feel defended, President Reagan discussed the moral dilemma involved in threatening to kill millions of innocent civilians in retaliation for an attack on the United States and in the 1980s raised hopes that defensive technologies might be developed that could defeat offensive attacks. This technological breakthrough had not materialized in the 1990s, and economic realities continued to make defense against a great-power attacker impractical. Defense against terrorist and small-scale rogue attack, however, was potentially different. The Bush 43 administration put high priority on repealing the anti–ballistic missile treaty so that this sort of defense effort could be mounted.

After 9/11, the administration also decided that "homeland security" was needed—that potential targets in the United States such as utilities, communications centers, and commercial hubs needed to be protected. It did not take long for defense officials in the Bush administration and most commentators on homeland security to realize, however, that there were too many valuable targets in the United States that were vulnerable to many different types of attack or sabotage to defend them all from all types of attack with very much confidence.[37] High priority could be put on homeland defense—and Bush moved to create a new Homeland Security Department with a cabinet-level secretary in charge—but top Pentagon officials made clear that this was not enough. Confronted with adversaries who had shown on 9/11 that they could and would inflict large-scale civilian casualties on the United States, Washington, according to prominent conservatives and neoconservatives alike, needed to go beyond reliance on deterrence and beyond what physical homeland defense it could mount. It needed to go on the offense by attacking potential adversaries before they could strike.[38] This strategy of preemption would include attacking such adversaries' sources of funding and disrupting their planning cells worldwide, as well as using military force to assassinate suspected terrorists and physically destroy their material capabilities. It would also mean attacking states that supported or gave sanctuary to terrorists.

Liberals in Congress understood the logic of preemption and endorsed in principle the idea of stopping mass murderers before they struck, but in practice they worried about the implications of this offensive, preventive strike doctrine for both civil liberties at home and international stability abroad. Nevertheless, declaring that America was at war, the Bush administration exercised extraordinary powers to detain suspects in the United States and to attack what the government identified as funding sources for terror. The debates these activities raised about due process and legal fairness are beyond the bounds of this chapter. Neoconservatives argued that the logic of preemptive defense in foreign policy meant that the United States should extend the war on terrorism by overthrowing Saddam Hussein's regime in Iraq. Although targeted assassination of terrorists in Middle Eastern countries such as Yemen did not provoke major debate within Washington, the idea of attacking a foreign country with the explicit intent of compelling a change in regime did.

Iraq Too?

Neoconservatives on the Bush team, who had made the overthrow of Saddam Hussein a high priority from the outset, argued in favor of attacking Iraq as part of the initial response to the attacks of 9/11.[39] Deputy Secretary of Defense Paul

Wolfowitz, for instance, is reported to have made this argument at an initial planning session at Camp David in late September.[40] Conservatives, including Secretary of State Powell, argued against this preemptive expansion of the war and in favor of concentrating on al-Qaeda and Afghanistan.[41] At that time, the uniformed military's argument in favor of doing one thing at a time and the uncertainty of how quickly the campaign in Afghanistan would succeed convinced President Bush to leave Iraq for a later day. According to Bob Woodward, Bush worried that trying to do too many things at once might lead to a lack of focus and increased risk. He was also reported to have wanted not to let the desire of senior advisers such as Cheney and Wolfowitz to settle old scores with Saddam Hussein affect the planning for the war on terrorism.[42] Vice President Cheney and Secretary of Defense Rumsfeld, although anxious to oust Saddam, accepted this war-time strategy, although they expressed their determination to go after state sponsors of terrorism, especially Iraq, in the near future. They also asserted that Iraq was closely linked to al-Qaeda—a claim that generated substantial debate within the intelligence community.

Conservatives argued that attacking Iraq early in the war on terrorism would undermine the international coalition that had supported the U.S. campaign in Afghanistan and would also inflame anti-American sentiments among Arab and Muslim nations at precisely the moment those nations' cooperation was needed in identifying and defeating al-Qaeda operatives. Colin Powell described the smart sanctions policy he had revived in spring 2001 as part of a strategy of regime change in Iraq, implying that more direct action was not a high priority in the short term.[43] These arguments assumed that the United States had important interests in the Arab world that should be protected by accommodating Arab nationalist sentiments. This assumption, although shared by many liberals, was not endorsed by neoconservatives in the Bush administration. Once the initial decision was made to leave Iraq until another day, this disagreement about U.S. interests in the Arab world had its biggest impact on U.S. policy toward the Israeli-Palestinian conflict.

Israeli-Palestinian Conflict

Immediately after 9/11, Americans were outraged, and emotional desires for retaliation and defense ran high. Although left-wing critics pointed to U.S. imperial policy and described the attacks as violent blowback, this was a very unpopular position. More common was the interpretation that the terrorists were simply fanatics who hated all that was good about America—freedom, democracy, and modern values. President Bush, by all accounts, responded very much as the typical American did, wanting to take action, and not just symbolic action. His extemporaneous statements at Ground Zero, telling rescue workers and the country that very soon the people who had knocked these buildings down would be hearing from America, was in perfect harmony with popular sentiment. Bush did not whip up nationalist furor—al-Qaeda had done that—but he appeared to be exactly in step with it and led by giving voice to this sentiment. He described the situation in stark terms as a struggle between good and evil, and he evidently entertained no doubts about the righteous position of the United States or the unequivocal evil of the enemy. His moralistic formulation of the situation and his language at times were so strong that, although they appealed to the wounded pride of Americans, they reportedly worried senior advisers at the State Department and leaders of the uniformed military, who felt that leadership required more restraint and composure in the storm.

Although sharing the anger and emotion generated by the attacks, conservatives who were expert on the Middle East and foreign policy in general felt that describing the scene in black-and-white terms, although popular, would not be an adequate guide for policy. For them, the attacks were connected to a broader strategic problem, the widespread perception in the Arab world that the United States was an imperial power. These conservatives believed that too many Arabs and Muslims were angry about U.S. foreign policy in the region, especially its support for Israel and its failure to make headway in resolving the Arab-Israeli dispute. It was not clear if President Bush shared this concern. Little in his public statements suggested that he did, but prior to 9/11 his comments on Middle East policy had been fairly brief. His attention had been elsewhere, and it is possible that his views of the Middle East were crystalizing in the context of the post–9/11 crisis. Neoconservatives did not disagree about the widespread anti-Americanism in the region, but they argued that it would exist regardless of Washington's policy toward Israelis and Palestinians.

Although some neoconservatives outside government attributed this anti-American hostility to Islam and to the failure of Arab culture to embrace modernity, prominent neoconservative voices within the Bush administration blamed it on the dictatorial regimes in the Muslim world and the propaganda and educational systems they employed. The Israeli issue, they argued, was used as a scapegoat by these dictators to justify their corrupt and exploitative rule. Rather than appeasing the Arab nationalist sentiment whipped up by these dictators, according to the neoconservatives, the United States should meet these hateful expressions with force, expose the vile nature of these leaders, and eventually bring down their corrupt regimes. Hard-line Israelis, such as Ariel Sharon, had since the early 1980s argued that if corrupt leaders dependent on populist demagoguery to cover their own failings could be removed from power and neutralized, more democratic and modern Arab leaders would emerge. Israel's invasion of Lebanon in the early 1980s was partly based on this premise. The situation had not worked out as expected in Lebanon, but that may have been because so much of the rest of the Arab world—the vast majority—remained under such awful leadership.

Paul Wolfowitz, among other neoconservatives, began in the late 1990s to write of the need for a sea change in the Arab world, with the U.S. promoting democratic transition, starting in Iraq. Wolfowitz argued that such a strategy had worked in Indonesia when he had been ambassador there and that it would work in the Arab world as well, once the dictators were pushed aside and the Arab population yearning for modernity and change was liberated.

The view that Arab nationalism was mostly a legitimating symbol in the hands of dictatorial Arab demogogues appealed to neoconservatives, but conservatives and liberals were skeptical that it had such shallow roots. As the Bush team began to build an international coalition to attack al-Qaeda, they announced on 2 October 2001 that the administration had been intending to push forward a plan creating a Palestinian state. This appeared to be an effort to win over Arab help in the face of the al-Qaeda threat. Prime Minister Sharon of Israel compared this U.S. move to the European appeasement of Hitler in the 1930s, warning Washington that Israel would go it alone if necessary. The White House reprimanded Sharon, calling his remarks unacceptable, and in his address to the United Nations on 11 November, President Bush reiterated his administration's interest in the creation of a Palestinian state and called for an end to violence on the part of both Palestinians and Israelis. Within a week, the president received an open letter from eighty-nine senators urging him not to restrain Israel's reaction to Palestinian attacks. Three days later, on 20 November, Secretary Powell announced that the administration would dispatch its first high-level mission to mediate the Israeli-Palestinian dispute. At this point, the line between conservatives and neoconservatives was fairly clearly drawn.

Secretary Powell dispatched to the Middle East Assistant Secretary of State William Burns and Special Envoy Anthony Zinni. These representatives went to the region to work with both sides to stop the escalating cycle of violence and push the process back toward negotiations. Conservatives in the administration and most liberals in Congress felt that progress on this issue would contribute to Washington's mobilization of Arab support against al-Qaeda and the Taliban. They also felt that Israel needed to compromise on the issue of land and that Palestinian and Arab nationalist sentiments should be accommodated. Neoconservatives emphasized the importance of allowing Israel to defend itself and demonstrating to Palestinians and Arabs more generally that violence would not lead to Israeli concessions but rather to the defeat of the Palestinians. As it turned out, Burns and Zinni were not able to make headway in halting the violence or in obtaining concessions from either the Israelis or the Palestinians. To the contrary, the violence seemed to escalate while they were in the region, as did the debate back in Washington over what they should try to accomplish.

Neoconservatives did not want the United States to wrest concessions from Israel to placate Arab opinion. Instead, they urged Washington to compel Arab acceptance of Israel's preferences regarding land and the terms of settlement. Conservatives, on the other hand, put high priority on Israel's security but felt its occupation of the West Bank and Gaza did not contribute to prospects for peace. To the contrary, they, like many liberals, believed that Israel's occupation provoked as much violence as it stemmed. Moreover, they felt that Israel's position toward the Palestinians made Washington's relations with the Arab oil-exporting states more complicated. As the war in Afghanistan wound down, the fighting among Israelis and Palestinians escalated, and Burns and Zinni returned to Washington in December empty-handed. Neoconservatives were not disappointed. They wanted the United States to endorse, or at least not oppose, the Israeli decision to crush the violent Palestinian resistance. This meant not treating the Palestine Authority and its leader, Yasir Arafat, as legitimate partners in a peace process but rather casting them into the same terrorist category as al-Qaeda.

Zinni returned to the region in January and again in March but made little headway. The Palestinian attacks on Israel continued unabated, and at the end of March 2002, Israel had Arafat's headquarters in Ramallah under siege. Prime Minister Sharon was discussing the possibility of exiling the Palestinian leader, while Israeli forces took control of Bethlehem and Nablus. Conservatives worried that allowing the situation to deteriorate further would undermine Arab-American relations and Washington's coalition to fight al-Qaeda. They were unable either to stop the Palestinian violence or to constrain Israel's policy, however, as the Likud government was responding to public outrage in Israel and was supported by powerful neoconservative allies in Washington. At this point, the debate within the administration moved past the tactical agreement that had sustained the attack on Afghanistan and evolved toward a more fundamental strategic dispute about how to proceed next in the war on terrorism. By summer, the most significant rethinking of U.S. policy in the Middle East in decades was underway. It certainly involved the prospect of attacking Iraq, but it went far beyond just preemption. The question on the table now was how to get out of the political dilemma the United States faced in the Middle East—that is, how to deal with the anti-American sentiments of Arabs and Muslims and initiate processes that would lead to stability in the long run.

Dealing with the Strategic Dilemma in the Middle East

Although President Bush had entered office anxious to focus U.S. foreign policy on core geostrategic interests and to lessen what was seen as a preoccupation with the Middle East and Third World nation-building, by summer 2002 the Middle East and nation-building in Afghanistan and even Iraq had come to dominate his foreign policy more than it had President Clinton's. Indeed, the Middle East was now the defining center of the Bush foreign policy, the front line of the war on terrorism. As the leading edge of the next phase in that war, the question of attacking Iraq now dominated discussion in Washington. And, as the debate turned to initiating a preemptive war, basic assumptions about U.S. interests in the region and about how ambitious the United States should be came to the surface in a way that they had not done since the end of the Cold War.

The Strategic Dilemma

The United States became involved in the Middle East in the second half of the twentieth century largely as part of the effort to contain communism. The fear that the Soviet Union might choke off the free flow of oil and thus disrupt NATO and U.S. Asian alliances became a central strategic concern—one that made Saudi Arabia especially important. Israel, too, became important for both instrumental strategic reasons as a military ally and as an ally with which many Americans felt an emotional affinity. When the Cold War ended, American leaders continued to place a high priority on relations with Saudi Arabia and Israel even though the strategic nature of the threat had changed. Regional powers did not present the same sort of threat to the oil supply that Moscow had, because they would still need to sell oil even if they were to establish hegemony in the region. There was no reason to rethink U.S. interests in the region in the 1990s, since the costs of maintaining the status quo were not high and inertia was strong. The 9/11 attacks and the subsequent debate about attacking Iraq, however, raised a public discussion of costs and drew attention to the nature of U.S. interests and the strategic dilemma that Washington faced in the region.

Although Washington's strategic thinking for decades had focused on the threat posed by Moscow and then Iran and Iraq, the attacks on New York and Washington were carried out by individuals from Saudi Arabia and Egypt. Weapons of mass destruction in the hands of radical anti-American regimes and/or terrorist groups suddenly became an immediate tactical priority. In fact, the fear that 9/11 might be repeated with weapons of mass destruction seemed to be the scenario that drove most of President Bush's thinking, as it certainly dominated his statements. There is no reason to doubt that this fear motivated him and good reason to believe that he was aware that should a second attack occur when he had not done everything in his power to prevent it, including taking preemptive measures, he would be condemned by the American people.

Although the president may have been focused on the tactical issue that would have greatest impact in his own place in history, senior advisers in the administration also worried about a deeper strategic problem that derived less from the weapons themselves and more from the will in the region to use them. To contain communism and anti-Israeli and anti-American Arab and Islamic populism, Washington had relied on nondemocratic governments that suffered persisting legitimacy deficits. Authoritarian regimes in Egypt and Saudi Arabia might have contained threats in the past, but they had also spawned al-Qaeda. Paradoxically, to move against state sponsors of anti-Israeli and anti-American terrorism was thought by many in Washington to endanger the stability of Arab regimes presumably friendly to the United States. How to define and defend U.S. interests in a region where popular opinion defined Washington as an unwelcome imperial power was controversial indeed.

Conservatives in the Bush administration were initially ready to continue the balancing act that had characterized U.S. diplomacy in the Middle East for years. In this approach, Washington would continue to provide financial and military assistance to the nondemocratic regimes in Cairo and Riyadh in return for their cooperation in providing stable oil flows and moderate policies vis-à-vis Israel. This aid might also allow these regimes to respond with both sticks and carrots to domestic nationalist or Islamist complaints that they were too soft on Israel and too accommodating to the United States. Of course, in this formula it was important not to push too far the need for these Arab allies to repress public opinion in their own countries. Washington also needed to demonstrate that it could deliver on issues important to Arab and Islamic sentiments, particularly progress on the Palestinian issue. Without some movement toward resolution of this problem, the Arab regimes allied to the United States would be vulnerable to charges of having "sold out" their brethren.

For conservatives, the proposed attack on Iraq was risky because it threatened to stoke Arab and Muslim fears of American imperialism at precisely the moment the United States was trying to elicit Arab and Muslim support against al-Qaeda. At the same time, no progress was being made on the Israeli-Palestinian front, and no prospects for breakthrough were in sight. On the contrary, the peace process was in a tail-spin. In this situation, conservatives were not keen to deal with the additional complication of a war on Iraq, especially when this would be seen in the Arab world as designed to overthrow an Arab government and serve Israeli interests and U.S. oil interests. If Iraq were shown to be closely tied to al-Qaeda, then a case for action might be made. Most conservatives, however, were not persuaded. Convinced that Iraq was already contained, they did not see a compelling reason to take on the near-term risks of a preemptive war—certainly not a war without UN support or the backing of NATO allies. For conservatives, U.S. interests in the Middle East were important but not necessarily the anchor around which other U.S. interests in Europe and Asia should revolve.

Neoconservatives put a higher priority on U.S. interests in the Middle East, and they were ready to adjust U.S. relations with Europe and Asia according to the instrumental role Europeans and Asians played in the Middle East. They thought the anti-Americanism within the region itself to be as much a product of dictatorial leaders as of nationalism or inherent cultural tendencies. Prominent neoconservative voices in the administration argued that many Muslims wanted political change and would endorse democracy if given the chance. The solution to America's problem, in this perspective, was not tinkering with the old formula but a bold break with the past. Washington should use its power to initiate major political change in the region by ousting the blatantly anti-American and anti-Israeli rogue dictators who threatened to acquire weapons of mass destruction and opposed the United States or Israel. At the rhetorical level at least, this plan also included the promotion of democratic reform in states allied to the United States, but obviously this consideration took on less importance in the context of greatly increased projection of U.S. power. This imperial move to extend U.S. influence and presumably to promote progressive political change, neoconservatives argued, was the best way to put longer-term U.S. interests on a more solid footing.

Democracy and the Israeli-Palestinian Conflict

The neoconservative program for change began with Iraq and the Palestinian Authority. Both Saddam Hussein and Yasir Arafat were described as sponsors of terrorism rather than representatives of Arab nationalism. Saddam was clearly an enemy of both the United States and Israel, Arafat an enemy of Israel and probably the United States as well. Beneath each of these leaders, the neoconservatives argued, were more democratically inclined Arabs who might attend to domestic issues and find a way to compromise with Israel and the United States, especially if Washington played a role as an agent of change.[44] Many conservatives and liberals found this perception of the situation overly optimistic if not simply wishful thinking. They noted that hard-line Israelis had been searching for these more accommodating Palestinians to replace Arafat for decades and that this entire characterization of the situation was reminiscent of European imperial arguments of a bygone era.

Liberals favored the emphasis on political reform but were skeptical that the United States could credibly lead this process of change, given its past history in the region and the widespread popular view of Washington as a self-interested imperial power. Clearly, the early focus on democracy in Iraq and Palestine, liberals felt, would do nothing to defuse Arab cynicism about American motives. Liberals were quite sure Arabs would see this new American emphasis on democracy in these cases simply as window-dressing, covering over the use of superior military force by Israel to compel Palestinian capitulation and by the United States to take control of Iraq and its oil. To demonstrate a commitment to democratic political reform that extended beyond self-serving tactical advantage, liberals argued for multilateral, institutional approaches in which Washington's European allies would take the lead, along with agencies of the United Nations.

The involvement of European and UN brokers was very unpopular with the Likud government in Israel and with neoconservatives in Washington. Preferring to settle the conflict with Palestinians from a position of undisputed Israeli superiority and fearing that the Europeans and the United Nations would favor Palestinian preferences more than Washington would, they attacked both European and UN involvement as pro-Arab, if not driven by underlying anti-Semitism. As the violence between Israel and the Palestinians continued, emotions intensified on these issues. Conservatives warned that it would be extremely difficult to mobilize Arab support for an attack on Iraq at a time when the violence in Israeli-Palestinian relations was escalating, and they suggested putting new pressure on Israel and the Palestinian Authority to compromise. Neoconservatives, of course, found this evenhanded approach unacceptable, demanding instead that the Palestinians be increasingly pressured to stop using violence and Israel be supported in its use of force to enhance its security.

With the tension between conservatives and neoconservatives in the administration breaking into public view, a decision was made to send Vice President Cheney to the Middle East. He represented many of the sentiments of the neoconservatives but also had had previous relations with key Arab leaders both in his role as secretary of defense during the previous Gulf War and, afterwards, as an executive of a major oil company. Officials at the State Department, who thought that Cheney's staff, like neoconservatives at the Pentagon, often underappreciated the strength of Arab nationalist sentiments, were also eager to have Cheney get a first-hand view of the anger mounting in the Arab world and the difficulty of assembling a coalition to attack Iraq. Cheney's visit to nine Arab countries, as well as Turkey and Israel, between 10 March and 20 March 2002 was presented as an effort to build support for attacking Iraq. Cheney, after all, had played this role in 1990. This trip, however, did not succeed in this objective. Instead, everywhere the vice president went, except Israel, he heard arguments against attacking Iraq and for concentrating instead on the Palestinian issue and directly combating al-Qaeda.

In April 2002, Secretary Powell tried again to salvage the Israeli-Palestinian peace process and bring about a cease-fire that might hold. Despite strong Israeli and neoconservative objections, Powell met with Yasir Arafat as part of this process. Although this intervention produced some tactical headway on lifting the Israeli siege of Bethlehem, it had little strategic impact.[45] By this point, the government in Israel and neoconservatives in the Bush administration had decided that Arafat must go and a new Palestinians leadership must be found.

In early June, violent Palestinian attacks on Israelis had not abated, and Israeli forces were back on the doorstep of Arafat's headquarters. On 24 June 2002 President Bush called for an end of Arafat's rule and urged Palestinians to replace Arafat with a leader not connected to terror. A few days later, Israeli forces destroyed the

Palestinian headquarters in Hebron, and in September they did the same to Arafat's headquarters in Ramallah. In this context, the Bush administration promoted the democratization of the Palestinian Authority as a way to produce a new Palestinian leadership. It appeared that the neoconservative perspective now prevailed on this issue and that Washington would join Israel in searching for a more accommodating Palestinian leadership. In the meantime, Washington would not criticize Israel's use of force to persuade Palestinians to give up their violent tactics.

Conservatives in the Bush administration may not have been comfortable with this one-sided approach to the peace process, but they did not mount a successful alternative policy. In conjunction with the European Union, Russia, and the United Nations, they prepared a plan for a three-year transition to a Palestinian state, but this plan was not formally released—at least not in 2002. The Israeli-Palestinian conflict was framed instead by the Bush administration almost entirely as part of the war on terrorism, with the Palestinian use of force seen as part and parcel of the terrorist threat Washington faced. It was to be met by force and crushed. With this process underway, neoconservatives turned their attention to Iraq—now it was time, they argued, to overthrow Saddam Hussein.

Attack Iraq?

Although conservatives and liberals saw attacking Iraq as adding fuel to the fires of anti-Americanism in the Middle East, neoconservatives regarded it as part of the overall strategy of defeating radical anti-Israeli and anti-American regimes.[46] Overthrowing the regime in Iraq would demonstrate America's overwhelming power, thus deterring future challenges and reducing current resistance. At the same time, it would liberate Iraqis from a murderous dictator and allow them to focus on domestic reconstruction. Where conservatives worried about the internal risks friendly Arab regimes would face as the United States did battle in Iraq, neoconservatives saw an opportunity.[47] These so-called friendly regimes, they argued, were actually promoting anti-Americanism in their schools and propaganda. Neoconservatives outside the administration, who could express their opinions freely, called the Saudi Arabian regime, for instance, an enemy of the United States.[48] It is not clear how widely this view was shared within the administration, but it was given prominent play at the Pentagon by Richard Perle. In any case, many believed that the nature of these regimes was more a part of the problem than of the solution.

The ambitious agenda of democratizing the Arab world starting with Iraq and then moving on to countries such as Saudi Arabia and Egypt might be promoted as a way to improve the climate for Israel and the United States, but it would be a radical departure for an administration that took office convinced that the Clinton White House had paid too much attention to nation-building in the Third World. Conservatives also worried that sudden liberalization would unleash as many, probably many more, anti-Israeli and anti-American voices than pro-Western democrats in the Middle East. They feared that this grand strategic vision would put U.S. interests in the Arab world at serious risk and that it might simply be part of an Israeli effort to end the balance in U.S. policy between its Israeli and Arab commitments. If the Arab world were to become unremittingly hostile to the United States, then Likud-minded Israelis might reason that the concern about offending Arab nationalism that they often heard in Washington would finally end and that the United States would align definitively with Israel and other non-Arab states such as Turkey.

While all of this grand strategic theorizing filled the time of neoconservatives, conservatives, and liberals in the think tanks all over Washington, it did not convince the American public, the president, or the secretary of state that war with Iraq was necessary. To pay the price of war, more immediate and concrete interests needed to be at stake, so the argument turned to Saddam Hussein's connection to al-Qaeda and his possession of weapons of mass destruction. The claim that Saddam was closely connected to al-Qaeda was not supported by publicly available evidence nor by the Central Intelligence Agency. When neoconservatives in the Pentagon initiated intelligence gathering on this matter within agencies of the Department of Defense,[49] this effort fueled not only bureaucratic competition but charges on both sides that the production of intelligence had been politicized in a fashion not seen since the mid–1970s, when neoconservatives had pressed for a B-team to evaluate Soviet military strength.

It was not the connection to al-Qaeda that eventually took center stage in the Bush administration's argument in favor of war, however, but the claims that Iraq had weapons of mass destruction, that it was close to having nuclear weapons, and that Saddam Hussein had shown previously that he would use such weapons and was not reliably deterred by typical rational calculations. The United States, conservatives and neoconservatives alike argued, could not allow the regime in Baghdad to have possession of such weapons, nor could it wait until after an Iraqi attack had been launched and horrific damage already done before acting. Vice President Cheney, articulating an especially hawkish position in late August 2002, declared that Iraq was a mortal danger that could not be left to a subsequent administration.[50] Cheney's stridency reportedly caught the president off guard and frustrated conservatives in the administration, including Secretary Powell.[51] On 4 September, however, President Bush announced that he would seek congressional approval for military action against Iraq, and on 12 September at the United Nations he declared that Saddam Hussein could either disarm or be disarmed by force but that, in any case, the United States would not wait long to ensure that Iraq did not have weapons of mass destruction.

President Bush's decision to take the case against Iraq to the United Nations was a victory for the conservatives within the administration. That case revolved around disarmament and compliance with previous UN resolutions, not the removal of the Hussein regime. On these issues there was a reasonably good chance of pulling together an international coalition and a chance that the threat of force would compel Iraq to allow UN weapons inspectors to return to Iraq to proceed with the process of insuring Iraq's disarmament. Neoconservatives were unhappy with taking this route both because they had little confidence that the UN's inspections could adequately insure that Iraq did not have weapons of mass destruction and because along this route Saddam Hussein might be allowed to stay in power, thus postponing political reform.[52] Bypassing the United Nations, however, would assure that the administration would face tough international opposition to an attack on Iraq even from its close NATO allies. It would also reduce the level of support for war among the American people, who wanted to be sure that war was the last resort.

On 10 October 2002 Congress approved President Bush's request for authorization for the use of all means, including force, to insure that Iraq was disarmed. Although liberals worried that this move granted the president too much discretion in deciding whether Iraq was complying with the UN inspection regime, neoconservatives, conservatives, and many liberals as well figured that the credible threat of force was the only condition under which there was any likelihood that Iraq would comply with the UN effort.[53] Inspectors returned to Iraq on 14 November, under the auspices of a new UN resolution no. 1441, and Iraq delivered to the Security Council a declaration of its weaponry on 7 December. It did not take long for the Bush administration to find the declaration woefully incomplete and declare Iraq in material breach of UN resolutions.

By this point, American military preparations for war were far along, and the onset of war seemed imminent. Neoconservatives welcomed the opportunity to overthrow the Iraqi regime, while conservatives, although still concerned about the risks, were determined to disarm Iraq if for no other reason than to sustain U.S. credibility. Liberals argued that the United Nations needed to determine Iraqi compliance, not Washington alone, and that action to enforce UN resolutions should be agreed upon in the Security Council, not in the White House. The liberals, of course, were not represented in the Bush administration, and Congress had already authorized the use of force.

Conclusion

President Bush had little experience in foreign policy before taking office, having been more concerned about domestic issues and relationships in the Americas. Reflecting popular conservative sentiments, he initially expressed reservations about becoming deeply involved in nation-building and regional conflicts abroad, especially in the Middle East. September 11th changed that, making foreign policy and homeland security the defining issues for the Bush presidency. This focus placed even relations with the great powers into an instrumental secondary status, as NATO allies, such as France and Germany, were to be judged in some important measure by the roles they played in the war on terrorism and, to a lesser extent, in the war on Iraq. The Middle East came to dominate the agenda, trumping other threats, such as that posed by North Korea's withdrawal from the nuclear non-proliferation treaty. Because of P'yongyang's military strength and South Korea's opposition to a confrontational strategy, the Bush administration worked on that crisis through more diplomatic means. The administration also tended to describe the threat posed by P'yongyang in terms of the danger that North Korea might transfer weapons to groups in the Middle East, although clearly there was also some concern about the danger in Asia.

In the highly charged atmosphere following 9/11, popular mobilization for war and for imperial moral missions to change the nature of politics in far-off lands was at least conceivable in ways that it had not been prior to the terrorist attacks in New York and Washington. This was an important consideration, because among the uniformed ranks of the Pentagon and among conservatives generally, one lesson that had been learned about using force was that before asking soldiers to engage, politicians needed to be sure that vital interests were at stake and that the public would sustain the endeavor. It was not clear how long the public would stay aroused, which, for neoconservatives, meant that the clock was ticking.[54]

After the defeat of the Taliban in Afghanistan, neoconservatives turned quickly to changing the regime in Iraq, an issue they had granted high priority since the first days of the Bush administration. In the context of the war on terrorism and the failure to capture Osama bin Laden, neoconservatives made the case for attacking Iraq and won over the president. Traditional conservatives within the uniformed military and among the former generals now running the State Department counseled caution, pointing out the risks of war, not just in the Middle East but vis-à-vis broader U.S. interests in Europe, Asia, and beyond.[55] They had come into office determined to refocus attention on these matters and to put Middle East affairs into this broader context, but the 9/11 attacks and the war on terrorism that followed derailed this effort. These factors instead put the Middle East at the center of American foreign policy, focusing attention on the instrumental value Russia and China and even NATO allies played in regard to Washington's policy in the Middle East rather than on the intrinsic importance of these other relationships.

The president's National Security Strategy, released in September 2002, stressed the primacy of the war on terrorism but went far beyond the conservative agenda of protecting the homeland and its allies. The strategic statement announced that the United States had a mission larger than merely its own defense—a moral mission that included the promotion of human values taken to be universally valid, including individual freedoms and democratic processes. In December 2002, Richard Haass, the director of Secretary Powell's planning staff gave a high-profile speech laying out America's moral obligation to promote democracy in the Middle East.[56] In an unusually frank appraisal of past U.S. policy, Haass argued that Washington had not made democracy a high priority in the past but that it now needed to do so, even if this meant that in the short run political parties and leaders hostile to the United States would come to office.

With war against Iraq looming, political reform in the Middle East became a visible part of the new Bush strategy. President Bush's foreign policy retained some traditional conservative inclinations but now gave higher priority to the neoconservative agenda than had any previous administration. The appointment in December 2002 of Elliot Abrams, a long-standing neoconservative, as director of Middle East affairs at the National Security Council only strengthened the neoconservative bent. The president himself was said to incline in this direction personally, persuaded partly by his strong Christian religious convictions. The administration was openly planning the post-Saddam future of Iraq, working closely with Iraqi opposition groups, and it appeared determined to disarm and change the regime in Baghdad. President Bush had mobilized a majority of the American public in support of the war effort, and few doubted that the United States had the military ability to succeed. What the costs, both direct and indirect, would be remained uncertain, but that this had become the central issue defining Bush's years in office was clear. Whether the war would eventually polarize the already deep fault lines in his administration and in the general public or rally the country to a new imperial agenda, only history would tell.

President Bush announced the commencement of Operation Iraqi Freedom on 19 March 2003. The American-led war proceeded quickly and met limited Iraqi resistance. Contrary to worst-case fears, the Iraqi army did not fight house-to-house in Baghdad but surrendered the capital city in the face of overwhelming U.S. firepower. Saddam Hussein went into hiding, and on 1 May 2003, President Bush, aboard the USS *Abraham Lincoln* declared that major combat operations in Iraq had ended and that the U.S.-led coalition was now engaged in securing and reconstructing Iraq. At this point, the president's popularity ratings at home were high, and it appeared as if the liberal and conservative fears may have been misplaced. This surely was the spin put on events by the neoconservatives and the White House.

Securing and reconstructing Iraq, however, quickly proved to be just as hard as liberal and conservative critics of the war had warned. They had said throughout the prewar debate that winning the military campaign would be the easy part;

winning the peace would be hard. The initial postwar situation in Iraq was more chaotic than the Bush administration had anticipated, as law and order collapsed across the country. In what appeared to be a change in plans, the administration in early May announced that it was recalling retired Lt. Gen. Jay Garner, who had been sent to lead postwar reconstruction and humanitarian assistance. L. Paul Bremer was sent as a civilian governor to manage Iraq. He explained that the transition to Iraqi sovereignty would take time, perhaps a year or two. Instead of allowing whatever Iraqi leaders might be able to grab power to do so, the United States said that Iraq needed time to decompress and establish a social context in which liberated Iraqis could participate in democratic processes.

The United States named an Iraqi Council to participate in governance and planning during the occupation but quickly faced mounting demands for the provision of security and economic recovery. It also faced increasing terrorist attacks, which made use of weapons that had not been used to defend Baghdad but evidently were taken home and hidden for a later day and guerilla activities. Between 1 May and 31 October 2003, the U.S. military suffered more casualties in Iraq than it had during the period President Bush referred to as major combat. As terror attacks became common events in Iraq and the bill for the continuation of the occupation came due, President Bush faced tougher questions regarding the wisdom of the war and especially the quality of postwar policy.

As the costs of the Iraqi campaign came into focus, the causes of the war became less clear. When chief U.S. weapons inspector David Kay delivered his interim report on 2 October 2003, his team of more than 1,400 inspectors still had not found evidence that Iraq had deployed weapons of mass destruction. The president spoke more often of the human rights and moral purpose of the war and outlined the ambitious plan for remaking the Arab world in democratic fashion that had been the vision of neoconservatives for some time. Although Congress in October 2003 approved an additional $87 billion for the Iraqi campaign, many members did so complaining that they saw little choice. The country was stuck in a credibility trap. It had gone to Iraq and overthrown the regime and could not just walk away. At the same time, the cost was much more than anticipated and there was no exit strategy in sight. Neither France nor Germany had come around to support the war or let Washington off the hook for the costs subsequently, as the administration had said they would.

The United States under George W. Bush had taken on a grand imperial mission to remake the neighborhood in the Middle East. It had done so, however, without the clear support of the American people. They gave support for an attack on Iraq that was couched in terms of protecting the country from an imminent threat of weapons of mass destruction and Iraqi links to al-Qaeda. The evidence for these threats was thin before the war and was not bolstered in the immediate postwar period. As the 2004 presidential campaign opened, Iraq and

America's mission in the Middle East were the central issue. By this point, Washington was still facing daily attacks in Iraq, and the road map for peace between the Israelis and Palestinians that President Bush had launched in Aqaba, Jordan, in June 2003 was at a dead end. No one doubted that America needed to make good on what it had started in Iraq, but how much to pay for this, whether to surrender unilateral U.S. control in exchange for international help, whether to press Israel to appease Palestinian nationalism or stick with a plan to remake the neighborhood by force were the questions already at the forefront of the presidential campaign.

No one could know for sure how the American people would answer these questions. Whether they would pay the price for what Secretary of Defense Rumsfeld, in a memo in mid-October 2003, called a "long, hard slog" that could go on for decades, however, would go a long way in answering another question that would be front and center in 2004. That was whether to reelect the president that had led the country into war in the Middle East.

Notes

1. See the second 2000 presidential debate between George W. Bush and Al Gore at Wake Forest University, Winston-Salem, N.C., 11 October 2000, www.debates.org/pages/trans2000b.html.

2. George W. Bush, "Address to a Joint Session of Congress and the American People," Washington, D.C., 20 September 2001, www.whitehouse.gov/news/releases/2001/09/20010920–8.html.

3. "Joint Statement by President George Bush and President Vicente Fox towards Partnership for Prosperity," Washington, D.C., 16 February 2001, www.whitehouse.gov/news/releases/2001/02/20010216–3.html.

4. See second 2000 presidential debate.

5. On U.S. policy, see William B. Quandt, *Peace Process: American Diplomacy and the Arab-Israeli Conflict since 1967* (Berkeley: University of California Press, 1993), 335–58; and Steven L. Spiegel, *The Other Arab-Israeli Conflict: Making America's Middle East Policy, from Truman to Reagan* (Chicago: University of Chicago Press, 1985), 395–429. On Israel's invasion, see Ze'ev Schiff and Ehud Ya'ari, *Israel's Lebanon War* (New York: Simon and Schuster, 1984).

6. Caspar Weinberger, *Fighting for Peace: Seven Critical Years in the Pentagon* (New York: Warner Books, 1990).

7. Alexander Haig, *Caveat, Realism, Reagan and Foreign Policy* (New York: Macmillan, 1984).

8. George P. Shultz: *Turmoil and Triumph: My Years as Secretary of State* (New York: Scribner's, 1993), 43–84.

9. See James Baker III, with Thomas M. Defrank, *The Politics of Diplomacy: Revolution, War & Peace, 1989–1992* (New York: Putnam, 1995), 115–31; and George Bush and Brent Scowcroft, *A World Transformed* (New York: Knopf, 1998).

10. See Daniel Pipes, "Why the U.S. Should Bolster Iraq," *New York Times*, 31 May 1987, 29; Daniel Pipes and Laurie Mylroie, "Back Iraq," *New Republic*, 27 April 1987, 14–15; and Laurie Mylroie, "After the Guns Fell Silent: Iraq in the Middle East," *Middle East Journal* 43, no. 1 (Winter 1989): 51–67.

11. David Halberstam, *War in a Time of Peace: Bush, Clinton, and the Generals* (New York: Scribner's, 2001).

12. See Ole R. Holsti and James N. Rosenau, *American Leadership in World Affairs: Vietnam and the Breakdown of Consensus* (Boston: Allen & Unwin, 1984). Also see Richard K. Herrmann, "The Power of Perceptions in Foreign Policy Decision Making: Do Views of the Soviet Union Determine the Policy Choices of American Leaders?" *American Journal of Political Science* 30, no. 4 (November 1986): 841–75.

13. For an extreme example, see Patrick J. Buchanan, *A Republic, Not an Empire : Reclaiming America's Destiny* (Washington, D.C.: Regnery, 1999).

14. See Nicholas Lemann, "Inside Bush Administration Foreign Policy," *New Yorker*, 25 March 2002; Justin Brown, "A Gulf Opens around Colin Powell," *Christian Science Monitor*, 23 January 2001, 1; and Janine Zacharia, "All the President's Middle East Men," *Jerusalem Post*, 24 January 2001, 5B.

15. On the views of the uniformed military, see Peter Feaver and Christopher Gelpi, *American Civil-Military Relations and the Use of Force* (Princeton: Princeton University Press, 2003); and Halberstam, *War in a Time of Peace*.

16. Dana Milbank, "Who's Pulling the Foreign Policy Strings?" *Washington Post*, 14 May 2002, A19. Also see Julian Borger, "Washington Hawks Get Power Boost," *The Guardian*, 17 December 2001.

17. Ed Vulliamy, "Hawks and Doves Fight for Control of Campaign," *The Observer*, 30 September 2001.

18. See Dale Russakoff, "Lessons of Might and Right," *Washington Post Magazine*, 9 September 2001, 23–39.

19. George W. Bush, "Statement by the President on American Plane and Crew in China," Washington, D.C., 2 April 2001, www.whitehouse.gov/news/releases/2001/04/ 20010402-2 .html.

20. Barry Bearak, "Afghanistan: US to Help Remove Mines," *New York Times,* 21 April 2001, A6.

21. Barbara Crossette, "US Sends 2 to Assess Drug Problem," *New York Times,* 25 April 2001, A5.

22. Bob Woodward, *Bush at War* (New York: Simon and Schuster, 2002), 38–39.

23. Condoleezza Rice, "Promoting the National Interest," *Foreign Affairs* 79, no. 1 (January/February 2000): 45–62, at p. 47.

24. Jane Perlez, "Powell Shifts Emphasis of Mideast Policy," *New York Times,* 21 April 2001, A10.

25. "Remarks by the President and Prime Minister of Israel Ariel Sharon," Washington, D.C., 26 June 2001, www.whitehouse.gov/news/releases/2001/06/20010626–12.html.

26. Jane Perlez. "Taking a Breather on the Mideast," *New York Times,* 5 July 2001, A6.

27. Robin Wright, "Bush's Foreign Policy Team Is Split on How to Handle Hussein," *Los Angeles Times*, 14 February 2001, A1. Also see Eli Lake, "Pentagon Seeks to Take Over Iraq Policy," UPI, 21 March 2001; and Amos Perlmutter, "Flux at the Foreign Policy Helm," *Washington Times*, 15 March 2001.

28. Susan Baer, "An Abiding Goal: Topple Hussein," *Baltimore Sun*, 12 May 2002, 1F.

29. Rice, "Promoting the National Interest," 60.

30. Colin Powell, "Remarks at the National Newspaper Association's 40th Annual Government Affairs Conference," Washington, D.C., 23 March 2001.

31. George W. Bush, "Address to a Joint Session of Congress and the American People," Washington, D.C., 20 September 2001.

32. George W. Bush, "Remarks by the President to the United Nations General Assembly," New York, 10 November 2001.

33. Suzanne Daley, "NATO says US Has Proof against bin Laden Group," *New York Times*, 3 October 2001, A1.

34. David Sanger and Patrick Tyler, "Wartime Forges a Unified Front for Bush Aides," *New York Times*, 23 December 2001, A1.

35. Thomas Ricks, "Desert Caution," *Washington Post*, 28 January 2003, C1.

36. Department of Defense, *Quadrennial Defense Review Report*, Washington D.C., 30 September 2001.

37. Deputy Secretary of Defense Paul Wolfowitz, "The War on Terrorism," speech to American Institute of Aeronautics and Astronautics," Washington, D.C., 19 February 2002, www.defenselink.mil/speeches/2002/s20020219-depsecdef.html.

38. Although deterrence and defense dominated the main objectives laid out in the *Quadrennial Defense Review* in September 2001, offense and preemption as the best way to conduct a war on terrorism dominated the logic and objectives laid out in President Bush's National Security Strategy statement issued in September 2002.

39. James Fallows, "The Unilateralist: A Conversation with Paul Wolfowitz," *Atlantic Monthly*, March 2002, 26–28.

40. Woodward, *Bush at War*, 83–84. Also see Bob Woodward and Dan Balz, "At Camp David, Advise and Dissent," *Washington Post*, 31 January 2002, A1.

41. R.W. Apple, "Piece-by-Piece Coalition: Rumsfeld's Delicate Mission," *New York Times*, 4 October 2001, A1.

42. Woodward, *Bush at War*, 84–85.

43. Gerard Baker, "Interview with Colin Powell," *Financial Times*, 14 February 2002. Also see Robin Wright, "Bush's Team Targets Hussein," *Los Angeles Times*, 10 February 2002, A1.

44. Paul Wolfowitz, "Bridging the Gap with the Muslim World," speech to the Asia Security Conference: The Shangri-La Dialogue, 1 June 2002. In an earlier interview, Wolfowitz estimated that if Iraqis had the chance to vote freely, more than 95 percent would agree with a decision for change and liberation. See "Interview with Paul Wolfowitz," Fox News, U.S. Department of Defense News Transcript, 25 May 2002, www.defenselink.mil/news/May2002/t05282002_t0525dsd.html. Also see Thom Shanker, "Key U.S. Pentagon Officials Calls for Ties with Moderate Muslims," *New York Times*, 5 May 2002, 22.

45. Alan Sipress, "Policy Divide Thwarts Powell in Mideast Effort: Defense Dept.'s Influence Frustrates State Dept.," *Washington Post*, 26 April 2002, A1.

46. See Richard Perle, "Why the West Must Strike First against Saddam Hussein," *London Daily Telegraph*, 9 August 2002. Also see Joshua Micah Marshall, "Bomb Saddam? How the Obsession of a Few Neocon Hawks Became the Central Goal of U.S. Foreign Pol-

icy," *Washington Monthly*, June 2002.

47. See Seymour Hersh, "The Debate Within," *New Yorker*, 11 March 2002.

48. Victor Davis Hanson, "Our Enemies, the Saudis," *Commentary*, July–August 2002, 23–28.

49. See Robert Dreyfuss, "The Pentagon Muzzles the CIA," *American Prospect*, 16 December 2002.

50. Richard B. Cheney, "Remarks by the Vice President to the Veterans of Foreign Wars 103rd National Convention," Nashville, Tenn., 26 August 2002, www.whitehouse.gov /news/releases/2002/08/20020826.html.

51. Woodward, *Bush at War*, 344–46.

52. Paul Wolfowitz is reported to have asked the CIA to investigate the performance of Hans Blix, the chairman of the UN inspection team, as part of the neoconservative opposition to relying on the United Nations. See Walter Pincus and Colum Lynch, "Skirmish on Iraq Inspections, Wolfowitz Had CIA Probe UN Diplomat in Charge," in *Washington Post*, 15 April 2002, A1. Also see Julian Borger, "US Hawks Try to Sully UN Inspector," in *The Guardian*, 16 April 2002.

53. Paul Wolfowitz explained the consensus this way: "Let's acknowledge that there is a seeming paradox here. The simple truth is, our only hope, and let me emphasize—our only hope—of achieving that peaceful outcome is if we confront the Iraqi regime with a credible threat of force behind our diplomacy. To be effective, the two must be part of a single policy. They are not two separate policies." Paul Wolfowitz, "Speech at the International Institute for Strategic Studies," Arundel House, London, 2 December 2002, available at www.IISS.org.

54. Public support for attacking Iraq spiked to over 70 percent in November 2001. By August 2002, it had declined to nearly pre–9/11 levels. See David Moore, "Majority of Americans Favor Attacking Iraq to Oust Saddam Hussein, But Support Has Declined to Pre–9/11 Level; Four in 10 Now Opposed," *Gallup News Service*, poll analysis, 23 August 2002.

55. Jeffrey Donovan, "U.S. Generals Said to be Cautious About Hitting Iraq" in *RFE/RL*, 14 June 2002; and David Rennie, "Military Chiefs Defy Bush on Iraq," *The Telegraph*, 25 May 2002.

56. Richard Haass, "U.S. Has Responsibility to Promote Democracy," speech to the Council on Foreign Relations, 4 December 2002, State Department Press Release and Documents, Federal Information & News Dispatch. Also see Richard Haass, "Defining U.S. Foreign Policy in a Post-Post-Cold War World," remarks to Foreign Policy Association, New York, 22 April 2002.

CHAPTER 9

Bush and Interest Groups
A Government of Chums

Mark A. Peterson

WHEN GEORGE W. BUSH did his Texas amble into the White House, he entered a capital often characterized as being awash in particularized interests. Oft repeated references to the "K Street Corridor" and "Gucci Gulch" capture the imagery of high-powered—and lavishly paid—lobbyists, plying their trade on behalf of well-heeled interests. Looking into Congressional Quarterly's *Washington Information Directory*, one finds identified a far more varied legion of labor unions, trade associations, organizations representing public and nonprofit institutions, citizen groups, advocacy centers, think tanks, and the like. Many are located figuratively and literally between the Oval Office and Capitol Hill, as well as between the Executive Office of the President and the agencies of the executive branch.

Even a deep textual examination of the U.S. Constitution will not reveal a single mention of either political parties or interest groups. Yet both play profound roles in the nation's politics and policymaking, influencing dramatically the context of presidential leadership. Organized interests are often spoken of disparagingly as "special interests" or "pressure groups" that thwart the pursuit of reasoned policymaking in the public interest. To be sure, such organizations do pose challenges and dangers to a president. Organized opponents to a chief executive's agenda can find allies among other elected officials and exploit the myriad veto points of the highly decentralized system of American government to help block a president's preferred courses of action. It is not surprising that some chief executives—President Ronald Reagan being a prime example—have tried to use their leverage to defund and politically defang groups they have identified as instrumental adversaries.[1] Even interest groups among a president's own electoral constituency can wreak havoc, acting to prevent the compromises on specific policy issues that an administration may determine to be substantively sufficient and politically advantageous. Democratic President Jimmy Carter complained, for example, that "when you don't measure up a 100 percent with those so-called liberal groups, they demand a gallon of blood. There's no compromise with them."[2]

In a governing system without much glue joining institutions and officials together, however, where successful leadership is predicated upon the continuous building of supporting coalitions in a number of institutional venues, organized interests can serve as influential allies of presidents. When such groups work in concert with the White House, their ties to other elected officials and capacity to mobilize constituencies can be used to forge winning alliances that bridge the institutional divides of American government. They can also help presidents reach out to segments of the public to burnish their images, enhance their credibility, and secure their roles as both head of state and head of government.

These patterns of what I refer to as "interest group liaison" between the White House and groups have been firmly established in the tool kit of presidential leadership for the past several administrations. They were routine features of governing as George W. Bush survived the crisis in Florida voting and assumed the powers of the presidency. His White House organization inherited several features of communications with interest groups that had been established earlier. Before the new administration unfolded, however, it was not obvious what overall strategy would guide the new President Bush's relationship with the interest group community. Would he and his administration make overtures to a broad range of organized interests to facilitate overcoming the questions of legitimacy created by the 2000 presidential election, which cast him as the first elected chief executive since Rutherford B. Hayes in 1876 to enter the Oval Office without having won the popular vote? Or, enjoying the first unified Republican government in two generations, would he pursue an activist agenda in Congress, fashioning alliances between Republican-led legislative coalitions and organized interests with similar ideological and partisan sympathies? Despite the balanced logic of these questions, the answer harbors no suspense. From the actual nature of George W. Bush's programmatic agenda and engagement with corporate and right-wing organized interests, one might have assumed that he and his Republican counterparts in Congress had just won a stunning and unambiguous landslide. The president may be, in his words, "a uniter, not a divider," but that assertion seems to have meant only that he would emphasize unity within the business and conservative ranks.

To provide the basis for judging the nature and import of President George W. Bush's relationships with the interest group community during the first years of his administration, I begin by providing analytical background on the context, means, and purposes of White House–group relations as they pertain to the new Bush administration. I describe the broadly transformed social and political world that Bush and his immediate predecessors confronted and how it has posed both political risks and openings for group coalition building. Next I consider the process by which formal linkages to organized interests became a standard feature of White House operations in the postwar period and a fully developed instrument available for Bush to amend and exploit for his purposes on the political terrain he confronted. I then present a generic typology of interest group liaison initiated by the White House that identifies the ways in which different types of presidential objectives and political conditions trigger quite varied group strategies. An activist president wishing to pursue a major and contentious legislative agenda, for example, turns to politically compatible and influential groups as participants in a "governing party" coalition. A chief executive with less-divisive programmatic initiatives can approach diverse organized interests to nurture policy consensus. The mechanisms of interest group liaison can also be used by presidents for more symbolic or representational purposes, either to reach out to marginalized interests counted among their electoral constituencies or to secure support from a wide array of mainstream groups in order to protect or recapture the political authority of an administration under siege. Using this conceptual framework for interest group liaison by the White House, I elaborate on how these relationships, and the president's leadership of them, could be affected by alternative interpretations of Bush's objectives and the context in which his presidency began and then evolved. Turning to the record of his first term, reported in the remainder of the chapter, I assemble evidence that shows a president who for the most part actively pursued a distinctly partisan programmatic agenda cultivated through close, often intimate, links to interests deeply embedded in the Republican electoral coalition. Where Bill Clinton succeeded primarily in "splitting friends" and "unifying enemies," George W. Bush has offered a government of chums.[3]

Social Institutions, Interest Groups, and Government

If George Washington, by popular adage, was the father of the United States, by most accounts it is fair to claim that President Franklin Delano Roosevelt begat what we now refer to as the modern presidency. Even within that convention, however, by the time a Bush entered the White House—either father or son—the generic requirements of presidential leadership and the environment in which it is practiced had proved far more complicated. When FDR served in the White House, state political party leaders played a significant role in selecting nominees and orchestrating successful campaigns. The president spoke to the public in occasional "fireside chats" via the new medium of radio, but public opinion polling was not yet routine; transportation technology limited the reach, frequency, and timeliness of the chief executive's travels throughout the country; and the dominating image and words of a president on television remained years in the future.[4] Although voluntary associations are as old as the republic itself, and group mobilization flourished in the late nineteenth and early twentieth centuries, often nurtured by democratic institutions and government itself,[5] the nation's capital was not awash in organized interests, advocacy centers, ideological think tanks, corporate public affairs offices, and lobbying firms. The primary groups of concern to presidents were significant blocs among their electoral constituencies. In both political parties there were few effective challengers to business interests other than the emerging labor movement, which gained federal protection during FDR's administration. Politically marginal groups, such as African Americans, were given only the most subtle access to policymaking and the presidential establishment.[6] Others enjoyed no entrée at all.

The six decades between Roosevelt's sudden death and George W. Bush's controversial ascension to office witnessed a profound transformation of the structure of social organization in the United States, with important implications for the relationship between interest groups and the contemporary presidency. The public became vastly more educated and thus more primed for direct and targeted communications from particular interests rather than just the mass mobilization of political parties, trade unions, or occasional broad-based movements such as the antialcohol temperance movement. In 1952, only six in ten adults twenty-five years old and over had gone beyond elementary school, and just 15 percent had any college-level education. In 2000, almost everyone enjoyed more than a grammar school education and over 50 percent had attended college.[7] Technological progress also altered the means of public communication and group organization. At first the rapid spread of television ownership in the 1950s and 1960s, picking up broadcasts over a limited number of channels, offered administrations a particular political advantage—no one else could command or dominate the medium as thoroughly as the president could. Jet airplanes, computer-assisted polling, advanced telecommunications, satellite transmissions, the shift toward cable television, and the rise of the Internet all accelerated unmediated interchange between the electorate and the president, but also between the public—more specifically a vast array of specialized publics—and both the administration's allies and its adversaries among groups and within Congress. Improvements in computer, telephone, direct-mail, and television technologies greatly enhanced the capacity of organizational entrepreneurs to identify and communicate with more easily identified potential supporters and members, no matter how narrow the niche of interests.

Broad patterns of social change in the 1960s and 1970s overwhelmed the traditional political party organizations, shifting the nomination process for the presidency and for congressional offices from state and local party leaders to a primary system that was based more than before on personal campaigns, utilization of the new technologies of communication with the electorate, and movement politics. In FDR's time, the congressional parties were tied closely to the party apparatus in each state, leading to important divisions in the Democratic ranks between southern conservatives, who were often in alliance with Republicans, and more liberal northerners; similar differentiation emerged between moderate urban Republicans and their colleagues. The social and demographic changes reflected in the new group system also resulted in altered parties in Congress as the twentieth century came to a close. While conservative southern districts and states elected more Republicans and fewer Democrats, and urban Republicans lost ground to Democratic challengers, congressional Republicans became more uniformly right-of-center and Democrats became more consistently left-of-center, yielding a House and Senate that were far more ideologically polarized along party lines.[8]

The organizational dynamism of the interest group system is especially noteworthy. Just in terms of raw numbers, the scope of organized interests grew dramatically by every available measure. The number of voluntary organizations listed in the *Encyclopedia of Associations* jumped fourfold, from 5,843 in 1959 to 23,298 in 1995. Forty percent of the organizations included in the 1981 edition of *Washington Representatives*—entities with a formal presence in the nation's capital—reported founding dates since 1960; a quarter arrived on the scene during the decade of the 1970s. These numbers do not even fully incorporate the massive proliferation in nonmembership advocacy outfits, legal action centers, think tanks, corporate public affairs offices, and for-hire lobbying and law firms often representing numerous clients.[9]

More important, the growth in the system has not been a matter of more of the same. The civil rights movement, which gained momentum in the 1950s, not only led to a massive expansion of political participation by African Americans, but also furnished the training ground and paradigm for successful social action subsequently exploited first on the left by the women's, consumer, environmental, and gay rights social movements and later by the Christian right and its compatriots, all of which spawned new sets of enduring formal organizations to represent these interests both in the streets and in the established corridors of power. The social movements of the 1960s and 1970s yielded myriad new "citizen groups" that challenged existing interests, especially those representing the for-profit and business sectors. They disrupted old monopolies in various policy areas and were potential allies of activist Democrats. Because of entrepreneurial leadership aided by wealthy benefactors, foundations, government agencies (through grants or contracts), and other "patrons of political action" (to use Jack Walker's term), they achieved a more secure organizational footing than similar groups had in the past.[10] While the number of voluntary associations representing the profit and nonprofit sectors grew by around 60 percent between 1960 and 1995, and unions remained fairly stable, the number of citizen groups such as the National Organization for Women, Citizen Action, Friends of the Earth, and the National Council of La Raza, jumped 180 percent.[11] The complexion of the interest group system shifted again, as the emergence of increasing numbers of organizations derived from liberal social movements stimulated a response on the right, with the formation of conservative think tanks (the Heritage Foundation), legal action centers (the Washington Legal Foundation), and advocacy entities (the Family Research Council) and mobilization of grass-roots conservatives (best illustrated by the Christian Coalition), all of which could help solidify Republican coalitions.[12]

Strategic approaches for influencing policy and politics also began to blur. At first, the liberal citizen groups and their social movement forbears concentrated on "outside" strategies that included grass-roots mobilization of adherents at the community level, while commercial and other traditional interests relied on "inside" strategies, such as more quiet backroom lobbying of government officials. By the 1990s conservatives had their own broad-based, pro-Christian, antigovernment, antitaxation movements. Commercial interests such as the banking, insurance, and telecommunications industries began using new consulting firms (and the more sophisticated polling and telephone technologies) to launch what appeared to be grass-roots popular responses favoring their policy agendas—often called "Astroturf mobilization" to suggest its stimulated, often targeted, and less than authentic quality. Environmental, women's, consumer, and even gay rights organizations, meanwhile, had become "establishment" enough to have direct access to the president and Congress.[13] Amid this ferment on both the left and right, however, came declines in "peak associations" that could speak for significant segments of the polity and that were sources of traditional broad-based organizational strength in support of liberal and conservative issues. For example, organized labor, the backbone of the drive for much liberal social policy and a mainstay of Democratic electoral coalitions, watched union membership drop from nearly 30 percent of the workforce in the 1950s to less than half that at the dawn of the 1990s (and from a third of self-identified Democrats in 1960 to just 11 percent in 1990). In 2000, only 9 percent of employees working for private business belonged to a union. The figures are even lower in the South; unions in North Carolina represent a paltry 3.6 percent of the state's workforce. To many members of Congress, the AFL-CIO is "just one more PAC," or political action committee, among hundreds. On the other side, closer to Republican ranks, the American Medical Association was long the voice of medicine (as well as unfettered free enterprise), with almost all practicing physicians counted as members and few organizational challengers. By the early 1990s, though, it could claim just over 40 percent of doctors as members and struggled with myriad organizational competitors.[14]

As had been the case for Bill Clinton before him, when Bush became president the interest group terrain as a whole thus defied simple characterization.

There were a vastly larger number of relevant organizations, and more specialized policy niches, and yet there was also arguably much greater ideological and partisan division among interests. In this context, by virtue of the technological advances and demographic changes, Bush would have the means to communicate both with the public en masse and through specific messages to myriad targeted audiences, but so would organizational interests and their legislative allies who were antagonistic to him and his programmatic agenda. Still, the new president had a mobilizing advantage over his predecessor. Clinton's New Democratic approach to policymaking ran against the grain of both affiliates of his own party and many organized interests with issue-oriented ties to the Democrats: his support of free trade encountered opposition from organized labor; his promotion of competition among private insurance plans in health care reform antagonized most liberal consumer groups and other organizations supporting universal coverage; his focus on personal responsibility prompted distrust by advocates of the poor. Bush, on the other hand, emphasized themes from his campaign—tax cuts, defense build-up, energy production, education reform, and market-oriented strategies overall—that were more likely to meld commercial interest and conservative social movement groups into a cohesive whole than to drive them apart.[15] If there were serious coalitional weaknesses to be found in the interest group community, it was among the president's opponents. The earlier rise of citizen groups strengthened the organizational armament of Bush's liberal adversaries, but trade unions had lost much of their reach within the electorate and much of their influence with members of Congress. Further, in addition to now facing a countermobilization of social movements on the right, the liberal citizen organizations are often, as Theda Skocpol has noted, "staff-led, mailing-list associations" with checkbook memberships, devoid of labor's previous ability to conduct face-to-face grass-roots mobilization. Ironically, it was the old staid business interests, likely allies of Bush, who had learned to exploit the grass-roots mobilizing techniques of the left, made all the more effective when they join forces with the energized social movements on the right.[16]

Past Presidents, Bush, and the Group System

To enhance their sway in the realm of politics and many domains of policy, chief executives, especially in the modern era, have employed three general strategies in interest group relations: intimidating the opposition, promoting and winning friends, and mobilizing allies to achieve specific political or policy objectives.[17] Bush would not need to experiment; he just needed to choose his weapons.[18]

Ronald Reagan pursued the most aggressive strategy of any modern president for enfeebling the organized interests perceived to be working at purposes contrary to those of his administration. As reported by Peterson and Walker,

[T]he Reagan administration launched a campaign to "defund the left." . . . [It] sought to inhibit the growth and reduce the financial resources available from the government for interest groups operating in Washington. Strenuous efforts were made to prevent federal agencies from providing grants, contracts, or consultancies to interest groups. In collateral moves, the Office of Management and Budget (OMB) sought to change regulations concerning the political activities of federal contractors, and the Internal Revenue Service (IRS) altered the bases under which tax exemption was granted to make it more difficult for nonprofit groups to engage in anything resembling partisan political activity.[19]

In one sense, these efforts were successful—federal government funding was reduced for "types of groups most likely to oppose the administration's principal goals." In other respects, though, the attack turned out to be poorly aimed, hitting not "leftist" or liberal citizen groups, which had never relied heavily on government largesse, but instead "mainly associations of social service professionals in the nonprofit sector [and others] that were the most heavily dependent on government financial support." These organizations had been largely nonpartisan and far less political, but the cutbacks tended to alienate and politicize them in response to the administration's threat.[20]

Coming to the scene when labor was weakened and conservative groups firmly established, Bush had less incentive than Reagan to drive a stake through the heart of the opposition. Nonetheless, early in his administration he pursued some institutional and legal changes that would either impair opposing interests or reduce their access to government. Recognizing the gender gap in which women voters favored Democrats more than men did, Bill Clinton had established the White House Office for Women's Initiatives and Outreach to focus particular attention on women's advocacy groups. As soon as Bush took over the White House, however, he abolished this office (unbeknownst to feminist organizations until a couple of months later) and folded representation of women back into the Office of Public Liaison. One of the president's advocates explained that the "Bush administration does not intend to treat women as a coalition. At 52 percent of the population, we are not a special interest group." The administration did establish a "White House Women's Information Network," but, although neutral sounding, this network clearly does not target all women or their perspectives. Instead it focuses largely on corporate CEOs and small-business leaders, and it is supported in spirit by the National Federation of Republican Women and RightNow!—another GOP women's group with a Web site, www. politicalchicks.com. These ties imply a take on women's issues that, in fact, favors Republican coalition building.[21] Similarly, Andrew Card, the White House chief of staff, told *USA Today* early on that the administration was terminating the

Office of National AIDS Policy and the Initiative for One America (focused on race relations), which also had been created by the Clinton White House and were especially pertinent to Democratic constituencies. Shortly thereafter, however, "moving to quell a public relations squall," the president's press secretary announced that Card had "made a mistake. It happens."[22] These operations would remain active, at least in some form, but their relative standing in the Bush White House was made apparent.

The Bush administration saved its most serious "attack" for unions, the organizational backbone of the Democratic opposition. By March 2001, labor leaders identified a dozen Bush initiatives that challenged their interests, from endorsement of "paycheck protection" legislation (requiring that members give unions explicit permission to use dues for political purposes) and congressional repeal of new ergonomics regulations to executive orders governing federal contracting and terminating a labor-management partnership for federal workers. Said one labor expert, "It's as if several of these actions have been taken to insult the AFL-CIO." Labor leaders interpreted this overall effort as "retaliation," a form of "punishment for their backing Al Gore."[23]

More important, these officials believed, these initiatives were motivated by coalition-building strategies of the administration, presented "as part of a broader strategy to weaken organized labor on national issues in general and in politics in particular" in order to foster "an unfettered field for corporate interests."[24] Later, unions would claim that the Bush administration was using legislation that authorized creation of a massive new Department of Homeland Security "as a backdoor attempt to erode worker protections" because of its inclusion of personnel provisions that circumvent existing civil service "pay and performance rules" and thwart union organizing.[25] Finally, just after the November 2002 congressional elections, the administration announced plans to open about half of federal jobs to competition from contractors in the private sector. The head of the American Federation of Government Employees retorted that the president had "declared all-out war on federal employees."[26] To be sure, President Bush has at times sought to build alliances with various unions or favored their positions. But in each of these specific cases—reaching out to the Teamsters in support of drilling for oil in the Arctic National Wildlife Refuge (ANWR), the United Auto Workers in opposition to raising fuel efficiency standards, and the United Steel Workers of America in favoring tariffs against foreign steel imports—labor was on the same side as industry.[27]

All presidents in one way or another have engaged in activities that are designed to promote and win friends, including within the interest group community. To some extent that objective is easiest to fulfill in personnel decisions, most notably by the use of patronage to fill government offices at all ranks, over which presidents had considerable control until the introduction of the civil service in the late nineteenth century.[28] Bill Clinton, of course, famously sought to appoint to the cabinet and senior agency positions individuals who would "look like America"—and, one might add, more like the constituencies of the Democratic Party.[29] Unlike his father and other Republican presidents before him, the current President Bush has incorporated diversity among senior appointments similar to that witnessed under Clinton, at least with respect to physical appearance. His appointees, in many respects, *look* like America, too. Still, there is no mistaking which interests are indeed friends of the administration.

Consider the financial contributors to the Bush campaign during the 2000 presidential election. Enron Corporation, of course, rings a bell. According to the Center for Public Integrity, Enron CEO Kenneth Lay and other executives ensured that the firm was "the single largest patron of George W. Bush's political career. . . . Bush received $774,100 from Enron's PAC and executives—including $312,500 for his two gubernatorial campaigns." Other contributions totaling more than $1 million flowed into campaign coffers from various legal, accounting, and banking enterprises employed by Enron. Overall, according to Texans for Public Justice, the "George W. Bush campaign. . . raised more money than any other political candidate in history, twice as much as any presidential candidate before him." Much of that funding came from the campaign's "Pioneers"— more than two hundred individuals who were responsible for raising at least $100,000 each. About half of them were business executives, and almost all represented corporate interests, including forty-four lawyers and lobbyists, thirty-eight individuals from the finance industry, and twenty-eight from energy and natural resources concerns, followed by other commercial interests.[30]

After the disputed election was settled by the Supreme Court, the *National Journal* published "Corporations, K Street Throw a Party," describing how companies and lobbyists representing them contributed nearly $25 million to help pay for Bush's inauguration. About 160 "corporate and individual underwriters. . . [include]. . . big names from the financial services sector, the oil and gas industry, real estate companies, and computer interests. . . . K Street-based associations are well represented, too, including the American Bankers Association, the American Insurance Association, the American Trucking Association, and the Pharmaceutical Research and Manufacturers of America."[31] The flow of people as well as dollars clearly reflected the nature of the Bush coalition. Just as had occurred under Reagan's orchestrated personnel strategy, during the transition, advisory teams for executive departments were joined by myriad major-industry lobbyists and were "also chock-full of corporate executives, fund-raisers, big donors, conservative think-tankers, and former GOP officials." They, or individuals of similar backgrounds, went on to be tapped for political appointments in the Bush executive branch (as becomes apparent in the later discussion of particular policy areas). Democrats sought to "gain some traction [with] the general thematic charge that he's a President for the special interests," with polls showing concerns that he "will go too far with policies that favor the rich and corporate interests over the middle class." When a similar claim was made by Democrats that Bush was a "captive of corporate interests" in the development of his Medicare drug-discount initiative, the administration responded that the president was merely "harnessing the expertise and ingenuity of private industry."[32]

In forming a government, Bush—the recipient of an M.B.A. from Harvard Business School and himself a former corporate executive—turned to members of the business community, with whom he is familiar, among whom he feels comfortable, and who share both his approach to decision making and his policy preferences. He also solidified his alliance with conservative interests that extend beyond the business world. Perhaps the best example is his creation of the White House Office of Faith-Based and Community Initiatives immediately upon taking office. Social and religious conservatives have long sought to bridge the separation between church and state and to make far greater use of faith-based organizations in promoting and implementing social policy. The significance of this constituency for Bush is underscored by his use of an executive order to institute this new office, an approach that Kathryn Dunn Tenpas and Stephen Hess report is rarely used by presidents for such single-policy, constituency-based operations within the White House establishment.[33]

Thus far, like Clinton, Bush has not yet gone from catering to existing friendly interests to the next step taken by John Kennedy, Lyndon Johnson, and Ronald Reagan, of actively reshaping the community of interests to their advantage. Much of the women's movement, for example, organizationally sprang from conferences, state Commissions on the Status of Women, and funding organized or promoted by the Kennedy White House.[34] Johnson's Great Society programs, such as the War on Poverty, which included provisions for Community Action Programs, required the maximum feasible participation in program implementation by the populations receiving social services. These initiatives failed to fulfill their explicit policy objectives, but they nonetheless helped to inaugurate the development of new leaders and organizations—especially among African Americans—that would ensure the presence of additional institutional allies for liberal programs in the future.[35]

Reagan, naturally, wished to do the opposite. His administration "sought to disrupt the ties that bind the Democrats to major social groups" and tried "to expand the constellation of interests that are tied to the GOP." According to Benjamin Ginsberg and Martin Shefter,

> In this endeavor they [Reagan, followed by the first Bush] have not been limited to working with a predefined political universe. Political leaders can undertake to destroy established centers of power, reorganize interests, and call

new groups into being. Recent Republican administrations have attempted to transform the political identities of established groups, to create new political forces by dividing existing groups, and to construct new interests by uniting previously disparate forces.[36]

Reagan's strategy along these lines involved "reunifying business," switching "middle-income suburbanites . . . from beneficiaries [of government programs] to taxpayers," reorienting blue-collar voters from "workers to patriots," and enticing southern whites through their "evangelical religious affiliations." The new Republican coalition would link Evangelical Protestants with Catholics to combat abortion, and meld business with the professional class to serve economic interests, all intending to "reconstitute society," recast who is represented, and alter how alliances are formed within the interest group community.[37] Presidential and congressional electoral politics were remade as a result of these efforts. Given Reagan's achievements in this regard, which were further cemented by conservative Republican congressional majorities after the 1994 election and invigorated by the right-wing attacks on Clinton, few business or even meaningful conservative social groups have had difficulty mobilizing or gaining access to influential policymakers. Bush has not needed to do any more to encourage a vigorous interest group domain favorable to GOP interests.

The signature feature of the modern presidency in relations with interest groups has been the third strategy—the increasingly institutionalized process of seeking to mobilize existing organizational allies to use their representational and lobbying resources in support of presidentially defined political and policy goals. The stature and relevance of such ties to groups is best indicated by the establishment of the Office of Public Liaison (OPL) at the outset of Gerald Ford's administration, following the resignation of President Richard Nixon, and its continuation in every White House since. After the creation of the Executive Office of the President (EOP) in 1939, some of FDR's assistants were designated informally to maintain ongoing communications with blacks, Jews, farmers, and other constituencies within the president's electoral coalition. The Johnson and Nixon White House staffs expanded on that representational function to include more explicit efforts to win the active backing of groups of various kinds in promoting the administration's goals. But the OPL formalized both of these functions and provided staff specifically intended to fulfill the associated responsibilities to "communicate, articulate, and support the President's programs, policies, and priorities in order to mobilize support for them."[38] The general task of interest group liaison remains largely the province of staff members scattered throughout the units within the EOP, and in most administrations is done more effectively by people outside of the formal Office of Public Liaison, but the enduring presence of the OPL underscores the significance of instrumental links to interest groups for all contemporary chief executives.[39]

Presidents, of course, can have a number of diverse needs and objectives, with different implications for how relationships with various kinds of groups are to be pursued. We can bring some conceptual order to interest group liaison approaches, and thus to Bush's particular tactics, by identifying four different kinds of strategies and the goals and incentives that are likely to motivate each one. Two primary characteristics distinguish among White House approaches to coalition formation using organized interests: First, there is the purpose of the engagement with groups—whether it is intended to marshal support for the president's programmatic initiatives, such as legislation proposed to Congress, or whether it serves to promote the president's role as an elected representative, such as improving and maintaining an incumbent's political standing with various constituencies. Second, there is the breadth of interactions with the interest group community—whether they are inclusive, extending broadly across an ideological or partisan spectrum of groups, or whether they are exclusive, focused on a more narrowly drawn, politically homogeneous subset of interests.

As shown in figure 9.1, combining these two dimensions yields a fourfold typology of interest group liaison by the White House. With the first type, *liaison as legitimization*, presidents seek ties to organizations representing interests well beyond their electoral coalitions in order to improve or consolidate the appropriateness of their roles as national leader and head of state, which may be in question or under threat. President Ford, for example, approved the establishment of the OPL as a way to develop group ties that would help buttress his difficult position as an appointed vice president who had been brought to the highest office by the resignation of his predecessor. Unusual adverse political circumstances and a desire to win public approval for his new role as chief executive dictated the kind of group strategy President Ford would pursue. *Liaison as outreach* also advances the representational function of the presidency, but in response to quite different circumstances and for quite different purposes. In this instance, presidents are secure in their own political standing but use interest group liaison to reach out to a select set of groups that traditionally have had limited access to the core centers of policymaking but that have demonstrated support for the president and could be important elements of the reelection coalition. FDR, Kennedy, and Johnson opened White House doors to African Americans; Johnson to consumer representatives, women, and environmentalists; Carter to women and gays; and Reagan to the Christian right. The third approach is *liaison as governing party*, in which case the collection of targeted groups is also limited but the goal is to stimulate advocacy and use of group resources—lobbyist, grass-roots capabilities, electoral connections—to help forge assertive alliances outside of government that will promote the emergence of successful

FIGURE 9.1   Typology of White House Liaison with Interest Groups

		Breadth of Group Interactions	
		Inclusive	Exclusive
Purpose of Group Interactions	Representational	Liaison as Legitimization	Liaison as Outreach
	Programmatic	Liaison as Consensus Building	Liaison as Governing Party

coalitions inside government. The president wants to pass a piece of legislation, for example, and the task is to bring under a governing-party umbrella the collection of organized interests, constituencies, and members of Congress who can secure enactment of the bill. This approach to group relations became a centerpiece of Carter's White House when the president, articulating a full policy agenda, suffered early legislative defeats and strove to improve his effectiveness with Congress in subsequent legislative encounters. It was also instrumental to Reagan's successful effort to enact major tax and budget cuts in his first year, pulling together an active alliance of organizations that shared the administration's policy convictions and had the financial and staff resources, as well as lobbying experience, necessary to ensure congressional attention. The final form of liaison is *consensus building*, which differs only in the expectation that enough agreement can be generated across diverse interests that it is worth more extensive and more inclusive communications with organized interests to promote a consensus coalition in favor of the president's preferred policy action. For example, when promoting civil rights and overcoming the problems of the poor were popular in the 1960s, and a growing economy produced an increasing flow of revenues for the government without raising taxes, Lyndon Johnson wanted to unite as many groups as possible by bringing together, for instance, community activists, civil rights groups, service providers, and the construction industry to support public housing.[40]

Which approach to interest group liaison is attempted by presidents, therefore, depends on what presidents wish to achieve—are they activists intent on reordering federal policy or are they defenders of the status quo? On the prevailing conditions specific to individual presidents are they well supported by the public and does their party have considerable influence in Congress, or is their own political standing precarious? And on the attributes of the issues under consideration are there deep partisan or ideological divisions within Congress and the electorate, or is it possible to achieve a consensus? In addition, these characteristics are likely to vary both across issues and over time within a single administration, so all presidents are likely to engage in all four approaches, but to varying degrees. All of these considerations resonated at the beginning of the Bush presidency.

Competing Scenarios for Bush and Interest Group Liaison

Let us cast ourselves back to 13 December 2000, the day after the U.S. Supreme Court's ruling that effectively determined that George W. Bush would become the forty-third president of the United States. Knowing the themes on which candidate Bush had campaigned, the results of the congressional elections for the partisan control of Congress, Bush's loss to Al Gore in the presidential popular vote, the uncertainty of the electoral college results due to the voting irregularities and ambiguities in Florida, and the resolution of the electoral outcome by a 5–4 vote in the Supreme Court (with the conservative majority, appointed by previous Republican presidents, having decided the case in contradiction to its usual principles on states' rights), what might we have expected to be the dominant strategy that the Bush administration would pursue with respect to interest group liaison?

Two distinct scenarios were possible. On the one hand, the political context in which Bush assumed office posed what could have been serious constraints on his ability to claim fully the office and assert effective presidential leadership. At the very least, these constraints suggested strong incentives to secure his standing among a broad base of groups, well beyond his natural allies in the business community and among movement conservatives. Four factors in particular pointed toward the need to establish an inclusive strategy for engaging groups. To begin with, as the first president in more than a century to win office while losing the popular vote, and as the first president ever to have his electoral fate determined by the unelected Supreme Court (and by the narrowest of majorities in a strangely argued opinion),[41] Bush's legitimacy as chief executive could have been called into question. Just as Gerald Ford had reached out to interest groups from across the ideological spectrum in an effort to overcome the stigma of being an appointed president, Bush might have been expected to pursue liaison as legitimization—inviting inclusive interactions with diverse organized interests to promote the representational dimensions of his presidency. Organized labor, environmentalists, minority groups all come to mind. It would also have contributed to cementing his standing with the electorate before launching what could be a contentious programmatic agenda. Second, the manner in which the institutional apparatus of the White House Office of Public Liaison has evolved since the 1970s would have reinforced this legitimization approach. Across Democratic and Republican administrations, officials in OPL have acquired ongoing responsibility for providing formal links between the White House and African Americans, women, Latinos/as, senior citizens, consumers, Asian Americans, and various other ethnic or underrepresented groups.

A third feature of the political and institutional context that could have prompted the continuation of an inclusive approach to interest group liaison was that, during the presidential campaign, Bush had identified himself as a "compassionate conservative," implying a programmatic agenda that would combine the smaller-government and market-based approaches associated with the right with a commitment to using targeted government action to rectify the social injustices usually of concern to liberals and moderates. This apparent predisposition was reinforced by Bush's claims to be a "uniter, not a divider," intent on rising above and changing what he described as the destructive partisan tone in Washington. And fourth, although Republicans had managed to hang onto control of the House and Senate in the 2000 elections, their majorities were slender at best—221–212, with two independents, in the House; 50–50 in the Senate—and reduced since the GOP had captured Congress for the first time in forty years in the 1994 elections. (Since that time, Republican ranks in the House had dropped steadily from 230 to 221; they had risen from 52 to 55 in the Senate, before falling to 50 in 2000.) In the Senate the Republicans had to rely on Vice President Cheney to break tie votes, and they fell well short of the sixty seats needed to ensure a working majority. The loss of Republican control of the Senate four months into the administration, when Senator James Jeffords departed the Republican caucus and declared himself an independent, only underscored the vulnerability of Republican legislative leadership. Bush's campaign rhetoric and his party's precarious hold on Congress, following on the problematic results of the presidential election, defined a situation in which liaison as consensus building—engaging interest groups of all stripes to engender support for legislative proposals that could attract endorsement from a broad swath of Congress—would have seemed prudent.

There was another way, however, to read the political tea leaves, producing a dramatically different imperative for interest group liaison.[42] One starts with the substance of Bush's campaign (the policy issues and specific proposals), not its rhetoric (the generic appeals to unity, inclusion, and compassion). The campaign's policy dictates, translated into the new president's programmatic agenda, were sweeping in scope. They were unmistakably conservative in thematic structure and driven by the substantive preferences of Bush and his Republican allies, not the reauthorization schedule of existing statutes. This agenda focused on tax cuts, energy development, environmental adjustment, redesigned primary and secondary education, reform of Social Security and Medicare, and military expansion. All of these initiatives were firmly rooted in Republican and conservative traditions, sure to be opposed by Democrats and like-minded interests, and they represented an effort to roll back the eight years of Bill Clinton's impact on public policy. They incorporated specific policy approaches refined in conservative think tanks and favored by Republican constituency interests, with an emphasis on wealthy entrepreneurship, private institutions, market incentives, and faith-inspired charity. Preferred alternatives included ending the estate tax and cutting other taxes paid largely by the wealthy; emphasizing extraction of carbon-based fuels (oil, coal, and gas) and nurturing nuclear power; promoting private property rights and deregulation in environmental matters; breaking down the wall separating church and state by infusing faith-based organizations into the provision of public services and opening private schools to publicly financed vouchers; establishing private accounts in Social Security and expanding private health plans in Medicare; providing Medicare drug coverage through subsidies to private carriers; building up the military in general and deploying a missile defense system. This forceful agenda and the solutions that Bush proposed would require a strong emphasis on the programmatic objectives of the presidency, facilitated by forging close alliances with like-minded interests: corporations, small businesses, and social conservatives. This approach would entail liaison as governing party—joining Republican elected officials with their conservative counterparts in the interest group community.

However precarious for Bush it might have appeared on the surface, the political and institutional environment offered some openings for prosecuting such an exclusive and programmatic set of relationships. First, Republicans had not enjoyed unified control of government since the first two years of the Eisenhower administration, 1953–54. In the postwar period, the typical pattern had been one of Republican presidents facing Democratic majorities in Congress from the moment they took the oath of office. Ronald Reagan had been the lone exception, enjoying a Republican Senate as his administration began and, despite nominal Democratic control, a working conservative majority of 189 Republicans and over 30 conservative Southern Democratic "boll weevils" in the House. He pursued a muscular conservative programmatic agenda and empowered it with interest group liaison as governing party.[43]

Neither Bush nor his GOP congressional allies, frustrated earlier by Clinton's successful vetoes, wished to defer exploiting this new opportunity created by the 2000 elections. Conservative Republicans in Congress now had the conservative Republican president they had lacked in the 104th Congress, when Clinton stymied the massive changes Speaker Newt Gingrich had shepherded through Congress and forced Republicans to suffer in the court of public opinion for the shutdown of government that occurred during their confrontation. Second, Bush could turn to conservative partners in the interest group community who were an even more effective resource than they had been under Reagan. The Reagan coalition had included the newly mobilized Christian right and social conservatives in general who did not yet have major access to the Washington establishment. One of the functions of the Reagan White House was to reach out to these interests—liaison as outreach—and bring them to the policymaking table, as Carter had done and Clinton would do for marginalized groups on the left, such as gays and lesbians. By the time George W. Bush entered office, the Christian right, evangelicals, and right-wing analysts all had become prominent parts of the Republican mainstream, and six years of a Republican Congress had also given them direct access to policymaking and helped embed them in government itself. As William Kristol, conservative editor of the *Weekly Standard*, put it, "For conservatives, the good news is you don't need to be a rebel anymore."[44] Thus there was less need for outreach by the new Bush White House and greater confidence in incorporating these groups, many possessing the resources of grass-roots mobilization, into an exclusive interest group coalition assembled for programmatic purposes. That ideological orientation was further strengthened by the fairly narrow base that had energized Bush's primary victories against John McCain and had brought ultimate electoral success.

Given these parameters, Bush could thus choose to deemphasize the liaison-as-legitimization strategy that otherwise would have seemed so appropriate on a first reading. Subsequent events, too, would resolve remaining concerns about his political authority and legitimacy. The terrorist attacks of September 11th and his response to them transformed his national standing, and congressional Democrats lined up behind the president. His erstwhile and potential future opponent, Al Gore, lengthened his own period of self-imposed silence, giving the president nearly full reign over the political and programmatic agendas. The percentage of the public giving Bush a favorable job approval rating soared from 51 percent just before the attacks to 90 percent shortly thereafter—the highest level recorded by the Gallup poll for any president since it began asking this question during the Franklin Roosevelt administration.[45]

Bush Interest Group Liaison in Practice

What strategy, in fact, did Bush choose in his relations with interest groups? Encompassing and serving the representational role of the chief executive, as suggested in the first scenario? Or narrowly targeted and programmatic, the far more provocative stance? Despite the uncertain political terrain that originally greeted the new president, there is no evidence that the Bush White House made the first possibility—liaison as legitimization—even a modest priority in its relations with organized interests. At best one can see that the institutional imperatives of broad-based group interactions established by previous administrations and formalized in the White House Office of Public Liaison carried forward into the

Bush administration. As noted earlier, the administration felt compelled to continue (after first indicating otherwise) task forces of particular interest to African Americans and gays, although women as a constituency, given a particularly high profile in the Clinton White House, had their representation folded back into the Office of Public Liaison. My search of the World Wide Web revealed the usual litany of minor events organized by OPL, where either OPL or other administration officials met with or addressed sessions for a broad spectrum of associations and constituencies with little obvious connection to the Bush electoral base or the administration's programmatic agenda. They included the National Black Chamber of Commerce, Operation Hope, breast cancer research advocates, various organizations representing the disabled, the National Council of Asian American Business Associations, the American Coalition for Filipino Veterans, Japanese-American individuals and organizations supporting preservation of World War II internment sites, Serbian-American organizations, the National Polish American–Jewish American Council, Armenian-American leaders, the nonprofit community, firefighters, general aviation pilots, and the like.[46] However, few attempts were made to build *systematic* relationships with politically influential interests that had not explicitly supported the president in the 2000 election. Unlike the Ford administration, the current White House has not used interest group relations primarily, or significantly, or even moderately to elevate Bush's political, representational standing in the country as a whole.

The real story of the Bush administration is how much it has emphasized the other alternative identified earlier: interest group liaison as governing party. Indeed, this approach to interest group relations has been the dominant, nearly exclusive, strategy pursued by the White House. Fairly early in the administration, one of the president's advisers commented, "Sooner or later, people were going to realize this guy isn't Eisenhower."[47] Whatever the campaign rhetoric, George W. Bush and his team had a well-defined and assertive policy agenda to pursue that is tied closely to the constituency base of his campaign contributors, electoral activists, business allies, and conservative supporters. The entire White House apparatus was immediately set up to advance a sharply drawn governing-party approach to political messages and coalition building. The administration established the new Office of Strategic Initiatives in the White House to "devise long-term political strategy" under the direction of Karl Rove, Bush's top political strategist from the campaign and well before. Previous presidents have committed staff resources to protecting their political core constituencies and furthering their own political standing, but this administration "has clearly taken a different approach by thoroughly integrating Karl Rove into the White House chain of command."[48] The Office of Public Liaison, directed by Lezlee Westine, reports directly to Rove, who, in combination with his leadership of the overall political apparatus of the White House, has seemed to play a measurable policy role. John DiIulio Jr., the former director of the Office of Faith-Based and Community Initiatives in the Bush White House, commented that Rove is "enormously powerful . . . There is no precedent in any modern White House for what is going on in this one: a complete lack of a policy apparatus. What you've got is everything, and I mean everything, being run by the political arm. It's the reign of the Mayberry Machiavellis."[49] Whether the president's policymaking is informed by analysis, by Bush's predispositions, or by the preferences of his supporting constituencies, it has been pursued in close collaboration with the administration's ideological compatriots in the interest group community.

The commitment to an exclusive and programmatic approach to interest group liaison by the Bush White House is in evidence in almost every policy domain in which Bush has attempted to shape the agenda. I start with an analysis of energy policymaking, where all of the contours of the governing-party strategy are exhibited in stark relief. The tight web of relationships goes back to the campaign. The Center for Responsive Politics, for example, reports that *"78 cents out of every dollar"* contributed by the oil and gas industry to major-party candidates in federal elections over the past ten years has gone to Republicans, and that "President Bush was the *No. 1 recipient* of the industry's money during the last election"—and cumulatively for the entire previous decade. From 1999 to 2000, oil and gas gave a total of $25.6 million in hard-money and soft-money contributions to Republican candidates and the party. Electric utilities followed suit, contributing 7:1 to Bush over Gore, and the coal industry also made Bush its leading recipient of contributions. Ditto nuclear power generators.[50]

Once in office, Bush took "the unusual step of managing energy issues out of the White House," for an administration in which the president, vice president, and secretary of commerce, among others, all had significant personal, experiential ties to conventional energy producers. Indeed, no less than thirty "former energy industry executives, lobbyists, and lawyers [were appointed] to influential jobs in. . . [the] administration." In the words of a senior energy company executive, "The people running the United States government are from the energy industry." Bush called upon Vice President Dick Cheney to head the task force—the National Energy Policy Development Group—that was given responsibility for crafting the administration's energy plan, which was released on 17 May 2001. From the beginning, Cheney and the administration sought to keep the deliberations of the task force far from public view, holding in secret the identities of the individuals from the energy industry and elsewhere who met with Cheney, the task force, or its staff. At the request of members of Congress, the General Accounting Office (GAO) attempted to obtain this information, resorting to a lawsuit against the vice president that thus far has been unsuccessful (a Bush-appointed federal judge dismissed the GAO suit in December 2002).[51] The task force in one way or another "met with more than 400 people from more than 150 groups," but by all accounts with "little input" from environmental organizations or consumer groups. The *National Journal* described "big oil's White House pipelines" when covering the task force, noting that "oil and gas industry leaders have been streaming into Washington for talks with Cheney, Lundquist [the executive director of the task force], and congressional leaders." Between the start of the administration and 17 May 2001, Secretary of Energy Spencer Abraham alone held meetings with "more than 100 representatives from the energy industry and trade associations."[52]

Most telling is the consistency between the president's final energy plan and the preferences of oil, gas, nuclear power, and mining companies and their trade associations. According to the *National Journal*, "faced with a choice between environmental protection and energy production, Bush has consistently sided with industry." The provisions of the energy plan itself—including deregulation, financial incentives to industry for production, and opening the Arctic National Wildlife Refuge (ANWR) to oil exploration, along with some modest support for conservation and production of alternative sources of energy—adhered closely Bush's campaign statements and fit so closely with the ideas of energy producers that the president of the Natural Resources Defense Council (NRDC) asserted that "big energy companies all but held the pencil for the White House task force." The administration's "new energy policy," suggested the *National Journal*, even "treats nuclear power as a national treasure." "Dig beneath the surface of the Bush administration's energy policies," says another account, "and you fill find a broad seam of coal." Some examples of energy policymaking illustrate the depth of the links between the administration and its friends among commercial interests in the energy domain. Based on documents obtained under a court order, the NRDC, for example, found that Executive Order 13211 issued by President Bush, pertaining to oil policy, "is nearly identical in structure and impact. . . and nearly verbatim in a key section" to a draft included in a 20 March 2001 e-mail message from the American Petroleum Institute to an official in the Department of Energy.[53]

All of this collaboration between industry interests and the administration yielded an energy plan in which 80 percent of the provisions were regulatory adjustments that Bush could implement administratively without congressional action. For the remaining elements, in classic liaison-as-governing-party mode, "Republicans joined energy industry and business groups to back the task force's recommendations for increasingly long-term production of oil, coal, natural gas, and nuclear power." In support of the president's energy plan, the American Petroleum Institute, the American Gas Association, the National Association of Manufacturers, the National Mining Association, the U.S. Chamber of Commerce, and other major industry trade associations established the Coalition for Energy, Environment, and the Economy, which was expected to spend something on the order of $10 million for a lobbying campaign. The largest oil companies also supported Arctic Power, a group promoting drilling in the Arctic National Wildlife Refuge.[54] Even the most tightly organized approach to liaison as governing party, of course, does not guarantee legislative success. The 107th Congress came to a close in 2002 without enacting the legislative features of the president's plan, such as drilling in the ANWR, and little of the plan advanced in the 108th.

A similar pattern of White House–interest group engagement is readily identified in many other policy areas. Consider the policy complement to energy: environmental protection. On the surface, Bush appeared to promise that in this area he would be reaching out to a broader spectrum of the electorate and organized interests than was the case for his energy program. Much of Bush's campaign oratory offered support for environmental issues, including a pledge to limit carbon dioxide (CO_2) flowing from facilities generating electricity. Once in office he swooned over the Florida Everglades, commenting that "[t]hey are here to be appreciated, not changed. Their beauty is beyond our power to improve. Our job here is to be good stewards of the Everglades, to restore what has been damaged and to reduce the risk of harm." Major environmental groups were also to be invited to meet with Vice President Cheney. During Bush's second year in office, the administration indicated "plans to promote its initiative on air pollution control by trying to enlist the help of a number of minority, labor and environmental organizations that it believes can rally public support." The draft plan, dubbed "Clear Skies," even suggested that "[environmental groups] should have the lead on all meetings."[55] All these signals seemed to suggest that, for environmental policy, the more inclusive approach of liaison as consensus building would be the norm.

Actual practice, however, proved quite different from the public overtures. As before, one can start by examining the flow of campaign contributions and identifying the personnel brought into the administration. Funding from the timber and forest products industry fit the same profile as that described earlier for the oil, gas, coal, mining, and utility firms in supporting Republicans and the Bush campaign. With regard to appointments of federal officials, the *New York Times* reported that "President Bush has filled several senior environment-related jobs in his administration with pro-business advocates who have worked on behalf of various industries in battles with the federal government." From the secretary of the interior to subcabinet posts in the Departments of Interior and Agriculture (which includes the Forest Service), on to positions in the Environmental Protection Agency (EPA) and in relevant White House offices, one finds a long list of individuals who previously worked for or lobbied on behalf of the oil, natural gas, coal, mining, timber, chemical-manufacturing, pesticide, electric power, and cattle industries or served at libertarian think tanks and advocacy centers. The legislative director of the American Conservative Union noted, "We're real happy with the team that Bush is putting in." Overall, these appointees share Bush's probusiness approach to "free market environmentalism." Said Bush, "This new approach is based on this common-sense idea: that economic growth is key to environmental progress, because it is growth that provides the resources for investment in clean technologies." In this view, the states rather than the national government should be the source of environmental leadership, private property rights should take center stage, and constraints on business should be based on incentives and voluntary action using "market discipline."[56]

In the pursuit of environmental policy, Bush has joined and worked with the key commercial interests involved. Catering to automobile, energy, and power production interests, he backtracked on his pledge to control CO_2 emissions. Agreeing with industrial leaders, he opposed the Kyoto treaty on global warming. In developing his Clear Skies proposal, he sought to reshape fundamentally the approach to air pollution control by shifting from regulation to market-based "cap-and-trade" provisions for various pollutants. His approach "drew applause from the nation's utilities . . . ; the National Mining Association; the National Association of Manufacturers and other business groups who called the plan balanced and realistic." Needless to say, environmental groups were not so enthused.[57] This overall theme of coordinated policy approach and industry support played out, as well, in the use of public lands and in approaches to Superfund cleanup of toxic sites. With respect to the first issue, Bush was "aggressively encouraging more drilling, mining, and logging on much of the 700 million acres controlled by the Interior Department and the Forest Service, . . . as green activists despair of even keeping track." On Superfund, which was suffering a revenue shortfall, "Bush and Republican congressional leaders are siding with industry in opposing reinstatement of the levies on polluting firms that previously had paid for the large-scale clean ups."[58] As in the energy policy case, even with strong support from allied commercial interests, the president was not successful in passing legislation such as the Clear Skies provisions during the 107th Congress, but much was accomplished using executive authority.

A third major area of government policy—general regulation of industry—continues the same story. President Bush immediately pushed his deregulation agenda by halting for review, and perhaps withdrawal, new and pending regulations written by the Clinton administration. Once again, reported *CQ Weekly*, "environmentalists and consumer activists say they fear the formation of a new triad—composed of industry officials, the White House and GOP committee chairmen—that leaves them out of the equation," a clear signal of a governing-party approach to interest group liaison. One primary example illustrates the point—the collaboration of organized interests from industry with the Bush White House and congressional Republicans to repeal the new ergonomics regulation designed to reduce repetitive-stress and other similar workplace injuries that had been issued by the Clinton administration, after many years of study, just before it left office. Soon after Bush's inauguration, representatives of numerous in-dustries and leading large employers and small-business trade associations began meeting and, as part of the National Council on Ergonomics, launched an inside-lobbying as well as grass-roots campaign of phone calls, e-mails, and media. The lobbyist for the U.S. Chamber of Commerce warned, "Capitol Hill is going to see some big-time grassroots on this issue." This broad-based partnership of business interests was taking on a coalition of labor unions, the National Organization for Women, the American Nurses Association, and the American Public Health As-sociation. With the president's support, however, Congress—on party-line votes—exploited a little-used law to repeal the ergonomics regulation in March 2001. About a year later, the administration "unveiled a new workplace safety policy . . . that calls for no mandatory steps by industry and instead relies on voluntary ac-tions by companies to reduce injuries from repetitive motions on the job. . . . Busi-ness groups . . . were mostly pleased."[59]

On trade policy, approximately the same coalitional battle lines were drawn in early 2001. According to the *National Journal,* "the White House, the business community, and their allies in Congress are launching a major push for free trade, while organized labor, public-interest groups, and their congressional allies are digging in for a massive campaign of resistance." Bush and his corporate con-stituents won on this one, too. Facing strong opposition from within his own party, Bill Clinton several years earlier had requested that the Republican Con-gress "postpone indefinitely" renewal of the "fast-track" trade negotiating author-ity previous presidents had enjoyed. Not burdened by similar problems, on 6 Au-gust 2002 President Bush signed legislation, which passed on a partisan vote, granting him "authority [through 2007] to negotiate trade deals with foreign countries without interference from Congress."[60]

In the realm of health care policy as well, Bush joined forces with commer-cial interests. Initiating a series of proposals to provide some abatement of phar-maceutical costs for Medicare beneficiaries, he offered a plan to provide $48 bil-lion in block grants to the states to finance coverage for those with low incomes. Then, in summer 2001 he joined forces with "five big health care companies" to make drug discount cards available through a privately administered plan. Com-peting with Democratic plans for pharmaceutical coverage that would be in-cluded directly in the government-provided Medicare benefit package, he also in-troduced his own initiative, which, embodied in legislation passed by the House, "would give insurers and health plans a subsidy to offer a prescription benefit. The idea is that pharmaceutical companies would compete for this business, thereby lowering prices." This approach, free of government price-setting and adding dollars to the prescription drug market, was greatly favored by the indus-try. However, by the end of July all drug coverage plans had failed in Congress, including the administration's. Reviving its initiative in the summer of 2003, the

Bush administration continued the emphasis on using private plans for the delivery both of drug coverage and of services, hoping thereby to shrink the administrative and regulatory role of "traditional" Medicare in favor of the market and commercial enterprises. Democrats attacked what they described as an effort to privatize one of the nation's most popular social programs.[61]

The president's allies in the defense industry fared better. Under Bush, and especially in the wake of the September 11th terrorist attacks, government funding has been flowing to firms that both benefit from and give considerable support to the president's policy positions. According to the *National Journal*, "the vast increases in homeland security and defense spending proposed by the Bush administration have many companies seeing dollar signs. . . . The perception is that there is gold in these here hills—and the administration is doing nothing to discourage that perception." In response to Bush's defense spending plans for 2003, the stock-market value of shares in major defense-contracting companies rose, although it was too early to tell just how lucrative the growing defense budget would be for these firms.[62]

What about President Bush's single most significant domestic policy victory—the enactment in 2001 of his multi-trillion-dollar tax-cut proposal? It bears more the signature of traditional, large-scale Republican versus Democratic, left versus right ideological politics, than of specific group-based alliances. Nevertheless, the tax reductions as proposed and enacted reward important segments of the Bush electoral coalition, both conservatives who fought to end what they, and the president, called the "marriage penalty" and more affluent taxpayers who are more likely to support Bush's ideological commitment to smaller government. For example, Citizens for Tax Justice, a nonpartisan, nonprofit research and advocacy organization, stated in a 12 June 2002 report, "By 2010 [the last year of the law's authorization], when (and if) the Bush tax reductions are fully in place, an astonishing 52 percent of the total tax cuts will go to the richest one percent—whose average 2010 income will be $1.5 million." People in the lowest 20 percent income group would receive 1.2 percent of the value of the cuts. The reductions in the top marginal tax rates on personal income, the additional deductions for two-income married couples, and the eventual elimination of the estate tax were all favored by the president's "governing party" commercial and conservative alliances. Small-business interests were especially pleased, although large companies and social conservatives wanted Bush to go further in support of their particular concerns. Big business, however, anticipated that it and those who invest in its enterprises would be beneficiaries of the next round of tax changes, as indeed played out in part with the cuts in taxes on dividend earnings and capital gains signed by Bush in May 2003.[63]

Finally, under this liaison-as-governing-party motif it is useful to spend a moment focusing specifically on the religious right and social conservatives, interests that—like the corporate community—are very much part of President Bush's coalition of organized interests in a serious, substantive way. As before, a revealing place to begin is with the appointments Bush has made to government positions. A core example is former Missouri senator John Ashcroft, an archconservative favorite of the social and religious right wing, who became attorney general. On the White House staff, Tim Goeglin, who has intimate ties to religious conservatives and their organizations, was appointed special assistant to the president and deputy director of the Office of Public Liaison. In an interview given shortly after the terrorist attacks to the American Center for Law and Justice, an organization founded by televangelist Pat Robertson, Goeglin commented, "We've heard a lot of good and evil, a lot of talk about justice and righteousness [from the president]. This is an outgrowth of his faith. This is the genuine article. This is George W. Bush." When his interviewer suggested that "one of the things that is so clear here is God's hand in the whole process. And here we have you all in place, Bush is the President, and John Ashcroft is the Attorney General," Goeglin responded, "You're absolutely right—at the end of the day, this is a Providential choice, and we should all find a good measure in humility but thanksgiving in that."

Other "pro-family conservatives" include Wade Horn, former president of the National Fatherhood Institute, named assistant secretary of health and human services for family support, and Mike Gerson, an evangelical Christian who is "the president's chief speechwriter." By May 2001, on his television program, *The 700 Club*, Pat Robertson commented, "It's been a decade since conservatives had control of the White House, and now that they have it back, the conservative operatives who have been hanging around Washington for a long time are making the most of their opportunity." On the same program, Grover Norquist, president of Americans for Tax Reform and a leading right-wing activist, noted, "When I walk through the White House, I recognize as many people as when I would walk through the [conservative] Heritage Foundation." Elsewhere Kenneth Connor, president of the Family Research Council, claimed his organization is "afforded access to the highest senior officials."[64]

Bush's programmatic promises during the campaign fit with conservatives' preferred policy agenda, from school vouchers to major tax cuts, from building up the military to promoting "charitable choice" (permitting federal aid to pass through faith-based groups without disrupting their hiring practices—an approach that has been challenged by a coalition of organized labor, education associations, and civil rights groups, and some religious organizations), from privatizing Social Security to reforming Medicare in their terms. Bush also has made clear his opposition to abortion, both directly and through appointments. Conservative organizations have been involved on each of these issues, orchestrating grass-roots campaigns in support of the president's policy proposals. Thus far they have obtained less from their friend in the White House than they desired on issues such as school vouchers and charitable choice, but Bush has, nonetheless, advanced their agenda. The administration and social conservatives have been particularly unified when working in concert on foreign policy issues, including blocking funding for international family-planning programs and supporting the "hard-line stance of Israeli prime minister Ariel Sharon." Sometimes on international issues they have been at odds with other parts of the Bush coalition, as when differing with business on trade with China. However, as reported in *CQ Weekly,* "experts note that religious conservatives begin with a strong ideological advantage in pursuing their foreign policy agenda: a president whose core beliefs and philosophy of 'compassionate conservatism' closely mirrors their own." Concluded an associate of the Hudson Institute, a conservative think tank, "The influence of the religious right has never been more robust on foreign policy."[65]

All of the policy areas described earlier are ones in which President Bush has worked with, engaged, and in some cases been strongly influenced by a fairly ideologically cohesive set of interests—primarily corporate, business, and religious conservatives—following the patterns of interest group liaison as governing party, where the objective is to enact and implement a programmatic agenda. No modern presidency, however, pursues a single interest group liaison strategy to the exclusion of all others. Even the highly focused Bush White House varies its approach to interest groups, depending on the policy domain or its representational objectives. Consider, for example, education policy. Instead of pitting a narrowly drawn coalition led by the president against his ideological opponents, such as labor, environmentalists, consumer groups, civil rights organizations, and others, in this case there has been substantial consensus in support of the programmatic agenda.

A centerpiece of Bush's campaign and of his initial policy agenda, his education initiative focused on school testing and accountability, school choice, and streamlined and expanded federal funding. This issue gave the president one of his most significant domestic policy legislative successes. In this instance, unlike those discussed earlier, Bush immediately assumed a bipartisan pose and accepted substantive compromises in order to ensure legislative enactment.[66] Two factors seem to explain the adoption of this different approach for education policy. First, Republicans and Democrats in Congress agreed on a number of provisions to be included in the overall bill; Democratic Senator Evan Bayh asserted that "eighty percent of our proposals are common ground." When Bush unveiled his general plan a few days after taking office, "the praise on Capitol Hill was so widespread that swift passage almost seemed like a sure thing." He also reached out to liberal Democratic Senator Ted Kennedy to work toward a compromise that satisfied both parties. Second, Democrats had always done well against

Republicans in public opinion surveys about education, but Bush wanted to gain control of the issue. That would not prove possible in other areas, such as health care, where the public favored Democrats and the policy preferences of the two parties remained ideologically divided in almost every respect.[67]

There were, of course, a couple of deeply contentious issues affecting education. The president wanted to introduce vouchers that would permit parents with children in failing public schools to send their children to other schools, whether public or private, secular or religious, to give states more flexibility by using block grants instead of strictly targeted federal funding, and to offer faith-based organizations a larger role in general. These provisions, which were not acceptable to Democrats, fell by the wayside on the road to enactment of the eventual legislation by overwhelming bipartisan votes (381–41 in the House, 87–10 in the Senate). Whatever interest group contention there was on the issues—unlike its effect in other policy domains—split the respective Democratic and Republican coalitions of interests. Both the National Education Association (a teachers' union) and conservative groups objected to the national imposition of school testing, but neither group's protestations were enough to generate serious opposition in the ranks of either party. Social conservatives, stalwarts of the Bush coalition, were also deeply disappointed that vouchers were dropped from the "No Child Left Behind Act," but even Republicans in Congress were divided on their appropriateness.[68]

Finally, the representational functions for marginalized interests were also not entirely ignored by the Bush White House, which engaged in a bit of interest group liaison as outreach, but with an interesting twist. In the past, this form of White House–interest group relations—reaching out to an exclusive set of interests to solidify their symbolic links to the administration—was used to bring to the corridors of power groups that had supported the president but that lay outside the domain of the political mainstream. Over several administrations Democrats had employed this approach to give representation to blacks, Jews, women, gays, and atheists (the latter involving the Clinton OPL), before they entered the general policy-making system as politically recognized and accepted constituencies. Republican presidents did the same for evangelicals and other movement conservatives. Few such "outsiders" now remain, but the Bush administration, exploiting the apparatus of the Office of Public Liaison in particular, used outreach to connect with two supportive constituencies that were marginalized by other interests in the president's *own* coalition. One of these groups was the Log Cabin Republicans, conservative gays and lesbians who endorse Bush and the GOP more generally. On 18 April 2002, at the invitation of administration officials, fifty leaders of the group participated in a White House briefing with a number of relatively senior staff. As reported by the *Dallas Voice*, "it was the first time a Republican White House had ever held such a briefing." Some right-wing organizations were none too happy about the attention Bush was paying to such representatives of gays and lesbians, as reflected in their vituperative web sites.[69]

The other controversial constituency the White House reached out to was Muslim Americans. In another first, on 5 March 2001, President Bush commemorated Eid-ul-Adha (the Feast of the Sacrifice) with "members of the American Muslim community," thanking their organization "for its support during the 2000 presidential campaign." Later, in the immediate aftermath of September 11th, Bush made more overtures to Muslims in the United States and met with Muslim leaders at a local mosque. Months later, however, there was more tension in the relationship. Although Lezlee Westine, the director of OPL, claimed that there had been "a consistent outreach to the community," those same leaders complained in August 2002 that they were being ignored. Some of them, such as the executive director of the Muslim Public Affairs Council in Los Angeles, suggested that "there's sort of a right wing—whether Christian fundamentalists or pro-Israel groups—that tries to drive wedges between us and decision makers."[70] One would not expect that either conservative gays or Muslims would find a comfortable home at the core of the Bush coalition, but modern interest group liaison practices offered them some—if limited—engagement with the White House.

Conclusion

Leading scholars of politics long argued that strong political party organizations and an influential interest group system are mutually exclusive: potent parties overcome the particularistic nature of individual interests, while the existence of aggressive and effective organized interests is a sign of enfeebled political parties. Based on our empirical observations during the period of the Reagan administration, Jack Walker and I concluded, to the contrary, that muscular parties and an elaborated group system need not be at odds with one another. Indeed, because they reflect similar divisions and developments within the body politic, they can be mutually reinforcing.[71] The first two years of the Bush administration underscore this assessment. As the parties (best represented in Congress) have become more ideologically polarized in the nation's capital,[72] they have maintained close, symbiotic relationships with distinctive group bases. Bush has led, and is often influenced by, a readily identifiable set of business and conservative (often hard-right) interests. During the Bush presidency, this party-group alliance—the "governing party" motif—has typically been countered by at least a core of Democrats in alliance with, usually, organized labor, and then, depending on the issue, environmentalists, consumer groups, civil rights organizations, and other like-minded associations. Although not as cohesive or reliable, this party-group agglomeration might still be referred to as the "opposition party" counterpart to liaison as governing party.

The question for the remainder of Bush's first term and the run-up to the 2004 presidential election was this: would these party-group dynamics continue and strengthen, or would various sources of uncertainty on the political horizon challenge, and perhaps unravel, these networks of relationships? George W. Bush had finished the first two years of his presidency enjoying considerable (if weakening) popularity with the American public, which he apparently leveraged effectively to assist Republican congressional gains in the 2002 election. With the larger GOP majority in the House of Representatives and the new, albeit slim, Republican majority in the Senate, and based on the preceding analysis, what might be expected about the president's approach to organized interests and interest group liaison for the remainder of his term?

The early indications in 2003 were that all of the forces that had originally led the White House to focus on the "governing party" strategy became even more pronounced as the administration entered the second two years of the president's term. Bush and his "chums" in the community of corporate, small business, and social conservative interests seemed more unified than ever. Gone were any worries about the need to shore up the president's standing or legitimacy. All that remained was the push to enact the significant elements of the administration's programmatic agenda that had stalled in the last Congress and to build further in directions thoroughly consistent with its previous successes. Even more than before, Bush's partisan, ideological coalition of interests entered 2003 chomping at the bit.

Bush made it clear that he would pursue his policy agenda aggressively in both the legislative and administrative realms—the Republican Congress would give him both new opportunities to enact legislation stymied by the previously Democratic Senate and added protection against congressional involvement when he chooses to effect selected policy outcomes through executive decisions. With regard to legislation, Republicans on the Hill quickly showed their determination to enact laws much desired by the conservative and business interests that work in close collaboration with the White House. The list included welfare reform, changes in pension laws desired by businesses, enlarging the role of private plans in Medicare, adding new tax reductions, and making permanent the massive tax cuts, including elimination of the estate tax, passed in the 107th Congress but with an expiration date of 2011. The House, which in Bush's first two years led the legislative charge in advancing the president's program, would "continue to be the incubator of the GOP's conservative legislative agenda." Tom Delay (R-Tex.), the new majority leader and an extreme conservative, "promise[d] strict party discipline and a controlled message," facilitated by the departure of leading Republican moderates.[73] The resulting bills would now move to a Republican Senate, with Republican committee chairmen thoroughly compatible with, and closely tied to, business and conservative interests. The alliances the Bush White House continued to nurture with like-minded interests would be reinforced by the close proximity of those groups to the majorities in Congress.

The importance of the Bush administration's connections to the business community—both large employers and small firms—remained clearly evident in a number of policy domains. In the area of tax policy, for example, "more tax breaks for business [were] a near certainty now that Republicans control[led] both the administration and Congress." By the end of 2002, revenues from corporate taxes were already down considerably from 2000, in part because of "increased aggressiveness in claiming deductions in the face of a business-friendly Internal Revenue Service and a heavy sprinkling of favors for business scattered through the Homeland Security Act and other legislation," promoted or supported by the White House.[74] Adding to capital write-offs, relaxing rules regarding pensions, ending or reducing dividend taxes, and continuing the elimination of the estate tax permanently beyond the current 31 December 2010 sunset provision were being promoted and welcomed by businesses of all sizes, which would join forces with the administration to try to assure passage in Congress.

Corporate interests were central to the health policy domain as 2003 progressed. Two issues reported in the media early on signaled the vitality of the Bush-business alliance in this area. Shortly after the 2002 election, *American Medical News* reported, "Now that Republicans control both the House and Senate, President Bush's health care plans are expected to take center stage, according to political analysts." Among the most important initiatives included on the president's agenda was a prescription drug benefit that would rely primarily on competing private plans under a fundamentally reorganized Medicare program. The *New York Times* observed that "having spent more than $30 million to help elect their allies in Congress, the major drug companies are devising ways to capitalize on their electoral success by securing favorable new legislation . . . . The industry's No. 1 goal is to shape legislation that both parties advocate to provide prescription drug benefits to the 40 million elderly and disabled people in the Medicare program." The White House, the major pharmaceutical companies, and their trade association, the Pharmaceutical Research and Manufacturing Association, continued working in concert with the Republican majorities in Congress (the predominant recipients of the industry's campaign contributions) to fulfill their shared objectives, although the conference to reconcile divergent House and Senate bills dragged on late into the fall.[75]

Bush proposals to deflect some payroll-tax funding of Social Security into private accounts—greatly favored respectively by the administration's corporate allies among health insurers and investment firms—received some attention early in 2003.[76] So, too, did energy legislation predicated on fossil-fuel production and nuclear power and drilling in the ANWR, as well as regulatory relief for oil, gas, and mining firms, the prime example of liaison as governing party as described earlier.[77]

In addition, significant features of the policy agenda were pursued administratively by the Bush White House in accelerated fashion after the 2002 election results made it substantially more difficult for Democrats to challenge these provisions. As reported in the *New York Times,* "Seeking to reinforce support from his core constituency, while at the same time possibly widening the Republican Party's appeal, President Bush is sidestepping Congress to advance the domestic policy issues he brought to the White House two years ago." In December 2002 the White House identified over 300 existing federal regulations that could be amended or terminated. As before, business support for relaxing federal environmental standards had a high priority. Even before the announcement, Bush administratively changed "new source review" rules for electric power plants in ways highly favorable to industry and permitted new drilling in the Padre Island National Seashore. "The environmental community," said a *New York Times* editorial, "already battered by two years of struggle with the Bush administration, is expecting the perfect storm when the 108th Congress convenes in January."[78] Also in December 2002, the president issued an executive order to accomplish a goal greatly desired by the religious right that he had not been able to get through the previous Congress. He forbade federal agencies to deny funds to faith-based organizations that provide social services, concluding that under current law becoming federal contractors "does not require religious groups to give up their right to hire on the basis of religious belief."[79]

Despite this initial alignment of factors strongly favoring the Bush agenda and the administration's exclusive, programmatic alliances with ideologically compatible interest groups, emerging sources of uncertainty could disrupt these relationships. Continued economic problems and rising (indeed, record) federal budget deficits could pit elements of the Bush coalition against one another, as missile defense, unexpectedly expensive military operations abroad, and domestic initiatives such as private Social Security accounts make permanent or additional tax cuts, including those for business, untenable. Although the 2003 war with Iraq came to a rapid conclusion and at first bolstered the president's popular support, ongoing instability and violence in that nation, requiring a lengthy and dangerous deployment of tens of thousands of U.S. troops, weakened Bush politically and could loosen his remarkably cohesive coalition, with its not always entirely overlapping interests of corporate enterprises, Main Street businesses, and religiously oriented right-wing organizations.[80] Economic dislocation and war have long histories of unsettling previously established patterns of politics and policymaking. So far, however, there are no signs that President Bush's government of chums is at serious risk.

Notes

Invaluable assistance was provided by my research assistant, Audrey Bazos, who was instrumental in identifying and assembling most of the materials referenced in this chapter. I am most grateful for her contributions.

1. Mark A. Peterson and Jack L. Walker, "Interest Group Responses to Partisan Change: The Impact of the Reagan Administration upon the National Interest Group System," in *Interest Group Politics*, 2d ed., ed. Allan J. Cigler and Burdett A. Loomis (Washington, D.C.: Congressional Quarterly, 1986).
2. Interview with author.
3. Mark A. Peterson, "Clinton and Organized Interests: Splitting Friends, Unifying Enemies," in *The Clinton Legacy*, ed. Colin Campbell and Bert A. Rockman (New York: Chatham House, 2000), 140–68.
4. Gregory L. Hager and Terry Sullivan, "President-Centered and Presidency-Centered Explanations of Presidential Public Activity," *American Journal of Political Science* 38 (November 1994): 1079–1104.
5. Alexis de Tocqueville, *Democracy in America* (Garden City, N.Y.: Anchor Books, 1969); Theda Skocpol, "America's Voluntary Groups Thrive in a National Network," *Brookings Review* 15 (Fall 1997): 16–19; and Gerald Gamm and Robert Putnam, "Association-Building in America, 1850–1920," paper presented at the annual meeting of the Social Science–History Association, New Orleans, 10–13 October 1996.
6. Kevin J. McMahon, "Altering Interpretation: Presidential Policy toward the Judiciary during the Administrations of Franklin Roosevelt, Richard Nixon, and Ronald Reagan," paper presented at the annual meeting of the American Political Science Association, Washington, D.C., 28–31 August 1997.
7. Mark A. Peterson and Jack L. Walker, "The Presidency and the Nominating System," in *The Presidency and the Political System*, 3d ed., ed. Michael Nelson (Washington, D.C.: Congressional Quarterly, 1990), 238–39; and U.S. Bureau of the Census, *Statistical Abstract of the United States, 2001* (Washington, D.C.: Government Printing Office, 2001), table no. 217, 140.
8. Frank R. Baumgartner and Beth L. Leech, *Basic Interests: The Importance of Groups in Politics and in Political Science* (Princeton: Princeton University Press, 1998); Terry M. Moe, *The Organization of Interests: Incentives and the Internal Dynamics of Political Interest Groups* (Chicago: University of Chicago, 1980); Jack L. Walker, *Mobilizing Interest Groups in America: Patrons, Professions, and Social Movements* (Ann Arbor: University of Michigan Press, 1991); David W. Rohde, *Parties and Leaders in the Postreform House* (Chicago: University of Chicago Press, 1991); Kay Lehman Schlozman and John T. Tierney, *Organized Interests and American Democracy* (New York: Harper & Row, 1986); and Margaret Weir, ed., *The Social Divide: Political Parties and the Future of Activist Government* (Washington, D.C.: Brookings Institution and New York: Russell Sage Foundation, 1998).
9. Baumgartner and Leech, *Basic Interests*, 103; Schlozman and Tierney, *Organized Interests*, 75; Walker, *Mobilizing Interest Groups*; James A. Smith, *The Idea Brokers: Think Tanks and The Rise of the New Policy Elite* (New York: Free Press, 1991); Andrew Rich

and R. Kent Weaver, "Advocates and Analysts: Think Tanks and the Politicization of Expertise," in *Interest Group Politics*, 5th ed., ed. Allan J. Cigler and Burdett A. Loomis (Washington, D.C.: CQ Press, 1998), 235–53.

10. Moe, *Organization of Interests*; and Walker, *Mobilizing Interest Groups*.

11. Baumgartner and Leech, *Basic Interests*, 111; and Walker, *Mobilizing Interest Groups*.

12. Jean Stefaneic and Richard Delgado, *No Mercy: How Conservative Think Tanks & Foundations Changed America's Social Agenda* (Philadelphia: Temple University Press, 1998); Matthew C. Moen, *The Transformation of the Christian Right* (Tuscaloosa: University of Alabama Press, 1992); and *The Christian Right and Congress* (Tuscaloosa: University of Alabama Press, 1989).

13. See Walker, *Mobilizing Interest Groups*; Jeffrey M. Berry, *Lobbying for the People* (Princeton: Princeton University Press, 1977); Ken Kollman, *Outside Lobbying: Public Opinion & Interest Group Strategies* (Princeton: Princeton University Press, 1998); and Kenneth M. Goldstein, *Interest Groups, Lobbying, and Participation in America* (New York: Cambridge University Press, forthcoming).

14. Margaret Weir, "Political Parties and Social Policymaking," in *The Social Divide: Political Parties and the Future of Activist Government*, ed. Margaret Weir (Washington, D.C.: Brookings Institution and New York: Russell Sage Foundation, 1998), 1–45; *Statistical Abstract of the United States, 2001*, tables no. 637, 639, pp. 411–12; Alan Greenblatt, "Labor Wants Out of the Limelight after Glare of Probes, Backlash," *Congressional Quarterly Weekly Report*, 28 March 1998, 787–91; Richard Sammon, "Fall of Striker Bill Spotlights Doubts about Labor Lobby," *Congressional Quarterly Weekly Report*, 20 June 1992, 1810; Paul Starr, *The Social Transformation of American Medicine* (New York: Basic Books, 1982); and Elton Rayak, *Professional Power and American Medicine: The Economics of the American Medical Association* (Cleveland: World Publishing, 1967), 2, 12.

15. Peterson, "Clinton and Organized Interests."

16. Greenblatt, "Labor Wants Out of the Limelight," 790; Theda Skocpol, "The Toqueville Problem: Civic Engagement in American Democracy," *Social Science History* 21 (Winter 1997): 473; idem, *Boomerang: Clinton's Health Security Effort and the Turn against Government in U.S. Politics* (New York: Norton, 1996); Weir, "Political Parties and Social Policymaking"; Peterson and Walker, "Interest Group Responses," 163; Kirk Victor, "Asleep at the Switch?" *National Journal*, 16 January 1993, 131–34; and Kollman, *Outside Lobbying*.

17. An earlier version of this section and the next one, extensively revised and updated here, appeared in Peterson, "Clinton and Organized Interests," 143–53.

18. Mark A. Peterson, "Interest Mobilization and the Presidency," in *The Politics of Interests: Interest Groups Transformed*, ed. Mark P. Petracca (Boulder, Colo.: Westview, 1992), 221–41.

19. Peterson and Walker, "Interest Group Responses,"163.

20. Ibid., quoted on 173, 175.

21. "Closed Due to New Ownership," Minnesota Women's Press, Inc., News Notes, 11 April 2001, www. Womenspress.com/newspaper/2001/17–2newsnotes.html; Cynthia E. Griffin, *Entrepreneur*, December 2001, at Entepreneur.Com, www.entrepreneur.com/Magazines/Copy _of_MA_SegArticle/; "RightNow! Congressional Reception," 27

February 2002, at www.politicalchicks.com/public/pages/; and quoted in "The White House Is Women Friendly," National Federation of Republican Women, at www.buncombegop.org/friendly.html.

22. James Gerstenzang and Marlene Cimons, "AIDS, Race Offices Will Remain Active," *Los Angeles Times*, 8 February 2001, A19.

23. Steven Greenhouse, "Unions See Bush Moves as Payback for Backing Gore," *New York Times*, 25 March 2001, 33.

24. Ibid.

25. Adriel Bettelheim, "Workers' Rights Issues Looming over Homeland Security Debate," *CQ Weekly*, 7 September 2002, 2294–97.

26. Richard W. Stevenson, "Government May Make Private Nearly Half of Its Civilian Jobs," *New York Times*, 15 November 2002, A1.

27. John Cochran and Rebecca Adams, "Fresh from a Set of Hill Victories, Can Labor Keep the Momentum?" *CQ Weekly*, 2 September 2001, 2004–9; and Gebe Martinez, "Bush Breaks with Position, Moves to Protect Steel Industry," *CQ Weekly*, 9 March 2002, 655–75.

28. Stephen Skowronek, *Building a New American State: The Expansion of National Administrative Capabilities, 1877–1920* (New York: Cambridge University Press, 1982).

29. Elizabeth Drew, *On the Edge: The Clinton Presidency* (Touchstone, 1994), 24; and Richard Willing, "A Year of 'Highs' for African-Americans in Clinton's Cabinet," *Crisis* 101 (February/March 1994): 32–34.

30. "Enron's Blackout Cuts Power behind Numerous Thrones," *Lobby Watch* (a publication of Texans for Public Justice), 4 December 2001, 1; Brody Mullins, "Enron-Linked Firms Gave Heavily to Bush," *National Journal*, 26 January 2002, 251; and "The Pioneers: George W. Bush's $100,000 Club," Texans for Public Justice, www.tpj.org/pioneers/.

31. Peter H. Stone, "Corporations, K Street Throw a Party," *National Journal*, 13 January 2001, 116–17.

32. For a brief analysis of how the Reagan White House centralized the personnel appointments process, gave it ideological direction, and incorporated it into a larger strategy of executive branch control, see Peter M. Benda and Charles H. Levine, "Reagan and the Bureaucracy: The Bequest, the Promise, and the Legacy," in *The Reagan Legacy: Promise and Performance*, ed. Charles O. Jones (Chatham, N.J.: Chatham House, 1988), 102–42. Information about the Bush appointments comes from Peter H. Stone, "Surprise! Bushes are Everywhere," *National Journal*, 6 January 2001, 44; Rebecca Adams, "GOP, Business Rewrite the Regulatory Playbook," *CQ Weekly*, 5 May 2001, 991; James A. Barnes, "Is Bush Poisoning His Well?" *National Journal*, 14 April 2001, 1121; and Robert Pear, "Bush and Health Care Companies Promise Medicare Drug Discounts," *New York Times*, 13 July 2001, A1.

33. Kathryn Dunn Tenpas and Stephen Hess, "The Contemporary Presidency—The Bush White House: First Appraisals," *Presidential Studies Quarterly*, September 2002.

34. Walker, *Mobilizing Interest Groups*, 31.

35. J. David Greenstone and Paul E. Peterson, *Race and Authority in Urban Politics: Community Participation and the War on Poverty* (New York: Russell Sage Foundation, 1973).

36. Benjamin Ginsberg and Martin Shefter, "The Presidency, Interest Groups, and Social Forces: Creating a Republican Coalition," in *The Presidency and the Political System*, 3d ed., ed. Michael Nelson (Washington, D.C.: CQ Press, 1990), 339.

37. Ibid., 339–47; and Peterson, "Interest Mobilization and the Presidency," 232.

38. Joseph A. Pika, "Interest Groups and the Executive: Presidential Intervention," in *Interest Group Politics*, ed. Allan J. Cigler and Burdett A. Loomis (Washington, D.C.: Congressional Quarterly, 1983), 298–323; and Memorandum from William Baroody to President Gerald R. Ford, 23 August 1974, quoted in Robert M. Copeland, "Cultivating Interest Group Support: Public Liaison in the Ford Administration," paper presented at the annual meeting of the Midwest Political Science Association, Chicago, 1985.

39. Mark A. Peterson, "The Presidency and Organized Interests: White House Patterns of Interest Group Liaison," *American Political Science Review* 86 (September 1992): 612–25.

40. For details on the typology, the approaches used by previous presidents, and an empirical analysis of President Reagan's use of liaison as governing party, see ibid. It is also useful to note that this typology accommodates mobilization for both interventionist, expansionist approaches to government and for those designed to shrink the scope and activities of existing government. In each case the purpose is programmatic instead of representational. For expansionist presidents, depending on their overall incentives, the strategy may be inclusive (Johnson's approach to much of the Great Society) or exclusive (Reagan's approach to the defense buildup). Agendas that involve building-down the state, however, have to involve an exclusive strategy of relationships with groups. Given the stakeholders favoring existing governing programs, one cannot imagine "liaison as consensus building." One would instead have to concentrate on a targeted "governing party" coalition versus the interests supporting the threatened programs.

41. Linda Greenhouse, "The Legal Spectacle: Divining the Consequences of a Court Divided," *New York Times*, 17 December 2000, Week in Review, p. 1.

42. See Gary Bauer, "Run to the Right, Not the Middle," *New York Times*, 15 December 2000, A39.

43. Peterson, "Presidency and Organized Interests."

44. Helen Dewar, "GOP Departures Signal Arrival of a New Era For Conservatism; Senators Hand Power to Next Generation," *Washington Post*, 16 September 2002, A4.

45. Gallup Poll and CNN/*USA Today*/Gallup Poll, reported at www.pollingreport.com/BushJob.htm.

46. These are some examples of information found at Internet sites: National Black Chamber of Commerce, www.nationalbcc.org/events/conv2001agenda.htm; Ohio Statewide Independent Living Council, www.ohiosilc.org/news/2002/020307_jfa_teachers.html; National Council of Asian American Business Associations, //national-caaba.org/new.html; Armenian Assembly of America, www.aaainc.org/press/02–22–02.htm.

47. Barnes, "Is Bush Poisoning His Well?" 1120.

48. Tenpas and Hess, "Bush White House."

49. "Ex-Aide Insists White House Puts Politics Ahead of Policy," *New York Times*, 2 December 2002, A16. DiIulio later issued a formal apology, saying his comments were "groundless and baseless due to poorly chosen words and examples." "Ex-Bush Aide Offers Apology for Remarks," *New York Times*, 3 December 2002, A27.

50. "A Money in Politics Backgrounder on the Energy Industry," Center for Responsive Politics, available at www.opensecrets.org/pressreleases/energybriefing.html (italics in the original); and Peter H. Stone, "Big Oil's White House Pipelines," *National Journal*, 7 April 2001, 1043.

51. Adam Clymer, "Judge Says Cheney Needn't Give Energy Policy Records to Agency," *New York Times*, 10 December 2002, A1.

52. Margaret Kriz, "Shock Politics," *National Journal*, 10 February 2001, 394; Don Van Natta Jr. and Neela Banerjee, "Bush Policies Have Been Good to Energy Industry," *New York Times*, 21 April 2002, sec. 1, p. 22; Jill Barshay, "A Closer Look at GAO vs. Cheney: Politics and the Separation of Powers," *CQ Weekly*, 2 February 2002; Katharine Q. Seelye, "Bush Task Force on Energy Worked in Mysterious Ways," *New York Times*, 16 May 2001, A1; and Peter H. Stone, "Big Oil's White House Pipelines," *National Journal*, 7 April 2001, 1042–44.

53. Margaret Kriz, "Power Struggle," *National Journal*, 31 March 2001, 942; Don Van Natta Jr. and Neela Banerjee, "Review Shows Energy Industry's Recommendations to Bush Ended Up Being National Policy," *New York Times*, 28 March 2002, A18; Margaret Kriz, "Nuclear Power Gets to Go to the Ball," *National Journal*, 19 May 2001, 1501; Rebecca Adams, "Coal Takes Stronger Position in Nation's Energy Strategy," *CQ Weekly*, 1 June 2002, 1440; and "Heavily Censored Energy Department Papers Show Industry Is the Real Author of Administration's Energy Task Force Report," Natural Resources Defense Council, at www.nrdc.org/media/pressreleases/020327.asp.

54. Adams, "Coal Takes Stronger Position," 1442; Chuck McCutcheon, "Bush Urged to Shift Emphasis to Fuel Efficiency Standards," *CQ Weekly*, 19 May 2001, 1153; and Stone, "Big Oil's White House Pipelines," 1042–43.

55. Frank Bruni, "Bush Carries Environment-Friendly Tone to Everglades," *New York Times*, 5 June 2001, A16; and Katharine Q. Seelye, "Bush to Seek Unlikely Allies in Bid to Alter Clean Air Act," *New York Times*, 9 June 2002, sec. 1, p. 26.

56. Katharine Q. Seelye, "Bush Is Choosing Industry Insiders to Fill Several Environmental Positions," *New York Times*, 12 May 2001, A10; Margaret Kriz, "Working the Land," *National Journal*, 23 February 2002, 535–37; Margaret Kriz, "A New Look at Land Use," *National* Journal, 27 January 2001, 258–59; Rebecca Adams, "Lack of Carbon Dioxide Regulation Spurs Criticism of Bush's Clean-Air Plan," *CQ Weekly*, 16 February 2002, 473; and Margaret Kriz, "Bush's New Green Toolbox," *National Journal*, 3 February 2001, 348–49.

57. Rebecca Adams, "Bush's Decision Not to Curb Carbon Dioxide Casts Shadow on Emission Control Legislation," *CQ Weekly*, 17 March 2001, 607–8; Adams, "Lack of Carbon Dioxide Regulation," 473; and Margaret Kriz, "Burning Questions," *National Journal*, 6 April 2002, 976–81.

58. Kriz, "Working the Land," 532; Margaret Kriz, "Superfund Slowdown," *National Journal*, 1 June 2002, 1625; and Katharine Q. Seelye, "Bush Proposing Policy Changes on Toxic Sites," *New York Times*, 24 February 2002, sec. 1, p. 1.

59. Peter H. Stone, "Block Those Regs!" *National Journal*, 17 February 2001, 484–87; Rebecca Adams, "GOP, Business Review the Regulatory Playbook," *CQ Weekly*, 5 May 2001, 990; Rebecca Adams, "GOP-Business Alliance Yields Swift Reversal on Ergonomics Rule," *CQ Weekly*, 10 March 2001, 535–39; and Steven Greenhouse, "Bush Plan to Avert Work Injuries Seeks Voluntary Steps by Industry," *New York Times*, 6 April 2002, A1.

60. Colin Campbell, "Demotion? Has Clinton Turned the Bully Pulpit into a Lectern?" in Campbell and Rockman, *Clinton Legacy,*, 64; Charlie Mitchell, "Hot Trade Winds Are

Blowing," *National Journal*, 12 May 2001, 1413; and Elisabeth Bumiller, "Bush Signs Trade Bill, Restoring Broad Presidential Authority," *New York Times*, 7 August 2002, A5.

61. Mary Agnes Carey, "Drug Plan's Low-Key Launch Signals Bush May Be Open to Deal," *CQ Weekly*, 3 February 2001, 281–82; Pear, "Bush and Health Care Companies"; Mary Agnes Carey, "Much Variety, Little Traction in Medicare Drug Plans," *CQ Weekly*, 13 July 2002, 1848–49; and Robert Pear, "Senate Kills Plan for Drug Benefits through Medicare," *New York Times,* 1 August 2002, A1; and Robert Pear, "Medicare Debate Focuses on Merits of Private Plans," *New York Times*, 9 June 2003, A1.

62. Carl M. Cannon, David Baumann, and Shawn Zeller, "The Deficit Difference," *National Journal*, 9 February 2002, 386; and Chuck McCutcheon, "Defense Contractors Suit Up for Air vs. Sea Funding War," *CQ Weekly*, 9 February 2002, 405.

63. "Year-by-Year Analysis of the Bush Tax Cuts Shows Growing Tilt to the Very Rich," Citizens for Tax Justice, 12 June 2002, at www.ctj.org/html/gwbo60s.htm; Daniel J. Parks, "Bush May Test Capitol Hill Clout Early with Expedited Tax-Cut Proposal," *CQ Weekly*, 6 January 2001, 41–42; and Lori Nitschke, "Tax Plan Destined for Revision," *CQ Weekly*, 10 February 2001, 318–21; and Alex Berenson, "No Big Rush to Stocks after Cuts in TwoTaxes," *New York Times*, 24 May 2003, C1.

64. "ACLJ Exclusive," American Center for Law and Justice," 18 September 2001, at www.aclj.org/news/nr_010918_geoglein.asp; Joel C. Rosenberg, "Flash Traffic: Political Buzz from Washington," World on the Web, 21 April 2001, at www.worldmag.com/ world/issue/04–21–01/opening_5.asp; "Robertson and Right-Wing Allies Brag of Control Over Bush Agenda," People for the American Way, 3 May 2001, at www.pfaw .org/pfaw/general/default.aspx?oid=1732; and Judith Stacey, "Family Values Forever: In the Marriage Movement, Conservatives and Centrists Find a Home Together," *The Nation*, 9 July 2001, 26.

65. Alexis Simendinger, "Reminders from the Right," *National Journal*, 6 January 2001, 35–37; David Nather and Megan Twohey, "Ashcroft Is Bush's Charitable Choice," *National Journal*, 20 January 2001, 202; Martin Davis, "Faith, Hope, and Charity," *National Journal*, 28 April 2001, 1228–35; "Bush Plan to Promote Faith-Based Charities Creates Dilemma for Both Parties," *CQ Weekly*, 3 February 2001, 283–85; and Miles A. Pomper, "Religious Right Flexes Muscles on Foreign Policy Matters," *CQ Weekly*, 13 July 2002, 1893–96.

66. Enacting legislation in Congress does not necessarily mean that the policy itself will be successful in its implementation. The ways in which this law requires states to measure public school performance and identify "failing" schools may create educational havoc in the states and results counter to the expressed objectives of the program. For those suspicious of every motive guiding the administration, noted a member of a state board of education, this outcome might be viewed as "a cynical attempt by the Bush administration to build in failure and use that as an argument for vouchers," Bush's preferred policy approach. Michael A. Fletcher, "States Worry New Law Sets Schools Up to Fail," *Washington Post*, 2 January 2003, A1.

67. David Nather, "Broad Support Is No Guarantee for Bush Legislative Leadoff," *CQ Weekly*, 27 January 2001, 221–25; idem, "Bush's Education Plan Unveiled in House amid Muted Dissent," *CQ Weekly*, 24 March 2001, 659–60; Siobhan Gorman, "Bush's Big Tent," *National Journal*, 24 February 2001, 549–53; and Juliet Eilperin, "House Passes

Education Reform Bill; Bipartisanship Hailed," *Washington Post,* 14 December 2001, A8.

68. Helen Dewar, "Landmark Education Legislation Gets Final Approval in Congress," *Washington Post,* 19 December 2001, A8.

69. Caryle Murphy, "Atheists Assemble to Lobby and Share Beliefs," *Washington Post,* 13 June 1998, C1; "White House Hosts Log Cabin Meeting," *New York Blade,* 3 May 2002, at www.nyblade.com/national/020503b.htm; and David Webb, "Dallasites at Log Cabin Confab Praise White House," *Dallas Voice,* at dallas.logcabin.org/news4.htm.

70. "President to Meet with Muslim Community Leaders," *Friday Brief,* Islamic Institute, 2 March 2001, 1; "U.S. Muslims Say Bush Ignores Them," Fox News, 18 August 2002, found at www.foxnews.com/story/0,2933,60700,00.html.

71. Peterson and Walker, "Interest Group Responses."

72. Gary C. Jacobson, "Party Polarization in National Politics: The Electoral Connection," in *Polarized Politics: Congress and the President in a Partisan Era,* ed. Jon R. Bond and Richard Fleisher (Washington, D.C.: CQ Press, 2000).

73. Derek Wills, "Nurturing the GOP Agenda," *CQ Weekly,* 9 November 2002, 2930–31.

74. David Cay Johnson, "Key Questions on Tax Breaks: How Big? Who Gets Them?" *New York Times,* 16 December 2002, C4.

75. Joel B. Finkelstein, "Elections Boost GOP Health Care Agenda," *American Medical News,* 25 November 2002, at www.ama-assn.org/sci-pubs/amnews/pick_02/gvl11125.htm; and Robert Pear and Richard A. Oppel Jr., "Election Gives Drug Industry New Influence," *New York Times,* 21 November 2002, A1, A28.

76. For Social Security, see Robert Kuttner, "The GOP Revives Social Security Privatization Ploy," *Los Angeles Times,* 6 December 2002, B17.

77. James Gerstenzang, "Bush Circumventing Congress on Domestic Policy," *New York Times,* 15 December 2002, A42.

78. Ibid.; Katharine Q. Seelye, "White House Identifies Regulations that May Change," *New York Times,* 20 December 2002, A27; and "Environmental War Clouds," *New York Times,* 25 November 2002, A24.

79. Richard W. Stevenson, "Religious Groups Face Fewer Curbs in Bush Aid Plan," *New York Times,* 13 December 2002, A1, A28.

80. Howard Fineman, "What Will Iraq Cost Bush?" *Newsweek,* November 3, 2003, 24–25; Susan Sachs, "Postwar GI Death Toll Exceeds Wartime Total," *New York Times,* October 30, 2003, A12; Jeffrey M. Jones, "Slight Majority Says Bush Deserves Re-Election," Gallup Poll Analysis, October 22, 2003, www.gallup.com/poll/pr031022.asp.

CHAPTER 10

George W. Bush and the Politics of Gender and Race

David Canon and Katherine Cramer Walsh

GEORGE W. BUSH faces a difficult challenge in improving the Republican Party's appeal to women and minorities. A gender gap has favored Democrats in national elections since 1980, and the gulf between Democrats and Republicans in minorities' voting patterns is even wider. The task is complicated by two factors. First, Bill Clinton is a tough act to follow; he was very popular among women and minorities at both the elite and mass levels. Second, and more important, the Republican Party's policies are widely perceived as being hostile to the interests of women and minorities. President Bush knows that he cannot be another Bill Clinton on race and gender issues and that he is unlikely ever to win the support of civil rights and women's group leaders as Clinton did. Therefore, Bush has tried to shift the negative perceptions of the Republican Party by appealing to women and racial and ethnic minorities in the mass public under the themes of "compassionate conservatism" and the "big tent." By emphasizing issues such as school vouchers, faith-based charity, and homeownership, he can play to traditional Republican strengths of individualism and opportunity while appealing to women and minorities on issues that they care about.

Assessing the success of this effort depends on the normative lens through which one is looking. From the perspective of leaders of the civil rights and women's movements, the second Bush administration is an abject failure, but from the perspective of the Republican Party, it may be somewhat successful. Bush's appeal to women and minorities at the mass level has remained true to the Republican Party's core principles and operated within the constraints of internal party politics. The approach may not pay large dividends in the short run, but as a strategy to expand the base of the Republican Party, it is a reasonable approach—probably the best available. The first electoral confirmation of this appeared in the 2002 midterm elections, in which the party's gender gap shrank to 2 percent (although the racial gap remained large).[1]

Our assessment of George W. Bush's presidency on the issue of race and gender has a chronological and thematic focus. Chronologically, we identify four distinct periods in the evolution of President Bush's approach to gender and racial politics: the 2000 campaign, the aftermath of the Florida deadlock, and governing before and after the terrorist attacks of 11 September 2001 (which we will refer to throughout this chapter as 9/11). Thematically, we examine the historical context of racial and gender politics, women and minorities' electoral and public support for Bush, his appointments and inner circle, and his policy positions and actions. This thematic organization will reveal that the dynamics of racial and gender politics are very similar in some respects; in others they differ substantially. The key similarity has to do with our fundamental argument: The president's appeals to women and minorities are rooted in traditional Republican themes of individualism, self-sufficiency, and opportunity. In making these appeals, Bush has adopted a "going public" approach that bypasses the interest groups that are opposed to his policies. We elaborate these points later, but we begin with the historical context of the racial and gender basis of the parties' coalitional politics.

The Historical Context of Racial and Gender Politics as a Political Constraint

For Americans born and raised in the last half of the twentieth century, it is not news to note that African Americans and women vote disproportionately Democratic.[2] This was not always the case, however, and to understand current race and gender politics, one must understand the dynamic of race- and gender-based partisanship by examining the partisan change that occurred historically.

Law and discrimination severely limited African Americans' electoral participation until the 1960s. But from the Civil War until the 1930s, blacks primarily supported the Republican Party, the "party of Lincoln," in opposition to the Democrats, who were the party of southern segregationists. In many black families, supporting a Democrat was considered political treason. As recently as 1932, three-fourths of blacks still voted for the Republican presidential candidate over the Democrat, FDR.[3] All of the blacks elected to Congress during Reconstruction and then in the early twentieth century were Republicans. The first black Democrat elected to the House of Representatives was Chicago's Arthur Mitchell in 1917. Blacks began to move to the Democratic Party during the Roosevelt administration, when New Deal programs gave unprecedented assistance to black as well as white citizens to help them out of the depths of the Great Depression and also began to address racial discrimination.[4] Black support for the Democrats continued to build through the next several decades as the northern Democratic Party and its leaders, such as Harry S Truman and John F. Kennedy, proved consistently more antisegregationist than either the Republican or the southern Democratic Parties. But even as late as 1956, 40 percent of blacks voted for the Republican president, Dwight D. Eisenhower. The final blow to black Republicanism came in the 1960s when a Democratic president, Lyndon Johnson, and a Democratic Congress pushed through the crucial 1964 Civil Rights Act and 1965 Voting Rights Act. While a majority of Republicans in Congress supported this landmark legislation (and southern Democrats opposed it), the Republican Party became more conservative on civil rights legislation in the late 1960s.[5]

The racial divide in partisan patterns of voting was reinforced by the campaign strategies of Barry Goldwater in 1964 and by the campaigns and presidencies of Richard Nixon—especially his "southern strategy" of attracting white voters through thinly veiled racial appeals—and Ronald Reagan. Reagan made racially tinged attacks on "welfare queens," and his administration was criticized by minority leaders for lax enforcement of civil rights laws. Consequently, since 1980 about 90 percent of black voters have supported Democratic presidential candidates, even in the losing campaigns of 1980, 1984, and 1988 (see figure 10.1). Meanwhile, as racially exclusive policies faded, African Americans had become not only more Democratic, but also more politically active, prominent, and influential at all levels of politics, largely because of a substantial decrease in both legal and informal discrimination against African Americans in the political arena.

The gender basis of political affiliations and participation also underwent important shifts. The constitutional amendment guaranteeing women the right to vote nationally was ratified in 1920. African Americans faced much more substantial roadblocks when attempting to assert their right to vote than women did once the amendment passed. Nevertheless it still took a long time for women to vote at the same levels as men for many reasons, including lingering social norms against women's participation in politics, problems of generational replacement, and the gap in education and employment that lasted until late in the twentieth century. By the beginning of the post–World War II period, the difference between men's and women's voting turnout was down to about 10 percentage points (and never got larger), and since 1980 women have voted at the same or higher levels than men.

Gender differences in partisanship have never been as large as race differences; in fact, men and women have usually voted very similarly as groups. But where differences appeared, for example, in the 1950s, women tended to be a bit more Republican than men. This began to change in the 1960s, especially as the parties diverged more markedly in their levels of hawkishness on defense, their stands on social welfare, and their levels of support for civil rights and antidiscrimination policies. The 1964 Civil Rights Act, so important in race policy, was also perhaps the most important piece of legislation combating sex discrimination because of Title VII, which barred employment discrimination on the basis of gender. Although Richard Nixon was the president who first extended affirmative action programs to cover women as well as racial minorities, the two parties soon took contrasting stands on affirmative action. The parties became divided on many policies relating specifically to women and gender questions, including antidiscrimination policies, abortion, the ERA (the proposed amendment to the Constitution guaranteeing equal rights for women), and policies related to violence against women. Because of the disproportionately large incidence of poverty among women, social welfare politics should be included among policies related to women. Women's movement organizations have long defined poverty and social welfare policy in general as especially relevant to women.[6]

The actual policy and social changes of the 1970s were so great that they became a key focus of the conservative backlash that gained force during and after Ronald Reagan's campaign for the presidency in 1980 and eventually led to the "culture wars" theme of the Republican convention of 1992. In 1980, the Republican candidates took strong stands in favor of rolling back the welfare state, environmental protection policies, and affirmative action, and the Republican platform included for the first time a clear anti-abortion statement.[7] As a result of this combination of policies (plus the relatively hawkish Republican defense policies), the 1980 presidential and congressional elections produced the first noticeable "gender gap," in which men voted disproportionately Republican and women disproportionately more Democratic. Although the *degree* of gender difference in the vote has varied in subsequent elections, the strong tendency for men to vote more Republican than women has persisted (see figure 10.2).

Research shows that the emergence of gender differences in any given election depends on the specific context and the degree to which it happens to be laden with the kinds of cues that stimulate such differences. For example, the gender gap will be wider in a campaign pitting a liberal woman who has a strong record on women's issues against a man who is unsympathetic to these concerns.[8] These cues vary from election to election. Despite some moderation in Democratic stands, the parties have remained distinctly different on a combination of issues that encourages gender differentiation in the vote.[9] Even though gender differences in the *vote* do not emerge equally in every election, since the late 1970s men's and women's basic *partisan allegiances* have continued to differ.

At the same time that party divisions in voting patterns and policy issues became apparent, women's success in elective office, as well as their social and economic life, also changed substantially. In the first half of the twentieth century, women were largely excluded both from the workforce and from politics. In 1946, only 28 percent of women were working outside the home, only eleven women served in the House of Representatives, and none were in the Senate or the cabinet. (The only woman who had ever served in the cabinet had left office the year

FIGURE 10.1 Percentage voting for Republican Presidential Candidate, by Race and Ethnicity

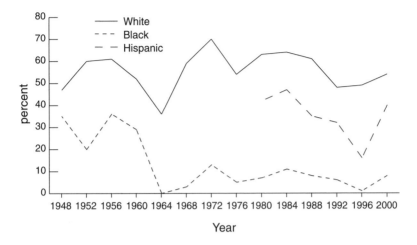

FIGURE 10.2 Percentage voting for Republican Presidential Candidate, by Gender

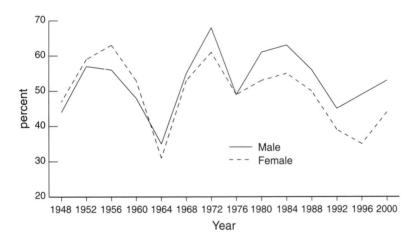

before.) In contrast, by 2000, a majority of women—even mothers of small children—were in the workforce. The proportion of women in public office had risen somewhat, although it was not close to parity; in 2003 women held 13.6 percent of the House seats, 13 percent of the Senate, and 22.6 percent of state legislative seats (in 2002), while twenty-seven different women had held cabinet posts. The women's movement, reborn in the late 1960s, had grown and become professionalized, and even if most women never labeled themselves "feminists," the majority of women persistently believed in the goal of increasing gender equality in the family, education, economic life, and politics and perceived that there was need for a women's movement to help achieve this goal.[10]

Thus, as George W. Bush was formulating his campaign for the presidency, one key element that would make a difference to potential success would be the structure of gender and race politics—and the opportunities and limitations that structure would place on any candidate at that time. Let us look briefly at the general strategic implications of the configuration of gender and race politics.

By the late 1990s, an important fact of political life was the erosion of the New Deal Democratic coalition at the mass level, as young white men, white ethnic men, and Southern men left in disproportionate numbers, while women and African Americans remained more resistant to the anti–welfare state, anti–affirmative action, and conservative "family values" messages. Thus black and female voters have offered a needed well of support for the Democratic Party and an increasing source of frustration for the Republican Party. Important differences between these two groups, however, hold different implications for Republican attempts to attract women and minority voters.

Women comprise a majority of the population (especially among the elderly), are geographically evenly distributed across the nation, support Democratic candidates only somewhat more than Republicans (and the gender difference depends on the specific context), and, since 1980, have voted at rates that are higher than or equal to those of men. African Americans comprise 12.3 percent of the population, are concentrated in specific geographic regions (especially the South and urban areas), and they overwhelmingly support Democrats, but they have relatively low voting rates—in recent elections, an average of 8 percentage points less than those of white voters.

Latino voters emerged as a growing political force in the 2000 presidential elections. Latinos now comprise the nation's largest minority group, at 12.5 percent of the nation's population, but they make up a smaller percentage of the voting population (about 4.7 percent) than do African Americans.[11] Their population is also concentrated in the Southwest, Texas, Florida, and large urban areas. Latinos have voted strongly Democratic in every election since 1980 (the first year for which good data are available), but not at levels that are comparable to African Americans. Also, there are differences across types of Latino voters. According to the 1989–90 Latino National Political Survey, the following percentages of each group who voted cast their ballots for the Democratic candidate, Michael Dukakis in 1988: 62 percent of Mexican Americans, 47 percent of Puerto Rican Americans, and only 14 percent of Cuban Americans.[12] This weaker (and variable) loyalty to the Democratic Party makes Latino voters a greater potential source of Republican votes than African Americans, especially given George W. Bush's success in attracting Hispanic voters in Texas.

Given this historical context, the general partisan electoral strategies on race and gender are clear. For Democratic candidates the key is to mobilize their base of strong supporters among women and minorities without alienating white men. For Republicans, the strategic challenge is just the opposite: they need to hold on to their base of white men, but in a fashion that will not completely shut off minority support and turn women away. In 2000, Republicans were especially concerned that Democrats had successfully poached on their turf by winning enough white men while mobilizing their base to win the 1992 and 1996 presidential elections. At the same time, they were increasingly worried about their own inability to attract women and minorities. George W. Bush's "compassionate conservatism" and the Republican "big tent" were strategies explicitly aimed at overcoming these deficiencies.

Race and Gender in the 2000 Election: Creating the Big Tent?

The 2000 presidential election was notable for its lack of attention to issues of race or gender. Racial profiling, hate crimes, and affirmative action came up during the campaign, but they clearly took a back seat to concerns about education, taxes, and the economy. However, Bush used his theme of "compassionate conservatism" to criticize the conservative wing of his party and to appeal to minority voters, especially Hispanics. Campaigning in April 2000 in California, Bush tried to repair some of the damage done by former Republican governor Pete Wilson's 1994 campaign in favor of Proposition 187, which had denied most public benefits to illegal immigrants. One Wilson campaign commercial in favor of that referendum, featuring the tag line "They keep coming," was especially offensive to Hispanic voters, who left the Republican Party in droves. In contrast, Bush condemned "the politics of pitting one group against another," and promised, "We will not use our children, the children of immigrants, as a political issue in this country."[13]

While African American voters were not courted quite as aggressively by Bush, his campaign did make a concerted effort to depict his nominating convention as more inclusive than previous Republican conventions. The Joint Center for Political and Economic Studies reported that eighty-five delegates to the 2000 GOP convention were African Americans, a 63-percent increase over 1996 and the second highest total ever (although this total still comprised only 4.1 percent of the 2,066 delegates). Several African Americans were given prominent speaking slots at the convention, including Colin Powell, Condoleezza Rice, and J.C. Watts. In his acceptance speech, Bush emphasized themes that were aimed at expanding the appeal of his party. He said, "We must tear down that wall" that separates those who are making it in this society from those who are mired in "poverty and prison, addiction and despair."[14]

The "compassionate conservative" title was also designed to attract women voters.[15] Bush portrayed himself as friendly to issues concerning women, and campaigned on education and "kitchen table" pocketbook issues such as Social Security and taxes.[16] At the same time, he avoided gun control, on which women tend to express liberal opinions, and like his opponent, Al Gore, avoided abortion as much as possible.[17] One exception was a period in September 2000, when the candidates had to distinguish themselves on abortion in the wake of the Food and Drug Administration's approval of the "morning after" pill, RU–486. Despite Bush's need to satisfy the religious right of the Republican Party, he stated before the New Hampshire primary that he would not use abortion as a litmus test for either his running mate or his judicial appointments if elected. Such an attempt to avoid alienating women was reflected in other strategies. He was advised to capitalize on women's exasperation with recent partisanship by emphasizing his outside-the-beltway status.[18] He attempted to connect with women directly by appearing as an hour-long guest on *Oprah,* one week after Gore had done so. He also reached out to women indirectly, by sending out Republican female lawmakers as his ambassadors. His mother, Barbara Bush, wife Laura Bush, and running-mate's wife Lynne Cheney also campaigned on his behalf on a "W Stands for Women" bus tour of three swing states in mid-October before the election.[19]

In at least two respects, the Gore campaign undercut what might have been a Republican advantage. Although Bush had an extra appeal among married women, Gore himself repeatedly talked about the importance of two-parent families. In addition, although polls had shown that women viewed Republicans as better at representing moral values, Gore chose as his running mate Senator Joe Lieberman of Connecticut, a man known for his principled moral views and devout Judaism.

Despite the effort to create the big tent, Bush did not make much headway in improving the Republican Party's position with women or minorities in the 2000 election. The gender gap persisted: National Election Study (NES) data show that 53 percent of men voted for Bush, compared to 44 percent of women. This 9 percent difference was smaller than the 14 percent gap in 1996 but larger than the gaps registered in elections in the 1980s (see figure 10.2). However, the Bush strategy may have paved the way for a Republican Party with greater appeal to Democratic women, as the gender gap closed to 2 percent in the 2002 midterms.[20]

It is an oversimplification to say that women preferred one party or candidate over another in 2000 or in 2002. Women in the mass public are far from unified in their perceptions of elected officials, leaving room for Bush to attract at least a portion into the Republican camp. During the 2000 campaign, a *New York Times* poll found that a *marriage gap* was more evident than a gender gap: while unmarried women leaned toward Gore, married women leaned toward Bush.[21] This was evident on Election Day: according to data from the University of Michigan's

National Election Study (NES), 51 percent of married women voted for Bush while only 29 percent of unmarried (excluding widows) women did so. The marriage gap was much less pronounced among men. While 53 percent of married men voted for Bush, 45 percent of unmarried men (excluding widowers) did so.[22]

The Bush vote displayed important divides among women in addition to the marriage gap. While 46 percent of middle-class women voted for Bush, only 33 percent of women identifying as working class did so. This gap was not evident among men. Proportions of middle-class and working-class identifiers among men who voted for Bush were 48 percent and 46 percent, respectively.[23] Also, while men who had children voted for Bush at rates similar to those of men who did not (51 percent and 48 percent respectively), a clear parent/nonparent divide emerged among women: 45 percent of women with children voted for Bush, while only 33 percent of women without did so.[24]

Although there was wide variation in Bush's ability to attract the votes of different subgroups of men and women, he made absolutely no progress in attracting African American voters (see figure 10.1). Since the NES surveys began in 1948, whites have voted for Republicans at higher rates than have African Americans; the size of this gap far surpasses that of the gender gap. It has not been smaller than 36 percentage points since 1964, and reached an apex of 53 percent in the 1984 and 1988 elections. In 2000, Voter News Service exit polls showed that only 8 percent of African Americans had voted for Bush, while 90 percent voted for Gore.[25]

However, Bush's success with Hispanic voters was substantially better than it was with African Americans. In the 1988, 1992, and 1996 elections, support for Republicans dropped below 20 percent of Mexican Americans, but Bush was able to attract approximately 39 percent of the Mexican American vote in 2000 (NES). According to White House pollster Matthew Dowd, exit poll data showed that 31 percent of the Hispanic vote for Bush came from people earning less than $30,000 per year, 37 percent from people earning between $30,000 and $75,000, and 46 percent from Hispanics earning more than $75,000.[26] However, only 2 percent of Hispanics earn more than $75,000 per year, while 76 percent earn less than $30,000. Therefore, while Bush is making inroads with Hispanic voters, Mexican Americans in particular, Republicans recognize that there is room for improvement, given that his appeal is mostly to the most affluent Hispanics.

On balance, the big tent strategy was not successful—the gender gap persisted and gains among minority voters were marginal. In naming George W. Bush its Person of the Year in 2000, *Time* magazine summarized Bush's frustration in these terms:

> Bush staged the most inclusive Republican Convention in memory, surrounded himself at every chance with poor schoolchildren whom he promised he would not leave behind, and in the end won a smaller percentage of

the African American vote than any Republican since Barry Goldwater. The comics joked that he won 100 percent of the black vote where it mattered most, on the Supreme Court, but Bush himself admits that the greatest misconception about him is that he is not racially sensitive.[27]

Fallout From Florida

The big tent strategy was not as successful as Republicans had hoped in the 2000 election, and it collapsed with amazing speed in the aftermath of the Florida deadlock. Whatever good will had been created during the campaign by the language of inclusiveness was destroyed by the allegations of racial bias in the conduct of the Florida election. With the presidency decided by a razor-thin 537-vote margin in Florida, the state's electoral process was put under a microscope. The nation was held spellbound for thirty-five days as hanging chads were counted, butterfly ballots were deconstructed, and legal challenges sped through the courts. The most disturbing and frustrating aspect of the process for civil rights advocates and Gore supporters was their firm conviction that Gore would have won if thousands of minorities had not been discouraged from voting and if the votes that had been cast by minorities had been counted at the same rate as nonminority votes. Ninety percent of African Americans who voted in the state supported Gore, but thousands of others were prevented from voting and 175,000 ballots were rejected statewide for various reasons. Hundreds of sworn statements were filed with the Justice Department concerning discrimination at the polls, and several lawsuits were initiated in the weeks following the election.

The allegations of bias fell into four categories: registered voters who were turned away or intimidated, felons who were not allowed to vote under state law, voters whose names had been erroneously placed on a list of state residents who had committed a felony, and voters whose ballots were rejected because of error, faulty and antiquated machinery, or inadequate assistance at the polls. It is difficult to determine how large the first group of voters was, but there is substantial anecdotal evidence of voters who were registered but were turned away from the polls because their names were not on the voter rolls. One poll worker, Edith Williams of Fort Lauderdale, said that she and five other poll workers "turned away about 100 people who did not appear on voters' lists and insisted they were registered." Attempts to get through to county officials to clarify the situation were unsuccessful because phone lines were jammed all day. "This was the first year we didn't get through. I was so disgusted," said Mrs. Williams, who had worked at the polls for more than twenty years.[28]

An Election Day roadblock set up by the Florida Highway Patrol near a predominantly black precinct outside Tallahassee was seen by the local residents as a blatant attempt to intimidate minority voters. Troopers stopped about 150 cars and checked drivers' licenses, issuing sixteen citations. Florida Attorney General Bob Butterworth said, "As far as I'm concerned, it's inexcusable. It's just flat-out wrong symbolism." Col. Charles Hall of the State Highway Patrol defended the roadblock, saying that officers had done nothing wrong, although he admitted that department policy on checkpoints had been violated because the location was not on the monthly list for checkpoints and local news media had not been notified as required.[29] Similar complaints were made about police intimidation in another black neighborhood in Tampa.[30]

While it is difficult to know precisely how many registered minority voters were not allowed to vote or were intimidated away from the polls, it is clear that the Florida state law prohibiting felons from voting even after they are released from prison disenfranched 170,000 blacks (out of 525,000 felons). Of those, 107,000 had served their time and were back in society. Only fourteen states have similar laws. A suit filed before the election alleged that the law had a discriminatory effect on minorities, as African Americans made up 14.6 percent of the state population but 32.4 percent of the felons in 2000. Thus, about a quarter of the adult male African American population in the state was disenfranchised for this reason.[31]

The third category is a combination of the first two: voters who were prevented from voting because they were erroneously on a list of "possible felons." Before the 2000 election, the State of Florida hired a company, Database Technologies (DbT; now owned by ChoicePoint), to produce a "scrub list" of voters who were currently registered to vote but should not have been on the rolls (felons, the deceased, and so on). The company provided a list of 175,000 people, including 57,700 who were labeled "possible felons." This latter group had been identified by matching the names and birth dates of known felons throughout the country with Florida voter registration lists. This crude methodology was made even less accurate because the state pursued a conscious strategy of erring on the side of including more names rather than fewer names. Clay Roberts, the director of the state's Division of Elections, said, "The decision was made to do the match in such a way as not to be terribly strict on the name."[32]

Database Technologies warned the state that the list of names would have to be verified, because it almost certainly contained errors. But the firm's comprehensive verification plan, which was contained in Secretary of State Katherine Harris's election files, had a handwritten note on it declaring, "Don't need."[33] Instead, as Clay Roberts testified under oath, verifying the accuracy of the lists was left up to the county supervisors. This shift of responsibility was in violation of the contract between the State of Florida and DbT, which clearly stated that the firm would be responsible for "manual verification using telephone calls." DbT did not make a single phone call to verify that any of the 57,700 people on its list were actually felons.

A comprehensive examination of the voter-purge list by an investigative reporter for *Harper's Magazine* revealed a pattern of errors that was truly stunning. *Harper's* found 325 names on the list for which the conviction date was in the future! State election workers noticed these errors, as indicated by an e-mail on the subject "Future Conviction Dates," which referred to the "bad news." The *Harper's* reporter, Greg Palast, says, "Rather than release this whacky data to the skeptical counties, Janet Mudrow, state liaison to DbT, suggested that 'blanks would be preferable in these cases.'"[34] Palast counted 4,917 blank conviction dates in the data set, so the 325 that remained must have been missed by DbT. The list also contained the names of another 2,873 persons who had moved to Florida after having been convicted of a felony in one of the thirty-four states that allow felons to vote after serving their time. Under the "full faith and credit" clause of the Constitution, which bars states from denying a right that is granted by another state, these people should have been allowed to vote in Florida. In fact, two rulings by the Florida State Supreme Court forbade the state from removing these ex-felons from the voting rolls. However, a letter from Governor Jeb Bush's clemency office on 18 September 2000 authorized the purge of these 2,873 names. After the election, when the matter was being investigated by the U.S. Commission on Civil Rights, Bush's office reversed course and allowed the ex-convicts from other states to vote in future elections.[35]

Another egregious error, admitted by DbT, was that 8,000 of the individuals named on the list had committed misdemeanors rather than felonies and therefore should not have been listed at all. However, the damage was done. Many counties simply removed the "possible felons" from their rolls without attempting to verify the accuracy of the list. Others sent out letters by certified mail, informing the registered voter that he or she was listed as a felon and would not be allowed to vote unless the charge could be disproven; if the voter did not respond, he or she was removed from the voter rolls. Some counties were so appalled at the shoddiness of the work that they did not use the lists. The elections supervisor of Madison County, Linda Howell, decided to ignore her county's list after discovering her own name on it! Other county lists included local judges and the father of another elections supervisor.[36] The one county that did verify all of the names on its list found that only 34 of the 694 names provided were actual felons who should not be allowed to vote in Florida. Based on this series of events, it is easy to see how an African American voter would be skeptical of the Republican Party's claims about diversity and inclusiveness.

The final means of disenfranchising minority voters was the one that received the most national attention and was the focus of the U.S. Civil Rights Commission's investigation: the rejection of 175,000 ballots statewide. The Commission concluded, by a 6–2 vote, that blacks in Florida were at least ten times more likely than other voters to have their ballots rejected.[37] The most sophisticated analysis of this problem was conducted by the *New York Times*, which discovered that black, Hispanic, and elderly voters had higher levels of ballot rejection that could not be explained by lower socioeconomic status and education or by differences in election technology. After taking all of these factors into account, ballots from heavily black precincts were still nearly five times as likely to be rejected as ballots from heavily white precincts. Even at the extreme levels of education, the pattern holds: in precincts in which 30 percent to 40 percent of the population had college degrees (the state average was 20 percent), 3.7 percent of the ballots in majority-black areas were discarded, compared to only 1.9 percent in majority-white areas.[38]

Of the 175,000 discarded ballots, only 25,000 clearly indicated the voter's intent—by, for example, a partially penetrated ballot or a ballot with a dimpled chad for the presidential vote that also included other dimples on the ballot. These ballots were proportionately distributed among white, black, and Hispanic voters, so a statewide recount, which under state law would focus on determining the intent of the voter, would not have redressed minority voters' disproportionate loss of voting influence. However, the *Times* analysis indicated that a statewide recount would have given Gore the election.

In September 2002, the NAACP settled its class-action lawsuit against election supervisors in seven counties and the Florida Secretary of State, Katherine Harris. The settlement built on the Florida Election Reform Act of 2001, which "included changes in registration list maintenance, provided funding for improved voter education and poll worker training, and created alternative voting and registration procedures."[39] The key additional improvement it called for was restoring to the voting rolls the people who had been wrongfully purged during the 2000 election. One week after the settlement was announced, however, Florida was mired in another voting morass. Chaos reigned in the 2002 primary elections: Hundreds of voters were turned away in precincts in Miami where some polls opened five hours late because poll workers could not figure out how to boot up the new touch-screen voting machines. Scores more could not vote in another precinct in which poll workers did not realize for several hours that the machines were plugged into a dead outlet.[40] Turnout in some precincts was recorded as 900 percent, while other precincts with 1,000 registered voters had no votes recorded because poll workers did not know how to work the machines. As a headline put it, "A Joke Is Wearing Thin for Voters in Florida."[41]

While the 2002 general election in Florida went much more smoothly than the primary (or the 2000 election!), there were many allegations elsewhere of attempts to suppress the African American vote. In Arkansas, Republican poll monitors snapped pictures of African Americans as they waited in line to vote and demanded to see photo identification cards. They told these voters that if they did not have their IDs, they could not vote; many believed them and went home, although Arkansas law does not require photo identification to vote. Similar demands were not made of white voters. In Maryland, black voters were told that they had to pay their parking tickets before they could vote, while in a hotly contested runoff election for a U.S. Senate seat, the Louisiana Republican Party paid for fliers that were distributed in New Orleans housing projects falsely informing voters that if they could not make it to the polls on Election Day (7 December), they could vote on 10 December. Complaints about similar practices were filed in Michigan and South Carolina. At the same time, Republicans charged Democrats with illegally registering Native American voters on reservations in South Dakota.[42] This racially charged atmosphere creates a difficult climate in which to build trust among minorities in the Republican Party.

"Going Public"

A subtle change in Bush's "big tent" strategy became evident after the fallout from Florida. President Bush realized that he would not be able to convince the leading civil rights organizations that he would be their champion. Indeed, they would probably never view his presidency as legitimate, given the tainted victory in Florida and the allegations of racial bias. Therefore, the only way to build the big tent would be by appealing to voters directly with a new set of policies upon which Bush had some credibility. (A similar strategy, labeled "going public" by political scientist Samuel Kernell, refers to a president's effort to go over the head of Congress by taking his case directly to the people.) In contrast, Bill Clinton's approach involved appealing directly to the "opinion leaders" who help shape the perceptions of the less attentive public.[43] Clinton obviously relied heavily on direct appeals to his female and minority supporters as well, but the indirect, two-step process of communication that was filtered through group leaders remained an important part of his coalition-building strategy.[44]

Bush's "going public" strategy is rooted in the observation that the leadership of women's and minorities' groups is "out of step" with their constituents. Feminist group leaders tend to be much more homogeneously Democratic, liberal, pro-choice, and pro–gay rights than women in the mass public. With respect to black leadership and the black community, every year the Leadership Conference on Civil Rights (LCCR) calculates support scores for members of Congress by picking about a dozen votes on issues that are important to its constituents and tallying up the number of times each legislator has supported the LCCR's position. On four of the fourteen votes tallied in the 103d Congress, however, the LCCR advocated positions that were actually opposed by a majority of blacks; differences of opinion emerged on school choice, abortion, and gay rights, for example. However, on issues that comprise the group's core agenda—affirmative action, opposition to discrimination, policies to aid the inner city, and government support for education and economic development—there were few differences between the LCCR and other groups such as the NAACP and their rank and file.

Therefore, President Bush had to be quite selective in the issues that he would use to try to expand the base of the Republican Party. Embracing the minority interest groups' core agenda positions would risk alienating the Republican base, so the strategy involved finding issues that would appeal to minorities, while remaining consistent with Republican values and policies. Exploiting the gap between the opinions of minority leadership and voters was also key. Bush therefore settled on three main issues that are consistent with Republicans' emphasis on individualism, opportunity, and limited government: faith-based initiatives, school vouchers, and homeownership. All three of these policies are popular with minority voters, and the first two are opposed by minority leaders.

Bush's "going public" approach did not imply that he was ignoring Congress. Indeed, Republican leaders in Congress were sympathetic to Bush's policy goals, and they also embraced the big tent philosophy. In fact, the Republican congressional leadership had attempted to expand its base two years before Bush was elected. In the post–midterm election leadership shuffle in 1998, when Jennifer Dunn announced her unsuccessful challenge to Dick Armey for the majority leadership of the House, she said, "We must broaden the base of the party by crafting a message that reaches out to everybody from every background." This reflected an explicit strategy by Dunn to "focus energy on helping the Republicans improve their standing among female voters."[45] In that same shuffle, the only black Republican in the House, Rep. J.C. Watts of Oklahoma, won the position of chair of the House Republican Conference, which is the number four position in the majority-party leadership; that too was widely seen as an attempt to broaden the Republican base.

Nevertheless, the big tent effort in Congress received three major blows during Bush's first two years. First came the defection of James Jeffords in May 2001, which gave Democrats control of the Senate. A moderate Republican from Vermont, Jeffords found the tent too ideologically restrictive, so he became an independent. Then in July 2002, J.C. Watts announced his retirement from the House. Critics charged that Watts had hit the "glass ceiling" in the House leadership. Watts had expressed an interest in the majority leadership position that had opened up with Dick Armey's retirement, but he was told that Tom DeLay was in line for the spot. In an article entitled, "Is the GOP's 'Big Tent' Move Losing Steam?" one critic wrote, "It [Watts's retirement] gives credence to what many have been saying about the Republican outreach effort, that beyond 'a few black faces' the effort is insincere."[46] Others said that Watts had become tired of the Washington life and wanted to spend more time with his family. Whatever the reasons, the Republican Party lost one of its most visible spokespersons for diversity. Third, Senator Trent Lott (R-Miss.) was forced to resign his position as majority leader after making comments at Senator Strom Thurmond's (R-S.C.) 100th birthday party that were widely perceived as expressing nostalgia for racial segregation. A firestorm of protest led to escalating apologies from Lott, but when President Bush distanced himself from the majority leader, declaring that any prosegregation sentiment is "offensive and it is wrong," Lott's days were numbered.

While Congress produced some obstacles to creating the big tent, a bigger challenge was posed by civil rights leaders who were not pleased with the "going public" strategy that left them on the sidelines. The NAACP was especially upset that President Bush did not attend its national convention either in 2001, 2002, or 2003, although he had done so when a candidate in 2000. Julian Bond opened the 2002 NAACP convention with an attack on Bush, announcing, "We have a president who owes his election more to a dynasty than to democracy. When he spoke to our convention in Baltimore in 2000, he promised to enforce the civil rights laws. We know he was in the oil business. We just didn't know it was snake oil." Bond was also critical of Attorney General John Ashcroft, calling him a "cross between J. Edgar Hoover and Jerry Falwell" and later referring to him as "J. Edgar Ashcroft."[47]

Bush's specific policies have also been criticized by black leaders. Representative Robert Scott, an African American Democrat from Virginia, for example, was very critical of the "poison pill" included in Bush's faith-based initiative. Scott pointed out that organizations that receive federal money must comply with nondiscrimination laws—for example, if a religious organization sought to hire someone to work in its food pantry that received a grant from the federal government, it would have to follow laws against discrimination based on race, gender, or ethnic origin. Under H.R. 7, the House bill sponsored by J.C. Watts and supported by President Bush, however, this organization would not have to comply with these laws if they conflicted with its religious practices. For example, it would not have to hire a pregnant single woman, a lesbian, or a non-Christian even if such a person were the best qualified for the job. Thus, while the policy of providing services through faith-based charities (which is strongly supported by a majority of African Americans) might look good on the surface, it may come with a price, Rep. Scott warned.[48] This was clearly an effort by minority leaders to counter Bush's "going public" strategy by placing Bush's new issues within the context of the civil rights movement's core agenda.

Appointments and the Inner Circle

Presidents as far back as Washington have attempted to achieve diversity in their administrations.[49] The original emphasis on geographic diversity has persisted, as presidents attempt to select teams representative of regions beyond the Beltway. However, since the late 1960s, an additional emphasis, on racial and gender diversity, has emerged.[50] This aspect of representation has been most pressing for

Democratic presidents, given their important base of support among racial and ethnic minorities and women.[51] Having run as "a uniter, not a divider," George W. Bush found himself required to demonstrate some truth in advertising once in office. In early December 2000, between Election Day and the final election decision, members of his campaign stated that they were seeking a diverse cabinet that would include Democrats, women, and racial and ethnic minorities. As then-candidate for the vice presidency Dick Cheney said, "We're going to want to emphasize diversity. We're going to want a broad cabinet."[52]

On the surface, Bush's inner circle was indeed diverse and inclusive of women in significant positions of power. Karen Hughes, director of communications during the campaign and then counselor to the president after the inauguration, was arguably Bush's closest adviser until her departure in late July 2002. She was just one of many women in the female-dominated communications department, which included Margaret Tutwiler as communications director and Lezlee Westine as director of the White House Office of Public Liaison. Vice President Cheney also enlisted a woman as counselor, Mary Matalin, a prominent Republican strategist. The administration included Condoleezza Rice as national security adviser and Margaret La Montaigne as domestic policy adviser. Cabinet appointments went to Ann Venneman as secretary of agriculture, Gale Norton as secretary of the interior, Elaine Chao as secretary of labor, and Christine Todd Whitman as Environmental Protection Agency administrator.

In addition to Rice (an African American) and Chao (an Asian American), the cabinet represented various racial and ethnic minority groups by the inclusion of African Americans Colin Powell as secretary of state and Rod Paige as secretary of education, Japanese American Norman Mineta as secretary of transportation, Arab American Spencer Abraham as secretary of energy, and Cuban American Mel Martinez as secretary of housing and urban development. Notably, Mineta is a Democrat who had also served in the Clinton cabinet. Additional diversity came with Alberto Gonzales, the first Hispanic American to serve as White House counsel.

The Bush campaign's promise to deliver on diversity came up against a tough precedent: Bill Clinton's administration had achieved the highest racial and gender diversity of any president's in history.[53] Despite its efforts, the Bush cabinet has not matched this level of diversity: women currently fill three of the fifteen seats (27 percent), a lower proportion than the five of fourteen positions (36 percent) held by women in the Clinton cabinet, somewhat lower than the Bush administration's own informal goal of 30 percent, and far lower than the 51 percent that women comprise in the U.S. population (according to the 2000 census).[54]

Although the Bush administration did not publicly claim that it had achieved greater gender representation than its predecessor, it did claim parity.[55] However, the evidence does not support this assertion. After one year in office, Clinton's top appointees were approximately 35 percent women and 22 percent minorities.[56] The Brookings Institution's Presidential Appointee Initiative, studying President Bush's first 126 publicly announced selections, found that 27 percent of his picks were women.[57] At the end of 2001, the Initiative released updated results with respect to Senate-confirmed nominees: just 26 percent were women, whereas 46 percent of such nominees under the Clinton administration had been women.[58] The two administrations were more comparable with respect to racial and ethnic diversity. The Clinton administration was 14 percent African American, 6 percent Hispanic, and 3 percent Asian-American, while the Bush administration was comprised of 9 percent, 8 percent, and 3 percent of these groups, respectively.[59]

Asking whether the Bush administration was diverse begs the question of the distinction between descriptive and substantive representation.[60] The former is achieved when representation mirrors constituents in terms of demographic characteristics; the latter occurs when representatives reflect constituents' policy interests. By claiming that he would create an administration that was diverse, Bush was promising descriptive representation, or a government that looked like the population. This by no means guaranteed substantive representation—the representation of a variety of the population's policy interests. Calls for demographic diversity implicitly assume that a diversity of ideas will follow. Critics of the administration argued that the promise of diversity was hollow, despite the demographic diversity of the Bush White House, because it did not result in a diversity of ideological perspectives. Wade Henderson, executive director of the Leadership Conference on Civil Rights, remarked, "There's a difference between diversity and appearance, between diversity of thought and action. The policies reflect the tight control of the administration."[61] Still others noted the fallacy in claiming that the administration was representing the interests of members of certain social groups by simply including individuals of similar color skin in the cabinet.[62]

Claims of diversity were also undermined by nominations such as that of John Ashcroft—a lame-duck senator from Missouri defeated for reelection by an opponent who had been killed several weeks before the election in a plane crash—for attorney general. Ashcroft's nomination set off a firestorm of criticism from civil rights and women's groups, who saw him as opposed to their interests. Civil rights activists mobilized to challenge the nomination, rallying around their criticisms of Ashcroft's leading efforts in the Senate to defeat the nomination of Missouri Supreme Court Judge Ronnie White, an African American, to the federal judiciary and his history of opposing the appointment of James C. Hormel, who is openly gay, as ambassador of Luxembourg. In addition, Ashcroft was assailed by a coalition of liberal groups for his opposition to abortion rights, desegregation efforts in Missouri, and gun control legislation, and for his acceptance of an honorary degree from Bob Jones University, which had prohibited interracial dating until 3 March 2000 and has publicly espoused anti-Catholic statements.

In the confirmation hearings, Ashcroft presented himself in moderate tones, promising to uphold laws, including civil rights and abortion regulations that he had actively opposed while in the Senate. "My primary personal belief is that the law is supreme; that I don't place myself above the law, and I shouldn't place myself above the law. So it would violate my beliefs to do it," he said.[63] Liberal activists and many Democrats on the committee were not convinced, however, and Ashcroft won confirmation by a narrow 58–42 margin, with all 42 votes in opposition cast by Democrats. Although Dick Cheney and others close to the Bush campaign had pledged to unify the election-torn nation by building an inclusive administration, the Ashcroft nomination renewed the divisions that had loomed in the 2000 vote.

Later battles would continue to highlight the tension between Bush's attempts to satisfy his conservative base and the opposition of civil rights and women's groups, though none reached the pitch of the Ashcroft confirmation process. These less prominent, yet contentious battles included the nomination of Thomas Dorr (accused of racial bias and evasion of farm subsidy payments) as undersecretary for rural development within the Agriculture Department, Gerald A. Reynolds (criticized for opposing affirmative action) to be the head of the Department of Education's Office of Civil Rights, Mary Sheila Gall (assailed for her reluctance to prosecute manufacturers for faulty children's products such as walkers and bunk beds) to head the Consumer Product Safety Commission, and Linda Chavez as secretary of labor. Bush's first defeat in this area came when Gall's nomination was turned down by the Senate Commerce Committee in August 2001. Chavez's nomination was highly contested by labor groups who pointed to her anti–affirmative action newspaper columns and policy actions as head of the U.S. Commission on Civil Rights under President Ronald Reagan. However, she withdrew her name from nomination after news emerged that an illegal immigrant from Guatemala had lived in her home, received money from her, and performed household chores.

The U.S. Civil Rights Commission became an arena for further struggles. In a June 2001 meeting with the Senate Rules Committee about its report on the 2000 presidential election, commission members argued bitterly over their report's conclusion that Bush had won the Florida vote and therefore the presidency because of systematic barriers against black voters. Then, in December, the Bush administration announced that it would add a member to the commission, even though no spot had become vacant, and despite the protests of the chairwoman, Mary Frances Berry. The addition would create a 4–4 split on the commission, undermining Berry's power. In May 2002 an appeals court ruled in favor of the administration, allowing the appointment of the new member, Peter Kirsanow, a labor lawyer and chairman of the conservative Center for New Black Leadership.

Judicial appointments are a crucial battleground for interest groups concerned about civil rights.[64] Although legislation such as the 1964 Civil Rights Act has made important strides toward ensuring civil rights, it is the courts that have enforced regulations protecting the rights of racial and ethnic minorities and women. In addition, federal judges are appointed for life, making it possible for a president to influence the interpretation of the law and the protection of civil rights for decades to come. On the assumption that social group membership is correlated with judicial opinions regarding civil rights, the diversity of federal appointments is of interest.

Bush has attempted to promote diversity on the federal bench. According to data posted on the Alliance for Justice website as part of its Judicial Selection Project, as of 6 September 2002, the Bush administration had filled seventy-three vacancies on the federal courts. Of those appointments, sixteen (22 percent) had gone to women, and thirteen (18 percent) to racial and ethnic minorities (two women and eleven men).[65] However, these appointments were not on par with the descriptive representation of the previous administration. During Clinton's first term, 31 percent of judicial appointments went to women and 28 percent to racial and ethnic minorities.[66]

Under the Bush administration, liberal and conservative interest groups alike watched judicial appointments intently, since appointments to the federal circuit and appeals courts are widely perceived as precursors to the three likely appointments to the U.S. Supreme Court that Bush is expected to make during his term in office.[67] The most prominent battle to date ended in a Bush defeat when the nomination of Judge Charles W. Pickering Sr. to the 5th Circuit Court of Appeals in New Orleans reached the Senate Judiciary Committee after control of the Senate had gone to the Democrats (following Senator Jeffords's switch). Abortion rights and civil rights groups opposed the nomination of the federal trial judge from Hattiesburg, Mississippi, on the basis of a record they perceived as hostile to their interests.[68] Despite Bush's public support for Pickering, the Senate Judiciary Committee voted 10–9 along party lines to defeat the nomination. However, early in January 2003, after Republicans regained control of the Senate in the midterm elections, Bush resubmitted Pickering's nomination to the Senate. Many Washington observers were surprised at this move, expecting that Bush would want to keep a lower profile on racially charged issues in the wake of the resignation of Senator Lott, who had been Pickering's strongest supporter in the Senate. On 2 October 2003, the Senate Judiciary Committee approved his nomination in a 10–9 party-line vote. However, Democrats blocked the nomination in the full Senate with a filibuster. When Republicans attempted to bring the nomination to a vote, only 54—not the 60 necessary—voted in favor of doing so.

Several other heated battles followed over judicial appointments relevant to civil rights issues. Bush's nomination of Judge D. Brooks Smith, the chief justice of the U.S. District Court for the Western District of Pennsylvania, to the U.S. Court of Appeals for the 3d Circuit was approved, despite opposition by liberal groups on the basis of Smith's relationship with conservative groups, involvement in cases in which he had financial interests, public opposition to the Violence against Women Act, and membership in an all-male gun club despite a vow that he would resign.[69]

After Republicans took control of the Senate, Bush renominated two conservatives whose appointments had been turned down by the previously Democratic-controlled Judiciary Committee. Priscilla R. Owen, nominated to the 5th Circuit Court of Appeals, had been rejected on the grounds of her opposition to abortion rights and probusiness judicial activism. Miguel Estrada, nominated to the District of Columbia Circuit Court of Appeals, had been turned down because of both his conservatism and, according to the Congressional Hispanic Caucus, his lack of commitment to concerns of Hispanics. Lacking the majority but resolving to continue their opposition to these appointees, Democrats countered their renomination by using a filibuster and winning enough votes to block the nominations from coming to a vote. The controversy over the Estrada and Owen nomination underscored the quandary facing the Bush administration: in order to ensure reelection, Bush needed to appeal to women and racial and ethnic minorities as well as to his conservative base. The solution arrived at was to create a diverse administration descriptively but not substantively. At the same time that the White House could point to a demographic profile that was at least competitive with that of the previous administration, it continued to nominate individuals with proven conservative credentials to policymaking and judicial positions, especially at the lower ranks.[70] Appointment battles continued, however, as Democrats remained unwilling to allow Bush to fill the government with conservatives just to gain descriptive representation.

The First Lady

The challenge facing Bush was to appeal to the mass electorate, pursuing antifeminist policies without arousing the active opposition of women's groups. This tension played out in the unofficial office of "first lady." Whether guided by electoral strategy or not, the approach Laura Bush brought to the role was consistent with the overall strategy of the Bush administration. She mixed the traditional and the contemporary in ways that had public appeal though not the full approval of either liberal or conservative interest groups. During the campaign and in her first years as first lady, Laura Bush was measured against both her predecessor, Hillary Rodham Clinton, and her mother-in-law, former first lady Barbara Bush. Hillary Clinton was the most activist of recent first ladies, while Barbara Bush played a more private and traditional role. When asked whose shoes she expected to fill, the second President Bush's wife replied simply, "I think I'll just be Laura Bush."[71] Instead of abandoning the traditional role in favor of a new approach to first-spouseship, she appeared to be revising it in ways that maintained its appeal to the party's conservative base.

A comparison of her behavior before and after 9/11 shows that the sudden change in national circumstance and climate did not substantially alter her behavior, but rather enabled her to continue performing the traditional role while gaining national attention for doing so. Prior to 9/11, Laura Bush's public actions included launching the first National Book Festival in September 2001, introducing the Ready to Read, Ready to Learn initiative promoting early childhood education, and advocating new teacher recruitment. These activities revealed her as a much less activist first lady than her predecessor. Headlines such as "Comforter in Chief"[72] and "Laura's Moment: The New First Lady's Quiet Strength Keeps the President Humbled and Anchored"[73] touted her as a full-time helpmate, not a policy leader.

After the attacks, the task of providing comfort became both more public and more newsworthy. In addition to figuring as a "rock" of stability for her friends and family,[74] the first lady was portrayed as performing that service for the nation as a whole. Despite this more public persona in the post–9/11 era, however, she continued to opt for a conservative version of that role. When she did speak out on behalf of women, it was only when the country was unified behind the war in Afghanistan, and her remarks addressed the situation of foreign, not American, women. In November 2001 she became the first first lady to deliver an entire Saturday radio address as she spoke on behalf of the rights of Afghan women.[75]

When Laura Bush edged toward proclaiming her own views on controversial issues, however, she was held tightly in check by attentive conservative groups. Two days before the inauguration, she revealed to NBC's Katie Couric on the *Today* show that she did not believe *Roe v. Wade* should be overturned. In response, conservative groups cried out to the administration for reassurance of the president's pro-life stance.

After 9/11 the public responded positively to the first lady, likely stimulated in part by the surge in approval for the president. After the terrorist attacks, a large segment of the public felt favorable toward her, and, at the same time, more people were willing to offer an opinion about her when asked. In response to the question, "We'd like to get your overall opinion of some people in the news. As I read each name, please say if you have a favorable or unfavorable opinion of this person—or if you have never heard of him or her. How about—Laura Bush?" favorable responses rose from 30 percent in August 2000, to 77 percent November 2001. The proportion of people unable to give a response dropped from 41 percent to 15 percent across that time. By June 2003, her favorability dropped slightly but remained high at 69 percent (with 18 percent unable to give a response).[76]

According to public opinion polls, the public viewed Laura Bush as "caring," "supportive," "nice," and "concerned," while women in particular described her as "intelligent."[77] Eventually, the White House appeared to try to capitalize on this perception. Before 9/11, President Bush had claimed that his wife was not part of a "coordinated campaign where she and I are at the top of our respective organizations and we sit down and plot strategy."[78] Later, however, the administration did appear to orchestrate her public actions judiciously. When the first lady publicly defended her husband against criticism of the administration's handling of warnings of terrorist attacks prior to 9/11, observers wondered whether it was coincidence that the president's top counsel and chief strategist, Karen Hughes, was traveling with her in Budapest.[79] In addition, they noted that as his term in office progressed, the president had begun including references to his wife as a regular part of his stump speeches.[80]

Clearly, Laura Bush has gained mass appeal, especially after 9/11. Whether or not her behavior in the role of first lady will improve Bush's standing among women remains to be seen, however. Opinion polls show no clear signal about what the public wants in a first lady. There are indications that a sizeable but not overwhelming portion of the public approves of a more activist, woman-with-an-agenda first lady. In June 2002, a Pew Center study conducted by Princeton Survey Research asked, "Thinking of the last four American first ladies, who comes closest to your image of what a first lady should be . . . Nancy Reagan, Barbara Bush, Hillary Clinton, or Laura Bush?" Only 19 percent picked Laura Bush, while 30 percent favored Hillary Clinton.[81] However, even among Democrats, only 51 percent picked Hillary Clinton as what a first lady should be.[82] Republicans also indicated no clear sense that Laura Bush is the ideal—in fact a larger proportion named Barbara Bush (35 percent) rather than Laura Bush (29 percent).[83]

Whether or not the administration's use of Laura Bush wins votes among women, it is clear that her actions in the role of first lady will do little to advance women's rights. Any support she holds personally for pro-choice policies has been silenced, and even Bush's lavish praise of her is described by some observers as more patronizing than complimentary.[84] Although she remains popular with the American public, she has not become a beacon for the cause of women nationwide. This moderate image appears to reflect the intent of the administration. Although she was showcased prominently during the 2002 midterm campaigns, her assigned task was seemingly not to address women's issues, but to appear as a woman promoting the top issues of the administration, such as homeland security.[85]

Governing Before and After 9/11

This section examines George W. Bush's policy agenda as it directly concerned women and minorities before and after 9/11. By emphasizing issues that were consistent with Republican themes and values, the president was able to try to build support among minority and women voters while not alienating his base. The issue agenda for minorities included homeownership, school vouchers, and faith-based social services, while the women's issues that received attention included women's health initiatives, support for women in business, and increasing funding for the Women, Infants, and Children (WIC) nutrition program. While Bush continued to focus on these issues after 9/11, the amount of attention directed to them waned substantially.

To assess the level of commitment to and interest in various issues of concern to women and minorities, we conducted searches of the whitehouse.gov Web site. A search in September 2002 revealed 74 "hits" for *African American*, 28 for *Latino*, and 176 for *Hispanic* (there was some overlap between these three categories, leaving 238 unique hits). Two general observations are worth making. First, a majority of the entries concerned symbolic politics: Bush meeting with various minority groups, pictures of the president with minority children at a public school, the transcript of Bush's attendance at the first National Hispanic prayer breakfast, announcements of National Hispanic Heritage Month and National Black Music Month. One amusing anecdote reveals that even symbolic politics did not appear to have a very high priority among Bush's White House staff early in his presidency: June 2001 was designated Black Music Month in a press release dated 29 June—with only one day left in the month, there was not much time to recognize black music! The next year, they got it right: June 2002 was designated Black Music Month in a nearly identical press release, but this one was dated 31 May.

Second, a surprising proportion of the hits occurred before 9/11. We anticipated that there would be a significant shift in attention away from domestic issues generally and racial issues specifically once the war on terrorism was under way, but even discounting for the flurry of activity that occurs at the beginning of any administration and for the subsequent focus on the war on terrorism, the differences were surprisingly large. Of the 238 hits, 165 (or nearly 70 percent) originated before 9/11; on the other hand, only 38.5 percent of the time period of our search occurred before 9/11. There was only one press release containing the term *African American* between 11 September and 29 December 2001.

While much of the focus was symbolic, and even this was diluted after 9/11, the Bush administration did make a serious effort to reach minority voters, especially in its early days. One of Bush's big pushes in his first six months was on the issue of education. He visited schools across the country, often in urban areas that had typically not been visited by Republican presidents, to tout his support for school vouchers that would allow poor, urban children to attend schools of their choice. As noted earlier, this policy initiative is opposed by minority leaders (and most Democrats), but it is supported by a majority of voters from minority groups. Similarly, Bush's faith-based initiative has popular support among minorities but is viewed with skepticism by minority leaders. This policy agenda, however, has received little attention from the Bush administration since 9/11. A search conducted on 15 January 2003 produced 2,428 hits on *faith based*. Sorting by date the top 100 selected by relevance, we found that only 14 of those 100 had been posted on the White House Web site after 9/11. A search on *community initiative* (the phrase is usually "faith-based and community initiative") yielded 2,824 hits (some of which were were not related to the faith-based initiative and were not counted in the top 100); only 15 of the top 100 appeared after 9/11.

Bush has proposed two other policy initiatives that are supported by both minority voters and their leaders. One, increased homeownership, is still on Bush's agenda, while the other, racial profiling, has taken on a decidedly different tone since 9/11. In a 15 June 2002 radio address President Bush could have been mistaken for a civil rights leader when he said, "Yet today, while nearly three-quarters of all white Americans own their homes, less than half of all African Americans and Hispanic Americans are homeowners. We must begin to close this home ownership gap by dismantling the barriers that prevent minorities from owning a piece of the American dream." Bush offered a comprehensive plan to increase the number of minority homeowners by at least 5.5 million before the end of the decade. It remains to be seen whether Bush will provide the necessary leadership to get the required legislation through Congress, but it is a serious proposal that addresses one of the persistent problems facing the minority community: quality housing.[86]

President Bush surprised many people when he called for an end to racial profiling in his 2001 State of the Union message, announcing, "Earlier today I asked John Ashcroft, the Attorney General, to develop specific recommendations to end racial profiling. It's wrong, and we will end it in America." This declaration was more assertive than President Clinton's order to compile data on racial profiling, but within a few weeks it appeared that the White House was backing away from the promise when White House spokesman Ari Fleischer pointed out, "It's not as if there is one federal police force that the president can wave a magic wand and make a very, very difficult problem go away. It involves a lot of local jurisdictions that the United States government does not have direct control over."[87] In a 31 January 2002 press conference Fleischer was asked if the president had forgotten about his commitment to ending racial profiling. He responded as follows:

> In the president's address to Congress last year, upon taking office, the president called for a ban on racial profiling. And the president remains committed to that. As a result of the war that began on September 11th, the Department of Justice, which had jurisdiction and purview over this, which was working very closely with a lot of local governments, as well as federal entities and agencies, has gotten distracted to other issues, of course. The priorities of fighting the war on terrorism has taken the Justice Department away from this mission. . . . The war has intervened, but the president has not forgotten the promise; it's a promise he intends to keep.

Nevertheless, the commitment to end racial profiling became much more difficult in the wake of the terrorist attacks. The Justice Department implemented several controversial initiatives that involved profiling citizens, permanent residents, legal visitors, and illegal aliens of Middle Eastern descent. Most of the Justice Department's efforts have focused on illegal aliens; for example, one program sought to round up 6,000 illegal aliens of Middle Eastern descent who had overstayed their visas or been deported for other reasons.[88] However, another program requested 5,000 visitors from the Middle East to voluntarily submit to questioning about their views on terrorism and radical groups. At the same time, Bush urged Americans not to make judgments based on appearances and implemented security policies in airports that included random searches rather than profiling.

One positive effect of the war on terrorism for President Bush has been that his support among minorities has risen along with that of the rest of the nation. A public opinion poll taken by Black America's Political Action Committee (BAM-PAC) showed that Bush's approval rating among African Americans increased by 22 points between July 2001 and July 2002 (from 19 percent to 41 percent). Other polls with smaller sample sizes have found even higher levels of support for Bush among blacks. However, another poll by CBS News found that blacks were more concerned than whites about the possible loss of civil liberties in the war on terrorism.[89] Therefore, President Bush will have to tread carefully to take advantage of this newfound support.

Bush also pursued a two-tiered strategy of appealing to women: he pursued policies that played to his conservative base, while at the same time behaving in a way that seemed to gesture, symbolically, to women. In the first part of his term, Bush's policies ran directly against the grain of advancements in women's rights: On his first day as president, Bush signed an executive order banning U.S. foreign aid to international organizations or groups in foreign countries that provide abortion services and/or counseling. In spring 2001 he closed the Office for Women's Initiatives and Outreach.

In his first months in office, when Bush was criticized from the left for policies contrary to women's rights, he and his staffers raised the composition of his inner circle as a defense. For example, when Bush closed the Office for Women's Initiatives and Outreach, Karen Hughes responded to criticism by declaring, "In this White House, the women's office is the senior staff meeting."

After six months in office (toward the end of the summer of 2001), the Bush administration renewed efforts to attract the votes of women.[90] Observers had noted that many of the president's actions since taking office, especially the tax cut, were widely perceived as catering to the rich, and not the ordinary citizen, and especially not the moderate woman voter.[91] Plans seemed to be under way to counter this perception by emphasizing Bush's "compassion" through a discussion of values that was to be called "Communities of Concern" and through renewal of attention to education. However, the terrorist attacks of 9/11 soon superseded any such plan.

After 9/11, although the Bush administration did not pursue women's rights, it did proceed with symbolic gestures toward women, primarily by capitalizing on the war in Afghanistan. The result was an administration whose main acknowledgments of women's rights were made with respect to women abroad, rather than women within the United States. The White House Web site illustrates this irony. A search of the word *women* on the site in early September 2002 revealed 1,106 hits. Many of these mentions were attributable to speeches in which the president used phrases such as "men, women, and children," "our policemen and women," or "our men and women in the military." Of the 500 "most relevant" hits (as determined by the Web site), only 12 referred to substantive actions (excluding nominations of women). The others reflected symbolic gestures, such as proclamations declaring Women's Equality Day or Women's History Month, and appearances by Laura Bush at women's groups such as the Genesis Shelter Women's Day lunch in May 2002 in Atlanta, and the 90th anniversary gala of the Girl Scouts. The lack of attention to domestic policy with respect to women was even more clearly demonstrated in the fact that among the twelve pages that referred to policy related to women, six of the policies concerned women in other countries, namely relief efforts targeted toward Afghan women (the Afghan Women and Children and Relief Act) and funding for global HIV/AIDS programs that attempt to halt the transmission of HIV from mother to child.

Beyond the White House Web page, the administration's policies affecting women in other countries were greeted with criticism by the international community, not applause. In October 2002 the Bush administration cancelled a $34 million contribution to the United Nations Fund for Population Activities that had been approved by Congress. The money would have gone to support family planning, AIDS prevention, and activism against female genital mutilation. Then, in December, the administration further undermined international family planning efforts at a regional conference held by the United Nations in Bangkok. Representatives of the administration brought the proceedings to a standstill when they threatened to withdraw their support for an agreement, reached at a 1994 Cairo conference, in support of efforts to enhance the legal, economic, and physical health of women throughout the world and of efforts to reduce population growth.[92] At the Bangkok conference, after days of contentious debate—during which the representatives of the Bush administration argued that the Cairo agreement supported abortion—the U.S. delegation's attempts to alter the agreement were defeated by votes of 31–1 and 32–1.[93] Another blow to advocates of women's rights came when President Bush reversed course on his support for an important international treaty protecting women's rights. This treaty, the United Nations Convention on the Elimination of All Forms of Discrimination

(CEDAW), has been ratified by 170 nations; on 30 July 2002, the Senate Foreign Relations Committee approved U.S. ratification of CEDAW on a bipartisan 12–7 vote. However, conservative groups objected, and the White House policy is now being "re-reviewed" by John Ashcroft and the Justice Department.[94]

Bush did not completely ignore women in the United States. The White House Web site notes clearly that in 2001, Bush signed into law a budget that funded the WIC nutrition program at its current level (serving 7.2 million people) and then proposed a budget for fiscal year 2002 that increased that participation rate to 8 million. Also, in February 2002 Bush signed legislation that would enable women to make "catch-up" contributions to their retirement plans, if they had taken time off from the paid workforce. Another piece of legislation authorized by the president funded Medicaid benefits to Native American women who had been diagnosed with breast or cervical cancer through a government screening program. In addition, Bush advocated programs to support small business entrepreneurship and explicitly emphasized the benefits of this action for women.

Despite these actions, the relative lack of attention to policies geared toward women in the U.S. population both before 9/11 and afterward suggest that Bush's attempts to attract women voters were made primarily through symbolic and not substantive means.

Conclusion

President Bush's "going public" strategy may have some success. If he makes appeals on issues on which there is popular support among minority populations despite opposition from their leadership (school vouchers, toughness on crime, faith-based initiative) and on issues on which there is consensus among minority groups (increasing homeownership among the poor, eliminating racial profiling), he is likely to make some gains among minority voters. This approach is especially favored within the Republican Party because emphasis on these issues reinforces the party's philosophy of individualism, limited government, and opportunity. However, when Bush challenges traditional civil rights positions or is perceived as being unenthusiastic about enforcing existing civil rights laws, he is likely to lose some of the support that may have been gained through the more positive appeals.

There is certainly important symbolic value in having African Americans such as Powell and Rice in top government positions. But these appointments, while very visible, do not promote progress on the core civil rights issues. If Bush continues to appoint individuals such as Ashcroft, Pickering, and Owens, who are perceived by civil right leaders as being hostile to their agenda—and especially if he opposes policies that are supported by minority leaders and masses alike, such as affirmative action—the compassionate conservative/big tent philosophy may not work. When Bush announced in January 2003 that the White House would be filing a Supreme Court brief opposing affirmative action in higher education in a case concerning the University of Michigan, the big tent strategy seemed particularly in doubt. Some had predicted the president would not take this step because of the damage it would do to the Republican Party's push for inclusiveness and the difficult balancing act of the "going public" strategy.

With respect to women, it also appears that Bush is pursuing a two-tiered strategy. At the same time that he is pursuing policies consistent with the wishes of his attentive, socially conservative base, he is making attempts to convey the image of a woman-friendly leader. Bush has created an inner circle that includes women in highly visible positions, produced an appointment record that descriptively represents women at rates not drastically below those of his predecessor, strategically mentioned at opportune moments the popular first lady, and pursued pro-life policies most visibly in the international arena, in which the American public is least attentive. The challenge for the future is that although conservative activists have noticed and appreciated his anti-abortion actions while in office, liberal activists have also observed these actions and are not likely to forget them as 2004 approaches.

Notes

We would like to thank Kimberly Follett for superb research assistance.

1. Anna Greenberg, "Where Were the Women?" *The Nation*, 30 December 2002, 20–21, citing Election Day polling conducted by Greenberg Quinlan Rosner Research. The lack of Voter News Service exit poll data (due to system malfunctions on Election Day) prevents further analysis of the election results with respect to race, ethnicity, and/or gender.
2. Parts of this section are drawn from Virginia Sapiro and David T. Canon, "Race, Gender, and the Clinton Presidency," in *The Clinton Legacy*, ed. Colin Campbell and Bert A. Rockman (New York: Chatham House, 2000), 170–75.
3. Robert D. Loevy, *The Civil Rights Act of 1964: The Passage of the Law that Ended Segregation* (Albany: State University of New York Press, 1997), 12.
4. Doris Kearns Goodwin, *No Ordinary Time: Franklin and Eleanor Roosevelt: The Home Front in World War II* (New York: Simon and Schuster, 1994). At the same time, it is important to note that some New Deal programs, such as Social Security, were biased against blacks. See Theda Skocpol, "African Americans in U.S. Social Policy," in *Classifying by Race*, ed. Paul E. Peterson (Princeton, N.J.: Princeton University Press, 1995), 132–34. To the dismay of the black community (and Eleanor), FDR never threw his support behind the antilynching law. See Goodwin, *No Ordinary Time*, 164.

5. See Edward G. Carmines and James A. Stimson, *Issue Evolution: Race and the Transformation of American Politics* (Princeton, N.J.: Princeton University Press, 1989).

6. But see Beth Reingold, "Making a Difference: Legislative Behavior and the Meaning of Women's Political Representation," unpublished paper presented at the annual meeting of the American Political Science Association, Boston, September 1998, on the limitations of defining "women's interests" in terms of particular issue areas.

7. "While we recognize differing views on this question among Americans in general . . . and in our own Party . . . we affirm our support of a constitutional amendment to restore protection of the right to life for unborn children."

8. Virginia Sapiro, with Pamela Johnston Conover, "The Variable Gender Basis of Electoral Politics: Gender and Context in the 1992 U.S. Election," *British Journal of Political Science* 27 (1997): 497–523.

9. Carole Kennedy Chaney, R. Michael Alvarez, and Jonathan Nagler, "Explaining the Gender Gap in U.S. Presidential Elections, 1980–1992," *Political Research Quarterly* 51 (June 1998): 311–39.

10. Virginia Sapiro, "Feminism: A Generation Later," *The Annals* 515 (May 1991): 10–22.

11. This figure is from 1996. Rodolfo O. de la Garza and Louis DeSipio, *Awash in the Mainstream: Latino Politics in the 1996 Elections* (Boulder, Colo.: Westview, 1999), 1.

12. Rodolfo O. de la Garza, Louis DiSipio, F. Chris Garcia, John Garcia, and Angelo Falcon, *Latino Voices: Mexican, Puerto Rican, and Cuban Perspectives on American Politics* (Boulder, Colo.: Westview, 1992), table 8.18, p.124.

13. John Marelius, "Bush Tries to Mend Rift with Latinos in California." *San Diego Union-Tribune*, 8 April 2000, A1.

14. DeWayne Wickham, "GOP Croons to Blacks Off Key," *USA Today*, 8 August 2000.

15. Peter Wallsten, "GOP Hopes for Receptive Ears across the Gender Gap," *CQ Weekly* 58, no. 14, 1 April 2000, 748–751.

16. Wallsten; and Kate O'Beirne, "Clueless: What Women Don't Know about Politics," *National Review*, 9 October 2000.

17. Although women and men have similar positions on abortion, the issue is often viewed as an indicator of a candidate's receptiveness to women's interests.

18. Richard S. Dunham and Ann Therese Palmer, "The Furious Waltzing of Women Voters," *Business Week*, 16 October 2000, 52.

19. Mike Allen, "Confident Bush Shifts Right, Goes after New Ground," *Washington Post*, 16 October 2000, A8. The states the tour planned to visit were Michigan, Pennsylvania, and Wisconsin, but the Wisconsin leg of the tour was cancelled due to problems with Laura Bush's plane.

20. Greenberg, "Where Were the Women?"

21. Katharine Q. Seelye, "The 2000 Campaign; Women Voters; Marital Status Is Shaping Women's Leanings, Survey Finds," 20 September 2000, A23.

22. Independent samples, 2-tailed T-test for gap among women yielded $t = -5.264$, $p = .000$, but among men $t = -1.582$, $p = .115$.

23. Independent samples, 2-tailed T-test for gap among women yielded $t = 2.776$, $p = .006$ but among men $t = .431$, $p = .667$.

24. Independent samples, 2-tailed T-test for gap among women yielded $t = 2.666$, $p = .008$ but among men $t = .575$, $p = .566$.

25. Marjorie Connelly, "Who Voted: A Portrait of American Politics, 1976–2000," *New York Times*, 12 November 2000, WK–4.

26. Jill Lawrence, "Both Parties Are Hotly Pursuing Hispanic Voters," *USA Today*, 1 August 2002, A1.

27. Nancy Gibbs, "Person of the Year: George W. Bush," *Time*, 17 December 2000.

28. Mireya Navarro and Somini Sengupta, "Contesting the Vote: Black Voters," *New York Times*, 30 November 2000, A1.

29. Randolph Pendleton, "Harris Denies Election Blame; 'Laughable,' Says Panelist," *Jacksonville Times Union*, 13 January 2001.

30. Navarro and Sengupta, "Contesting the Vote."

31. David Usborne, "Blacks Sue Florida over Racist Voting Law," *The Independent* (London), 14 January 2001, 21.

32. Robert E. Pierre, "Botched Name Purge Denied Some the Right to Vote," *Washington Post*, 31 May 2001, A1.

33. Greg Palast, "The Great Florida Ex-Con Game: How the 'Felon' Voter-Purge List was Itself Felonious," *Harper's Magazine*, March 2002.

34. Ibid.

35. Ibid.

36. Pierre, "Botched Name Purge."

37. Katharine Q. Seelye, "Senators Hear Bitter Words on Florida Vote," *New York Times*, 28 June 2001, A20.

38. Ford Fessenden, "Examining the Vote: The Patterns; Ballots Cast by Blacks and Older Voters Were Tossed in Far Greater Numbers," *New York Times*, 12 November 2001, A17.

39. "NAACP Settles Dispute over 2000 Presidential Vote," Reuters.com, 3 September 2002.

40. Dane Canedy, "Again Sunshine State Is in Dark a Day after the Vote," *New York Times*, 12 November 2001, A17.

41. Adam Nagourney, "A Joke Is Wearing Thin for Voters in Florida." *New York Times*, 12 September 2002, A17.

42. Marie Cocco, "Republicans Are Still Playing the Race Card," www.newsday.com, 19 December 2002. Also see "The New Poll Tax: Republican-sponsored Ballot-security Measures Are Being Used to Keep Minorities from Voting," *American Prospect*, 30 December 2002, 26–28.

43. Elihu Katz and Paul F. Lazarsfeld, *Personal Influence: The Part Played by People in the Flow of Mass Communications* (New York: Free Press, 1955).

44. See Canon and Sapiro, "Race, Gender, and the Clinton Presidency."

45. Guy Gugliotta and Juliet Eilperin. "GOP Turns Attention to Contest for House Majority Leader," *Washington Post*, 10 November 1998, A1.

46. Anthony Asadullah Samad, "J.C. Watts' Exodus from Congress: Is the GOP's 'Big Tent' Move Losing Steam," *Black World Today*, 5 July 2002.

47. Lori Rodriguez, "Bond Opens NAACP Conference with Swipe at Bush 'Dynasty,'" *Houston Chronicle*, 12 July 2000, sec. 1, p.1.

48. Congressman Robert C. "Bobby" Scott, "Bush's Faith-Based Action Plan Contains Civil Rights Poison Pill," 29 January 2001, www.house.gov/scott/res_op_ed_01_30_01.htm.

49. Robert C. Byrd, *The Senate, 1789–1989: Addresses on the History of the United States Senate* (Washington, D.C.: Government Printing Office, 1988).

50. Stephen Hess, *First Impressions: Presidents, Appointments, and the Transition* (Washington, D.C.: Brookings Institution, 2000), 7.
51. Hess, *First Impressions*, 7.
52. Frank Bruni, "Contesting the Vote; The Texas Governor; Advisors to Bush Say He Would Use Appointments to Send a Message about Diversity," *New York Times*, 1 December 2000, A27.
53. Sapiro and Canon, "Race, Gender, and the Clinton Presidency."
54. Martha Brant, "Bush's 'Power Puff Girls,'" *Newsweek*, 7 May 2001, 36. For the personnel director's public claim that the administration was not using quotas, see Ellen Nakashima and Al Kamen, "Bush Picks as Diverse as Clinton's," *Washington Post*, 30 March 2001, A27.
55. Ibid.
56. Ibid.
57. Ibid.
58. Al Kamen, "In the Loop: Holiday Bender," *Washington Post*, 19 December 2001, A37.
59. Ibid.
60. Hanna Pitkin, *The Concept of Representation* (Berkeley: University of California Press, 1967).
61. Quoted in Roxanne Roberts, "Civil Rights Coalition Clicks on Tomorrow," *Washington Post*, 10 May 2001, C1.
62. Michael Eric Dyson, "Bush's Black Faces," *The Nation*, 29 January, 5–6.
63. "Ashcroft Examined: Excerpts of Senator's Opening Questions at his Confirmation Hearing," *Seattle Times*, 17 January 2001, A3.
64. Sapiro and Canon, "Race, Gender, and the Clinton Presidency."
65. See http://www.afj.org/jsp/cf/index.cfm.
66. Sapiro and Canon, "Race, Gender, and the Clinton Presidency."
67. Neil A. Lewis, "Judicial Confirmation Hearing Evokes Civil Rights Struggle," *New York Times*, 8 February 2002, A17; idem, "Senate Panel Seems to Vote against Bush Judicial Nominee," *New York Times*, 6 March 2002, A18; idem, "From Quiet Nomination to Noisy Test for Future Battles," *New York Times*, 26 February 2002, A19.
68. *The Nation*, a liberal newsweekly, publicized additional claims, including complaints that Pickering "signed an open letter declaring he was working along more genteel lines to maintain 'our Southern way of life'" and the statement, "At least eleven of the two dozen Pickering decisions overturned by the Fifth Circuit were rejected for violating well-settled principles of law involving civil rights, civil liberties, criminal procedures and labor rights." Neil A. Lewis, "Fighting Pickering," *The Nation*, 18 March 2002, 5.
69. Edward Walsh, "Court Choice Cleared with Democrats' Help; 12–7 Vote Frustrates Liberal Groups," *Washington Post*, 24 May 2002, A6; and Nan Aron, "Alliance for Justice Raises Serious Concerns about Judge D. Brooks Smith and His Nomination for the US Court of Appeals for the 3rd Circuit," Alliance for Justice press release, 26 February 2002, http://www.afj.org/jsp/news/release022602.html.
70. David Broder, "Trying to Piece Together a Puzzling Presidency; Scholars Praise Bush Staffing, Fault Public Message," *Washington Post*, 3 September 2002, A2, citing, in particular, work by Shirley Anne Warshaw of Gettysburg College.

71. Lois Romano, "A Twist on Traditional; Reluctant Celebrity Took Unconventional Route," *Washington Post*, 14 May 2000, A1.

72. Martha Brant, "Comforter in Chief," *Newsweek*, 3 December 2001, 34–35.

73. Kenneth T. Walsh and Angie Cannon, "Laura's Moment," *U.S. News & World Report*, 30 April 2001, 20.

74. Elaine Sciolino, "Laura Bush Sees Everything in Its Place, Including Herself," *New York Times*, 15 January 2001, A1.

75. Incidentally, Laura Bush is the first first lady to refuse an honorary membership in the American Newswomen's Club since its creation under Eleanor Roosevelt.

76. Gallup polls, 4–5 August 2000 (N = 1,051); 26–27 November 2001 (N = 1,025); 9–10 June 2003 (N = 1,029).

77. "Laura Bush's Changing Image: No Longer Just 'Nice,' No One Dislikes Her!" Survey Report, Pew Research Center for the People and the Press, 2 July 2002.

78. Walsh and Cannon, "Laura's Moment."

79. Elizabeth Bumiller, "Out of Lamb Chop and into Fire," *New York Times*, 10 June 2002, A20.

80. Ibid.

81. Conducted by Princeton Survey Research, 19–23 June 2001, N = 1212. Nineteen percent chose Nancy Reagan, and 26 percent named Barbara Bush.

82. "Laura Bush's Changing Image."

83. Ibid.

84. Jennifer Loven, "Bush Sings Praises of the First Lady," *New York Times*, 28 October 2002, A4.

85. Martha Brant, "Laura Bush and the Gender Card," *Newsweek* Web Exclusive, 31 October 2002.

86. Bush's radio address may be found at: http://www.whitehouse.gov/news/releases/2002/06/20020615.html. Also see the "home ownership fact sheet" at: http://www.whitehouse.gov/news/releases/2002/06/20020617.html.

87. Dana Milbank, "Bush Considers Move against Racial Profiling," *Washington Post*, 10 February 2001, A7.

88. Dan Eggen and Cheryl W. Thompson, "U.S. Seeks Thousands of Fugitive Deportees: Middle Eastern Men Are Focus of Search," *Washington Post*, 8 January 2002, A1.

89. Adam Clymer, "U.S. Attitudes Altered Little by Sept. 11, Pollsters Say," *New York Times*, 20 May 2002, A12.

90. Brant, "Bush's 'Power Puff Girls.'"

91. Frank Bruni, "After Six Months Bush Team Plans Change of Focus," *New York Times*, 5 August 2001, A1.

92. James Dao, "U.S. Raises Abortion Issue at Conference on Families," *New York Times*, 15 December 2002, A1.

93. James Dao, "Over U.S. Protest, Asian Group Approves Family Planning Goals," *New York Times*, 18 December 2002, A7.

94. Noy Thrupkaew, "Money Where His Mouth Is: Bush Talks a Good Game on Women's Rights, But Talk Is Cheap," *American Prospect*, 23 September 2002, 17–18.

CHAPTER 11

Bush II and the World

Graham Wilson

GEORGE W. BUSH GAINED the presidency at a moment when the United States enjoyed a degree of power in the world that was probably unprecedented. By every conceivable measure of power, the United States utterly dominated the world stage. In the nineteenth century, the British had an informal rule that their navy should be stronger than the next two most powerful in the world; in the early twenty-first century, U.S. military power was as great as the next *ten* most powerful militaries combined. In 2000 American military expenditure was greater than that of Britain, Russia, Japan, Germany, France, and China combined.[1] Roman legions had dominated the region from what is now Britain into the Middle East; United States forces either already dominated every continent or, as events in Afghanistan were to show, could project American might more or less anywhere on earth.

Contrary to fears expressed by academics such as Paul Kennedy, American power was not limited to the military sphere.[2] The GDP of the United States was greater than those of Britain, Russia, Japan, Germany, and France combined.[3] The American economy was not only the largest in the world but was also seen as the most dynamic. American growth rates were among the best in the world. At the start of the new century, the economies, particularly the Japanese and German, that had once been held up as superior examples of growth and efficiency that the United States might emulate were trapped in low growth and high unemployment. The American economy, in contrast, was hailed as a "jobs machine," generating large quantities of jobs that were not, it turned out, predominantly low-wage "hamburger flipping" jobs.

Perhaps uniquely among history's superpowers, the United States also enjoyed a considerable cultural influence that was not limited (as were the British or Romans in earlier times) to elites around the world but reached the masses. The ubiquity of American fast-food chains such as McDonald's was the aspect of this cultural triumph that was most widely noticed, but the dominance of cinema by Hollywood (and the comparable strength of American television companies in exporting their programs) extended American cultural influence into the lives and homes of the common people.

Indian princes might have studied at Oxford and played cricket for England, but American popular culture reached ordinary people on every continent. The collapse of the Soviet Union and the intellectual discrediting of communism served to emphasize American dominance. The Soviet military had been the only plausible threat to the United States; after the defeat of the Nazi and fascist powers in 1945, communism had been the only important, fully articulated alternative to the American creed of capitalism and democracy.

Any president of the United States taking office in 2001 would have been presented with the challenge of deciding how this power should be used. International relations theories about the behavior of utterly dominant ("hegemonic") powers suggested a variety of possible answers.[4] The first was that the hegemon take on the burden of making sure that the international system operated smoothly. In part, this would be a matter of military power, of policing the world effectively. In the nineteenth century, the British Royal Navy had kept world sea-lanes safe and had conducted operations against activities that had come to outrage civilized opinion, such as the slave trade. But this world leadership role also required attention to economic problems. Charles Kindleberger has argued on the basis of historical evidence that the world economic system needs a hegemon to steer the system through potential crises by making or guaranteeing loans and by providing markets for struggling economies.[5] Some suggested that a distinctive feature of American hegemony was that it was generally exercised through international organizations rather than unilaterally. The International Monetary Fund (IMF) was perhaps the best example. While the United States dominated the Fund through its large block of votes, it was the IMF that took the heat publicly for controversial actions such as dictating economic policy to countries such as Argentina that applied to the Fund for loans to tide them over.

A second, more cynical view of hegemonic behavior suggested that the dominant superpower could exempt itself from rules and norms that were required of other countries. French President Charles de Gaulle had complained in the 1960s, for example, that the international monetary system that existed from World War II until the early 1970s (known as the Bretton Woods system) had allowed the United States to run large trade deficits with impunity. No other country could have done so within the Bretton Woods framework, which had been largely designed by the United States. In short, its dominance gave the United States the choice between accepting the burdens of world leadership on the one hand and giving itself privileges within the world system on the other.

George W. Bush's immediate predecessors had inclined toward accepting the burdens of leadership. His father, George H.W. Bush, with a little prodding from then British Prime Minister Margaret Thatcher, had accepted that as the hegemonic power, the United States had to take the lead in reversing the seizure of one sovereign state (Kuwait) by another (Iraq). In another classic move for a hegemonic power, Bush I, allegedly at the urging of his wife, had sent U.S. forces to Somalia to try to save its citizens from mass starvation. Bill Clinton had hastily withdrawn those troops from Somalia after they suffered casualties, but in general he had almost eagerly accepted the world leadership role that American dominance created. Clinton played a decisive role in attempts to bring peace to Northern Ireland. Again prompted by a British prime minister (Tony Blair), he used American military might to avert genocide and achieve peace in the Balkans. Clinton even endangered his support within his own party by pushing through two major international trade agreements. The first was the North American Free Trade Agreement (NAFTA) with Mexico and Canada. The second, potentially more important, provided for membership in the U.S.–designed World Trade Organization (WTO) and ratified the global trade agreements reached in the Uruguay Round. The WTO and the Uruguay Round were generally seen as the bedrock for the new, global economic order.

The New Administration

The new Bush administration was temperamentally and politically skeptical of this world leadership role.

Bush himself showed remarkably little interest in the rest of the world. Indeed, given that his father's jobs during his own youth had provided many opportunities for travel, it was extraordinary how little of the world Bush had seen. While this might reflect what at least one journalist who follows him closely sees as a general lack of intellectual curiosity, it is hard not to see Bush's failure to travel in Europe—so atypical of someone with his patrician family background—as a conscious rejection of the rest of the world. Bush came to the presidency not only with little background in foreign policy but with almost no experience—even as a tourist—of other countries. On his first official visit to London—when he was already president of the United States—Bush followed for the first time in his life a sightseeing itinerary that many young Americans of far more modest means have completed before they finish college.

In political terms, too, the new administration faced significant pressures from within the Republican Party to pull back from international leadership. While the Republican Party in Congress had been the bedrock of support for trade liberalization, the Republican right wing had long suffered from a deep suspicion of international organizations. Most of this suspicion had been directed at the United Nations; for those on the farthest shores of right-wing paranoia, black helicopters from the UN that would impose global government on the United States already roamed the skies. Even within mainstream Republican politics, there remained suspicion that crafty foreigners were able to use international organizations to advance their own interests at the expense of the United States.

With the exception of trade policy, the Republican Party showed signs of a tilt back toward its isolationist past, a past abandoned, it now seemed, only temporarily during the Cold War in order to combat communism.

The final and perhaps decisive influence on Bush was his father's electoral defeat in 1992. Bush II is said to been deeply depressed by this event.[6] The Bush family believed that it was due to Bush I placing a higher priority on foreign than domestic policy. Distracted by the Gulf War, Bush I had, in this view, failed to realize the political necessity of prioritizing action to bolster a sagging economy. Of course, the long boom that benefited Clinton had begun under Bush I, but the popular perception was that Bush I was too busy with world affairs to notice the impact of the recession on ordinary Americans. Bush II's top political adviser, Karl Rove, who had also worked in the Bush I administration, was likely to remember the lesson vividly.

This increased emphasis on domestic politics naturally concerned diplomats. Foreign governments almost always fear the arrival in office of a new American president. They have grown used to the last one, and their fears are multiplied by structural differences between the United States and the other democracies. Politicians without experience of national politics rarely become chief executives in most democracies; the norm is to have decades of experience in national government before winning the top job. In contrast, in the United States in recent times, most presidents (Reagan, Clinton, Bush II) have never held national office prior to their accession to the White House. Being a governor can be a great preparation for being a president, but it gives foreigners the impression that an ill-prepared ignoramus has suddenly become the most powerful person on earth. For, whatever their strengths, governors have little or no foreign policy experience. Bush II actually had more than most because of his efforts to cultivate friendship with his state's neighbor, Mexico. (President Vicente Fox was perhaps the only foreign leader Bush knew before taking office.) Yet the factors discussed earlier help explain why allies viewed the advent of Bush II with even greater concern than usual.

Personnel

It is a commonplace but true observation that many of the key personnel in Bush II's administration had played important roles in his father's. We have already encountered one such official—Karl Rove. Almost all the key personnel in foreign policy also fell into this category: Colin Powell had been chairman of the Joint Chiefs of Staff during the Gulf War; National Security Adviser Condoleezza Rice and Secretary of Defense Donald Rumsfeld had also served in the administration of Bush I. Foreign governments worried about the lack of experience of Bush himself were encouraged to look at the people who surrounded the president rather than at the president himself—in foreign policy, as in general, Bush II had assembled a very experienced crew. Yet any notion that the president could turn over foreign policy to this crew while he devoted himself to his never-ending quest for top personal fitness was complicated by the disagreements that existed among them. Rumsfeld emerged as an early proponent of what, depending on one's personal beliefs, were either strong and vigorous acts or reckless folly; his support for an invasion of Iraq was a case in point. Powell was regarded—probably to his delight—as the voice of reason in the administration for, for example, opposing an invasion of Iraq. Powell's natural caution (evident during his tenure as chairman of the Joint Chiefs) was no doubt reinforced by his responsibility as secretary of state to listen to the opinions of foreign (especially allied) countries as well as representing the United States to them. Finally, Karl Rove, though lacking any foreign policy experience, emerged as a keen advocate of placing consideration of domestic electoral politics ahead of foreign policy on a number of key issues.

In the early stages of the administration, it seemed that Powell would be the dominant influence on foreign policy. This was not the inevitable consequence of his office, as secretaries of state are not guaranteed ultimate sway in making American foreign policy. During the Nixon administration, Henry Kissinger had far more influence as national security adviser than was enjoyed by Secretary of State William Rogers. Nevertheless, Powell was clearly a more substantial figure than Rogers, as well as vastly more experienced than Rice. But the war on terrorism inevitably shifted the balance of power in the administration by making the military, and therefore the Department of Defense, more central to policy discussions and more powerful than it would have been in peacetime. In brief, the newly influential Department of Defense had been staffed by Bush with a preponderance of hard-line appointees who were more willing to use American military might and less worried about the attitudes of other countries than was Powell. In addition to Rumsfeld himself, his deputy, Paul Wolfowitz, was a passionate hawk, whom Bob Woodward, in his sympathetic account of the Bush administration, shows as pressing for using the attacks of 9/11 as a pretext for invading Iraq almost from 12 September 2001.[7] The influence of the Pentagon was obvious in shaping American policy in Afghanistan, where, by the summer of 2002, the emphasis placed on military operations and the neglect of policies aimed at improving life for the Afghans already threatened to turn world opinion against the United States.

The disagreements between Bush's foreign policy advisers were not necessarily damaging. On the contrary, studies of the presidency have often argued that competition and debate among presidential advisers may help the president by widening his choice of policy alternatives; FDR's administration is often cited as an exemplar of this competitive approach.[8] But this approach can work only when the president is willing and able to arbitrate between competing policy proposals, and George W. Bush's lack of interest in foreign affairs made it difficult for him to use this competition as a mode of control. The danger for a chief executive who tolerates disagreements among his subordinates but is unwilling or unable to resolve them is that his administration will seem to lack clear policies or purpose. Policy will seem to be made by the last person to speak to the president, or by the person who can command media attention, or simply by the last person in a position of authority to address the issue. The disarray on policy toward Iraq in the summer of 2002, when the administration seemed totally divided on whether or not to declare war, reflected the dangers of having competing and conflicting advisers reporting to a weak leader.

From Unilateralism to Multilateralism—and Back Again?

A British prime minister, Harold Macmillan, was once asked what was the greatest challenge in governing. "Events, dear boy! Events!" was his reply. One single event, the terrorist attacks on the United States on 11 September 2001, created a challenge that redefined the Bush administration in general and at first seemed to redefine its foreign policy in particular.

It is important, however, to start by describing the foreign policies that the administration had followed prior to 9/11 (as this event came to be called in the United States). In brief, the administration gave the clear impression that it had abandoned the foreign policy approach followed by previous administrations, which emphasized creating and maintaining alliances, and was instead pursuing a policy based more on unilateral action, asserting the primacy of American interests and values whatever its allies might say. This approach was pursued with a vigor—some would say a brutality—that startled loyal allies of the United States, particularly in Europe. A notorious example of this assertive unilateralism was the announcement that the United States was removing its signature from the Kyoto Treaty on measures to combat global climate change. The decision itself was not unreasonable, both because the Kyoto Treaty had no chance of ratification by the U.S. Senate (which had voted 98–2 against in a nonbinding vote) and because other advanced industrialized countries had considerable doubts about the treaty as well. The Bush administration thus could easily have walked away from Kyoto gracefully, noting that its chances of implementation internationally were negligible and calling urgently for a conference to produce a new and better treaty. Instead, the administration announced its decision to allied governments abruptly and without warning—in short, as offensively as possible. Neither would Kyoto have mattered so much if the episode had not seemed to many diplomats to be typical rather than atypical of the administration's approach to its allies, which it had demonstrated in announcing its withdrawal from a whole slew of agreements and treaties, including the treaty creating an international criminal court[9] and the agreement with Russia (negotiated when that country was part of the Soviet Union) to halt development of antiballistic missiles.[10]

Two other examples seemed to illustrate how the new administration's approach to foreign policy differed from its predecessors'. The first was the Middle East, where all American presidents struggle to balance U.S. support for Israel with its alliances with Arab countries in the region. Most American presidents have also sought a place in history as peacemakers; President Clinton had come agonizingly close to securing an historic peace agreement between Israel and the Palestinians. Bush II was much less interested. Soon after the administration took office, Condoleezza Rice echoed the president's wish to be less involved in troublesome conflicts when she remarked, "We shouldn't think of American involvement [in peace talks] for the sake of American involvement."[11] The participation of U.S. officials in attempts to revive peace talks remained episodic until the fall of 2001.

A further example of the administration's new approach was its reluctance to get involved in "nation building." It is hard to be clear about what the administration found so offensive about "nation building" or even to be sure what it meant by the phrase. What Bush himself meant by it remained unclear, but it was probably the use of American military and financial power in attempts to consolidate effective and acceptable government in crisis-torn regions. The administration's antipathy to nation building probably stemmed in part from a fear of casualties like those that had been incurred in Somalia (and were vividly dramatized in the popular movie *Blackhawk Down*, which was released early in its term). Its antipathy probably also reflected a belief that American might should be used to serve American interests, not to pursue more amorphous, even if desirable, goals around the world. Again, this seemed to reinforce the picture of an administration that was leaning more toward an isolationist rather than an internationalist tradition in American diplomacy.

9/11: The Impact of the Attacks on the United States

The terrorist attacks of 11 September 2001 have been described and discussed elsewhere in this book. My concern here is neither to describe nor to explain those attacks but to discuss instead their impact on the president and his policies.

It is hard to believe that any American president—or, for that matter, any foreign leader possessing similar military power—would have reacted to the attacks much differently than the Bush administration did initially. The continued existence of al Qaeda posed an immediate danger to the United States and its allies; the terrorist group made clear its eagerness to carry out similar attacks in the future. As the group operated from Afghanistan, it was urgently necessary for the United States either to secure the cooperation of the Afghan authorities or to act itself in destroying al Qaeda bases. As the extremist Taliban government showed no inclination to destroy the al Qaeda operation itself, American military action in that country became inevitable. How did that operation affect the president and his approach to foreign policy?

Several consequences of the attacks are evident, almost all of them deeply ironic in view of the administration's initial approach to foreign policy. First, and most obviously, the attacks transformed the president's interest and engagement with foreign policy. Whatever Bush II's unwillingness to be thought of—as he imagined his father had been—as a foreign policy president, history had now demanded that he give foreign policy his highest priority.

Second, the attacks transformed the president's standing with the American public. Prior to 9/11, Bush's approval ratings—around 50 percent in June 2001— were the lowest presidential approval ratings in five years, and particularly low for such an early stage of a presidency.[12] The president's initial response to the crisis was not impressive: accepting Secret Service advice not to return to the White House, an apparently bewildered Bush added to, rather than allayed, the public's fears in hasty press conferences held at military bases as he was moved around the country in *Air Force One*. Thereafter, however, he assumed the manner of a wartime president—strong, confident, and capable of simplifying the conflict to a struggle between good and evil in an effort to elicit popular support. Even his most partisan critics thought that Bush's televised address to Congress after the attacks was a success. Foreign policy had made the image of a president who had tried to avoid it.

Third, the administration needed allies, or at least felt that it needed allies. The United States made clear to its friends among the advanced industrialized democracies that it expected military as well as diplomatic support, and the allies responded. The British played the most prominent role: Prime Minister Tony Blair ordered a British missile-carrying submarine to join the initial attacks on Afghanistan, and British Special Forces and thousands of Royal Marine commandos followed. French, Canadian, Australian, and German troops also joined in the invasion of Afghanistan. Perhaps in part because of the goodwill that had been engendered overseas by his predecessor, President Clinton, Bush II had little difficulty in securing the practical support of America's allies despite the vigorous unilateralism that had characterized his own policies. The United States needed much more than diplomatic and military assistance from advanced industrialized nations, however; it needed help from the Islamic world. The United States could not afford to let its fight with al Qaeda be seen as a fight with Islam more generally, and for this, legitimation of its policies in Afghanistan from Muslim countries would be needed. Much more specifically, the United States required the cooperation of Pakistan, a nation whose very identity is based on its Islamic character. Without the toleration, if not support, of Pakistan, the invasion of Afghanistan could not have occurred.

Fourth, the administration found itself engaged in what promised to be an extensive and prolonged example of nation building. The Taliban regime soon collapsed under American and allied pressure, but the resulting situation was far from easy. Because Afghanistan had never been a truly unified nation state, the fall of the Taliban threatened the return of a power struggle among contending, regionally based warlords. Complicated ethnic as well as regional rivalries also threatened to divide the country. Determined efforts by the United States, allied nations—particularly, again, the British, who accepted initial responsibility for internal security—and the United Nations were clearly required in order, to use the dreaded phrase, to build a nation. Nation building was an even more formidable task in Iraq after the U.S. and Britain had invaded successfully. By late 2003 the administration had admitted that $87 billion was needed for the task, an estimate generally thought to be on the low side.

The final and most perplexing challenge that forced itself onto the president's agenda was the Middle East. A few American friends of Israel attempted to argue that attacks on the United States by Islamic extremists were unrelated to the large-scale U.S. military and financial aid to Israel. Most observers, however, believed that arranging a peace in the Middle East would reduce the threat of further attacks on the United States, or, to put it the other way round, that the continued dissemination of pictures of Israeli forces using American-supplied military equipment to repress Palestinians would produce a new generation of terrorists. Unfortunately, the Middle East moves to its own rhythms, and, as the administration's interest in promoting peace in the region increased because of pressure from Arab countries for measures to address Palestinian grievances, as their price for accepting U.S. policy, the problem became even more intractable. The great scholar of the presidency Richard Neustadt thought that Bush had committed the cardinal sin of undercutting his own power by demanding that the Israeli leader, Ariel Sharon, moderate his policies and pull back Israeli troops, only to have Sharon ignore that demand. A wave of suicide bombings by Palestinians directed against Israeli civilians was followed by waves of Israeli military campaigns that devastated cities and killed scores of Palestinian civilians. In June 2002, the administration decided that there was no hope of successful peace negotiations as long as Yasir Arafat remained the Palestinians' leader; Bush called for Arafat to be replaced in democratic elections. Arafat, however, proved to be very adept at clinging to power. Attempts to make him a figurehead, with real power in the hands of a prime minister more acceptable to the USA, failed ignominiously.

Bush and World Leaders

Modern diplomacy involves much more direct interaction between leaders than was the case in the past. In consequence, leaders' opinions of each other also matter. Bush was unusual in the way in which he expressed his opinions, but he was not unusual in being influenced to an important degree by his private reactions to foreign leaders. Margaret Thatcher, for example, was much affected by her personal assessment of the last leader of the Soviet Union, Mikhail Gorbachev, and passed her view that "We can do business with this man" on to Ronald Reagan. The younger President Bush, however, seemed more likely than most leaders to rely heavily on his personal impressions of foreign leaders individually. We have already encountered Bush's enthusiasm for Vicente Fox; his friendship with Tony Blair was somewhat more surprising. Blair had been a close friend and confidant of Bill Clinton; they were both proponents of "third way" politics that sought to escape the usual distinctions between right and left. Yet partly through his vigorous support of the United States after 9/11, Blair was able to develop a close and trusting relationship with Bush, which, like his predecessors, he prized as a means of preserving the "special relationship" with the United States that has given Britain more influence than richer and larger European countries enjoy.

Probably the most important example of Bush's personal assessment influencing diplomacy was his high opinion of the Russian president, Vladimir Putin. Bush announced that he had "looked Putin in the eye," had "been able to get a sense of his soul," and had found him to be "an honest, straightforward man whom Americans can trust."[13] For his part, Putin proved to be adept at making deals with Bush in which he himself refrained from grandstanding in return for very practical gifts from Bush, such as financial aid. The American withdrawal from the anti–ballistic missile treaty occasioned hardly a word of criticism from Russia and was followed up by an agreement to reduce the number of nuclear warheads that each country possessed. Putin's rapport with Bush brought substantive benefits to Russia; it also allowed Bush to claim some foreign policy successes independent of his response to the terrorist attacks. Putin was strikingly exempted from the policy of punishing prominent countires that had failed to support the U.S.–led attack on Iraq in 2003.

Just as there were, in Bush's view of the world, "good guys" among world leaders, so there were bad guys. After 9/11 (and possibly, if Bush was aware of the danger, before) Osama bin Laden and the leaders of the Taliban were naturally among this latter group, and Yasir Arafat, the Palestinian leader, joined them in this category in 2002. One long-standing criticism of American diplomacy has been its alleged tendency to view world politics in moralistic terms. Bush's own habit of dividing world leaders into good guys and bad guys arguably reinforced this tendency.

The Triumph of Unilateralism; the Supremacy of Domestic Politics

We might assume that the need to create and maintain a large international coalition would have brought an end to the unilateralism with which the administration had initially approached foreign policy. When the United States led complex coalitions against the Soviet Union and China during the Cold War, it frequently made concessions to its partners in order to maintain their loyalty and stability. It is often argued, for example, that Japan and newly industrialized countries were allowed to sell freely to the United States, while restricting imports from it, as part of a strategy to secure their support in the Cold War. Foreign aid to Third World countries was at least in part a weapon to keep them from allying with the Soviet Union. The precedent of American diplomacy during the Cold War therefore suggested that concessions would be made to other countries in order to maintain their loyalty in the campaign against al Qaeda.

In practice, however, post–9/11 American policy was remarkable for its indifference to those whom the United States might have been expected to court. The most obvious case was Pakistan. As we have seen, Pakistan was a Muslim country whose support was vital to the success of the American-led campaign in neighboring Afghanistan. In tilting toward the United States, the leaders of Pakistan took substantial risks—including, in a country in which assassination is an established practice, to their own safety—of alienating a population in which Islamic extremism had a substantial following. When these leaders asked the Bush administration to accelerate reductions in its tariffs on imported apparel and textiles, partly to show that they had obtained some payback from the United States and partly to avoid the increased unemployment that might fuel support for al Qaeda, the administration refused.

Arab friends of the United States also received little for their support. Islamic fundamentalism had a popular following that posed major problems for many Arab governments that tilted toward the United States. Again, any policy that indicated American understanding of Islamic concerns about U.S. support of Israel would have been useful. Following waves of horrendous terrorist actions directed against Israeli civilians, however, the Bush administration declared that the Palestinian leader, Yasir Arafat, was a barrier to peace because he would not take effective action against Palestinian terrorist groups. In a speech on 24 June 2002, Bush called for Arafat to be voted out of office. Frustration with Arafat was very understandable, and Bush's total support for Israel accorded with the views of most Americans. However, as Thomas Friedman noted, Bush had failed to balance his support for Israel with an unequivocal call for a halt in the creation of Israeli settlements on Palestinian soil. Such a message would have helped the leaders of Arab countries argue that U.S. policy was not entirely "pro-Zionist." Perhaps domestic politics were the explanation, as Friedman suggested, arguing that "Mr. Bush blinked because he didn't want to alienate Jewish voters."[14]

But Bush was being pushed to back Israel unequivocally not only by Jewish American organizations but also by religious fundamentalists active on the Republican right, such as Ralph Reed. Reed forged an effective campaign linking Jewish friends of Israel and right-wing Christian groups to exert pressure on the administration. While there were many ironies in this alliance given the far right's history of anti-Semitism, the fundamentalist Christians—who believe that the existence of the State of Israel is a necessary condition for the return of Christ— had considerable influence in the Republican Party. In the run-up to the 2000 nominating convention, Bush himself had been presented to the Republicans as a more moderate candidate who could win, rather than one tied to the party's socially conservative fundamentalist right wing. Because he therefore did not enjoy the instinctive support of the Republican right, including the religious right, Bush needed to offer some concessions to this group, and the tilt toward Israel provided an opportunity to make such a gesture.

European allies also were distressed by a series of foreign policy decisions that seemed both to show scant regard for their interests or opinions and to indicate a willingness on the part of the United States to promote its own interests by abandoning its principles. Here again it can be argued that the priority the Bush administration placed on domestic concerns was crucial.

For many years, Republicans had been committed to moving to a free market in agriculture. One of the party's major achievements after capturing control of Congress in 1994 was the "Freedom to Farm Act," which planned a phase-out of the subsidies and restrictions on production that had long been employed to raise farm prices. In 2002, however, President Bush signed a farm bill that provided for massive increases in farm subsidies. The White House even distanced itself from efforts by some Republicans in Congress to minimize the market-distorting impact of this policy by linking the subsidies more clearly to conservation rather than to production. Few thought that the 2002 farm bill was good public policy. It was costly to taxpayers at a moment when the government was rapidly heading back into heavy budget deficits. It also encouraged overproduction and the creation of agricultural surpluses that would depress prices on world markets, with devastating consequences for poor farmers in the Third World. The farm bill was useful, however, in boosting Bush's electoral prospects in farm states. A special meeting was held in October 2003 in Cancun to revive flagging negotiations for the "Doha Round" of trade liberalization. The talks broke down, however, when the U.S. refused to commit to reducing farm subsidies.

The Europeans, in common with many other allies of the United States, were even more distressed by the administration's decision to impose heavy tariffs on steel imports. This policy again departed from the principles that Republicans had regularly espoused—in modern times, Republicans in Congress had been very much more supportive of free trade than had Democrats. The policy also was a clear contravention of the rules of the World Trade Organization (WTO), the international trade–regulating body that the United States had taken the lead in creating. The WTO allowed the temporary imposition of special tariffs if there had been a flood of imports, but, although the Bush administration invoked this rule, the fact was that steel imports into the United States had been falling, not increasing, in the previous year. Pressures for protection from a part of the U.S. steel industry were not new: all previous administrations had faced calls for higher tariffs and import controls from the technologically outmoded sections of the industry. In practice, however, it had been easy to contain these pressures by mobilizing support for free trade within the modern, efficient, and competitive "mini mills" sector of the steel industry. Spokesmen from this sector were often encouraged to testify against protectionism. Bush, however, chose not to follow this tactic but to surrender to protectionist demands instead. His most probable motive—it was more or less proclaimed publicly by the White House—was an attempt to win votes in the midterm elections and in 2004 in states that he had lost narrowly in 2000, particularly Pennsylvania and West Virginia.

The return to unilateralism is not wholly explicable by reference to electoral politics, however, as can be seen in Bush's highly publicized campaign, beginning in July 2002, against the International Criminal Court (ICC). In the past, the United States had been instrumental in the creation of international tribunals to try perpetrators of war crimes and genocide. The Nuremberg Tribunal, which judged Nazi leaders; the tribunals that dealt with Japanese war criminals after 1945; and, most recently, those set up to try the perpetrators of genocide in Rwanda and the Balkans had all been created with American support and involvement. America's European allies strongly favored the creation of a permanent international court to try those accused of war crimes and genocide in very restricted circumstances and only when the appropriate nation's courts or authorities refused to investigate. The Bush administration, however, not only once again removed the signature of the United States from an international treaty— this time the Rome Treaty creating the ICC—it also threatened to end American participation in UN peace-keeping missions unless the international community agreed that no U.S. citizen could be tried by the court.

It is true that this policy resonated with the nationalist right wing of the Republican Party; conservative Republicans had introduced a resolution promising the use of force to rescue any American put on trial before the court. Citizens of the Netherlands, where the ICC is located, noted that as the court building is only a mile from the seacoast, an American invasion would be reasonably easy to carry out, if somewhat surprising since their country is a firm ally of the United States. Few observers around the world, however, would have noticed the issue if the administration had not highlighted it. It might be that Bush II's decision to make a loudly trumpeted attack on the new international court was intended to be a low-cost means of pleasing a group that Bush I had been accused of neglecting, namely, the conservative base of the Republican Party. If so, this was a particularly cynical use of foreign policy for domestic purposes. A more probable explanation is that the administration's behavior reflected its view of the privileged position of the United States in the world. As the *New York Times* noted,

The administration policy towards the court says much about how the lone superpower will project force abroad. It also presents America's partners and the world with a stark choice: if American military power is needed to quiet international trouble spots, the rules of that operation will be written by America.[15]

An American academic commented more succinctly, "An 800-pound gorilla just doesn't like anything to restrict its freedom of action, unless it thinks it can control it completely."[16] The Bush administration's policy, however, caused great political problems for even its most loyal allies, including the British prime minister, Tony Blair, the administration's sole partner in invading Iraq.

Finally, the administration made its belief in American predominance remarkably explicit in its version of a regularly issued document, *The National Security Strategy of the United States*, which it published in September 2002. That document declared openly that the United States would not tolerate any power attempting to equal or excel the military might of the United States.[17]

The Ultimate Test? Iraq

It would seem a contrivance unworthy of serious fiction to have the reputation of Bush II depend in large part on what happened in his dealings with Iraq. Bush I had won a great triumph in the Gulf War and in doing so had shown great diplomatic skill. His preparation of the American people for war and his creation of a mighty coalition against Saddam Hussein showed that Bush I had the foreign policy skills that his prepresidential resumé had promised. Unfortunately, Bush I failed to finish off the Iraqi dictator, who remained in power when his son entered the White House. In a manner reminiscent of a Shakespearean history play, Bush II was granted the opportunity to destroy his father's enemy utterly and to finish the task his father had begun. As Bush the son had earned a reputation as a wastrel in his younger days—and sustained it even in middle age—the obvious Shakespearean analogy is the *Henry IV/Henry V* sequence, during which the playboy Prince Hal morphs into the mighty warrior, Henry V.

Bush II had clearly been interested in trying to remove Saddam Hussein from power before 9/11. Indeed, in a meeting in the Oval Office in February 2001, he told speechwriter David Frum that one of his objectives was to "dig Saddam Hussein out of power."[18] But did Bush II possess either his father's skills or his determination? His administration's desire to overthrow Hussein was not accompanied by a clear political strategy. By late summer 2002, criticism of a proposed invasion was more evident among America's allies than was support. As usual, only the British seemed supportive, while generally dependable allies such as Germany were critical. Indeed, Chancellor Gerhard Schröder won reelection unexpectedly in 2002 by emphasizing his hostility to Bush's Iraq policy, an electoral strategy that was successful domestically but strained Germany's relations with the United States considerably. Capitalizing on Schröder's opposition, France moved to take leadership of a European bloc opposed to the war, thus furthering long-standing foreign policy goals of weakening U.S. influence. Not only Saudi Arabia but even the Iraqi Kurds, whose semi-independence from Hussein had been guaranteed by American and British airpower, came out against invasion.

Even more astonishing was the fact that in August 2002, prominent congressional Republicans such as Dick Armey, the majority leader in the House, declared that the case for war had not been made.[19] Former members of the Bush I administration, including Brent Scowcroft, also expressed unease at the direction U.S. foreign policy was taking. Even the administration itself seemed divided: the hawks at the top of the Defense Department (though probably not the military) favored war, while the State Department urged further diplomacy.[20] Almost every week brought a flurry of stories in leading newspapers such as the *New York Times*—reports that were clearly informed by sources within government agencies—detailing either how ready the plans were for invasion or, alternatively, how great would be the military difficulties and economic costs of war. Bob Woodward's sympathetic account of the administration's foreign policymaking on Iraq suggests that during the summer of 2002, the president was having difficulty in defining his own goals and opinions. In consequence, the administration's policy remained unclear as rival factions within it contended for Bush's support.[21]

By the late summer of 2002, it seemed that Bush II would fail the Iraq test, until a sudden flurry of activity in the early fall seemed to bring the situation back under control. According to opinion polls, the public continued to support the administration's foreign policy by a wide margin, and the disarray within the administration, so evident in midsummer, was also reduced. Republican leaders in Congress fell back into line behind the president, and Democratic critics in Congress were intimidated by the threat that they might actually be asked to cast a vote on war with Iraq before they faced the electorate in the November elections. U.S. allies were temporarily reassured by President Bush's decision to seek support from the UN Security Council rather than acting alone. The Security Council adopted a resolution (No. 1441) demanding that Iraq allow inspectors back in to ensure that it had no weapons of mass destruction and threatening serious consequences if the inspectors did not receive full cooperation. It was left unclear, however, what would constitute "a material breach" of the resolution. There was also uncertainty as to whether or not the Security Council would have to approve any action to punish such a breach by Iraq; members of the Bush administration contended that no further resolution would be needed, but even its staunchest ally, the British, said that it would. Still, with his administration reunited and the allies apparently mollified, Bush—not for the first time in his life—seemed to have risen to a challenge at the last possible moment.

In fact, however, the administration's policies remained handicapped by three failings that were central to Bush II's presidential style. The first was the administration's continuing inability to define its objectives coherently. Congress, the American public, and, above all, America's allies remained unclear on whether the primary objective was the disarmament of Iraq or the removal of Saddam Hussein from power. Administration statements—sometimes even the same speech by the president himself—could be cited to justify either interpretation. Second, the administration continued to have unusual difficulty in understanding the implications of its actions. Bush had agreed to go back to the United Nations in November to secure Security Council resolution 1441 giving Iraq one last chance to disarm and to allow UN inspectors to verify that this was accomplished. Surely it was foreseeable that other countries as well as large sectors of the U.S. populace would expect that the inspectors would be given time to accomplish their mission. Within weeks, however, the administration was arguing that the time had come to go to war, and another draft resolution to support this position was presented to the Security Council by the United States, Britain, and Spain in February 2003. This obvious inconsistency surely aided the organizers of massive demonstrations against U.S. policy that took place around the world on 15 February. Bush had made a tactical decision to go back to the UN in the fall without appreciating the costs of appearing to refuse to give the UN inspectors time to achieve their goals.

Third, administration representatives showed a complete inability to handle relations with America's allies: within eighteen months, they had turned the global wave of sympathy for the United States—"We Are All Americans Now," the French newspaper *Le Monde* had declared—into an unprecedented rift between the United States and most of its long-standing allies. President Bush clearly lacked the skills to win support among either the citizens or the elites of other countries. For all too many leaders and citizens around the world, the most pressing issue had become not the war on terrorism but how to restrain a mighty but reckless United States. Bush had, unfortunately, come a long way since he told Al Gore and the electorate in the 2000 presidential debates, "It really all depends upon how our country conducts itself in foreign policy. If we're an arrogant nation, they'll resent us. If we're a humble nation, but strong, they'll welcome us. And its—our nation stands alone right now in the world in terms of power and that's why we have to be humble."

In the event, the United States attacked Iraq in March 2003 without explicit authorization by the United Nations and supported by only a tiny "coalition of the willing" that contained a relatively small number of lesser-power allies (Australia, Spain, Portugal, Poland, and other eastern European nations) and Britain. Only the British contributed sizeable military forces to the campaign, taking responsibility for the capture of the city of Basra and southeastern Iraq. The impressive American-led military victory came at enormous diplomatic cost, however. Relations with

France and Germany—referred to disparagingly by Secretary of Defense Rumsfeld as "old Europe"—fell to a low level unprecedented since the Second World War. Indeed, it is no exaggeration to say that the whole fabric of multilateral relations between the United States and the rest of the world was a casualty of the war. Few in the Bush administration seemed to recall that the structure of multilateral institutions that now seemed so endangered was one that the United States itself had been instrumental in creating and sustaining over the previous half-century.

Nor was the estrangement between the United States and its erstwhile allies merely a matter of tension between elites. Surveys conducted around the world on behalf of the Pew Research Center in May 2003 showed an alarming decline in trust and affection for the United States in almost every country, the exceptions being its closest allies, Britain and Israel. The percentage of French and Germans holding a favorable view of the United States had dwindled to 45 percent and 43 percent, respectively, whereas, a year earlier, over 60 percent in both nations had held a positive view of the United States.[22] Iraq had been occupied, if neither completely pacified nor stabilized, but although America's alliances desperately needed rebuilding as well, the administration's initial response was instead to insist that countries such as France that had opposed its policies must be punished for their refusal to support the U.S.–led invasion.

Conclusion

As noted at the beginning of this chapter, all contemporary presidents of the United States must come to terms with the unprecedented dominance of their nation in the world today. George W. Bush approached this determination with reluctance, expressing no wish to be "a foreign policy president," in contrast to predecessors such as Kennedy and Nixon, who had embraced the challenge. Bush II was vividly aware of the possibility that a president could succeed overseas and be rejected at home; his own father was a case in point. Yet the rest of the world cannot be avoided. In this era of globalization, the United States is much more closely linked to the world economy than it was a few decades ago. The horrors of 11 September 2001 have also shown that the United States cannot wall itself off from the violence of the contemporary world.

It is striking that in spite of the need to create and maintain an international coalition to combat al Qaeda, the Bush administration did not fully retreat from its original foreign policy views. The concerns of even the closest allies would continue to be subordinated to domestic politics and the quest for reelection. The interests of the United States would continue to be asserted vigorously even if doing so conflicted with its own principles or with the urgings of international organizations that the United States had supported in the past. The decision to attack Iraq without widespread international support or explicit authorization from the United Nations was a striking example of the triumph of unilateralism. Rarely has the United States deployed its might with such little regard for the opinions of many of its traditional allies. In more technical terms, this stance might be described as enjoying the fruits of hegemony: because of its immense power, the administration feels able to pick and choose when to listen to allies and when to ignore them, when to ratify and honor international agreements and when to repudiate them.[23] At least some Americans welcome this approach to foreign policy. An uneasy feeling that the United States has been taken advantage of in world affairs by other nations is widespread in the country, so an administration that uses American hegemony to exempt itself from international law and from the decisions of international organizations is likely to be more popular than one that subordinates American interests to principle or to the wishes of allies. For the rest of the world, and especially the allies of the United States, however, the prospects of a self-centered American foreign policy make the challenges of living next to the "800 pound gorilla" all the more difficult. It must be doubted, moreover, whether this is in the long-term interest of the United States itself.

Foreign governments might seek comfort in reflecting on the general tendency for American presidents to become more internationally minded as time passes. Although there is little systematic research to support this claim, most scholars of the presidency would agree that the longer presidents remain in office, the more they are drawn to foreign policy and their relations with other world leaders. It is worth recalling that while Bill Clinton ended his presidency intensely involved in foreign policy, his administration had begun with a determined focus on domestic policy and an approach to foreign economic policy that also seemed nationalistic; Clinton's first commerce secretary, Ron Brown, was a great advocate of using American power to pressure other countries to buy American goods. There is no doubt that George W. Bush has had to pay far more attention to international affairs than he can possibly have imagined, let alone wished, when he took office. Might the necessity of devoting far more time to foreign policy—and to conversations with foreign leaders—make him more internationally minded and diplomatically adroit?

There were some grounds for optimism. An interesting straw in the wind of international economic policy came in September 2002, when the administration exempted a large number of imported steel products from the tariffs it had imposed so determinedly in the early summer. Although welcomed by European governments, the change in policy called into question the electoral payoff in November that the imposition of the tariffs had promised. Perhaps this reversal marked a tilt toward giving a higher importance to international factors than to domestic politics.

The recession that loomed over the United States in 2002 also pushed the administration toward a more sophisticated approach to foreign economic policy.

Bush II's first Treasury secretary, Paul O'Neill, had taken a very dismissive view of the difficulties of Argentina. That country, he argued, should be given aid only through the International Monetary Fund (IMF) and only when the IMF had imposed rigorous conditions on its economy. But when first Uruguay, then Brazil threatened an economic collapse that could further damage the American economy, the administration changed course and provided aid both directly from the United States and through the IMF (where the United States has overwhelming voting power).[24] Argentines might feel that this contrast in treatment was unfair—after all, Argentina had followed American-endorsed economic policies faithfully in the 1990s, and arguably its large budget deficit had resulted from implementing a decision to privatize social security that Republican economists in the United States had applauded. However, the "U turn" in providing aid to Brazil could also be interpreted as the beginnings of multilateralist wisdom; as Franklin Roosevelt memorably said in defense of Lend Lease aid to Britain in the darkest days of World War II, "Suppose my neighbor's home catches fire, and I have a length of garden hose 400 or 500 feet away. If he can take my garden hose and connect it up with his hydrant, I may help him to put out his fire."[25] Perhaps the loans to Brazil marked the realization by the administration that in today's interconnected world, even the United States needs to be attentive to the needs and concerns of its neighbors and friends. The firing of O'Neill as secretary of the Treasury—the administration's first major personnel change—was perhaps a further sign that multilateralism, at least in foreign economic policy, was triumphing.

The crisis that erupted over North Korea's announcement in the winter of 2002–03 that it would reactivate its nuclear weapons program and expel UN inspectors who were in place to oversee its closure was handled in a manner strikingly different from that displayed in the Iraq crisis. Bush had labeled North Korea part of an "axis of evil" that also included Iraq and Iran. By accelerating its development of missiles and nuclear weapons, its leadership had acted in a manner that was even more provocative than that of Saddam Hussein. In this case, however, Bush hastened to announce that the United States would not attack North Korea and that the problem could be resolved, with the help of other countries, through diplomacy. Indeed, Bush's policy toward North Korea was to refuse to deal with its representatives outside a framework for discussion that included South Korea and Japan. This was carrying multilateralism almost to an extreme.

For those in the administration such as Vice President Cheney, Secretary of Defense Rumsfeld, and his deputies, Paul Wolfowitz and Douglas Feith, the Iraq war demonstrated the virtues of unilateralism. Aided only by the British, the United States had proven its astonishing military strength in defeating and destroying in a matter of weeks an evil regime that the United States perceived as a threat. This offered a happy precedent, they argued, for dealing with similar regimes—perhaps in Iran or Syria—in the future. Ironically, however, the attack on Iraq may yet have the perverse effect of redirecting the Bush administration's approach to the rest of the world toward a more traditional posture. The rising impatience of the American public with the mounting financial and human costs of the occupation of Iraq made a repeat performance in another country unlikely.

The Iraq war had, for example, conditioned President Bush to working with foreign leaders. During the approach to the conflict and the war itself, British Prime Minister Blair became in effect a crucial member of the Bush team, with an influence on par with that of the president's most senior advisers. Blair's price for his support was a commitment by Bush to a peace plan for the Middle East, where Bush had refused to involve himself in a Clinton-like quest for peace over the first two and a half years of his term. As soon as the war with Iraq was over, however, Bush committed to a peace plan, the "road map"—for the first time in his administration placing his personal prestige behind the effort to bring peace between Israel and the Palestinians. In June 2003 Bush traveled to the Middle East, bringing together Prime Minister Ariel Sharon of Israel and the new Palestinian prime minister, Mahmoud Abbas, for peace talks. Blair's influence in Washington, the commitment to a Middle East peace process, and even the quest for allied help in bringing order to Iraq all seemed to offer some prospect that even this administration might return to the path of exercising American hegemony within a multilateralist framework. The surge of anti-Americanism in Europe and around the world in 2003 had illustrated that even for the American superpower, there might be costs in failing to do so. Yet it was not at all clear that the administration had truly returned to multilateralism. By October 2003 the Middle East "road map" to peace had been abandoned. In the face of continued Palestinian terrorism the administration drifted back to uncritical support for Israel. Tony Blair, under intense criticism in Britain for his support for the war on Iraq, saw the one concession he had obtained from Bush vanish. In the continuing struggle for the administration's foreign policy soul, apparent returns to multilateralism generally proved to be illusory.

Notes

1. "Present at the Creation: A Survey of America's World Role," *The Economist*, 29 June 2002, 8, table 2.
2. Paul Kennedy, *The Rise and Fall of Great Powers: Economic Change and Military Power 1500–2000* (New York: Vintage Books, 1989).
3. Ibid.
4. See Giovanni Arighi and Beverly J. Sills, eds., *Chaos and Governance in the Modern World System* (Minneapolis: University of Minnesota Press, 1999); Charles P. Kindleberger, *The World in Depression 1929–39* (Berkeley: University of California Press, 1973); and Robert Gilpin, *The Challenge of Global Capitalism: The World Economy in the 21st Century* (Princeton, N.J.: Princeton University Press, 2000). For more cautionary per-

spectives on American power, see Terence K. Hopkins and Immanuel Wallerstein, eds., *The Age of Transition: Trajectory of the World System, 1945–2002* (London: Zed Books, 1996); and Joseph S. Nye, *The Paradox of American Power: Why the World's Only Superpower Can't Go It Alone* (New York: Oxford University Press, 2002).

5. Charles P. Kindleberger, *The World in Depression 1929–1939,* rev. and exp. ed. (Berkeley: University of California Press, 1986).

6. Frank Bruni, *Ambling into History* (New York: HarperCollins, 2002).

7. Bob Woodward, *Bush at War* (New York: Simon and Schuster, 2002).

8. Richard Tanner Johnson, *Managing the White House* (New York: Harper and Row, 1974).

9. Julia Preston, "US Rift With Allies on World Court Widens," *New York Times,* 10 September 2002, A6.

10. Steve Erlanger, "Bush's Move on ABM Pact Gives Pause to Europeans," *New York Times,* 13 December 2001, A19.

11. As quoted in "Bush Diplomacy in the Middle East," *New York Times,* 30 June 2002, sec. 4, p. 4.

12. Richard Berke, "GOP Defends Bush in Face of Dipping Poll Ratings," *New York Times,* 2 June 2001, A19.

13. Patrick E. Tyler, "Putin and Bush Meet," *New York Times,* 17 June 2001, sec. 1, p.10.

14. Thomas L. Friedman, "The End of Something," *New York Times,* 30 June 2002, sec. 4, p.15.

15. Thom Shanker and James Dao, "US Might Refuse New Peace Duties without Immunity," *New York Times,* 3 July 2002, A1, A4.

16. Stephen M. Walt, as quoted in Serge Schmemann, "US vs. UN Court: Two Worldviews," *New York Times,* 2 July 2002, A8.

17. *The National Security Strategy of the United States,* www.whitehouse.gov/nsc/nss.html.

18. David Frum, *The Right Man: The Surprise Presidency of George W. Bush* (New York: Random House, 2003), 26.

19. Eric Schmitt, "Iraq Is Defiant as GOP Leader Opposes Attack," *New York Times,* August 2002, A6.

20. Todd S. Purdum, "Embattled, Scrutinized Powell Soldiers On," *New York Times,* 25 July 2002, A1.

21. Woodward, *Bush at War.*

22. Christopher Marquis "After The War; OPINION; World's View of USA Sours After Iraq War Poll Finds," *New York Times,* 3 June 2003, Section A, p. 19.

23. For a similar argument, see Andrew Moravcsik, "Why Is U.S. Human Rights Policy So Unilateralist?" in *Multilateralism and U.S. Foreign Policy,* ed. Stewart Patrick and Shepard Forman (Boulder, Colo.: Lynne Reiner, 2001).

24. "Lifelines for Brazil and Uruguay," *The Economist,* 10 August 2002, 33.

25. Radio broadcast, 17 December 1940.

CHAPTER 12

Presidential Leadership in an Era of Party Polarization — The George W. Bush Presidency

Bert A. Rockman

GEORGE W. BUSH is the second American president to be the son of a former president, John Quincy Adams (1825–29) being the other. There are some odd similarities between the two presidencies. For one, each son bears the given name of the father but not the same full name. Furthermore, each father served only a single term in office, each having followed a more renowned two-term president (George Washington and Ronald Reagan). A far more important coincidence, however—and one that is vital to the analysis offered in this chapter—is that both sons, John Quincy Adams and George W. Bush, were awarded the presidency after a disputed and drawn-out electoral process. Ultimately, neither election was settled by popular preference, but by other elites—politicians in the case of Adams and members of the U.S. Supreme Court in the case of Bush.

The process by which Bush came to be the nation's 43rd president provides essential context. The 2000 election revealed a nation that was very evenly divided in its political alignment, with political parties sharply demarcated from one another and closely matched in their shares of congressional seats. It also showed evidence of a potential electorate that was fairly evenly divided, into roughly one-third slices, among identifiers of each party and non-identifiers. However, those who identified with either of the parties at the mass level had stronger loyalties to their party than in earlier decades, a result to some extent of greater consonance in beliefs between party leaders and followers. But the parties have come to mean less to the electorate as a whole because fewer people are attached to them. Among the non-identifiers, the parties are often seen as too strident and combative. Each party can now count more on its passionate base, but each also has to struggle to attract the more indifferent element of the public that is frequently turned off by the perception of unproductive partisan struggle in Washington.[1] Under such circumstances, it may be more cost-effective for each of the parties to target its own base constituencies, to appeal to them, and to mobilize them than to appeal to the median, typically indifferent, voter.

The reinvigoration of partisanship occurred over a considerable period of time and came about from the interplay of mass and elite political phenomena, including complex sociopolitical forces at the mass level, sharpened interest-party alignments, powerful new ideas, more homogeneous and noncompetitive congressional districts, and an enhanced party leadership role in Congress, especially in the House of Representatives.[2] What could have been more reflective of the power of partisanship than the fact that in late 1998 when Republicans in the House of Representatives voted to bring charges of impeachment against President Bill Clinton, Clinton's popular approval rating soared to over 70 percent?[3] House Republicans were less concerned with that global figure than with the deep distaste that their party constituency—and undoubtedly they themselves—had for Clinton, and with the worry that if they deviated from the party line they might face competition encouraged by party leaders for nomination to present or higher office.

As other chapters in this book have noted, the appointments process for administrative positions (Aberbach) and, above all, for the federal bench (O'Brien) has in recent years become enshrouded in partisan controversy: greater political contentiousness surrounding appointments, more party-based interests lobbying, more delays in confirmation, and so on. In other words, the stakes of office have rarely been higher in American political history.

The waxing and waning of partisanship in American politics has complex causation. When partisanship is at high tide, it is usually the consequence of a set of elements—issue intensity, political mobilization, strong incentives to follow party leadership, relatively clear lines of cleavage that both deepen and extend over a broader array of issues—coming together in "a perfect storm." David Rohde has noted that alteration in lines of cleavage (southern whites becoming more Republican as a consequence of southern blacks becoming politically mobilized), the elite movement of a more ideological issue agenda (Reaganism), and changes in the rules and structures of power within the House of Representatives coalesced a set of forces to produce a powerful vector in the direction of more partisanship in that body.[4] Critical to these ups and downs in the intensity of partisanship, however, is leadership.

How much leeway do leaders have? That is a matter about which we can speculate endlessly. Leaders' motives and cognitions are both crucial, however. Two leaders with the same motivation may cognize the same situation dissimilarly and so arrive at different courses of action. There also are contexts in which the incentives for acting in certain ways are powerfully compelling, and they are similarly cognized. My argument in this chapter is that we are living in a time in which the contextual determinants of presidential behavior are especially powerful, yet that does not mean that choice is predetermined by the political context. George W. Bush is his own political personality with his own leadership style, which is very different in many respects, for example, from that of his father. To examine the role of George W. Bush as a political leader, we must therefore consider the interaction between Bush's political personality and the political context of his leadership.

Political Context and Political Personality

One of the most perplexing tasks involved in the analysis of leadership behavior is to differentiate the causal influences of specific features of the context that leaders inhabit from their own values, styles, or cognitive processes. Typically, we know a good bit about one (the context) and virtually nothing that is firm about the other (leaders' political personalities).

Contexts have their own logics. They make choices more or less probable. For example, all political leaders are forced to put together governing coalitions in one way or another. In periods of relatively low partisanship, presidents may be more apt to play to the center in the expectation that there is shared space there across the parties. Alternatively, in periods of high levels of partisanship, presidents may be more likely to shore up their political bases. The incentives are there to do that, and it is likely but not necessary that such behavior will follow. In the first two years of his administration, George H.W. Bush sought to assure the broader public that he was not Ronald Reagan. In the last two years he sought to assure his Republican Party base that he was. By this time, however, it was too late. Bill Clinton and Britain's Tony Blair thought they could be more appealing by discarding their parties' traditional red-meat doctrines by appearing to be moderate, respectable, and sober—and to be where the mass of citizens and commentators claim the public is, namely in the middle. Actually, few people are in the middle unless they are indifferent or ignorant, or both, about the issues. People who have opinions are rarely moderate about them. Clinton's and Blair's strategy was to make the opposition appear to be extreme and to make even some members of their own parties appear extreme in the opposite direction so that they could appear to be reasonable, moderate, even statesmanlike. In sum, people generally approve of moderation and reasonableness on matters about which they themselves have no opinion.

Social science ways of thinking about leadership emphasize the principle of Occam's Razor. The idea is to try to explain the most with the least by seeking the most parsimonious explanation possible. Generally, social science leads us to look at the structures and circumstances that create incentives, presuming that rational people are likely to follow them and, hence, behave in predictable ways. Some analysts in this tradition would go so far as to say that while people are different, their differences do not themselves make a difference.[5]

Commentators and journalists, on the other hand, tend to cover the person and find the story to be a function of the leader's political personality. What kind of leader is this person? What do we need to know about him or her? A book such as this one, focusing on the George W. Bush presidency invites its readers to expect that it will emphasize aspects of the Bush persona rather than the contextual climate of the Bush presidency. I will not extinguish those expectations entirely, but I will dampen them considerably.

To a considerable degree, the extent to which we place emphasis on the individual leader primarily or on the context is related to the extent to which we believe that leaders are more or less free agents or, alternatively, are like pinballs mainly moving in a direction in which they have been propelled. When we see leaders as having significant free agency or discretion, we want to focus on their values and perhaps also on their cognitive capabilities. We believe under these conditions that political leaders can make a powerful *independent* impact. If so, then certainly we need to know more about them. What manner of person is this or that leader?

Alternatively, if we think that leaders basically respond to strategic situations, then what we need to know are the specific incentives promoted by the strategic context. In competition with one another, especially in primary elections, political candidates position themselves as a function of who else is in a race. Each candidate has some prior baggage that influences the extent to which he or she can adapt to the other candidates within that context. Some—let's say a Ronald Reagan or a Ted Kennedy—would be perceived to carry a lot of baggage. They have recognition and well-developed political images. Even modestly informed voters would likely recognize Reagan as a conservative and Kennedy as a liberal in the peculiar parlance of American politics. But what about a Jimmy Carter or a Bill Clinton? Neither had a powerfully etched political past. In the crowded 1976 Democratic primary, Carter nestled himself between the candidate of the right, Senator Henry Jackson, and a set of contestants on the left, Rep. Mo Udall, Senator Birch Bayh, Governor Jerry Brown, Senator Frank Church, and others. Carter looked centrist, shifting leftward a bit when the more conservative Jackson was his prime adversary and rightward a bit when the more liberal Brown and Church became his remaining opponents. At one point, a survey showed that Carter was perceived to be liberal by liberal voters in the Democratic primaries, centrist by centrist voters, and conservative by conservative voters. That, by any standard, constitutes effective positioning.

Similarly, as the governor of a small state, Clinton was little known to a national mass public. But he too benefited by having other candidates project clearer images to the left and right of him, especially Senator Tom Harkin to his left and former Senator Paul Tsongas to his right (at least on fiscal issues). The past tethers a candidate, and even, to some extent, a political leader. Strategic circumstances make some roads "less well traveled" for good reason. Candidates without well-known pasts may be more nimble, but as leaders they also may have less-loyal followers and may have to prove themselves constantly. Both Bush I and Carter were affected by these problems of weak definition when things got bad, whereas Reagan had the Reaganites who were increasingly dominant within the Republican Party and Clinton had Newt Gingrich to play off against—a perfect foil.

The fact is that we simply do not know precisely how much leaders are affected by context and how much they seek to alter the context—that is, to rearrange the existing parallelogram of forces. Clues come to us occasionally. When George W. Bush proposed massive federal income tax cuts during his campaign in 2000, the United States was experiencing considerable prosperity, with high growth rates and low unemployment and with the government having turned the huge federal deficits of the 1980s and early 1990s into big surpluses. Candidate and then President George W. Bush's mantra was that the government's surplus—a product of the booming economy, the increased tax rates legislated in 1993, and the spending restraints required by the Balanced Budget Act of 1997—should be turned back to "the people." When the economy soured—partly a natural result of the collapse of the earlier bubble and partly the fallout of the September 11th terrorist attacks—Bush II's mantra became another round of massive tax cuts in order to stimulate the economy. So, whatever the question, the answer became more tax cuts. Clearly, the relevant context did not lie in the economic conditions.

Maybe it was that Bush himself was a strong believer in small government and tax relief for the most affluent sectors of the population. Or maybe it was that, unlike his father, Bush first wanted to shore up support among his party's core activist constituency and its leadership in Congress, for whom massive tax cuts, especially for the most well-off, and constricted revenue flows for government were articles of faith. One can only infer the most direct triggering mechanisms, but it is generally safe to say that politicians, more than most people, are well schooled (or perhaps just instinctual) in considering whose support they need and then crafting policies or taking positions accordingly.[6] If this supposition is true, then the significance of party polarization as critical backdrop for comprehending the George W. Bush presidency is apparent. Bush's nomination was the result of his being perceived as the truest of the Republican candidates; his (s)election was made possible by appearing to be otherwise; and his presidency has largely, though not exclusively, been molded by the need to remain connected to the activist Republican core.

Although the party polarization context is vital to comprehending the George W. Bush presidency, it is not fully determinative. For example, while Paul Tsongas, the most conservative Democrat in the race for nomination in 1992, claimed that a Democratic president had the right to counter the Republican revolution on the judiciary by nominating judges likely to be loyal to liberal ideological doctrines, Clinton's eventual appointees, on the whole, were remarkably moderate, although this may have been a function of his relative inattentiveness or inconstancy in gaining support for his nominees.[7] Nevertheless, his appointments were held up in the Senate as some Republican senators sought a coequal share in the nomination and confirmation process.[8] And, as Joel Aberbach noted, Clinton's administrative appointments were more notable for their diversity along ethnic, racial, gender, and sexual-preference lines than they were for any clear ideological direction.[9]

How presidents manage the White House and the ways in which they make decisions are especially apt to be reflective of their personalities, although even these aspects of behavior do have a powerful party component.[10] Bush II likes to decide and to take risks; he favors clear-cut management practices and is uninterested in details. However, his father preferred to be prudent and avoid risks. They both belong to the same party. Thus, we are left with a distinction that largely rests on the person. In this regard, Clinton liked to debate and discuss issues and options; he loved the detail and often delayed decisions. He was more a risk-avoider than a risk-taker. Carter liked to read voraciously and to respond in detail. The decisions he made were not always ones that made a "51/49" mind comfortable, so another decision to reverse the prior one might be forthcoming, at least until "indecisiveness" or "inconsistency" in decision making became a media stereotype of the Carter presidency.[11]

Presidents also vary in intellect, and especially in their appreciation of the implications of their decisions. Some suffer from "paralysis by analysis," whereas others, such as Harry Truman, Ronald Reagan, and George W. Bush, have not hesitated in making decisions and remain either unaware of, or not bothered by, or otherwise immune to alternative possibilities. Presidents also vary in their buoyancy and in their political skills. Some seem to be natural politicians who shine and impart confidence in their leadership—Roosevelt, Kennedy, Reagan, Clinton, and George W. Bush. Others appear out of touch (George H.W. Bush), or morose and reticent (Nixon and Johnson), or sometimes bumbling (Ford, and even Eisenhower, in whom confidence was largely based upon his previously earned prestige as Supreme Commander of the Atlantic Theater during World War II). In sum, leaders do differ and may even react to similar circumstances in different ways, but certainly they are different in their styles of leadership.

Given the emphasis I place on the political context of party polarization, most of this chapter focuses on how George W. Bush maneuvered through various stages in his run for the White House and at different stages during his presidency. I examine critical moments of choice during the Bush II presidency from the standpoint of modifying or reinforcing the prevailing political climate. I then return to particular features of President Bush's style as a leader and their implications, while also noting that some features of his leadership style are not at all random and are more typically associated with Republican than Democratic presidents. Finally, the chapter ends with an assessment of President George W. Bush's handling of the somewhat discordant roles of party leader and national leader.

George W. Bush as Presidential Candidate

Prologue: Markers on the Path to Intense Partisanship

The process by which the partisan cycle gets ratcheted up is, as noted, complex. The present upsurge in partisanship is the product of underlying but deep changes in the composition of electoral and elite cleavages, which are typically stimulated by a critical set of issues and reinforced by changes in institutional rules that strengthen party forces against competing ones, such as committee autonomy in Congress. Candidates, issues, and events all can serve to mobilize further the existing forces that have been set in motion. The conservative Goldwater candidacy of 1964 and, above all, the identification of the Republican Party in that critical election year as a resisting force to the civil rights revolution helped establish the GOP as the party to which southern whites would likely gravitate if Republicans continued to cultivate that constituency. Thus, as blacks who entered the electorate in the South following the 1965 Voting Rights Act overwhelmingly identified with the Democrats, the Republicans over time were able to anchor themselves more fully among southern whites and to mobilize them. The country club Republican elites and those who settled in the South from northern settings more hospitable to Republicans eventually gained the company of the Dixiecrats from the countryside, who supported Strom Thurmond in 1948 and George Wallace in 1968.

Manifesting ambivalence toward the civil rights revolution and its results, the Nixon administration moved to enforce rights in the North (perhaps hoping to turn white workers away from the Democratic Party) and, more publicly, to evoke a "southern strategy" of going slow in desegregating the South. The Republican Party, founded as the party of national union and with its traditional strength in the industrial North, was evolving in the South, and more slowly in the rest of the country, to become in the main the "white" party, while the Democrats, traditionally the party of white supremacy and the "solid South," but consummating their New Deal reformation under Franklin Roosevelt, were evolving to become the party of "minorities." However, Gary Jacobson notes that these trends firmed up at the mass level in the 1990s following the sharpening of congressional party divisions in the 1980s.[12] The implication, clearly, is that elites, not mass publics, define the alignments. But once these are sharply defined, mass publics tend to migrate along lines of conflict given definition by elites.

Another precipitant to growing partisanship may have been the Watergate crisis of Richard Nixon's second term. Although that episode, which forced Nixon to leave office under threat of impeachment, had, by its end point in August 1974, induced a general consensus that Nixon's conduct of the office of the presidency had violated the law in egregious ways, the view that he had been railroaded by longtime Democratic foes may have been a more lasting perception among Republican elites. Nixon, after all, still enjoyed the approval of nearly one-fifth of the public even as he was preparing to pack his bags.

The congressional electoral results of 1974, in the wake of Nixon's political demise, brought forth a throng of new, overwhelmingly Democratic, members and generated an enthusiasm and opportunity for the return of the party caucus on the Democrats' side of the aisle, especially in the House of Representatives. As is often the case, this transient majority misunderstood its status as permanent and, therefore, did what it could to increase the power of existing majorities. The Democrats in the House, especially, sought to use the party caucus to become as cohesive a party as the Republicans were in their party conference. They hoped that if a new Democratic president were elected in 1976, they would have the opportunity to generate legislative majorities for their preferences. Above all, the new Democrats sought to have a significant voice and input in the legislative process. The liberals among them and among the incumbent Democrats also looked forward to the breakup of the conservative coalition between most Republicans and conservative southern Democrats that had largely dominated the Congress, especially the House, since the late 1930s. As matters eventually turned out, they got their wish. And as such matters often turn out, they did not necessarily like the outcome.

As fate would have it, the new Democratic president who eked out electoral victory in 1976, Jimmy Carter, was one of the least partisan presidents of the twentieth century. His defining issues were ones involving collective goods that set the Democrats in Congress against one another by virtue of whether, for example, they came from regions that were energy suppliers or energy users. He lacked passion for the Democrats' red-meat concerns about enhancing social protections and labor rights, often posing questions about what such initiatives might cost.

While the Democrats in Congress floundered during the Carter administration in their last throes of party disunity, the Republicans, who were typically more unified to begin with, found a clarion voice in Ronald Reagan, who appealed to the party's growing southern and western base and, ironically, simultaneously to both its libertarian (NRA) and its statist (Christian fundamentalist) wings. Reagan made it clear what he was about, and that was, as best he could, to dismantle the welfare state developed in the New Deal administration of Franklin Roosevelt and bolstered especially during the Great Society administration of Lyndon Johnson. The Reagan agenda also included starving the government of future revenues through tax cuts, lowering marginal tax rates on the most affluent taxpayers (actually shifting the tax burden from higher-income to lower-income taxpayers), massively increasing military spending, and prosecuting the Cold War with the Soviet Union to its fullest.

The Reagan era helped finish off the southern Boll Weevils (conservative Democrats) in the Democratic Congressional Caucus and sharpened party divisions in Congress by virtue of the issues it sought to do battle on. While rapidly diminishing in number in the southern congressional delegations, the remaining southern Democrats were far more liberal than their predecessors and closer to the national party, and they were increasingly more African American in their ethnic profile. Meanwhile, Mountain State delegations were becoming more Republican at the presidential and congressional levels. On the other hand, Democrats were doing better along both coasts. The Reagan era thus deepened the prevailing cleavages and created new ones along the country's secular/fundamentalist cultural divide.[13] It also brought foreign policy divisions into play in such a way that these matters ultimately became as important and divisive (and for a while even more so) as domestic issues on congressional roll calls.[14]

Reagan's successor, George H.W. Bush, was more a traditional than a movement conservative. As a result, he and the more radical wing of his party never found a comfort zone. As Reagan's vice president and heir apparent, Bush I had to appear to adopt the Reaganite mantra on taxes, which he used effectively on the primary trail in 1988 against his strongest competitor, Senator Robert Dole. Dole had become his party's leader in the Senate and had previously served as chair of the Senate Finance Committee, but he was skeptical of the doctrines of "Reaganomics." Bush I rapidly adopted the Reaganite doctrines, including the famous, if ill-advised, "read my lips, no new taxes" pledge at the 1988 Republican Convention in New Orleans. But the elder Bush was not totally at ease with the new forces in his party, and, more important, they were not at ease with him.

Bush I began by rounding the edges of the Reagan era. His appointments were more moderate, his tone was more conciliatory, and he indicated respect for Washington institutions. Above all, George H.W. Bush knew that he was going to have to confront the magnitude of the budget deficits resulting from the earlier tax cuts and the inexorable growth in public entitlement funding. Yet, while Bush I was veering more toward the traditional conservative he really was, his party's core in Congress, especially in the House, was moving in a more radical and combative direction, pushing to the forefront a new generation of leaders—

Newt Gingrich, Dick Armey, Tom DeLay—who were determined not to live with the Democrats as a more or less permanent minority, but to topple them from the majority.

During the time of Operation Desert Shield in the Persian Gulf (late 1990), Bush I was facing a struggle at home on domestic issues, particularly on the budget, that was set into motion when Bush and House Ways and Means chair Dan Rostenkowski (D-Ill.) began sending signals that a deal could be had on the budget and that, by implication, Bush's lips might become unsealed. The deal would require Bush to propose revenue increases and the Democrats to harden firewalls and offsets on the spending side. Traditionally conservative Republicans might have been inclined to think they got the better of the deal by forcing spending constraints while moving toward a balanced budget—but these were not the new breed of Republicans. The deal being offered, they concluded, would get them nowhere politically, just more of the same. Opposition to taxes, not the old warhorse of balanced budgets, was the new doctrine, and compromise was decidedly out. As a result, Bush I needed Democratic majorities to pass the budget bill in early 1991, a bill on which he tried to keep hands-off to the extent possible.

From the time of the budget bill's passage onward, Bush was in trouble with his party's core constituency despite the hugely successful outcome of the first war with Saddam Hussein. After that victory, Bush I's approval ratings shot up to about 90 percent, similar to those his son would attain immediately after the terrorist attacks of 11 September 2001 and, later that year, following the successful prosecution of the war against the Taliban regime in Afghanistan. In the aftermath of the Gulf War, Bush I faced a set of decisions much like those his son would later confront: he could maintain the moderate conservative posture he had adopted in the first half of his term or he could play to the mobilized core and the increasingly powerful movement-conservative wing of his party in Congress. Fearing that he was losing the latter, Bush began to court them by establishing the Competitiveness Council under Vice President Dan Quayle to review (meaning oppose) agency regulations on business, nominating Clarence Thomas to the U.S. Supreme Court, and offering initial resistance to proposals for extending provisions of the Civil Rights Act that had come up for renewal. In sum, Bush I was moving rightward fast as the 1992 election approached.

Despite a record of moderation (except on cultural issues)—in fact, frequently adopting Republican-favored measures—the next president, Bill Clinton, became a lightning rod of partisanship. Clinton's ascendancy came at a time when the Republican congressional revolutionaries were attaining the leadership of their party, particularly in the House. After the Republicans' congressional sweep in 1994 and the Contract with America platform on which they ran that year, the Republican congressional majority became the dominant agenda setter in Washington. Reduced months later to a plaintive cry that he was still relevant to the governing equation, Clinton thereafter brought his political adeptness into play. No longer able or, thus, required, to push legislation favored by the Democratic Party, he was now in an ideal position to adopt a "third-way" strategy. The genius of this expedient was to adopt the stated goals of much of the Republican agenda, bargain legislative proposals to the best terms a Democratic buy-in could possibly get, and reap the benefit of supporting, even taking credit for, Republican-initiated legislation—at least that part of it that had public support. "Slick Willie" was the sobriquet that Clinton's opponents applied to him, and perhaps there was a large element of truth to that label. Clinton demonstrated that he could lift those parts of the Republican agenda that were popular, make the Republicans look extreme and churlish, and so frustrate the Republicans' ability to create a national political majority. He beat them at their own game, an outcome that earned him both the enmity of the Republicans and the dissatisfaction of his own party loyalists. Nevertheless, the vulnerable Clinton of 1994 and early 1995 won solid reelection in 1996 and went on to benefit from the economic bubble of the late 1990s, which ensured his popularity during this time.

Clinton's political success frustrated Republicans, particularly because he didn't seem to pay much of a cost within his own political party for dabbling in Republican-initiated ideas. Imagining what the real article could be like, Democrats became grateful for small favors achieved through Clinton's dexterity and skillful acrobatics. But Clinton was immensely helped by the combative nature of the Republican Party leadership in Congress: he appeared reasonable, and they didn't. However, the fundamentalist Christian right constituency within the Republican Party was also upset by Clinton's personality traits. Or, perhaps to put it more cynically, they were disturbed by his cultural agenda and used his character flaws as a lever to oppose him. When the President's liaison with White House intern Monica Lewinsky surfaced in early 1998—the culmination of a long history of such affairs—the Republican core constituency and its congressional leadership smelled blood. It pursued especially a perjury link between Clinton's testimony in the Paula Jones deposition (another sex episode dating back to the period of Clinton's governorship in Arkansas), but in fact, the Republicans had had a tail on Clinton and his wife since an investigation opened on their role in a real-estate development venture known as Whitewater. The independent counsel in place (also a Republican) was removed by a panel of federal judges and replaced with Kenneth Starr, who seemed deeply motivated by a passion to bring Clinton down. Starr's charge to investigate Whitewater then expanded suddenly to encompass Clinton's life generally, including his apparently insatiable sexual appetites.

Most people were appalled at Clinton's behavior—whether his morals, his duplicity, or merely his sense of taste and discretion. His personal approval ratings were weak even as his presidential approval ratings remained high—very much the reverse of how an earlier predecessor, Jimmy Carter, was seen. On the question of precisely what his behavior added up to, Republicans and Democrats sharply disagreed both at the elite level and to a lesser, but still significant, degree at the mass level. The Republican leadership in the House, led especially by the party whip, Tom DeLay of Texas—whose sobriquet, appropriately, was "the Hammer"—went after Clinton tooth and nail, even as Clinton's presidential approval ratings kept rising. Congressional Democrats, seeking to go on record with some form of disapproval of Clinton's behavior, chose to introduce a resolution of censure, but the Republican leadership, fed by Starr, wanted a full impeachment proceeding. Thus, despite his New Democrat, so-called third-way politics, Clinton turned out to be as sharply polarizing a figure as there has been in the White House.

The impeachment process galvanized each party's core constituencies and generated a powerful division between the parties, inasmuch as the House Republicans refused to let the censure resolution come to the floor—an outcome that was preferred by virtually all Democrats as well as some of the Republicans, thus likely to gain a majority. Absent the resolution, which was discarded by the Republican leadership and its Judiciary Committee chair, Rep. Henry Hyde of Illinois, only up-or-down votes on the four articles of impeachment were permitted—an option that especially pressured relatively moderate Republicans from competitive districts.

In the end, the only officials brought down were Newt Gingrich, the fiery Republican Speaker of the House, and Bob Livingstone, the House majority leader and Gingrich's would-be successor—both wound up exposed for extra-marital affairs of their own. The impeachment proceedings displayed the dysfunctional lengths to which party polarization had proceeded in a system that requires compromise to work. The poisonous upshot of the impeachment affair was that among party activists and elites, Democrats came to despise the Republican leadership, not merely to differ from them, while Republicans continued to believe that Clinton was getting away with murder, at least figuratively speaking. Indeed, they continued to pursue him even after his departure from office in 2001, blustering over his use of the presidential pardon power upon leaving office.

This long prelude to the entrance on the scene of the protagonist, George W. Bush, is essential to understanding the political atmospherics enveloping his candidacy, his campaign tactics, and the conduct of his presidency—and, above all, the inconsistencies that would surface between his campaign and his governance.

Act I—The Primary Election Context

Each party headed into the 2000 campaign with one establishment candidate and one major reputable challenger. The Democrats' establishment candidate, Al

Gore, the incumbent vice president and likely successor to Bill Clinton, faced a persistent challenge from a former senator and basketball star, Bill Bradley, who appealed to constituencies a bit to the left of Gore. Bradley sought to project a big-picture image for the party after Clinton's success in playing to smaller, incremental issues. But he failed to do so in a coherent or consistent way. Although he wanted to appeal to the left-leaning Democratic activists, he did not want to be labeled a leftist if he were to get the nomination. Ultimately, he did not have to worry about how to project himself in the general election, as Gore steamrollered his way through the primaries, forcing Bradley off the road.

The Republican situation was a bit more complicated, although it did not initially seem that way. With access to his father's Rolodex, George W. Bush gathered in money by the bushel—so much that he chose to reject federal financing along with its constraints. Bush seemed to be lacking in obvious traditional credentials of experience: he had rarely stepped out of the country, and he had been known as a "party man" in a strictly nonpolitical sense. Having been an unsuccessful candidate for the U.S. House, an operative for his father in the Bush I White House, and part-owner of a major league baseball team, he was in his sixth year as governor of Texas, a large and complex state whose governor is, nevertheless, a relatively weak figure. What the younger Bush may have lacked in political experience and knowledge of issues, however, he more than made up for by possessing other attributes. First, he was thought to be reliable and unlikely to rock any boats, in contrast to his chief opponent for the Republican presidential nomination, Senator John McCain of Arizona. Second, a popular governor of the nation's second largest state, he was known for his politically ebullient personality. Third, for a Republican candidate in Texas he had managed to attract an unusually large measure of support among Hispanic voters. Fourth, he had developed a reputation for being conservative on issues but moderate in demeanor and able to work with Democrats in the Texas legislature. Fifth, he had gathered enormous amounts of money and so had become a formidable candidate. Sixth, he had clearly developed the right message for the outside world—"compassionate conservatism," which made him look like a "third way" Republican.

Bush's primary opponent, Senator McCain, was a former naval officer and aviator and the son and grandson of naval admirals. As young adults, both candidates had become known for personalities that could best be described as fun-loving. During active service in Vietnam, however, McCain had undergone a seven-year incarceration in Hanoi after his aircraft was brought down, during which time he was subjected to considerable physical and mental abuse. His credentials seemed the stuff of a dream presidential candidate. Moreover, McCain's record in the Senate was solidly conservative.

He ran, however, as a reformer, particularly stressing campaign finance reform and loosening the grip of the fundamentalist Christian wing on the Republican Party as his signature issues. For these reasons, McCain attracted much independent support and even some crossover Democrats, and his unexpected strong showing was built on sources of support that were necessary for a general election but more problematic for the primary run.

By demonstrating unanticipated crossover appeal, McCain forced Bush to reposition himself as the party stalwart. Bush had geography and time working for him with the big rush of southern states coming early in the primary season. In South Carolina, he made a controversial appearance at Bob Jones University, a fundamentalist bastion that forbids mixed-race dating and carefully controls the lives of its students. In sum, Bush knew that he would have to rally the party base on his behalf, and to do that required playing to its core instincts. That was the tactically rational thing to do under the circumstances. Perhaps any politician would do it, but it was also a natural course for Bush, who had long been reputed to believe that his father's political downfall was the result less of mere circumstance (being caught in a recession at a critical point) than of poor political strategy—failing to feed and nurture the party base. Thus, like his father in 1988, Bush II positioned himself as the candidate of the new Republican orthodoxy against an opponent whose credentials as a conservative were strong. Like Bob Dole in 1988, however, McCain was an old-school conservative who occasionally strayed from the new party orthodoxy. After dispatching McCain in South Carolina, the problem that George W. Bush faced was how to work his way back to his original strategy of portraying himself as a Clintonesque antidote to Clinton—a "new" third-way politician who would put the kibosh on the intense partisanship in Washington. He had succeeded in establishing his orthodox credentials. Now he had to sell himself to a broader public.

Act II—The General Election Context

With the nomination settled, Bush and his political advisers had to plan a strategy for the Republican Convention. The party conventions no longer are arenas where candidates actually get nominated, except in the most nominal sense. The primaries settle these matters much earlier. And the conventions are no longer covered gavel-to-gavel on television either, except for the most dedicated political junkies willing to watch them on C-Span, PBS, and news cable. The key event is the candidate's speech accepting the nomination and the expectations that have been built up preceding it. Low expectations tend to work in a candidate's favor, since they can usually be beaten.

George W. Bush had a perilous tightrope to cross. First, he had to pick a vice-presidential nominee who would not divide the party. Tom Ridge, the governor of Pennsylvania, seemed an obvious candidate: coming from a big northeastern state, he was a Catholic, a Marine officer in Vietnam, a Harvard Law graduate, a popular political figure in his home state, and a moderate. For a candidate seeking to say that he was a new kind of Republican, Ridge would have been an ideal running-mate. Ridge, however, had a major liability: he was pro-choice on the abortion issue. That stance would have mobilized in opposition the fundamentalist wing of the Republican Party, whose shoe leather and activism, not to mention its votes, are quite essential to the party. It was therefore an early signal of the kind of president that George W. Bush would become that Ridge was eliminated from contention for the vice-presidential nomination. Instead, Bush chose the chair of the search committee himself, Dick Cheney, an arch-conservative with strong governmental credentials in precisely the areas in which Bush needed tutoring. Cheney was a former defense secretary under Bush's father, a former White House chief-of-staff under President Ford, and a former member of Congress from Wyoming, and his voting record in the House was among the most conservative in the House Republican Conference. But Cheney was respected for his intelligence and his experience and his familiarity with the ways of Washington.

Bush's second task was to project an image of himself as a paragon of diversity. He had learned lessons from the experience of the former Republican governor of California, Pete Wilson, whose nativist, anti-immigrant policies had alienated the state's Hispanic population and helped ensure Democratic dominance there. Recognizing that the Republicans looked like a white-bread party, Bush wanted to emphasize the party's openness to non-Anglo populations, especially Hispanics, who had a greater potential for sympathy with Republican positions on cultural issues if they were not alienated on other matters. George W. Bush had also learned from the 1992 Republican Convention in Houston that nominated his father that tight control over the convention speakers and proceedings was a must. George H.W. Bush had paid the price for allowing extremists such as Pat Buchanan and Pat Robertson to command the airwaves, projecting a face of the Republican Party that looked gruff and mean, especially when the speakers attacked Mrs. Clinton, who was not (yet) running for anything. George W. Bush therefore was keenly aware of what kind of convention he wanted—one that was fine-tuned, positive, tolerant, and in line with the nominee's message. The fact that the diversity of the people trotted out on stage looked nothing like the delegates sitting in the seats on the floor demonstrated, above all, that the party conventions had become elaborate free advertising, public relations events.

A third thing that Bush needed to do was to emphasize "compassionate conservatism," a slogan that was as soothing and mellifluent as it was alliterative. Compassionate conservatism, by design, sounded good, but what did it mean? Mainly, it echoed the "thousand points of light" that Bush's father had articulated in his 1988 acceptance speech, except that, on this occasion, George W. Bush also could appeal to the party's religious wing by converting the thousand points of light—often derided by Democrats as "a thousand pints of lite"—into "faith-based initiatives." Another way of thinking about the faith-based initiatives idea was that it was a clever scheme to privatize social welfare through religious groups that would then be immunized from the civil rights laws and protections afforded government workers. Bush was careful, however, not to threaten popular programs. Instead, he paid homage to them. In his acceptance speech at the convention, for example, he claimed, "We will strengthen Social Security and Medicare for the greatest generation, and for generations to come. Medicare . . . reflects the values of our society [and] we will . . . make prescription drugs available and affordable for every senior who needs them." One might have thought that Bush had accidentally wandered into the wrong party convention.

A fourth move that was necessary was to placate the fundamentalists, which the vice-presidential nomination and the faith-based initiatives idea were designed to do. The key here was to take an unstinting, but not highly visible, position in support of anti-abortion planks, including the so-called red-button partial-birth plank—so-called because the term is a political, not a medical, one. In his acceptance speech, Bush made "partial-birth" (his term) the issue, not *Roe v. Wade*, which, if placed front-and-center, might have frightened away more voters from his cause than it could hope to mobilize. Bush would show compassion for the religious right wing. He preferred that they understand that well in advance of the convention and, in turn, avoid making any scenes during the convention that would be embarrassing to his candidacy. And they more or less complied, with the notable exception of his own state's delegation, which was rife with fundamentalists. The Texas delegation caused the one stir during the convention when they looked away from the podium and bowed their heads in prayer during a speech by Jim Kolbe, a gay member of Congress from Arizona. (Kolbe's speech had nothing to do with any issue remotely related to his sexual preference.)

A fifth necessity for Bush was to have an agenda. As with Reagan, tax cuts would be the centerpiece of the George W. Bush agenda. Supply-side economics, associated with the Reagan era, would be revived. However, unlike the period during which Reagan touted tax cuts as a tonic for an ailing economy, Bush was running in prosperous times. Although the economy had begun to slow down during the election year, times were still good, and budget surpluses had replaced the massive deficits incurred during the Reagan years that had hit the fan by the time George H.W. Bush came to office. George W. Bush therefore sold tax cuts not as a stimulus (his present effort on Tax Cut: The Sequel) but as an effort to give back to the taxpayers their own money. Moreover, the tax cuts presumably would take away slack for any significant new government expenditures as well, compatible with Republican professions in favor of "small government."

By most standards, the Republicans should have had a massively uphill struggle on their hands to win the White House in an era of prosperity and economic growth, when the outgoing president of the other party was leaving office with high levels of popular approval. Bush needed to make an issue of the negative atmospherics around Clinton, stressing by implication the loss of dignity in the White House under the Clinton administration and the lack of clear policy direction from a president who had been forced to play defense for the better part of his tenure. On the lack of dignity, there was, to be sure, a notorious lack of discipline in the Clinton White House, both organizationally and individually on the part of the president. Policy discussions frequently had taken on the appearance of all-night poker games, with no outcomes forced by a president who liked the discussing more than the deciding. And, of course, Clinton himself had led a wildly libidinous life in the White House, chronicled by Kenneth Starr in a fashion designed to titillate and released by the House Judiciary Committee for (avid) public consumption of the breathless details.

Clinton also had appeared to lack clear direction, in part because of his status as a "New Democrat," a condition which might be described as Republican envy—most especially, the envy of winning presidential elections. But a much bigger part of it was that the Republicans had controlled both chambers of Congress for six of Clinton's eight years in the White House, meaning that his posture was largely defensive. In basketball parlance, Clinton had specialized in the "take away," a defensive maneuver typically performed by a player with speedy feet and even quicker hands. What Clinton did was to take away the most popular aspects of the Republican agenda, rework them, and take credit for them. Not linear direction, but clever adaptation. In the process, he had made Democrats happy that he was there to prevent worse things from happening. Bush emphasized these aspects of the Clinton persona in his acceptance speech at the Republican Convention, noting that from a political standpoint, Clinton's tendencies were to take the path of least resistance, a path that Bush claimed was "always downhill." He summed up Clinton's eight years in the same way that a good number of rabid Democrat activists might have done: "So much promise, to no great purpose." And Bush was careful to evade his party's responsibility for the impeachment fiasco while also making sure that Clinton's personal tawdriness lingered in the public mind: "When the moment for leadership came, this administration did not teach our children. It disillusioned them."[15]

Finally, the strategy was to portray Bush as someone who could end the intense partisanship in Washington and the climate of noncooperation, as though Bush's own party had had nothing to do with the creation of that climate. But his ability as governor to get along with the then Democratic majority in Texas seemed to be a selling point on his behalf. Again, in his acceptance speech, Bush ticked off a number of accomplishments during his gubernatorial regime in Texas, topping it off with this line: "I don't deserve all the credit and don't attempt to take it. I worked with Republicans and Democrats to get things done."[16] Bush would come back to the theme of bipartisanship in his speech to the Texas legislature after the Supreme Court settled the election outcome of 2000. It was nearly the last time that theme would be credible.

Bush began the election campaign disadvantaged by the country's prosperity but made hopeful by signals of economic slowdown. He was advantaged to an unknown degree (probably small but crucial) by the relative clumsiness of his opponent, the sitting vice president, Al Gore. Gore had a reputation for being an intelligent student of government and policy, but he also seemed uncomfortable in his political skin. If Bush was nimble and scripted, at least he had a good script. An astute politician is never obvious about manipulation, but Gore went from white shirts and ties to earth-tone golf shirts, partly to emphasize his buffed physique and partly to show that despite his years in Washington, he could be folksy and populist, too. What it actually may have indicated was that he never felt comfortable with who he was.

Gore had much of Clinton's tendency for being a policy wonk but none of his adeptness or cleverness in turning issues to his advantage. The debates between the candidates reflected their diverse styles. Gore was challenged by high expectations that he would use his superior knowledge to demolish Bush in the debates. Bush was advantaged by low expectations that he must show himself able merely to hold his own. Bush's handlers had a well-honed script, and their candidate stayed on message, yet seemed relaxed. Gore, by contrast, tried to pin Bush down to arcane specifics. A defining moment during the debates occurred when Bush chimed in that he was for a patients' bill of rights, which had been advanced by the Democrats as a way of capturing the popular outcry against health maintenance organizations (HMOs) and medical insurers. Gore thereupon poached on Bush's podium turf, enveloped him like Count Dracula about to suck his victim's blood, and, long past his allotted time, queried Bush as to where Bush stood on a specific piece of patients' rights legislation known as Norwood-Dingle for the bill's sponsors, Reps. Charles Norwood (R-Ga.) and John Dingle (D-Mich.). Outside the Washington Beltway, only a handful of people knew what Norwood-Dingle was. Gore seemed to have mastered the ability to lose his point, whereas Bush seemed to have mastered speaking to the point, staying on it, and saying nothing extraneous that could get him into uncharted waters and, therefore, potential trouble.

While it is true that debates change few minds, mainly because they are watched by the more passionate voters whose minds are already made up, the sound bites and the spin can influence the less passionate, on whom elections in a tightly divided electorate often can turn. Bush came through as human and succinct; Gore did nothing to relieve himself of his reputation for lacking political touch.

Act III: The Post-Election Context

What followed on the night of the general election of 2000 is legendary. The election produced a nearly 50/50 split across the board in Congress and in the

presidential contest. The results could hardly have been tighter or less definitive. The presidential election contest continued to depend on the outcome
in the state of Florida, where a significant number of irregularities were reported, including an unusual number of ballots counted for Pat Buchanan,
the independent far-right candidate, in districts where he was distinctly unpopular. The ensuing seven-week hiatus between election night and a result was
unprecedented.

During this time, the Bush entourage was relentless in its pursuit of the
White House and also in its preparation for governance. It had purpose and it
had drive. It had gained the upper hand by appearing to be the winner in
Florida, even though, of course, the vote remained too close to call. But the
Bush campaign was able to make Gore look like the challenger instead of the
holder of an equal share of the possible outcome. In Dade County (greater
Miami), one of the key counties where chads hanging from the punch ballots
were being examined to verify the initial election results, the national Republican
Party unloaded operatives to demonstrate in protest against that reexamination, which they hoped to characterize as an illegitimate activity—implying, of course, that any recount was illegitimate. In the meantime, the Democrats, not wanting to look unpatriotic, caved in to allow the counting of undated
absentee ballots coming from servicemen and women out of state. The fact is,
we will never have a definitive answer regarding this most unusual election
night, but we do have an answer as to how the post-election struggle was waged,
and that was a harbinger of things to come for the soon-to-be-anointed Bush
presidency. The Bush post-election campaign pursued political advantage relentlessly and single-mindedly, making clever use of tactics to put the Democrats at a disadvantage. This was likely to be a very partisan and very politically
astute presidency.

The way in which the outcome was resolved could never have been thought
to be fair by the losers, whichever party or set of candidates the losers turned out
to be. High-stakes political processes decided through the courts rarely are perceived as fair unless the ground rules are well understood *ex ante*. In this case,
however, the U.S. Supreme Court overrode directives of the Florida Supreme
Court to continue counting the chads in three South Florida counties, and it did
so in a way that was completely consistent with its own liberal-conservative ideological divide. This inevitably aggrieved the losers even more. The Court majority concluded, ironically, that an outcome—any outcome, but especially the
one it deemed to have in hand—was preferable to further drawn-out vote-count-
ing processes, whatever their accuracy—which, at this point, probably was not a
matter about which anyone could be assured.[17] In any event, it is fair to say that
the Bush team played effective hardball in the post-election hiatus, and the U.S.
Supreme Court's disposition of the case would always be perceived as unfair and
unjust on the part of the losers and, especially, their strongest supporters.

Act IV: Signs—Bush as President-Elect

Now, less than two weeks before Christmas, it had become clear that George W. Bush would be president after all. What was this presidency going to be about? In reality, the answers to that question are usually less dependent upon the person in office than upon the events and conditions that arise and require presidential attention. Clinton's presidency, for example, might have looked different without six years of Republican control of Congress. Nevertheless, Bush gave off unusual hints of ambivalence. There was the seemingly bipartisan, compassionate conservative Bush. But when push came to shove under threat from John McCain in the Republican primaries and from the Gore-Lieberman ticket in the election aftermath, Bush had shown that he could play partisan hardball as sharply as anyone, that he could be remarkably petulant (as when Gore called him to retract his concession on election night), and that he would cultivate his party base—the base that he thought his father had neglected.

For those hoping that the election with its disputed outcome might usher in a new era of reconciliation and moderation, Bush's victory speech before the Texas state legislature (where he was still governor) gave hope that he would lead a presidency of reconciliation at a moment when the country seemed to be in need of that. Here is some of what Bush said that evening:

> Tonight I choose to speak from the chamber of the Texas House of Representatives because it has been a home to bipartisan cooperation. Here in a place where the Democrats have the majority, Republicans and Democrats have worked together to do what is right for the people we represent.
>
> We've had spirited disagreements. And in the end, we found constructive consensus. It is an experience I will always carry with me, an example I will always follow. . . .
>
> The spirit of cooperation I have seen in this hall is what is needed in Washington, D.C. It is the challenge of our moment. After a difficult election, we must put politics behind us and work together to make the promise of America available to every one of our citizens.
>
> I am optimistic that we can change the tone in Washington, D.C.
>
> I believe things happen for a reason, and I hope the long wait of the last five weeks will heighten a desire to move beyond the bitterness and partisanship of the recent past. . . .
>
> I know America wants reconciliation and unity. I know Americans want progress. And we must seize this moment and deliver. . . .
>
> We have discussed our differences. Now it is time to find common ground and build consensus to make America a beacon of opportunity in the 21st century.

I was not elected to serve one party, but to serve one nation.

The president of the United States is the president of every single American, of every race and every background.

Whether you voted for me or not, I will do my best to serve your interests and I will work to earn your respect.[18]

I quote portions of this speech at considerable length simply to emphasize the first hopeful signs of a George W. Bush presidency—recognition of the unusual events that resulted in this informal victory speech, the close divisions that prevailed in the American electorate, and a promise to avoid contributing to these deep partisan divisions. For moderate Republicans and all but the most rabid Democratic activists and their interest group allies, Bush's speech offered signs that maybe this could be the "third way" Republican counterpart to Clinton's presidency, minus Clinton's self-destructive personal tendencies and minus the congressional opposition eager to delegitimize the president.

The next set of signs would come in the appointment process. What people would Bush bring in? And where would they be placed? Would this presidency be predominantly moderate or would it cater to the far-right-wing activist base? The signs were ambivalent: like most presidencies that have to cater to both party activists and to public respectability, the George W. Bush administration would make appointments responsive to both needs. Among recent presidencies, only the Reagan administration set out with nearly missionary purpose to make appointments reflecting its principal's radical objectives. As time wore on during the Reagan administration, of course, these missionaries often got themselves and the administration into trouble, and the respectables came to displace them. Such is the life cycle of would-be revolutions.

Bush's preinaugural appointments were a mixture of moderates and hard-core conservatives. To the national security team came Colin Powell and Condoleezza Rice, notable on the one hand for being the first two African Americans to hold the positions of secretary of state and national security adviser to the president. Powell was known as a moderate voice, a sober former chairman of the Joint Chiefs of Staff and a highly regarded practitioner of bureaucratic politics. Powell was a conservative in the traditional meaning of the term—cautious, sober, certain that the odds were overwhelmingly with him before committing to a course. The foreign policy team at the first-rank level was nearly a replay of the administration of Bush's father. It had lots of Washington experience on its side, and for a president who promised that the United States would become less rather than more risk-taking in foreign affairs, it appeared appropriately cautious.

In his other appointments, Bush seemed to balance conservatives with moderates. To head the controversial Environmental Protection Agency, he appointed Christie Whitman, the moderate governor of New Jersey. At the Department of

Health and Human Services, Governor Tommy Thompson of Wisconsin, a genuinely compassionate conservative, was named secretary. And Bush even kept one holdover from the Clinton administration in the cabinet, albeit in the new position of secretary of transportation—Norman Mineta, a former Democratic member of Congress from California. But in many other positions, Bush went for people who resonated well with his party's right wing—recently defeated senator John Ashcroft of Missouri for attorney general, Linda Chavez for secretary of labor (who ultimately withdrew her name under fire), Gale Norton as secretary of the interior, and defeated senator Spencer Abraham of Michigan as secretary of energy. Beneath the first tier, the second-tier officials, especially in the Defense Department and the National Security Council staff, were people whose ideas tracked well with those of the Reagan administration, in which many of them had served. From this mixture, it remained open as to precisely what sort of presidency Bush's would be. The appointment of Ashcroft, which was highly controversial in the Senate, was a sign that Bush would bring to Washington his version of Texas-style justice, with its casual attitude toward procedural regularity and its passion for the frequent exercise of the death penalty.

By the time Bush delivered his inaugural speech on 20 January 2001, the new administration was beginning to take shape, but some uncertainty remained. Unlike Ronald Reagan's first inaugural address, which clearly signaled an agenda—government was not the solution but the problem—Bush's signals were not radiantly clear. While he did stipulate in the address key elements of the Republican agenda—lower taxes, more funding for defense, and emphasis on the role of religion and voluntarism—he also signaled themes that cut across the partisan divide. For example, he emphasized "a concern for civility," the responsibilities of government "for public safety and public health, for civil rights and common schools," and he took note of "the pain of poverty."[19] These observations were not adopted from the sayings of Ronald Reagan. But how authentic were they? And what did they mean in terms of public policy? Knowing the value of soothing words, Bush and his handlers may have been engaging in a form of deceptive advertising. On the other hand—and this seems at least equally plausible—the emphasis on private good works and deeds was reflective of Bush's tag line "compassionate conservatism," thus promising a government incapable of running programs but also a flourishing, essentially religion-based voluntaristic sector engaged in providing soup and saving souls.

George W. Bush as President

Act I: The Pre–September 11th Presidency

Before the national tragedy of September 11th, the Bush administration moved more notably in a strong conservative direction than toward a reconciling moderation. The Clinton presidency, as do most, had left office in a flurry of sudden executive orders involving, among other things, the permanent conservation of large amounts of land (based on legislation from the era of Teddy Roosevelt) and ergonomic regulation of the workplace (favored by labor unions).[20] Bush quickly rescinded Clinton's most controversial orders, which he could do with the slender Republican majorities at hand. There is nothing illegitimate in such reversals, inasmuch as major changes in policy are more appropriately settled through legislation than by executive fiat. What Bush's swift reaction indicated, however, was that continuity would not be a hallmark of the new administration. Indeed, it planned to make its mark as abruptly and sharply as it could.

In the nearly nine months leading up to the September 11th turning point, five elements emerged to begin to shape the Bush presidency. The first was Bush's monumental tax cut proposal, on which he had insisted from the primary season onward. The Democrats failed to change the conversation. Instead, concerned about the deadly "tax and spend" label that the Republicans had successfully pinned on them, they kept racheting upward the maximum tax cut they would accept until, finally, they settled on a figure far closer to Bush's starting point than to their own. One thing became clear—once Bush defined a purpose, he was willing to stay the course, and the Democrats, fearing that they would be maligned for any opposition, caved massively. The tax-cut exercise gave Bush a feel for the softness of his opposition and also for his presidency's and his party's rhetorical advantage in labeling the Democrats as "taxers and spenders."

The second element was the general pro-business, anti-labor tilt to the George W. Bush administration. There were no Nixonian efforts to capture a labor union vote. Unions in the private sector were in sharp decline; those in the public sector were in proportionate ascendancy, and many of these unions were middle-class and professional. If you wished to diminish and delegitimize the public sector and also weaken the Democrats' political base, a broad effort to strengthen business claims and weaken labor ones was especially advantageous. One way to do this, of course, was to appoint judges, as well as members of various regulatory commissions and boards, who were notably favorable to business interests and unfavorable to labor ones. This, of course, was an old struggle between the parties, but given new legs in recent years. As Republican presidents and members of Congress increasingly come from "right to work" states with weak labor unions, they have little involvement with labor elites or with its constituencies and so see them largely as an impediment to doing business as well as to promoting efficiency in the public sector. And, of course, the unions are a core constituency of the Democratic Party. The Republicans increasingly find themselves wanting to go for the trifecta: solidifying their connections with business and with privatization advocates for public services while weakening the political opposition.

The business-labor schism was not the only one, however, in which the Bush administration's early positions and policies tilted heavily toward business interests. The new administration set forth generally to weaken restrictions on business, including reduction through redefinition of CAFÉ standards for fuel efficiency in vehicles, scaling back inspections of food processors, and support for the efforts of the new FCC chair, Michael Powell (son of Colin Powell), to relax restrictions on multimedia ownership in local markets, among others.

Probably the most salient issue, however, was the administration's effort to open up wilderness lands for energy exploration, a position that was strongly opposed by interests that claim to act on behalf of the environment. In a set of remarks about the controversy that were remarkable as much for their lack of political sensitivity as for their content, Vice President Cheney reportedly claimed that conservation might make for a sense of moral virtue, but it was not an energy policy.[21] In essence, according to the Cheney doctrine, an energy policy was one-dimensional, and that dimension was exploration and development. Indeed, prior to making this proclamation, the vice president had formed an energy policy task force, whose list of members and documents the administration fought to keep secret despite efforts by Congress and by the director of the General Accounting Office (GAO), David Walker (himself a Republican), to obtain them, based on the presumptive congressional right to supervise the operations of the executive branch. Cheney refused the GAO request, and the GAO went to court, but it eventually withdrew after an unfavorable judicial decision. It does appear, however, that the task force meetings were overwhelmingly populated with energy executives rather than with a broader array of energy constituencies.[22] Reaganism was back in Washington.

Furthermore, the contretemps over the energy advisory committee indicated clearly that a third element of the George W. Bush presidency—following here in the footsteps of the father's administration—was that it would be secretive and closed to probing from the outside. It would offer little; it would hold the press at bay, granting few news conferences; and it would keep the president on script. In short, this administration, much like the Reagan administration, had a clear strategy for controlling the story: it revealed little that it didn't want to have revealed, and it relentlessly kept its message where it wanted to be. That takes discipline. Despite George W. Bush's partying past, he had clearly developed a fine sense for keeping order,[23] and this, certainly by contrast to the Clinton administration, became one of the early hallmarks of the second Bush presidency. Every presidency, of course, tries to put its story out front. Some fail because they don't have a story, some because they can't keep order—the two are related, because the lack of a story line leads various actors within an administration to offer their own.

A fourth element of the early George W. Bush presidency—one that would be deepened later—was its aggressive unilateralism in international affairs.

Quickly, the Bush administration worked to create a missile shield (or to operate as if it could) that would abrogate the treaty against the use of defensive missiles reached in 1972 between the United States and the Soviet Union. The grounds the administration pursued were that the treaty was no longer valid because there no longer was a Soviet Union, despite the fact that Russia was the obvious successor state in possession of a vast proportion of the nuclear weapons that had been under the control of the former Soviet government. The Bush White House also flatly rejected the Kyoto accords on reducing so-called greenhouse emissions in the atmosphere. President Clinton had signed the agreement, but it had not been ratified by the Republican-controlled Congress. Indeed, Clinton had signed the accords probably on the calculation that Congress would not ratify them because they would have been wildly unpopular had they been implemented, thus allowing him to build credits with the environmental lobby without facing consequences. Regardless of what one thinks of the Kyoto accords, Bush could have sought to launch a renegotiation, since a treaty on public goods to which the United States was not a cooperative signatory could never amount to much. Instead, the Bush administration clearly signaled that it would pursue a purely unilateralist path, expecting others to do as it wished while not respecting the wishes of others. Another such flap had to do with an international tribunal formed for the explicit purpose of prosecuting war crimes. The United States, under the new administration, explicitly asserted that it would not allow any of its citizens to be tried by the International Criminal Court, and, indeed, pushed (perhaps bullied) a number of states into bilateral accords that would explicitly exempt U.S. citizens from facing such an international tribunal. Thus, even early in its tenure in office, the George W. Bush administration was acquiring a reputation for not playing well with others, whether externally or internally.

By contrast with both his father's administration and the Clinton administration, the Bush II administration stayed away from diplomatic or peacekeeping efforts, and its passivity was particularly evident as relative quiescence erupted into bloodshed between Israelis and Palestinians and as instability persisted and worsened in sub-Saharan Africa. While the new Bush administration was unequivocally unilateralist, until the events of September 11th, it was also largely isolationist. The isolationism would turn to interventionism thereafter, but the unilateralism would remain. The underlayer of neoconservative intellectuals in the foreign policy apparatus of the Bush administration, perhaps led by Vice President Cheney, guaranteed a lot of unilateralism, and, as the opportunity arose, a lot of interventionism.

As a foreign policy president, however, Bush was not well defined. He was inexperienced in foreign affairs and showed little interest in the subject—this in vivid contrast to his father who, along with Nixon, thought that foreign policy was what the presidency was about. In fact, George W. Bush, as noted, had rarely been out of the U.S. The isolationist aspects of his early foreign policy seemed to reflect his own tastes. What would happen under crisis? And what kind of crisis?

Despite these tendencies, there also were some signs that Bush still had compassionate conservatism in his repertoire—this was the fifth element shaping his presidency. Eventually, his administration collaborated with Senator Edward Kennedy, the patron saint of Senate Democrats, to pass education legislation that would impose mandates on the states but would also provide additional funding from the federal government. Some of the Republicans in Congress objected, believing the legislation was closer to what Kennedy might desire than what they wanted.

In addition, the Bush administration brought in John DiIulio to head its faith-based initiatives program. A University of Pennsylvania professor with a background in criminology and social problems, DiIulio was both religiously and socially committed, and he had a firm intention to make the faith-based initiatives heavy on the initiatives side. Ultimately, however, his tenure was short, and as he made clear in an interview in *Esquire* magazine that he later partially retracted, he had vastly underestimated the Bush administration's political motives in pushing the faith-based initiatives program.[24] The administration, as subsequent moves made clear, was essentially interested in cultivating its religious clientele and privatizing social services. But these motives were less apparent in the early stages of the George W. Bush presidency.

Overlaying the first nine months of the Bush presidency was its leading man's seemingly convivial personality. As mentioned earlier, there were certain parallels in the lives of George W. Bush and Bill Clinton, including bouts of *Animal House* behavior. But Clinton had demonstrated political ambition early on and a desire, for good or ill, to serve a public purpose. Bush, despite coming from a family of considerable political lineage—perhaps second in recent times only to the four generations of Tafts—had pursued only episodic political interests. More important, however, were the differences between the two men. Clinton was born to modest circumstances. Indeed, it could be said that he came from a lineage of "bubbas." In American southern tradition, the bubba is a "good-old boy" with a common touch, coming from humble stock and exhibiting what might be regarded by outsiders as coarse manners and a lack of cultivation. Clinton had worked his way through life from his "bubba" origins to become a Rhodes scholar and Yale Law graduate and to build a reputation for being a "policy wonk"—someone with the knowledge to debate the fine details of policy and the consequences of policy proposals.

George W. Bush, on the other hand, was born to a family of significant political repute. His grandfather was Senator Prescott Bush, an Eisenhower Republican from Connecticut. His father, the former president, had pursued a long career of public service in elected and appointed positions, the latter concentrated in the national security and diplomatic roles in which he was greatly interested.

In fact, Bush's family reflects the evolution of the Republican Party in the United States over three political generations: like the Bush family itself, the party has migrated from its northeastern bastions to new outposts in the Southwest. It has moved progressively rightward from the days of Senator Bush in the 1950s and early 1960s to the nearly three-decade career of George H.W. Bush, culminating in the party led by George W. Bush and, effectively, in the House by Tom DeLay. The party has moved from being the party of Wall Street (a good bit of which now supports the Democrats) and even Main Street to being a party with strong populist overtones, despite its connection to wealthy interests. The party managed to become an advocate of the "right to bear arms" (and thus the NRA), and it was increasingly favored as the party that was tough on crime and more willing to use force to further national security interests. It became the party, especially, of the angry white male (along with others less angry, of course).

Thus, while Clinton went from bubba status to the policy elite, George W. Bush moved in an alternate path from elite status to affecting a bubba style. Bush was personable; he liked to give people nicknames and to use so-called straight talk (the kind that can get you in trouble amongst the politically correct and diplomatically inclined). His straight talk played well with his natural constituency, but not so well in other quarters—especially abroad, where he was often seen as coarse and vulgar. His style was "just folks," and many Americans, reflecting their egalitarian culture, like that. In the end, the common touch would not help if economic or other conditions were to remain bad or dramatically worsen, but Bush's interpersonal and public style was certainly a plus for him. He was, on that level, a hard man not to like, indeed, a natural politician. If these traits couldn't hurt, how much they could help was another question. On the eve of September 11th, Bush's level of popular approval stood at about 55 percent—good but not great—and he was presiding over a deteriorating economy.[25]

Act II: The Post–September 11th Presidency

In the immediate aftershock of September 11th, George W. Bush's approval rating, in an intense rally effect, shot up to 89 percent in the Gallup poll, and not until the end of July of 2003 did it fall back to where it had been immediately before the crisis. Throughout 2002, Bush stayed at about two-thirds approval levels and rallied again to about three-quarters support in the follow-up to the dismantling of the Saddam Hussein regime in Iraq. On the whole, Bush, like his father, was perceived as being a more effective foreign policy than economic policy president. However, the continuing turmoil in Iraq and casualties incurred by American troops there have led to a slide in Bush's perceived foreign policy prowess as well.[26]

The journalist Bob Woodward suggests that the events of September 11th sharply concentrated the focus of the Bush presidency on national security affairs and on eradicating or at least weakening the terrorist apparatus of al Qaeda.[27] In times of external challenge, presidents are able to do what they do best, which is to represent the country in a unified way, above the political divisions of the day. The challenge, of course, has to be seen by the public in similar ways. The attacks of September 11th were indeed viewed with remarkable unanimity and concern, and Bush's finest moments lay in rallying the nation during a time of deep anxiety and insecurity. Following the attacks, the sympathetic support offered by America's traditional allies was exceptionally strong. Probably any president would have done well under those circumstances, but Bush's wordsmiths and his delivery, and perhaps even his robust physical appearance, helped. The successful prosecution of the war against the Taliban regime in Afghanistan that was harboring Osama bin Laden sustained and enhanced Bush's support.

The post–September 11th presidency produced, among other things, two interesting options for the president. One was to seize on a second opportunity—the first having been the aftermath of the deeply contested election and its deeply divided outcome—to seek a path of interpartisan conciliation on behalf of the larger cause of national unity in facing the unique challenges posed by large-scale terrorism. The second option was to play to the advantages of the presidency, especially a Republican presidency, and, thus, to wrap the Bush administration in a national security blanket. This option also could include a transformation of the administration's posture on international matters from unilateralist isolationism to unilateralist assertion. Events provided the trip wire for that movement—one that was, no doubt, supported by the neoconservative refugees from the Reagan administration who had been largely homeless under George H.W. Bush.

After a short interregnum of at most three months, however, partisan bickering resumed in Washington, and the Bush White House joined in as the parties jockeyed for advantage in the 2002 midterm elections. When September 11th offered him a new opportunity for compromise, unity, and reconciliation, Bush's choice, it is fair to say, was to cater to his party's expansive right wing.[28] Comparing George W. Bush's administration with that of his father, one leading movement conservative, Grover Norquist, asserted, "Every group that this president has kept faith with, the previous president double-crossed."[29] Similarly, another movement conservative, David Keene, claimed, "In the first Bush administration, the conservatives were asked to be spectators—and it was hoped that they would applaud the action in the field. In this one, they have a president who wants them to be part of the team."[30] The message garbled by earlier mixed signals was becoming abundantly clear: the George W. Bush presidency was Reaganism without Reagan. The Bush II administration gave no quarter to the opposition. It can be said that, in fact, it contributed munificently to the deepening harshness of partisan polarization in the contemporary United States.

On the national security front, the struggle to create a new administrative agency designed to coordinate domestic security measures was at first resisted by the Bush administration, as was the effort to replace the contract workers who screened travelers at airports with a new federal service (the Transportation Security Agency) requiring federal employees. The administration eventually accepted both initiatives. The TSA conflicted with the Bush administration's efforts to privatize increasing numbers—setting its goal ultimately at 850,000—of the federal workforce.[31] When a good number of Republicans on the Hill, however, indicated that they would defect on the issue of the federalization of airport security agents, the administration decided to adopt it. Homeland security was a more difficult issue, but the Bush administration found ways to turn that to its advantage as well. At first skeptical of the idea as another large-scale government intrusion, the administration later warmed up to it. The Bush White House created its own package, which turned out to be a massive reorganization, and it pressed to have normal civil service and other federal employee protections eliminated so that the directorate of the new organization would have maximum flexibility—and, not so coincidentally, also maximum opportunities for political patronage.

With the Democrats now holding marginal control of the Senate (as the result of Senator Jim Jeffords's defection from the GOP in the summer of 2001), the struggle over the homeland security legislation turned significantly on the issue of workforce flexibility and civil service protections. The Bush administration may have seen this as another opportunity to accomplish several goals at once: (1) link the Democrats with bureaucratic lethargy; (2) portray them as being soft on national security; (3) weaken further the government employee unions that are part of the Democrats' constituency; and (4) allow for further privatization of the federal workforce. In the end, having taken up the homeland security banner that had initially been foisted on them, Bush and his advisers successfully turned homeland security into an issue from which they might benefit. Eventually, the administration more or less got the security apparatus and labor conditions it had sought, and in the 2002 midterm elections Republicans were able to portray the Democrats as opposing the president on vital national security issues.

In the state of Georgia, in particular, Rep. Saxby Chambliss, the Republican senatorial challenger, used the homeland security issue by charging that his opponent, the Democratic incumbent Max Cleland, had opposed the president during a time of great threat. The media portrayed Chambliss's tactics as highly effective, although it is not clear if they necessarily were so. The impact of Cleland's loss sent shivers down what remained of the Democrats' spine, since Cleland was a poster boy for heroic sacrifice, having lost many of his body parts during his service as a young officer in Vietnam. The outcome had two effects: (1) in the face of strenuous Republican efforts to take advantage of the public perception of theirs as the party of national security, Democrats were chastened to lie low, since even those of their incumbents who were veterans and who had sacrificed so much could be defeated on national security grounds, and (2) further ill-feeling was generated between the parties, particularly as Democrats believed themselves to be unfairly targeted as being weak on national security.

Given these conditions, including an open mandate for hunting terrorists and destroying terrorism, and given the economic doldrums besetting the Bush II administration on the domestic front, could a president who was so dependent upon his and his party's advantage on national security issues fail to pursue that advantage, either through bellicose actions or belligerent rhetoric? In other words, operating within a declining economic environment and what surely would be declining popular approval for his presidency, was George W. Bush after September 11th dependent upon security challenges? Had the warpath become a political necessity? The real answers, as Richard Herrmann and Michael Reese note in their chapter in this volume, probably are to be found in the well-conditioned ideological premises of much of the administration's foreign policy and national security policy team. Yet it is equally clear that there was also political advantage to be had in appearing to be tough, and in some cases getting tough, against an assortment of some of the world's nastier regimes, beginning with the one in Iraq. September 11th had a variety of impacts. One of them was that it played exactly to the instincts of the Reaganite neoconservatives within the Bush II administration to remake the world as America would wish it to be and to feign shock at others who failed to see the righteousness of this mission. The other impact was that it put the administration on a more or less permanent war footing, which gave it a decided advantage over the Democrats.[32]

Returning to the question of the relationship between political context and political personality and leadership, it is probably fair to say that distemper across party lines is as strong as it has ever been in the lifetimes of those who have contributed to this volume. How much of that is George W. Bush's personal contribution as distinct from the pursuit of a political strategy derived from powerfully compelling incentives in the present political context is hard—in fact, impossible—to say. We can say, of course, that given similar choices in the first half of his administration, Bush's father more often chose the path of compromise and deal-making. We can also say that Clinton's policies and, above all, his judicial appointments were far more moderate than those of Bush II. Is it fair to say, then, that George W. Bush is merely Tom DeLay with a personality? (The House Republican floor leader, whatever his attributes, is largely perceived by Democrats as an utterly despicable scoundrel whose will to win overpowers all other considerations.)

Leaders do have choices, although contexts may provide powerful incentives. In an era during which political cleavages were much more complicated but also less intensely partisan, Eisenhower had to reach across the aisle to accomplish what he wished. Both Eisenhower's own tendencies and the political context of his times were more congruent than competing in this regard.[33] Bush II has different incentives, and they are ones in the main that dictate going the party route.

But the party divide was not the only context that Bush faced. Unlike any other president, he twice faced extraordinary circumstances calling for unity and national, rather than merely party, leadership, the first in the aftermath of the intensely divided 2000 election and the second in the post–September 11th climate. In each instance, whatever hope had been invested in Bush's ability to be a leader of national cohesion and reconciliation was dashed. He failed to take the steps that his earlier rhetoric had promised. If intense partisanship is the problem, Bush's presidency so far has only exacerbated the problem, not helped to resolve it. If, on the other hand, the longtime dream of some reformers of the American system is to create a party-based regime with little use for compromise, then the Bush II presidency has drawn closer to that ideal, especially during the periods when it has had majorities, however slender, in both chambers of Congress. What kind of man is George W. Bush? First and foremost, a party man.

It is extraordinary that a political leader whose path to the White House was deemed questionable by many of those who did not vote for him could engage in pursuit of a full-out partisan agenda during his presidency. The strength of a governing party, of course, is typically a function of the weakness of the opposition, and in this case, the Democrats' weakness was less a lack of numbers than a lack of purpose. Republicans grew their strength in proportion to the Democrats' fear quotient. More than two years into the Bush II presidency, however, Democrats began to stiffen their spines as a consequence of emerging bad news for Bush's policies and consequent declines in his public standing, and as nomination politics came to the fore.

The Electoral Incentive

The scent of an upcoming election leads politicians to look for popular initiatives that can help them look like leaders. Bush's father (Bush I) failed to latch onto any such gimmicks during his effort to get reelected in 1992. Instead, Bush I did two things: (1) he scrambled to regain support from the party core that he had lost over the budget bill and the tax increases that resulted, and (2) he claimed that there was no immediate governmental intervention that would "fix" the economy without, in fact, worsening it. While the latter stance was judicious, the result was that on the former he turned rightward when he needed to offer something with broader appeal. Bush II, whatever his intent (about which we can only speculate), reversed both of those directions. Having gotten himself in solid with his party's faithful in the early going, he could afford to deviate a bit from them in the run-up to the 2004 election. Thus, Bush moved to put a sliver of distance between himself and his party on issues such as Medicare prescription coverage, child tax credits, and agricultural subsidies.[34] This was partly a replay of Clinton's triangulation strategy—Bush II obviously had drawn lessons from Bill Clinton's playbook. Bush II could gain leeway only by building up credits from his party's demanding core. The lesson he learned from his father's misfortune was that by building loyal support early from his party base, he could move off of it as the election struggle neared. By contrast, not having built that base but in need of it as the nomination and electoral campaigns drew closer, Bush's father looked to be captured by the party's right at precisely the point he could least afford it. His need to build support from the base as the election campaign neared gave him less latitude to zigzag or to appear more attractive to wider audiences.

Bush II also learned from his father's fate that leaders should not simply stand there, but do something. Bush I, like Eisenhower, held to the supposition that when it came to the economy, government often could do worse by intervening than by standing aside. Bush II, on the other hand, claimed that Tax Cut II would stimulate economic growth (whereas Tax Cut I supposedly was conceived mainly to return to taxpayers the now vanished surplus). Eisenhower and Bush I were conservatives but not radicals. Since the Reagan economic doctrines took hold in the Republican Party, however, supply-side notions have been dominant among the party leadership. (The supply-side theory emphasizes cutting taxes, especially for the very well-off—presumably those with investment capital—on the grounds that it will stimulate investment and economic growth and thereby pay for itself in the greater tax revenues created by that growth. Its opponents refer to it as "trickle-down" economics.) In fact, there seems little reason to believe that any substantial short-term effect is to be had by fiscal stimulants, whereas staggering long-term deficits may actually discourage investments in the economy, especially from abroad.

Above all, the successive impacts of cuts in governmental revenue flows will likely bind the discretion of future political leaders by limiting existing programs while virtually eliminating the prospect of new ones that would require public expenditures. This, of course, may well have been Reagan's agenda, and George W. Bush's, all along. And it may be in tune with contemporary Republican ideals. In this sense, Bush II has shown the vision that Bush I presumably lacked. Ultimately, that vision will work against presidents of either party who need to show that they can initiate popular programs—ones that offer goods and services that are seemingly free but, of course, arise from government spending. Given the gap between what presidents or candidates will have the resources to do and what there may be a compelling need to do, it is likely that the distance between expenditures and revenue will widen.

George W. Bush's Leadership Style

My emphasis in this chapter has been far less on George W. Bush's unique political personality than on the political context that he inherited and has helped to reinforce. There are powerful incentives operating to move in the direction he has chosen, and that is a very big part of the story. But Bush II has had options to move in different directions that he did not pursue. Would a John McCain have done so? We cannot say. What part of his record was ideologically based (reflecting personal principles) and what part was strategically based (influenced by the perception of prevailing incentives) is hard to judge. It is doubtful, however, that Bush II was ever the moderate he allowed others to perceive him to be. Rather, his political career reflects the culmination of the geographic push of the Republican Party southward and westward (at least up to the eastern edge of the Sierras) and its sharpened ideological drive rightward. Bush II concluded that his father's fundamental failure was in not sufficiently heeding and comforting the party base. In the unlikely event that McCain had won the party's nomination, he would have continually faced that battle, and how he would have worked it out can only be a matter of speculation. The simple point is that party counts for a lot. And in our present era of party polarization, it counts even more.

But presumably there are aspects of the George W. Bush presidency that have to do with the personal characteristics of the man himself. It has been noted that George W. Bush brings to the office a brisk business efficiency and a corporate style, that he likes to delegate and not to spend much time on detail.[35] Although these traits surely do reflect the training and experience of the first M.B.A. degree–holder in the White House, they are actually fairly characteristic of party differences among presidents as well. Republicans are more attuned to orderly ways and strong, hierarchical staff systems; Democrats tend to spread ideas around like jam on the kitchen floor. They are messy, and they tend to be less hierarchical and less disciplined and cohesive. If governing is about bringing orderly processes to bear on the needs of society, Republicans know how to govern, although as Colin Campbell rightly points out in his chapter, a disciplined message is only the beginning and not the end of an orderly process of policy development. In sum, George W. Bush is, in this respect, fairly typical as Republican presidents go, even though he may be a little to the extreme on the orderly side of things.

Bush II and Clinton are virtual mirror images of one another as presidential personalities. Clinton liked to bury himself in detail, discussing it endlessly, pondering over its implications, holding seminars rather than meetings, and availing himself of professorial dimensions of timeliness (namely, virtually none at all). Clinton liked to think about decisions; Bush II likes to make them. George W. Bush likes to get to bottom lines quickly; he has great confidence in his judgments. He doesn't fuss a lot over details or consequences. He likes action, not contemplation. The devil in Clinton's case, aside from his outsized libido, was paralysis and indecision based on knowing too much. In Bush's case, the devil may be in the unforeseen (or in some cases the all-too-foreseen) consequences of knowing (or caring to know) too little. Bush is neither skeptical nor, as his father liked to say, prudent. Temperamentally, he is not in the least bit conservative.[36]

Much has been made of the assumption that Bush is the product largely of his handlers.[37] We can know more of this only later. The same thing was said of Reagan. Not proved, I think, would be the tentative verdict in either case. Clearly, George W. Bush does receive an exceptional amount of political advice that has so far worked well for him. But he does not appear to be heading anywhere he wishes not to. The same was true of Reagan. And while Bush may not have fully comprehended all the implications of the deeply intellectual and aggressive uni-lateralism that his neoconservative foreign policy advisers have made the hallmark of American policy in the world, there is every reason to believe that he is com-fortable with it at the level of application. Like many decisive leaders, including Ronald Reagan, Bush II seems very much at ease with himself and appears to be nagged not at all by doubts. He is a doer, not a doubter. His style is more provocative than prudent; more populist than patrician (even though his policies are certainly immensely beneficial to the patrician class). He embodies Reagan-ism without being identified as a Reaganite. He is, arguably, the most radical president of the past fifty years. Who would have expected this from a candidate who came in second-best in the popular vote?

A Final Word

What should we make of this president and this presidency, so unlike the politi-cal personality of Bush I and so unlike the style of that presidency?

There are consequences to rash behavior and to vindictiveness. Some of them were beginning to be felt in the aftermath of war in Iraq. An administration that disdained its traditional alliances might now be in need of them. An administra-tion that persisted in pushing the envelope might find the forces of resistance to be powerful. Democrats began searching for personal, as well as political, reasons to tie up more of Bush's most noxious (from their perspective) judicial appoint-ments. Ugliness is the product of political warfare. Sooner or later, the Democrats would likely find their version of Newt Gingrich and conduct the same sort of guerilla warfare operations against the Republican majorities in Congress as Gin-grich did against the earlier Democratic majorities. Sooner or later, too, Bush's approval ratings would dip and his opposition would be emboldened.

With the apparent support of the White House and the clear sponsorship of the aforementioned Tom DeLay, Republicans—especially in Texas, but also in Col-orado—have sought to seal themselves in place through the fine old American tra-dition of the gerrymander. In the past, however, gerrymandering was used to seal in incumbents of both parties to the extent possible and to gain political advantage until the courts or others ruled the procedures to be foul (a possibility that only arose forty years ago as a result of the initial one person–one vote Supreme Court ruling). Typically, once the redistricting had been settled upon, that was it. No longer is that the case. The Republicans in Colorado and Texas—states where the party controls both chambers and the governorship—have tried to push through legislation that would radically alter redistricting plans arrived at in 2002. Their effort to rewrite the congressional map in Texas caused the Democrats in the Texas House to hide out in Oklahoma to prevent a quorum while the Republicans gave chase through the police apparatus, including use (or abuse) of the resources of the new Department of Homeland Security. According to a news account in the *New York Times*, "Once Republicans took control of the state house in January, Mr. DeLay began pressing for a new Congressional map, spending several days in Austin, and dispatching the head of his political action committee, Jim Ellis, here to help draw a new map."[38] The idea, according to the story's version of the Republican perspective, "was to help remove centrist Democrats from Congress, leaving only the most liberal behind." According to a redistricting expert, the "plan basically envisions all Democrats elected to Congress being either from Hispanic-majority or African-American-majority districts." In the same story, a movement conservative spokesperson, Grover Norquist, was quoted as saying, "I want to take the partisanship in Washington and drive it into the fifty states."[39]

It is all too easy to say that things were once better than this. Nostalgia comes with age. While the parties were not as quarrelsome in the 1950s, 60s, and much of the 70s as they are now, there were plenty of deep conflicts in American politics, some much deeper than those operative at present, for example, the basic civil rights of African-American citizens. The issues of the day, however, were then not as clearly organized by party as they are now—for better or worse. They often involved cross-cutting coalitions. While it was never easy to put together compromises or coalitions, it was more possible to do both across party lines than it is now. The American system requires compromise and bargaining in the absence of conclusive majorities. It is a testament to George W. Bush's agility as a political leader that his agenda dominates and that much of it has come to pass. At the same time, if we judge leaders by the extent to which they struggle to create a different reality—not taking the path most easily traveled, but the one less so—Bush must be reckoned a successful party leader but a failed national leader. In view of the unusual opportunities he was given to do what he said he would do—reduce the partisan distemper in Washington, create conditions of political civility, and promote national cohesion—his failure on these matters has been profound, but apparently also intended. The conditions of his accession and those of national crisis created openings that were ignored. Bush did not come to office, as Reagan had, with an overt agenda and a reasonably clear victory. He came to office promising that he would be one kind of president, and he has very much been another.

Notes

1. See John Hibbing and Elizabeth Theiss-Morse, *Stealth Democracy: Americans' Beliefs about How Government Should Work* (Cambridge University Press, 2001).

2. For example, see David W. Rohde, *Parties and Leaders in the Post-Reform House* (University of Chicago Press, 1991). See also, Jon R. Bond and Richard Fleisher (eds.), *Polarized Politics: Congress and the President in a Partisan Era* (CQ Press, 2000), and especially in this book, the following chapters: Gary C. Jacobson, "Polarization in National Politics: The Electoral Connection," pp. 9–30, and John H. Aldrich and David W. Rohde, "The Consequences of Party Organization in the House: The Role of the Majority and Minority Parties in Conditional Party Government," pp. 31–72. It is worth focusing on Jacobson's conclusion to his chapter (p. 29) that was written before the election of 2000:

   > Party divisions in Congress have increasingly sturdy electoral roots, particularly among activists, as well as strong institutional reinforcement from the congressional parties. Both parties' holds on their respective branches [the Democrats then had the Presidency, and the Republicans the Congress] are tenuous, guaranteeing electoral competition across the board. . . . The party that achieves the upper hand has an excellent chance of winning control of the whole federal government. . . . With so much at stake, no partisan political advantage is likely to be left unexploited. The only constraint on undiluted partisanship is the fear of losing ground by *looking* [emphasis in the original] too partisan; if impeachment politics is any indication, it is not much of a constraint.

3. The Gallup Poll of December 19–20, 1998, for example, recorded 73% approval of Clinton's performance as president. For the compilation of data, see the Web site of the *Roper Center Presidential Job Approval Ratings*.

4. Rohde, *Parties and Leadership in the Post-Reform House*.

5. For example, Terry Moe claims that there have been excessive investments on the personal or leadership side of the presidency and too little on its institutional incentives for behavior. Terry M. Moe, "Presidents, Institutions, and Theory," in George C. Edwards III, John H. Kessel, and Bert A. Rockman (eds.), *Researching the Presidency: Vital Questions, New Approaches* (University of Pittsburgh Press, 1993), pp. 337–385.

6. David R. Mayhew, *The Electoral Connection* (Yale University Press, 1974).

7. David M. O'Brien notes that Clinton's initial appointments to the bench were of highly qualified individuals who also increased diversity on the bench. Over time, his options became increasingly constrained by Republican control of the Senate, resulting in abandoning confirmation struggles and making trades to appoint some judges opposed to his outlook but who were favored by key Senate Republicans. See David M. O'Brien, "Judicial Legacies: The Clinton Presidency and the Courts," in Colin Campbell and Bert A. Rockman (eds.), *The Clinton Legacy* (Chatham House, 2000), pp. 96–117, esp. p. 116.

8. O'Brien, pp.110–115.

9. Joel D. Aberbach, "The Federal Executive under Clinton," in Colin Campbell and Bert A. Rockman (eds.), *The Clinton Presidency: First Appraisals* (Chatham House, 1996), pp. 163–187.

10. Joel D. Aberbach and Bert A. Rockman, "The President and the Bureaucracy in the United States," in Edward D. Mansfield and Richard Sisson (eds.), *The Evolution of Political Knowledge: Theory and Inquiry in American Politics* (Ohio State University Press, 2003).

11. A characterization made of Carter by one of the senior officials in his administration during a "not for attribution" conference at The Miller Center, University of Virginia, Charlottesville, 1984 as part of the Oral History Project of the Carter Presidency.

12. Jacobson, "Party Polarization in National Politics," p. 26.

13. See Geoffrey C. Layman and Thomas M. Carsey, "Party Polarization and 'Conflict Extension' in the American Electorate," *American Journal of Political Science* 46 (October 2002): 786–802.

14. George C. Edwards III, "The Two Presidencies: A Reevaluation," *American Politics Quarterly* 14 (1986): 247–263, and David W. Rohde, "Partisan Leadership and Congressional Assertiveness in Foreign and Defense Policy," in David A. Deese (ed.), *The New Politics of American Foreign Policy* (St. Martin's Press, 1994), pp. 76–101.

15. Nomination Acceptance Speech of George W. Bush at the Republican National Convention, August 3, 2000. Transcript obtained via *www.whitehouse.org.*

16. Ibid.

17. Although the majority opinion of the Court cited 14th Amendment considerations of fair and due process, in the end it concluded that inasmuch as Florida law required all controversies to be settled by December 12, a date the Court noted was now at hand, an outcome was required. Supreme Court of the United States, 531 U.S., December 12, 2000. *George W. Bush, Et al., Petitioners v. Albert Gore, Jr., Et al.* Obtained from *Supct.law.cornell.edu/supct./html/00-949.ZPC.html.*

18. Victory Speech of December 13, 2000, Austin, Texas. Transcript obtained through *www.whitehouse.org.*

19. Inaugural Address of January 20, 2001, Washington. Transcript obtained through *www.whitehouse.org.*

20. Ken Mayer notes that presidents tend to issue executive orders disproportionately at the beginning and ending of their terms. Clinton left with a flurry; Bush began with one. See Kenneth R. Mayer, *With the Stroke of a Pen: Executive Orders and Presidential Power* (Princeton University Press, 2001), esp. pp. 88–90 and 96–102.

21. As quoted by Paul Krugman, "Cheney sneeringly dismissed energy conservation as a mere 'sign of personal virtue'." Cheney's actual remarks are from 2001. Paul Krugman, "Cheney and the Confidence That Comes before a Fall," *New York Times,* March 29, 2003; obtained through the *International Herald Tribune* Web site, *www.iht.com.*

22. "Energy Task Force Meetings Included More Executives than Previously Revealed," March 28, 2003. Obtained through the Web site of the Center for Responsive Politics, *opensecrets.org.*

23. For a succinct analysis of the Bush managerial style, see Donald F. Kettl, *Team Bush: Leadership Lessons from the Bush White House* (McGraw Hill, 2003).

24. The *Esquire* magazine interview appears in the January 2003 issue. In it, he emphasizes the George W. Bush administration's political rather than policy interests and also the powerful role of Karl Rove, the president's chief political adviser. Shortly after the flap broke, and after White House Press Secretary Ari Fleischer dismissed DiIulio's

comments, DiIulio rushed to issue an apology and some specific retractions, while not retracting his general critique. Scott Lindlaw, "Former Aide Tones Down Criticism of Bush," *Tallahassee Democrat,* December 2, 2002. Obtained from the newspaper's Web site, *http://www.tallahassee.com/mld/tallahassee/news/politics/4648910.htm.* See also, "Ex-Aide Insists White House Puts Politics Ahead of Policy: A onetime insider laments the power of Bush's political staff," *New York Times* (no byline), December 2, 2002, p. A-16.

25. *Washington Post*-ABC News Poll of September 9, 2001. Obtained from the *Washington Post* Web site, *http://www.washingtonpost.com/wp-srv/politics/polls/vault/stories/data071103.*

26. While by the second week of July, public approval of Bush's handling of the situation in Iraq had declined to 58% from a high of 75% at the end of April, approval of his handling of the economy stood at only 47%, with a small plurality (within sample variance) disapproving. By November the same poll data revealed that only 45% approved of Bush's handling of the economy. But support for Bush's handling of foreign affairs was mixed. Only 47% now approved of Bush's handling of the situation in Iraq, but 63% approved of Bush on the campaign against terrorism. *Washington Post*-ABC News Poll.

27. Bob Woodward, *Bush at War* (Simon & Schuster, 2002).

28. For example, see Jonathan Weisman, "In 2003, It's Reagan Revolution Redux: Embracing Big Tax Cuts and Deficits, Bush Moves Away from Compassionate Conservatism," *Washington Post,* February 4, 2003, p. A6; *www.washingtonpost.com.* Also see Adam Nagourney, "Bush , Looking to His Right, Shores Up Support for 2004," *New York Times,* June 30, 2003, pp. A1, A-17.

29. Quoted in Nagourney.

30. Ibid.

31. Richard Stevenson, "Government Plan May Make Private up to 850,000 Jobs: Goals Is to Lower Costs—Bush Aides May Seek Bids for Nearly Half of Work Force—Unions Are Infuriated," *New York Times,* November 15, 2002, pp. A1, A21.

32. Republicans have held a decided advantage over Democrats on national security issues. In a *New York Times*-CBS Poll taken a couple weeks after the 2002 midterm election, for example, 29% agreed that under a Republican Congress the U.S. will be more secure from terrorist attacks, whereas only 8% agreed that the U.S. would be less secure under Republican control. See Adam Nagourney and Janet Elder, "Positive Ratings for the G.O.P., if Not Its Policy: Poll Finds Unfavorable Views on Democrats," *New York Times,* November 26, 2002, pp. A1, A22.

33. An inference one might draw from Fred Greenstein's favorable assessment of Eisenhower as leader. This is not to say that Eisenhower lacked tempestuous conditions; it is to say that the most important and divisive issues he faced came from within his own party (McCarthyism), or required cross-party coalitions (civil rights), or required facing down a Democratic governor (Orville Faubus) in a state that at the time he had little chance of winning (nor needed). Of course, few presidents have come to the office with Eisenhower's stature or his conscious effort to place himself above the seamy side of partisan politics. Fred I. Greenstein, *The Hidden Hand Presidency: Eisenhower as Leader* (Basic Books, 1982).

34. See, for example, Robert Pear, "White House Says It Will Support Same Drug Benefit—Bow to Political Reality—Identical Prescription Coverage for People in Medicare and Those in Private Plans," *New York Times,* June 11, 2003, pp. A1, A24; Robin Toner and

Robert Pear, "Bush Seeks Medicare Drug Bill That Conservatives Oppose," *New York Times,* June 24, 2003, pp. A1, A21; David Firestone, "Bush Pressing House to Back Credits for Poor," *New York Times,* June 11, 2003, pp. A1, A24; Carl P. Leubsdorf, "Re-election Politics Drive Bush's Medical-Care Policy," *Columbus Dispatch,* June 22, 2003, p. C5.

35. Kettl, n.23 above.

36. See also in this regard, Bill Keller, "Not a Centrist, Not a Puppet, Not a Fool: The Radical Presidency of George W. Bush," *New York Times Magazine,* January 26, 2003.

37. See, for example, James Moore and Wayne Slater, *Bush's Brain: How Karl Rove Made George W. Bush Presidential* (Wiley, 2003). Also, see Elisabeth Bumiller, "Keepers of Bush Image Lift Stagecraft to New Heights," *New York Times,* May 16, 2003, pp. A1, A20; Joshua Green, "The Other War Room," *Washington Monthly,* April 2002, pp. 11–16.

38. David M. Halbfinger, "Across U.S., Redistricting as Endless Battle," *New York Times,* July 1, 2003, pp. A1, A21.

39. Ibid.

About the Contributors

Joel D. Aberbach is professor of political science and policy studies and director of the Center for American Politics and Public Policy at UCLA. He is cochair of the International Political Science Association's Research Committee on Structure and Organization of Government. His books include *Keeping a Watchful Eye: The Politics of Congressional Oversight* (Brookings Institution, 1990) and (with Bert A. Rockman) *In the Web of Politics: Three Decades of the U.S. Federal Executive* (Brookings Institution Press, 2000).

Colin Campbell taught for nineteen years at Georgetown University, were he held the rank of university professor. He has published nine books, three of which have won distinctions. The Brookings Institution published his most recent book, *Preparing for the Future: Strategic Planning in the U.S. Air Force* (coauthored with Michael Barzelay), in September 2003. He currently holds the Canada Research Chair in U.S. Government and Politics at the University of British Columbia, where he also chairs the U.S. Studies Program. Campbell is a fellow of the U.S. National Academy of Public Administration.

David T. Canon is a professor of political science at the University of Wisconsin, Madison. He received his Ph.D. from the University of Minnesota in 1987. His teaching and research interests are in American political institutions, especially Congress. He is the author of *Race, Redistricting, and Representation* (University of Chicago Press, 1999); *The Dysfunctional Congress? The Individual Roots of an Institutional Dilemma* (with Ken Mayer; Westview Press, 1999); *Actors, Athletes, and Astronauts: Political Amateurs in the U.S. Congress* (University of Chicago Press, 1990), and various articles and book chapters and has also edited several books.

George C. Edwards III is Distinguished Professor of Political Science and Jordan Chair in the Bush School at Texas A & M University. He is editor of *Presidential Studies Quarterly*. In addition to dozens of articles he has written or edited nineteen books, including *At the Margins: Presidential Leadership of Congress; Presidential Approval; Implementing Public Policy; Researching the Presidency;* and *On Deaf Ears: The Failure of the Bully Pulpit*.

Richard K. Herrmann is director of the Mershon Center and professor of political science at the Ohio State University. Articles from his research on American foreign policy have recently appeared in the *American Political Science Review, International Organization,* and the *Journal of Politics.* He served as a Council on Foreign Relations Fellow on the Policy Planning Staff at the U.S. Department of State during the first Bush administration

Gary Mucciaroni is associate professor in the Department of Political Science at Temple University and serves as Graduate Chair. He is the author of *The Political Failure of Employment Policy, 1945-82* and *Reversals of Fortune: Public Policy and Private Interests.* His current work is on the politics of legislative deliberation (with Paul J. Quirk) and the politics of gay and lesbian rights.

David M. O'Brien is Spicer Professor of Politics at the University of Virginia and the author of numerous books, including *Storm Center: The Supreme Court in American Politics,* the two-volume casebook *Constitutional Law and Politics,* and an annual *Supreme Court Watch,* and coauthor of *Government by the People.* He was a Judicial Fellow at the Supreme Court of the United States and has held Fulbrights at Oxford University and the University of Bologna, Italy, and in Japan.

Mark A. Peterson is professor of policy studies and political science, and chair of the Department of Policy Studies at the UCLA School of Public Policy and Social Research. His publications include *Legislating Together: The White House and Capitol Hill from Eisenhower to Reagan* (Harvard); "The Presidency and Organized Interests: White House Patterns of Interest Group Liaison,"in the *American Political Science Review;* and "Political Influence in the 1990s: From Iron Triangles to Policy Networks," in the *Journal of Health Politics, Policy and Law.* His current research focuses on institutional change and interactions and the politics of national health care policymaking. As an APSA Congressional Fellow, Peterson served as a legislative assistant to U.S. Senator Tom Daschle.

Paul J. Quirk is professor of political science at the University of Illinois at Urbana-Champaign. He is the author of *Industry Influence in Federal Regulatory Agencies* (1981), *The Politics of Deregulation* (1985), and numerous articles and essays on the presidency, presidential elections, public opinion, and public policymaking. He is co-winner of the 2003 Aaron Wildavsky Enduring Achievement Award of the Public Policy Section of the American Political Science Association. His current research concerns the processes and quality of policy deliberation in American politics.

Michael J. Reese is a Ph.D. student in political science at the Ohio State University.

Bert A. Rockman is director of, and professor in, the School of Public Policy and Management at the Ohio State University, where he also holds an appointment in political science. His books include *The Leadership Question,* which was awarded the Richard E. Neustadt Prize by the APSA's Organized Section on the Presidency. He is a past president of that section and is currently president of the Midwest Conference for Public Administration.

Barbara Sinclair is Marvin Hoffenberg Professor of American Politics at UCLA. Her publications on the U.S. Congress include articles in the *American Political Science Review,* the *American Journal of Political Science,* and the *Journal of Politics* and five books. Among the latter are *The Transformation of the U.S. Senate* (1989), winner of the Richard F. Fenno Prize and the D. B. Hardeman Prize; and *Unorthodox Lawmaking: New Legislative Processes in the U.S. Congress* (1997, 2000). She was an American Political Science Congressional Fellow in the office of the House majority leader in 1978–79 and a participant observer in the office of the Speaker in 1987–88.

Katherine Cramer Walsh received her Ph.D. from the University of Michigan in 2000 and is an assistant professor in the Department of Political Science at the University of Wisconsin-Madison. She is the author of *Talking about Politics: Informal Groups and Social Identity in American Life.* Her current projects include work on civic dialogue programs and gender and campaign advertising.

Graham Wilson was born and educated in Britain. He spent the first eleven years of his career at the University of Essex and moved permanently to the University of Wisconsin in 1984. He is the author of numerous books on interest groups, business and politics, and the relationship between bureaucrats and politicians. He has also written extensively on political leadership in both the United States and Britain. His current research focuses on how conflicts between U.S. foreign policy goals and domestic pressures and interests are resolved.